CONTEMPORARY EUROPEAN ETHICS

Selected Readings

Joseph J. Kockelmans was born in the Netherlands in 1923. After receiving his Ph.D. in 1952, he studied mathematics and physics for five years, followed by three years of advanced study in contemporary philosophy. Dr. Kockelmans was professor of philosophy at the Agricultural University of Wageningen (the Netherlands) before coming to the United States. He has taught philosophy at the New School for Social Research and the University of Pittsburgh, and is currently teaching at Pennsylvania State University.

Dr. Kockelmans has published three books and several articles in the realm of philosophy of science; one of the books, a study on the special theory of relativity, was awarded the gold medal of *Teylers Tweede Genootschap* in 1956. His most recent publications are in the area of contemporary continental European philosophy, and include, in addition to many articles, two books on Heidegger's philosophy, one on Husserl's philosophy, and one on Husserl's phenomenological psychology. He is the editor of the Anchor book entitled *Phenomenology*.

CONTEMPORARY EUROPEAN ETHICS

Selected Readings

Edited, Translated in Part, and Introduced

by

JOSEPH J. KOCKELMANS

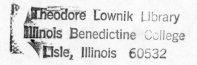
ANCHOR BOOKS
DOUBLEDAY & COMPANY, INC.
GARDEN CITY, NEW YORK
1972

The Anchor Books edition is the first publication of
CONTEMPORARY EUROPEAN ETHICS: Selected Readings

Anchor Books edition: 1972

PREFACE

A great number of textbooks and anthologies on ethics have been published over the past fifteen years. The fact that this book has been added to the long list does not have its origin in any criticism of the work done by other authors, but rather in a desire to fill a gap that has been felt by many of us for quite some time. To the best of my knowledge, all the existing anthologies in English that are intended to inform the reader and the student about contemporary ethical views, deal either exclusively, or for the most part, with English and American views; as far as continental European views are concerned, they are either absent altogether or are represented only by the views of Sartre, Marcel, Camus, and Buber. For this reason, the American reader and student could have the impression that ethics is a dead issue for most European philosophers or that the only views worth mentioning are those found in the works of certain "existentialists." However, a glance through the available literature shows immediately that the problem of ethics as such, and many individual ethical questions in particular, constitute a substantial part of, if not the main concern of, many leading European philosophers in France and in the German-speaking countries. That most of these views are not mentioned in readers and anthologies is understandable, since the original literature is not, or in some cases not yet, available in English. It seems to me that Vernon J. Bourke has already made a substantial contribution to changing this situation. In the last five chapters of his *History of Ethics*, he discusses many books written by European philosophers who have made an important contribution to the realm of ethics. This anthology is an attempt to bring the works of some of these authors closer to the American public; it consists for the most part of selections that until now have not been available in English. I hope that in the near future the works of some of these authors will be translated in their entirety.

In addition to the "one-sidedness" of this present anthology, which has its origin in the fact that it limits itself to a consideration of continental European theories, there is another "one-sidedness." The latter follows from two different sources: First, it appeared to be impossible to include all the authors whose work is unquestionably worthy of being studied seriously. Space limitations made a choice necessary. I can only hope that my choices have been reasonable ones. Second, I should like to have included some selections from Marxian and other socialist philosophers. I was unable to do so, however, because I was not able to secure the necessary rights. I was informed that the works of some of these authors (namely G. Lukács and E. Bloch) are in the process of being translated, and it would be undesirable to have a second translation of part of their works appear in English. An analogous remark must be made concerning Sartre's *Existentialism Is a Humanism*. The French publisher objected to my including the complete text of this popular essay. I am using as a substitute for Sartre's text a short paraphrase of the main argument and the pertinent commentaries and critical reflections of Francis Jeanson and Simone de Beauvoir.

In choosing selections from the literature, I have tried to combine two guiding principles: the selections were to be genuinely representative of the authors' views, and the anthology as a whole was to touch upon as many important ethical problems as possible. It was for this reason that in some instances I chose selections from material in which the authors in question had clarified their position in regard to ethics, whereas in other cases, namely where this basic conception of ethics could easily be characterized in a short introduction, I chose essays on particular ethical problems.

I have ordered the material under four general headings: spiritualist ethics, axiological ethics, the case of humanism, and situation ethics. Such an ordering is in some instances somewhat arbitrary. In most cases I have taken Bourke's suggestions in this regard as a guideline. I have purposely avoided such labels as "personalism," "existentialist ethics," "phenomenological ethics," and "religious ethics," which are often used in the literature. I do not deny that these labels indeed refer to vitally important characteristics in the philosophical conceptions of many of the authors represented here. Many authors have been, in fact, influenced by a certain "existentialism," many have used "phenomenological" methods, and almost all of them placed a great deal of emphasis upon the person and especially upon interpersonal relationships. Finally, most of the philosophers included do subscribe to a religious view.

Nonetheless, I feel that none of these labels really characterizes the *position in ethics* for which any of these philosophers stands. Furthermore, I wish to avoid the term "existentialism" altogether, because in my view it is the adequate label only for the philosophical position of Sartre and his disciples; as almost no one included in this book has much in common with Sartre, it seems to me that using the term in a broader sense to characterize the position in ethics of people other than Sartre and his followers is destined to cause confusion. As far as Sartre himself is concerned, I think his view should be characterized by the label "humanism," as he himself has stated explicitly on several occasions.

The term "phenomenological ethics" seems to me to be inadequate for two reasons: for most phenomenologists, the term "phenomenology" refers merely to a method to be used, not to a means to characterize the insights that might be brought to light by the use of this method. Furthermore, and this is much more important, the term is ambiguous, since it can be used to characterize the conceptions of Hegel, Husserl, Scheler, Hartmann, Heidegger, Sartre, and Merleau-Ponty—conceptions by no means identical or even similar. Another reason why I believe it is better not to use the term "phenomenology" in this context is the fact that most phenomenologists, Husserl included, have defended an axiological conception of ethics. Thus, in trying to characterize the basic conception underlying their investigations in the realm of ethics, it seems to me that the term "axiology" is by far preferable.

Finally, the term "personalism" is used in the United States mainly for the ethical view defended by Flewelling, whereas in France the term is used to characterize the conception of Emmanuel Mounier and his followers. Using the term in yet another sense would have, again, been a source of confusion.

I have kept my introductions as short as possible, limiting myself to giving some data about the authors and their works, as well as those insights I feel are necessary for an understanding of the selections chosen. Where we are dealing with book chapters, the introductions are slightly longer, because the reader deserves to have some knowledge of the chapters that preceded and followed the one presented here. Where an introduction to the selections chosen seemed to be superfluous, I have limited myself to indicating the source and the circumstances under which the essay was written.

In writing these introductions I have used a great number of books, encyclopedias, and essays. I wish to list some of these sources here instead of mentioning them time and again throughout the book. The following works have been very helpful in this regard: Vernon J. Bourke, *History of Ethics* (New York: Doubleday, 1968), Virgilius Ferm, ed., *Encyclopaedia of Morals* (New York: Philosophical Library, 1956), Ludwig Landgrebe, *Philosophie der Gegenwart* (Bonn: Athaneum Verlag, 1962), Colin Smith, *Contemporary French Philosophy: A Study in Norms and Values* (London: Methuen, 1964), W. H. Werkmeister, *Theories of Ethics* (Lincoln, Nebr.: Johnsen, 1961), and *The Encyclopaedia of Philosophy*, ed. Paul Edwards (New York: The Free Press, 1967).

Grateful acknowledgment is made to the publishers, authors, and translators represented here for their generosity in granting permission to reprint selections from copyrighted material and for their kind co-operation throughout the work.

Department of Philosophy   JOSEPH J. KOCKELMANS, PH.D.
The Pennsylvania State University

CONTENTS

Part I: SPIRITUALIST ETHICS

The term "spiritualist ethics" refers to the moral philosophy that has developed in the French movement called *la philosophie de l'esprit*. The origin of this movement goes back as far as Nicholas Malebranche (1638–1715) and Blaise Pascal (1623–62), and via both to Descartes (1596–1650). Other important sources of inspiration are the works of Maine de Biran (1766–1824) and Charles Renouvier (1815–1903). The contemporary movement thus labeled originated with a series of philosophical books edited by Lavelle and Le Senne (since 1934). Lavelle has characterized the movement briefly as follows: "The philosophers who founded this series in 1934 to which they gave the name *la philosophie de l'esprit*, had in mind to serve philosophy rather than to let a certain doctrine triumph. . . . The *philosophie de l'esprit* attempts to establish a closer relationship between ethics and metaphysics. . . . Philosophy is nothing but the reflection of the mind on the real, and this is inseparable from the reflection of the mind upon itself. . . . There is only one philosophy, but there are as many ways of philosophizing as there are philosophers."

The movement does not defend a clearly defined body of doctrines. The most characteristic aspect of the movement is its criticism of materialism, positivism, empiricism, and scientism, and its attempt to establish the rights of the "spirit" wherever possible. In this connection it is important to state explicitly that the term *esprit* does not have a good equivalent in the English language; it means spirit as well as mind, and in addition it refers also to that reality which can be discovered by the "higher" functions of man's consciousness. Furthermore, spiritualism is not identical with idealism; most "spiritualists" are realists in some sense or other. Also, the term "spiritualism" does not in any way indicate a denial or underevaluation of the rights of the body. Finally, the term does not imply Descartes's dualism of body and soul, a view that is rejected by all spiritualists and that most of them have explicitly tried to overcome.

In addition to Louis Lavelle, René Le Senne, Vladimir Jankélévitch, Pierre Lachièze-Rey, Aimé Forest, Jean Guitton, Maurice Nédoncelle, and Paul Ricoeur, one can also mention the names of Jacques Palliard, Gabriel Marcel, and Jean Wahl in this connection. The French movement has also had great influence in Spain and Italy, as well as in many Latin American countries.

Mainly because of space limitations, I have decided to restrict myself here to including some selections by Lavelle, one of the founders of the contemporary movement, and by Jankélévitch, Marcel, and Ricoeur, who in my view are the most important representatives of the movement as far as ethics is concerned. Since Le Senne's contribution to ethics is certainly axiological in character, I have decided to include a selection from his *Traité de morale générale* in Part II.

The reason why I have decided to include the work of Marcel and Ricoeur in this section is for many readers perhaps not a very convincing one. Let me begin by admitting that it has been quite difficult to make this decision and that I agree with anyone who would argue that the contributions to the realm of ethics made by Marcel, as well as by Ricoeur, are so unique and important that they deserve to be listed separately, without any systematizing label. On the other hand, I feel that in an introductory reader a moderate systematization is helpful. Finally, it seems to me that Lavelle's characterization of the spiritualist movement indicates quite clearly the basic concern of the ethical views of both Marcel and Ricoeur.

Chapter 1

INTRODUCTION

LOUIS LAVELLE (1883–1951) studied in Paris, where he was profoundly influenced by the work of Henri Bergson. Other influences on his thought came from Nicholas Malebranche, Maine de Biran, Octave Hamelin, and Maurice Blondel. Lavelle taught at the Sorbonne (1932–34) and later at the Collège de France (1941–51). He has written on a great number of subjects, but his major concern has always been the problem of Being, which he identifies with the Absolute. His main work, *Dialectique de l'éternel Présent*, consists of four volumes, which appeared between 1928 and 1951.

According to Lavelle, philosophy must be in a lively dialogue with the Absolute; the Absolute is Being itself. We encounter Being in each experience and in each activity focused on beings. The privileged experience in which we encounter Being itself is in the being of the ego. Being is not an object, but a subject, not a substance but an Act, the pure Act in which everything and I, myself, participate. Since everything, including man himself, is "rooted" in Being itself, it is possible for man to be in contact with things and his fellow man.

Each being takes part in Being. Being itself, however, is not the sum of all things. There is, and always will remain, a distance between Being and each individual being (*intervalle*). Lavelle often speaks of the "All" (*le Tout*); by this he means Being itself in so far as it is the transcendent *and* immanent source of all that is, which, although as the creative source of all that is, It allows everything to participate in its fullness, nonetheless maintains an unbridgeable distance (*intervalle*) between Itself and the various beings. Man's primitive experience is found in the mutual presence of the ego to Being and of Being to the ego. Man's essence consists in the never successful attempt to bridge the distance between himself and Being. This distance constitutes the world in which each man is anchored through his body. Body and world are the means that separate the finite ego and the Absolute, and as such, constitute the necessary means for all human activity, even and precisely those which aim at transcending the distance between Being and man.

From this it follows that Lavelle's philosophy ultimately ends up being a mysticism of participation. In each man there are two spontaneous activities: one has its origin in nature, the other in the spirit. They do not contradict one another, but neither are they necessarily in harmony with each other. The task of man's will consists in guiding the "spontaneity of nature" in such a way that it becomes harmonious with the "spontaneity of the spirit"; in so doing, the will must take into account the fact that nature is the necessary foundation of the spirit. Man's goal consists in trying to unite as closely as possible with Being (the pure Act), in which he takes part. In so doing, his will is motivated by love; self-love, on the other hand, attempts to separate the finite ego from the pure Act. In so far as genuine love urges man to unite with the Absolute (Being, pure Act), it leads to *morality*; in so far as it implies happiness, that is, once a man realizes that he is partly united with the Absolute, it leads to *mysticism*.

Thus the "life of the spirit," to which moral behavior must lead and which constitutes the goal of man's life, consists of a fighting toward gradual liberation from the passivity characteristic of the "spontaneity of nature." Man becomes fully man by subordinating natural spontaneity to reflection and rational discipline. Human freedom *originates* in this process, and this "conversion" of natural spontaneity into freedom is the real vehicle of participation. As spiritual being, man is endowed with possibilities for the accomplishment of his "pre-established essence." His vocation is to seek to make

his actual self coincide with the pre-established ideal predelineated in his potentialities.

The selection that follows is taken from *Evil and Suffering*.
This book consists of two independent but connected essays:
one on the problem of evil and suffering, the other entitled
"Those Who Are Separated and United." The selection forms
the first part of the first essay and, as such, needs no further
introduction.

THE PROBLEM OF EVIL

Louis Lavelle

1 THE SCANDAL OF EVIL

We may ask whether or not it is useful for the mind to turn its attention to the problem of evil, either to define, explain or evade it. If we consider it too closely, we give it a kind of reality; it then fascinates our consciousness which, by reason of the fear it experiences, feels attracted to evil. Is it not rather the thought of and the will to do good that alone ought to give our soul light and strength and, in occupying the whole capacity of our consciousness, deprive evil of the possibility of being born? It is only when generous activity begins to fail that an emptiness makes itself felt in consciousness, and there evil enters in. The most virile morality only knows positive precepts: it commands what must be done; it prohibits nothing.

However, we cannot hope that evil will disappear from our lives if we turn toward good. We encounter it everywhere, inside and outside ourselves. It is not limited to those moral transgressions which lie in our power to prevent. Suffering is an experienced evil we must submit to. Whatever be the purity of our will, there are in us evil tendencies that suddenly cross our thoughts like a flash and fill us with horror by their depth, by an obscure presence with which they con-

Reprinted, with permission of The Macmillan Company, from *Evil and Suffering*, by Louis Lavelle, translated by Bernard Murchland. Copyright © by The Macmillan Company, 1963. Originally published in France under the title *Le Mal et la Souffrance*.

tinuously surround and threaten us. Then, too, there is the suffering of others, their moral misery. Evil, no matter what we do, is part of our every gesture, of our most natural activities. It is perhaps an ingredient of our best actions. To fail to recognize evil in order to make the good the unique object of our activity would be to blind ourselves voluntarily, to expose ourselves to confusion when evil relentlessly confronts us, to fail in that courage of spirit necessary to look upon reality honestly and embrace it in its totality in order to understand it better and redirect it.

Evil is the object of all the protests of consciousness: of sensibility in questions of suffering and of judgment in questions of moral transgression; it is because we cannot cast aside our liberty that we have the power, even though we may at the same time reject it, of committing evil. Evil is the scandal of the world. It is our major problem. Because of it, the world is a problem for us. It imposes its presence upon us and we can do nothing about it. It spares no man. It demands that we endeavor both to explain and abolish it.

Might we say that the good is also a problem? This would not be a correct manner of speaking because good, as soon as it is recognized and accomplished, is rather a solution; it is by definition the solution to all problems. By a kind of reversal, it is only a problem for one who seeks it, while evil is a problem for those who have found it. For there is no will that, in pursuing evil, does not pursue a shadow of the good. Now it is by reflecting upon the interval that separates the good that we desire and the evil that we do that reflection enables us to discover simultaneously the meaning of our destiny, the very heart of our responsibility and the center of our spiritual life.

2 THE ALTERNATIVE BETWEEN GOOD AND EVIL

We can think of neither good nor evil in an isolated manner. They exist in relationship to one another like two contraries; each calls forth and excludes the other. No one can imagine evil without also imagining the good it makes us betray; and good, in its turn, cannot appear to us as good except in terms of a possible evil that risks seducing us and making us succumb.

It is impossible to imagine a world from which evil would be banished and in which only the good reigns. For a consciousness that had no experience of evil, there would be nothing to merit the name of good. In a perfect equality of value between all forms of being, there would be no value. Evil, like a shadow, permits us to perceive the light and determine its value. The very love that I have for the good would be impossible without the presence of evil from which I try to free myself and which never ceases to threaten me. Good gives meaning to the world in virtue of the very scandal of evil which makes me desire the good, which obliges me to imagine the good and imposes upon my will the duty of acting to realize it.

The alternative between good and evil is the source of my spiritual life. However lofty this be, there always remains in it some element of evil which obliges it to transcend itself. Evil is a constant peril that menaces our spiritual life. We pray that the Lord will deliver us from evil; and we constantly hope our intelligence will become so pure and our will so strong that we will cease to know and to do evil. But who thinks that good could ever exist in virtue of an ineluctable necessity? Would it make any sense if it were one day to become a law of nature, something given to us? With the impossibility of evil, good is annihilated. We end then with this extraordinary paradox; good, which gives everything that exists its value, meaning and beauty, calls forth evil as the condition of its very being. And yet evil, which is the negation of good, can justify itself only in terms of a process that denies it; thus it must exist; but it can exist only to be abolished.

Our emotional life is marked by the same law of the spirit, by the same rhythm of consciousness between a state which we love and a contrary state that sustains it, even though we try to abolish the latter with all of our strength. All men love pleasure and detest suffering, including the saint and the ascetic. The suffering they sustain or demand is never more than an element of or a means to a more perfect and purer joy. Everyone dreams of eliminating all the evil that exists in the world in order that pleasure alone may fill it. But it is a hopeless dream; whoever takes away the faculty of suffering also takes away that of enjoyment. This is not because pleasure is in itself a form of suffering as some philosophers think; rather, these two states are as inseparable as the two extremities of a scale; each minute oscillation carries the other with it and calls it forth. To want to disjoin the two terms and retain only one of them would be to abolish both. One who desires continuous pleasure finds only boredom. The keenest, deepest personalities are also those that conjointly experience the richest and the most intense pleasures and sufferings.

The intelligence seeks knowledge, that is to say, truth. But this truth is meaningful for us only in terms of the error from which it delivers us. Truth is necessarily a rectified error and never by itself a stable and assured possession. It is related to an act which depends on us, an act that we can refuse to perform or perform badly. In the latter case we deceive ourselves, and it is the possibility of deception which not only gives truth its value but is the cause of its very existence. There can be no truth for one who has not known error. The intelligence, like the will in the case of evil and the sensibility in the case of suffering, finds in error a negative term that it strives to abolish, but with which it cannot dispense, since without it the positive term toward which it tends could neither be conceived nor obtained.

3 Evil and Suffering

It cannot be denied that there is an immediate and primitive intuition of consciousness that identifies evil with suffering. But as consciousness develops, suffering and evil appear as two different realities, although the bond that unites them is never broken.

This is because suffering imposes itself upon us despite our efforts. This already shows that it is a mark of our passivity and our limitation, a curb on the development of our being. Further, consciousness repels suffering with all of its strength, whereas the present evil is clearly indubitable even before the faculty of judgment has pronounced it so. Though suffering is not the whole of evil, though it is not itself an evil, it is directly or indirectly linked to all forms of evil, including the most subtle and most complicated. The pessimist who curses life sees the world entirely given over to suffering, whether he looks upon the animal world where beasts devour one another or upon our civilization which increases the means of suffering in the measure that it becomes more refined.

Not only is suffering always joined to a protest, a revolt of consciousness which strives to drive it out; it is one with this protest and this revolt. Undoubtedly one could demonstrate that suffering is not itself evil, that it is not an absolute and radical evil, and even that it can be the condition of a greater good. Nonetheless, one is obliged to recognize that it is always an integral element of evil, and that, if suffering were suddenly to disappear from the world, it would be difficult to define what we might still understand by evil or to say just what a bad will was. Thus suffering seems to us to be the sign of the presence of evil. To be evil is to suffer. The wicked man voluntarily produces evil. We understand a good man to be one who suffers because of the suffering of others and who does everything he can to alleviate it. To be a pessimist is, in the final analysis, to see suffering as inseparable from consciousness or the very possibility of its exercise.

But we must not be too quick to identify evil and suffering. The existence of suffering does not present the mind with insurmountable difficulties. It is the ransom of our limitation. It breaks that harmony with ourselves and with the universe that had hitherto assured our interior peace. It disrupts that _élan_, that natural and confident expansion which continuously renewed our pleasures and our joys. It calls attention to a failure, a rending of the unity of our being. It is not difficult to understand that a limited creature, living in a world that transcends him, where so many impersonal forces are at work, be always exposed to suffer some conflict or some wound. And there have been those who thought that there was a kind of rationality in suffering, since they believed it warned us of a danger against which we could still defend ourselves.

Suffering in itself is not evil. We may bemoan the destiny of creatures given over to suffering in a blind and indifferent world. Such suffering could be the test of their will, the measure of its strength, its purity, and its beneficence. This cruel, austere, suffering world would not then be an evil world. We could not condemn it without being unjust. But if evil resides uniquely in the will, then the world could only be evil if it were the product of an evil will, if the suffering that exists were willed, if it were the very end toward which the will tends and not the means it needs to achieve its most significant realizations. There is perhaps no evil in the world that does not bear some relationship to suffering; but evil is not to be identified with suffering; it is the will's attitude toward it that matters. Sometimes the will lets itself be overcome by the suffering in question; sometimes it imposes it on others; and sometimes it accepts it in order to alleviate, enter, and transcend it. In the latter case it converts evil into good.

4 THE USE OF SUFFERING

If we only look at the suffering that fills the world—and we have no hope that it will ever disappear—and if we begin to identify this suffering with evil, then all is lost, consciousness is hopelessly thwarted, and our life, which is always exposed and threatened, can only be an object of malediction. Suffering taken in itself, independently of the use freedom can make of it and of the good it can serve, is both an absurdity and a cruelty. But it pertains to freedom to give meaning to everything it touches, to everything that can become the condition of its exercise and the means of its ascent. Our point of departure, then, must be the freedom which seeks the good and which, if it finds in suffering the means of its moral destiny, will succeed in restoring to it a spiritual meaning.

There can be no question here of condemning all those who are overwhelmed and vanquished by evil. For many, suffering has a destructive character; it saps their energies. It is

therefore the sign of a supreme peril and enslavement, although it can be a liberating trial. It gives us an extraordinary intimacy with ourselves; it produces a form of intro-
spection in which the spirit penetrates to the very roots of
life, where it seems that suffering itself will be taken away.
It deepens consciousness by emptying it of all the preoccupy-
ing and distracting objects that had hitherto sufficed to fill
it. Some people acquire a sensitivity, a seriousness, an interior
and personal value as a result of certain sufferings they have
undergone, while others who have not known such suffering
evince, in comparison, an indifference that is both impermeable and superficial. Relationships between two people have
an acuteness and a depth that is in direct proportion to their
common suffering, even when one has caused the suffering of
the other, as when, for example, in spite of the obstacles of
nature and character and beyond all the wounds and all the
pitfalls of self-love, they seek a purely spiritual communion.

We can perhaps be judged by our attitude toward suffering. In the difficulties it presents, in the anxiety it causes, in
the abrupt return it forces us to make into our individual and
separated self, it deprives us of every resource and every
strength but those which we can find deep within ourselves.
Also we might say that upon the meaning we can give suffering will depend the meaning the world will have for us, for
the world has no other meaning than the one we are capable
of giving it. If it were an object, a pure spectacle, it would
have no meaning. It has meaning only through my will which
prefers being to nothingness and which, at the price of suffering and even of life itself, undertakes to realize certain ends.
These ends in turn give to suffering, that is accepted and not
merely undergone, and to life, that is sacrificed and not
merely lost, their true spiritual meaning.

If all value depends upon an activity of choice and consecration, it is easy to understand that there can be no value
either in suffering or in life when this activity is absent. It is
easy to understand that both can be vitiated by the use I make
of them; it is necessary that both exist in order to be redeemed by a will which is the arbiter of good and evil, which

can convert all the good that enhances our nature into evil, and all the evils that continually plague it into good.

5 INJUSTICE

In general we may say that evil consists not in suffering but in the will to cause suffering. But in this case we demand that there be in the same consciousness a kind of equation between the evil it wills and the evil which affects it, that what we suffer be proportionate to what we do, that there always be some harmony between the active and passive parts of our being. But this, generally speaking, is not the case. Those who suffer the most are not the guiltiest. Evil, in its most serious form, consists precisely in that close bond that is established between two creatures and is such that when one does evil, it is the other who suffers it. This we take to be the very principle of injustice.

Our inability to establish a regular correspondence between sensible evil (which is suffering) and moral evil (which is sin) troubles human consciousness profoundly. If this correspondence always existed, evil would cease to surprise us, for it would be a kind of compensated disorder. But experience shows a strange disparity between happiness and virtue, a disparity which, if absolute and definitive, would appear to most men as the very essence of evil. We have always tried to explain it either by looking backward or forward: backward, to show how all suffering is the effect of an unknown and distant transgression whose effect still persists in an unpurified will; forward, to show that there is in this suffering a trial which, if overcome, will in the end produce some accord between sensibility and will. We may say that it pertains to faith to unite these two explanations and to carry itself from one to the other without separating the Fall from the Redemption.

However, no one will admit that in this life there is an irremediable conflict between happiness and the good, or that suffering and evil are always separated. We cannot credit to chance, by a kind of abdication of judgment, the extremely diverse relations that can be established between the decisions of the will and the emotions that accompany them. In reality these relations are always extremely complicated. The Greeks thought that the wise man and he alone was always happy; not that he was ignorant of suffering, but he alone was capable of accepting, understanding, and entering it. And we cannot reflect without trembling upon the double meaning of the word "miserable"; it can mean either the last degree of suffering or the last degree of abjection. These two extremes sometimes coincide. We may add two observations: first, however happy a man be who has done evil, he can never separate himself from his past, which many of our contemporaries effectively consider as an almost impossible burden; secondly, the good man, by a kind of reversal of the rule that demands that we treat others like ourselves, is not a good man because he pursues his own good but rather because he is concerned with the good of others. His contribution to the good of another constitutes his true happiness. Thus in the midst of the worst tribulations we cannot abolish all relationships between the good and happiness, at least insofar as this happiness is the effect of the good we have accomplished.

When we see the wicked happy and the good unhappy, supposing that this is possible, it seems that we are in the presence of a disorder that consciousness might well consider the essence of evil. This noncoincidence of happiness and goodness, of evil and suffering, is a scandal against which our will and reason protest. We cannot accept that the unity of our being can be so broken, that our sensible states fail to be a faithful echo of the acts which our will has accomplished, that a good action engender in us sorrow and an evil action, joy. Confronted with such effects, our logic as much as our virtue is offended. The happiness, even apparent happiness, of the wicked man and the unhappiness, even accepted unhappiness, of the good man, assail both intelligibility and justice. We cannot understand how consciousness can experience any growth or fulfillment when it pursues a destructive and negative end, nor that it can feel limited and constrained when its action is beneficent and generous. We would undoubtedly admit that the highest good can sometimes be attained only at the price of suffering experienced at another level of consciousness. Still, we not only desire that this suffering be accepted, but that we derive joy from submitting to it.

6 WICKEDNESS

We distinguish between evil and suffering to show that suffering is only an affection of the sensibility, and therefore something we undergo, while evil depends upon the will and is something we do. This suffices to indicate the close relationship that always exists between suffering and evil; for if suffering, insofar as we submit to it, is only an evil to the degree that it expresses a limitation in us, evil itself is a suffering that we impose, a limitation that we inflict on others. Suffering is always the mark of a limitation or a destruction which can be the means of purification and growth. The distance between suffering and evil is what separates an involuntary from a voluntary limitation or destruction.

One may then think that to define evil as the simple infliction of suffering is too restricted, that suffering can sometimes be willed in view of a greater good, and that perversity consists less in causing suffering than in degradation through the very use of pleasure. This, in effect, suffices to show that suffering is an evil only when it is merely the evidence of a diminution of being which was itself willed; and it is this diminution that perversity also seeks to attain. Pleasure can be the means by which it does so.

An analysis of wickedness proves beyond doubt that there is a bond impossible to break between suffering and evil. The wicked man's first objective is to make others suffer; and undoubtedly this suffering is a diminution of being in the one he sees suffering, a diminution of being which he has caused and which makes him aware of the power at his disposal. To this awareness is added a kind of satisfaction in seeing the suffering of a creature whose consciousness must bear witness to the state of misery to which it has been reduced. It may be said that such wickedness is rare, but it is possible that the most benevolent and pure spirits are to some extent contaminated by it. This is because the human condition obeys common laws from which no one is exempted.

Here we see the line of demarcation and the point of contact between suffering and evil. Evil can be defined, whatever one may think, not by its relation to sensibility, but rather by its relation to the will—although we must bear in mind that the will and sensibility imply each other. Sensibility is the testimony of the will's power or lack of power. Thus suffering itself is an evil only in relation to the will. When it is imposed by nature, it is considered an evil in the measure that it is an obstacle to our development, that it paralyzes and annihilates the will; and when it is the effect of another's will, we then experience a sentiment of horror as though, in adding a voluntary limitation to a natural one, the spirit was turning against its own specific end and contributing to its own defeat.

The wickedness of making others suffer is never an isolated phenomenon, but always has some external motive associated with it. We see this, for example, in the case of vengeance where the will to impose suffering on the person who has offended us is always allied either to the need of conquering after having been conquered or to the idea of a reestablished equilibrium and a satisfied justice. What shows that suffering is never anything but a sign of evil is that the most subtle and profound wickedness is not limited to suffering: it finds in suffering merely a means (which could be equally well served by pleasure) and has the further advantage of deceiving the other by false pretenses. What wickedness aims at is the diminution of being itself, a kind of inversion of the development of consciousness; it aims at corruption and degradation, although one cannot consider such a state free from a kind of secret suffering which the wicked person relishes beforehand.

7 THE DEFINITION OF EVIL

It is indeed remarkable that we can never define evil in a positive manner. Not only is it part of the couple of which good is the other term; but, further, it is impossible to define it without recalling the notion of good of which it is the privation.

Moreover, there exist, it seems, innumerable forms of evil, and we can fail to do good in many ways which are nominally the same. An ancient philosopher thought that good had a finite character, whereas evil had an infinite character. Here we recognize the common Greek opinion that the finite was the completed and perfect, that which lacked nothing, while the infinite was the indetermined, disorder, chaos, that which lacked everything that could give it meaning and value—that is, the act of thought which would enable man to organize, circumscribe, and take possession of it.

Let us pass over this dubious distinction. At least we must recognize that all forms of good converge upon one another. We could multiply virtues and even contrast them, insisting upon the diversity of moral vocations. Yet what is proper to all of these virtues is to produce a harmony between the different powers of consciousness, and what is proper to all moral vocations is to produce a harmony between different consciousnesses. Evil, on the other hand, is always defined as a separation, the rupture of harmony, either in the same being or between all beings. This is because every bad will pursues isolated ends which, sacrificing the whole to the part, always contaminate the integrity of the whole and threaten to annihilate it. It is understandable, then, that there are innumerable forms of evil, although they all possess the common character of dividing and destroying. We can observe this within the same consciousness where evil creates an interior rupture, where perversity itself gives us bitter pleasure, as well as in the interrelationships of consciousnesses that are in a constant state of conflict and enmity. The entente between criminals is no exception to this law, if it is true that such accord is always precarious and always turned against the rest of humanity. To the extent that it is a true understanding, it still imitates the good and is the foreshadowing of a moral society. This is true in such a way that if solidarity in good makes the unity of each being or the union of different beings closer and more complex, solidarity in evil cannot go on indefinitely without soon creating disharmony and discord, the result of which would be a state of conflict with ourselves as well as with the universe at large.

8 THE FUNDAMENTAL CHOICE

It is the role of the spirit to introduce value into the world. The word evil has no meaning except in relation to our spiritual destiny; and this destiny is nothing if it is not our work, if it does not depend on the successive deployments of our liberty. We cannot understand how this liberty could be exercised if the different ends proposed to its choice were juxtaposed on a horizontal plane. To choose is to establish a hierarchical or vertical order among our actions, such that each of our actions may be defined as an ascent or as a descent.

Thus the alternative between good and evil is directly related to our liberty. The experience of liberty is one with the experience of good and evil. For liberty is nothing if it is not the power of choosing. On the other hand, we could not choose if all the objects of the will were on the same plane. It is therefore necessary that there be differences of value to initiate the act of choice. But these differences would rupture and disperse the unity of the will if they were not all reducible to the multiple differences between good and evil. But the will itself secretly remains in that state of insensible oscillation by means of which we determine our destiny and feel capable of winning or losing all at every moment. Thus the perfect unity of the self resides in the possibility it has of choosing. But it can choose only between alternatives; and the self's unity is the living unity of the act which postulates and resolves this alternative. We see, therefore, that by a kind of paradox, our liberty can determine itself only by distinguishing between good and evil in the world. But in order that our liberty not become enslaved by this distinction, it is necessary that, in recognizing the value of good, it can nevertheless prefer evil in order to assert its independence by making a good of evil itself through an act of choice.

Life possesses value for us only if there is a place in it for a good that we can understand, will, and love. Evil, on the contrary, is something we can neither understand nor love, even if we have chosen it, something we condemn, when we have committed it, something which would be the condemnation of being and of life if it were their essence. Good and evil submit the real to the judgment of the spirit, for the real cannot justify itself unless it is found to be good. To say that it is evil would be to say that nothingness must be preferred to it. Good and evil thus both correspond to a right of jurisdiction which the spirit assumes over the universe. For there can be good and evil only for a will which considers the real in relation to a choice which it has made, a choice which the real sometimes confirms and sometimes belies. We agree, then, that the principle of good and evil is within us. But, either because the will is always associated in us with nature, or because it finds outside of us obstacles it cannot overcome, good and evil transcend its proper activity. This is what obliges the will to confront, in what concerns it, the problem of responsibility and merit and, in what concerns the universe, its very reason for existing.

Thus both good and evil are linked to the essence of the will which cannot determine itself unless the idea of the good sets it in motion. If this stimulus is lacking, either through lack of knowledge or lack of courage or by a perversion of that impulse which the good gives it, it then falls into evil. For the good cannot be a good for the will unless it remains to some extent elusive, either because the will has abused it or because it has turned away from good in still being attracted by its shadow.

That our liberty cannot be exercised without the presence of two opposite terms between which it constantly chooses is a source of suffering for us, because there is in choice an exigency which condemns us if evil prevails. Thus we prefer to predicate an essential, radical evil of the world rather than look into our will which, by its choice, causes it.

Pessimism is always a weak excuse. It is a failure of confidence and an abdication of our spiritual being that refuses to act and to give an object the meaning and value that depend on it alone. To recognize that there is evil in the world is to enable our spiritual activity to avoid it and thereby to acquire independence and vigor. Our spiritual activity constantly creates itself by opposing all that it encounters. It therefore runs the risk of always being buried, of being misunderstood and vanquished; but this risk is its very life; it draws nourishment from risk; risk bestows upon it its ardor and its purity. It is the nature of the life of the spirit to be invisible; it must always stand in need of support and regeneration and take the risk of always being rejected.

At any moment we can make materialism true by concentrating our attention upon objects outside of us and upon our instinctive nature within us. He who seeks the spiritual as an actual reality in the world might well complain that he never finds it. The world before us is devoid of spirituality, and this precisely because the spirit is a life which must penetrate the world, give it meaning, and transform it. The spirit is not a thing we display but an activity we exercise, in favor of which we choose and on which we gamble. It exists only for him who wants it and, in wanting it, brings it into being. It hides itself from him who denies it. Again, it bears witness to its essential nature by refusing to be found where it is not. Should we say that evil is present everywhere or that the spirit is not where it should be? But the judgment we pass on evil is also a testimony of the spirit which finds in evil its limit or its defeat. Evil is always known as evil by an act of the spirit which establishes a duality between the world and itself, and which finds in the world its opposite. But the spirit must have enough courage and confidence to accept the world as a trial, a task and a duty, as the condition of its separated essence, of the very activity by which it constantly creates itself, and of the victories which it never stops trying to secure.

9 ON THIS SIDE OF GOOD AND EVIL

If evil is a problem, we must try to learn how it is born within our consciousness. Its birth is a belated one and comes only with the emergence of reflection. We can imagine a dawn of consciousness where reflection is not yet active and where the distinction between good and evil is as yet unknown. This is the state of innocence described by Genesis in which the unity of consciousness has not yet been broken, its simplicity not yet tarnished, where it acts with a spontaneity that is both natural and spiritual. It is a state on this side of good and evil rather than beyond it. We sometimes think that the only evil for us is to have lost this innocence and that the true good consists in recovering it.

But let us beware of deception in this matter. Consider the innocence of a child: it is a negative innocence, the innocence of nature. The child has not yet begun to direct his life, but is rather directed by it. The child carries within him all the powers that he will one day exercise and is a victim of each of these in turn; the only unity the child has is the absence of any check that might curb this disorder. And yet man leans over the child's crib and admiringly and anxiously seeks in its face all the spiritual forces which he has lost, which he has wasted, blighted, and corrupted. But such a man has already made a choice. Those who preach "the return to childhood" do not want to be taken literally. The portrait of a child must not be that of an angel who has not yet come into contact with the world. Other more severe touches must be added, for the child is very close to the world but has not had time to raise himself much above it. Thus the child suffers. He is not self-sufficient; he is entirely the victim of the needs and distresses of organic life, of the pains of growth, of his impulses and biological needs. Moreover, the cruel probings of some psychologists discover in the child a formidable network of instincts, the fount of all those perversions we spend a lifetime trying to throw off and purify. The memory of this prereflective age never ceases to trouble and plague us.

But this account must be amended. The fact that the child enters the world like a lump of clay should not lead us to diminish in principle the value of our life. Life must have its roots in the most obscure and most profound regions of being in order to blossom forth one day into the brightest regions; it is good that the nobility of its destiny bear this relationship to the lowliness of its origins, and that the brute necessity to which life is at first bound give its liberty more force and impetus.

However, this nature in which life is, so to speak, buried is not in itself either good or bad, although it contains the germs of all the good and all the evil that will be born as soon as our liberty begins to operate. The adult can discover every imaginable perversion in this nature, but only after his reflection and will, having freed themselves from the senses, once again turn toward them to take pleasure in them and become their slave. The perversity of the child is often the perversity of the adult's thought. Just as the child has a kind of organic innocence before his consciousness is born, so too does he have a kind of spiritual innocence as soon as his physical needs are satisfied and his body permits him some leisure. Then he discovers the world in a disinterested fashion and begins to smile upon it. He opens himself to the world, already disposed to give and to receive, forgetting his body and seeking in things the echoes of that more intimate reality whose mysterious presence he experiences within him. But innocence becomes tainted as soon as the body and spirit, no longer pursuing separate careers, come together to choose their path. Then a choice must be made: and it becomes a question of knowing whether the body will show itself docile or if the spirit will allow itself to be overcome.

We sometimes dream that when our trials and tribulations are over wisdom will be a kind of rediscovered innocence. But innocence is never rediscovered. Once lost, it can only be transcended. There would be something impossible and even frightful in making it an object of desire. The experience of life makes us incapable of reconquering those primitive states to which we now attribute an inaccessible purity. Self-interest, passions, and memory have penetrated, enriched, and altered them. We never go backward; it is with all that we have become that we must now progress. Furthermore, any man who undertakes the enterprise of life wants to have self-consciousness, responsibility, and liberty. Otherwise he would merely receive the being which he has instead of giving it to himself, and so would be a thing rather than a being. We would not want to be victims of a spontaneity we could not control. We demand the power to do evil; no good is possible for us otherwise. We refuse to be content with a life that is a gift we need only accept. Would this be truly life for us? And could we call it our own?

The union of body and spirit is the condition of our liberty. Because of this union, we can become what we are by an act that depends on us. It is first of all because we are subjected to nature that the life of the spirit must be a constant liberation for us. If there is no ready-made liberty, if liberty can only be obtained and maintained as a result of much effort, it is evident also that it can give way to and justify determinism. This failure is in itself an evil. But the most radical and most secret evil lies in free choice which must be capable of betraying the good; otherwise the good, by becoming necessary, would disappear. Such is the grandeur of the life of the spirit: it can only be if it exists as ours. It coexists with a nature that resists and frequently scandalizes it. But this is inevitable. Spirit borrows from nature the strength it needs. It dwells in the use it makes of this strength, in the obedience and the ratification which it frequently gives nature, in the combat it carries on with it, from which it emerges sometimes vanquished, sometimes stronger and purer. It has no existence except by what it adds to nature, and it can add nothing to it except through reflection.

We must now study the origin of reflection, which sometimes has a purely critical, negative, and even destructive role, that dries up the springs of interior spontaneity and so often makes us unhappy and impotent. In its purest essence, however, it returns to the very source of our life and questions our activity in order to permit us to judge it and dispose of it. Our personal initiative is founded upon it, and in it the notions of good and evil begin to form.

10 THE BIRTH OF REFLECTION

Reflection has a triple origin in us. First, it may seem, as it has often been demonstrated and as the etymology of the word indicates, that when our spontaneity encounters an obstacle that obliges it to turn in on itself, to become aware of the end it seeks, and to interrogate itself on its possibility of attaining that end, then two persons are born within us, one of which discovers the other with a kind of astonishment. But the two persons soon separate and stand in judgment of each other. Secondly, reflection is, as it seems, inseparable from our awareness of time: I cease to become absorbed by what has been given to me as soon as I am capable of contrasting the present with the past and a future which can only be thought of and with which I begin to compare the present, since the past is an object of regret for me and the future an object of hope. Finally, reflection is born in a very special sense when I encounter others who, because they either resemble me or differ from me, oblige me to realize the image of what I am. Then unfathomable problems arise in me and multiply as my relations with others become closer and the demands of action more urgent.

We would be quite wrong to assume that reflection applies first and principally to the world of things, as the prestige of scientific method might lead us to think. This merely teaches me to recognize the relations of objects among themselves in order to enlist them in the service of mankind. But the most serious questions I ask myself bear on my conduct in regard to another person, whose consciousness is always to a certain degree impermeable to me, who is endowed with an inviolable liberty which I cannot even think of forcing or limiting, and with whom I continually seek a kind of accord and cooperation. As soon as my action begins to envisage persons about me rather than things, it becomes good or bad. Reflection, consequently, is naturally oriented toward the search for moral value. If my activity encounters an obstacle that limits it, my reflection might well rouse itself to transcend it; but reflection is not engaged in any decisive manner until it takes into consideration the destiny of self and the spiritual society it forms with all other selves.

Thus the difference between good and evil takes on real meaning as soon as reflection becomes operative. I can freely dispose of myself only through reflection. Until that time, nature acts in me and by me. With the birth of reflection, which makes me the author or the father of my own actions, which obliges me to justify them by reasons which I give myself, I experience the presence of nature as a slavery, that is to say, as a kind of humiliation and shame. Whence the tendency of traditional theology to consider nature itself as evil. This is because it imposes itself upon us in spite of our efforts. We have no choice but to suffer it. But nature is not evil; nature is rendered evil or perverse by the spirit which becomes subject to it and serves it. It makes an object of complacency out of the simplest and healthiest pleasures and degrades them in degrading itself. On the contrary, as soon as spirit illuminates nature from within and makes of it a means of its own progress, it transfigures and elevates it to its own level.

The life of the spirit and even the life of the self begin then with reflection. We might regret the loss of the innocent initiative of childhood and its spontaneous grace. But we should not like to purchase these at the price of distress and sufferings. There is little sincerity and little courage in such nostalgia. The paradise of childhood is an elementary and already falsified representation. Our nostalgia for it is a kind of contradictory desire. For it is less a question for us of returning to this instinctive and nebulous simplicity than of taking possession of all the resources that an adult consciousness can discover in it. Reflection is always present, seeking the path of least resistance, desiring to find enjoyment by not acting. But this ambition is prohibited. As soon as reflection is born, it imposes obligations on us that we cannot renounce. It creates a division in us but only to give us a light we had hitherto lacked, and it gives us a representation of the world only to oblige us to transform and improve it.

11 THE KNOWLEDGE OF GOOD AND EVIL

As soon as our activity ceases to be spontaneous, it is determined by knowledge. And evil originates in the relationship between knowledge and activity, as the unanimous tradition of all peoples recognizes. This is not to say that knowledge is evil in itself, as has been said. How could it, any more than nature, be evil? It is knowledge that enables us to gain access to the life of the spirit; with knowledge is born the condition of our liberty and consequently the undivided principle of both good and evil. Knowledge is undoubtedly not self-sufficient and is dangerous for us to the extent that we seek in it a pure satisfaction of the spirit. It sometimes happens, too, that it is more a distraction than a nourishment for us. Thought always tends to make of each problem a kind of game upon which it exercises its strength, a game that flatters our vanity either by the exercise itself or its success. Moreover, according to the author of the *Imitation of Christ*, knowledge is a difficult burden to bear. It can augment our egoism, our malice, our desire to dominate. And, in the most ancient myths, there is a kind of venom in knowledge. The relationship between evil and knowledge is without doubt singularly subtle. We cannot be content with thinking that nature is always good nor that knowledge, in seeking out its secrets, gives us only a means of doing evil. For it is the knowledge of good and evil and not the knowledge of things that engenders evil. When the good is present, it is not necessary to seek to know it in order to possess and enjoy it; too much light annihilates it, as we see in the myths of Pandora and of Psyche. But in the one as in the other, we find a very deep secret of the spiritual life which is this: the good is invisible, it cannot be grasped as an object, it is discovered mysteriously by those who desire it and not by those who scrutinize it. In the will which does good, the self goes out of itself and forgets itself; as soon as it seeks to know the good, it takes possession of it and makes it its own. But as soon as it begins to think about good, it ceases to do good. Thus we can understand that the knowledge of good and evil is already evil, since this knowledge changes good into evil by virtue of the very desire it has to appropriate the good.

This is because good and evil are not things that can be known. They are born of reflection, but only when reflection interrogates itself on its intention rather than its end. It is because the end can never be represented, because it can never be reached, that we are able to isolate the most spiritual and purest movement of the will. The end is merely the evidence of the will's momentary direction: it is merely an image or sketch which hides rather than reveals its deepest meaning.

It seems therefore that the distinction between good and evil is inseparable from the emergence of consciousness. This distinction, in the popular meaning of the word, is the proper object of consciousness and not at all the indifferent light which gives us a representation of ourselves and the world, as it is used in philosophy. But perhaps it might be shown that the second meaning derives from the first, and that we must know ourselves and the world in order to accomplish our spiritual destiny.

The distinction between good and evil gives pause to our thought and conduct; it causes the appearance of terror and anxiety in our consciousness; it obliges us, instead of being carried away by nature, to become responsible for what we are going to do, for what we are going to be. And this activity already judges us.

12 SELF-RESPONSIBILITY

It is characteristic of reflection to divide our spontaneous activity in order to create our interiority. We cease to trust in all of those forces which heretofore had carried us along in their wake. We have not yet encountered evil but only that extraordinarily lively and perpetually renewed emotion of discovering in our own depths not only an unknown and secret life but a life that depends upon us, a power of acting that is in our control and by which our destiny is to be shaped and the face of the world transformed. Reflection always measures the peril to which it exposes us. It separates us from the nature with which our being was formerly united. It obliges us to assume responsibility for ourselves. It gives our life an extraordinary keenness. Only in virtue of this do I exist as a center of initiative, as the author of what I am, that is to say, as consciousness, as liberty, as person.

In separating myself from nature which surrounds me, I separate myself from the nature that constitutes me. There is in me an individual, a being of instinct and desire with which I am no longer identified, although it is involved in each of my actions; it is both the matter and the instrument of my activity. I now force myself to assume responsibility for myself and for the world; for the spirit's activity does not permit of division. And since it does not abolish individual nature (rather it discovers it by transcending it), we can easily understand that it can choose between two alternatives: either it can consider the self as the center of the world and turn the world to its uses, or it can make the self the vehicle of the spirit by means of which the whole world must be penetrated in order to receive meaning and value. This is the supreme principle from which the opposition between good and evil is derived. This is enough to prove that evil is always present: it could disappear only if the spirit abolished nature. But, although nature always retains some hold on spirit, the latter, as soon as it begins to act, cannot dispense with nature; it is born while gradually freeing itself from nature; it develops by virtue of this obstacle which is also its support, and it is finally nature itself that is illuminated by spirit and serves its glory.

Thus in the problem of evil there are three different attitudes we can adopt toward nature. First, an attitude that is optimistic and charming, which consists in always praising it either in the admirable artistic spectacle it presents, or in the instincts it puts in us, and which thought always corrupts. However, it is still reflection that judges the beauty of this spectacle, and, since it can control our instincts, it also judges their rectitude. The second alternative is the reverse of the preceding: it adopts a pessimistic attitude toward nature and always considers it evil. There is at the bottom of many such attitudes an old Manichean dualism. But the same spirit which condemns nature is in conflict with it and does not always emerge victorious. Some may think that nature is reality while spirit is idealism which always topples when it is put to the test. But there is a third attitude which holds that nature in itself is neither good nor bad. Only the spirit, after it becomes active, consecrates nature's resources in order to dispose of them, but also in order to find in them sometimes an object of complacency and enjoyment and sometimes the strength and efficacy it needs and which nature alone can give.

We can say, in any case, that whoever considers nature either good or bad makes such a judgment only retrospectively. It is only when his will has come into play, when it has already chosen between good and evil, that he can say that nature is good or that it is evil in representing to himself all the actions which depend on nature as voluntary, and in distinguishing those which bear the character of goodness and generosity from those which give evidence of egoism and violence. It pertains to reflection to obligate everyone to become a problem to himself, to interrogate himself on the value of his life. Only the good can provide an answer to this problem and this interrogation. Evil not only leaves him without an answer, it further creates a scandal against which all the powers of consciousness protest.

SELECTIVE BIBLIOGRAPHY

La dialectique du monde sensible (1921) (Paris: Presses Universitaires de France, 1954)

La dialectique de l'éternel Présent
Vol.
      I: *De l'Être* (Paris: Aubier, 1928)
     II: *De l'Acte* (Paris: Aubier, 1937)
    III: *Du temps et de l'éternité* (Paris: Aubier, 1945)
    IV: *De l'âme humaine* (Paris: Aubier, 1951)

La conscience de soi (Paris: Grasset, 1933)

La présence totale (Paris: Aubier, 1934)

L'erreur de Narcisse (Paris: Grasset, 1939)

Le mal et la souffrance (Paris: Presses Universitaires de France, 1940). English: *Evil and Suffering*, trans. B. Murchland (New York: Macmillan, 1963)

Les puissances du moi (Paris: Flammarion, 1939)

Introduction à l'ontologie (Paris: Presses Universitaires de France, 1947)

Traité des Valeurs, 2 vols. (Paris: Presses Universitaires de France, 1951–55)

Quatre Saints (Paris: Albin Michel, 1951). English: *Four Saints*, trans. D. O'Sullivan (Notre Dame, Ind.: University Press, 1963)

De l'intimité spirituelle (Paris: Aubier, 1955)

Conduites à l'égard d'autrui (Paris: Albin Michel, 1957)

Chroniques philosophiques: Morale et Religion, 3 vols. (Paris: Albin Michel, 1960–67)

Manuel de méthodologie dialectique, ed. G. Brelet and G. Varet (Paris: Presses Universitaires de France, 1962)

Chapter 2

INTRODUCTION

VLADIMIR JANKÉLÉVITCH (1903–   ) has written a great number of books, among which are seven works on music (mainly on the music of Fauré, Ravel, and Debussy), and at least fifteen works on philosophy. Most of these philosophical writings are devoted to a "systematic" exposition of his own philosophy, whereas the remainder focus on topics connected with the history of philosophy; among the latter is an important book on Bergson and a remarkable work on Schelling.

Jankélévitch was inspired by the philosophy of Bergson; from a methodological point of view, however, he might be called a phenomenologist. He has always had a great interest in ethical problems, but in his view the careful study of these problems leads unavoidably to the domain of metaphysics and a philosophical study of man.

According to Jankélévitch, we must make a distinction between two types of human experiences. The first presents itself as a unity of being, unaware of itself because it is still undivided against itself; the second type is found in the various stages of our explicit and reflexive consciousness. When a man acquires knowledge about himself by acquiring knowledge about something else, he is forced to divide himself and thus to destroy the unity of the unreflective stage of consciousness. As long as man is in the original state, not divided, not self-conscious, he is in a state of innocence. This state of innocence is obviously precarious, because according to his own essence man has to act, and thus become self-conscious, and then the mind's coincidence with itself is destroyed.

From then on, there is a gap between man and world, and a gap between man and himself as object of consciousness. This basic detachment taken in its double sense is the origin of pain and evil, which can be alleviated only by irony.

Detachment, however, takes place on two different levels. First, there is the complete detachment that man accomplishes only in theoretical, disinterested contemplation. This type of consciousness, by taking the situation out of the flux of time and rescuing it from complete immersion in the present, frees us from the oppressive presence of the concrete situation and from consequent readaptations. The other type of consciousness, "half consciousness" (demi-conscience) or also "bad consciousness" or "bad conscience," is only half-detached from the concrete content, since it remains closely bound up with the passage of time and realizes that the fleeting present becomes necessarily transformed into a solidified, immutable, and irrecoverable past, at the same time bringing upon us a still-uncertain future. But this means that consciousness sees itself fundamentally frustrated in its basic desire for eternity—the desire that seeks to perpetuate a state of contentment. Pain and evil are unavoidable on this level.

However, it is possible to carry part of the disinterested contemplation into the practical situation by conceptualizing or banalizing the irremediable ills, by denying the uniqueness of our predicament and behaving as if the inescapable evil we encounter is just one case of evil necessarily connected with the universal and inescapable fate common to all of us. This "consolation of resignation" plays an important role in reconciling ourselves to misfortune and disappointment; the discovery that one's plight is the common lot makes innumerable ills tolerable. Genuine consolation, however, requires more than this; it implies a conviction of one's innermost self, and is not just a matter of rational assent. The Christian compensation in an eschatological future provides us with one solution; another is found in irony. Where half consciousness is a condemnation, because it holds us prisoners in the semelfacticity of the lived experience and offers its occurrence once and for all as an object of saddening contemplation, irony is complete detachment and thus "good conscience," which offers us a legitimate possibility of escape. Irony recognizes the necessity of our limitations in time and space, but at the same time realizes that there is a possibility of being elsewhere and later. It localizes our present within a temporal process consisting of an infinity of moments and thus reduces the intensity of the tragic "here and now." Furthermore, it makes us realize that each one of us has his proper place in the scheme of things, which he shares with everyone else. There is some consolation in this awareness, and it gives us a certain feeling of freedom. But even this kind of consolation is not really genuine. Such consolation is found only in the realm of a religious view. Within the perspective of such a view, it is possible to take up the partially undesirable, which the obstacle is, as the means of living. This is the attitude of the "serious man."

In Jankélévitch's philosophy a number of dual opposites appear. The basic dualism seems to be the one to which he refers with the terms the *Quid* and the *Quod*. The *Quid* refers to a world in which we can distinguish basic types and structures that allow us to account for things and events in a rational, mostly causal way. The *Quod* refers to a radically contingent world that is mainly the world of our action. Using this basic distinction, Jankélévitch has developed a "first philosophy" as well as an ethical theory.

In the selection that follows, the author describes conscience in terms of the pain connected with the fact that we realize that we have done something. The selection was preceded by a chapter in which he described duty as the pain connected with having to do something.

ON CONSCIENCE,

or On the Pain of Having-Done-It

Vladimir Jankélévitch

We must now try to grasp in its most intimate sense that intangible moral reality we have tried to capture in its most critical tension, that is to say, in the violent future incumbent upon it. This intimate tribunal is conscience. The will taken as *conscius sibi* or *secum* is the will no longer considered as oriented toward its ideal tasks and toward the construction of its having-to-be, but as interior to itself and, rather than absorbed in itself, existing *with itself* and, at the same time, *within itself*. In a word, the soul of the soul.

I SELF-CONSCIOUSNESS

With and *within* . . . , but neither merely "with," nor solely "within." *Within*: consciousness would then not be consciousness, but again vegetative and lethargic subjectivity. *With*: consciousness would then be two consciousnesses just as Siamese sisters are two persons, and we would then need a third consciousness, which would be consciousness of the two unconsciousnesses, or perhaps the guardian angel standing before the two half-conscious twin sisters. Plotinus had an intimation of this absurdity of an infinite regress, *eis apeiron*; and rather than admitting outside the Spirit, outside the *Nous*, a second *nous* whose task it would be to think the first and, little by little, a third one to think this thought

This essay is from *Traité des vertus*, by Vladimir Jankélévitch (Paris, 1968), pp. 143–77. Copyright © 1968 by Bordas/Mouton. The present essay was translated into English expressly for this edition by Joseph J. Kockelmans.

(*noein hoti noei hoti noei*), he condensed into one unique
intuition (*mia prosbolē*) this double thought, that which
thinks itself and that which thinks what is intelligible.[1] In
fact, however, this is merely a means of coming to a standstill
while avoiding the absurd (*atopon*), and it is admitting the
priority of the relationship characteristic of consciousness
over what is represented and what represents, over the pure
object and the pure subject. It is intimacy that is the most
secret interiority, which constitutes the ultimate instance that
alone is capable of sparing us the emptiness gaping between
the two selves: in this way we escape from the infinite, sub-
tilizing, and cancerous undoubling of the *idea ideae*.
The *tête-à-tête* of the two unconsciousnesses does not yet
fabricate one consciousness. But if an undoubled self is two
selves, then a redoubled self, that is to say a self repeated
twice, is merely *duplex* in an arithmetical sense, *solo nu-
mero*; for it is as alone as he who stands before a mirror.
Consciousness is the mystery of the unique in two, the same
thing being itself and another; however, not in turn (as is
the case in the alternations of personalities), but together. A
mystery of the same order found in generation designates
the ungraspable threshold of the procreator and the procre-
ated: before, there is only one organism and one individual,
and afterward there are two, without our being able to pin-
point the moment at which the miraculous doubling takes
place. In consciousness, the mystery of the duplication is no
longer a "limit," as is the case in procreation, and it does not
give birth to an independent offspring: rather, it is the light
and the spiritual *aura* in which bathes a subject-object that
has a dialogue with itself, *heautōi dialegomenos*. Rather than
reiterated *ego*, rather than a populated and inhabited ego,
consciousness is this animation of the virtual duo, which is
never a society, although it is always a silent dialogue. The

[1] *Enneads*, II, 9, 1. Cf. Spinoza, *Ethics*, II, 21: "Simulac enim
quis aliquid scit, eo ipso scit se id scire, et simul scit se scire quod
scit, et sic in infinitum." [Thus if a man knows anything, by that
very fact he knows he knows it, and at the same time knows that
he knows that he knows it, and so on to infinity.]

ego anceps, the undoubled but not doubled ego, is in conversation with this It-self which one calls the *self* and which is the ego "bent back upon itself." The ego is not an other than its own self, no more than the model is not an other than its own image in the mirror, no more than the subject in the nominative becomes an other when he is object or complement. However, the original does not form that free and living unity with its copy which is characteristic of the bond between the ego and the self of this ego; and on the other hand, in the order of consciousness, no one can say which one is the model and which is the duplicate, inasmuch as that ego and self have a meaning that is even more relative than Aristotle's matter and form: each one of the two, at the very same moment that it posits itself, detaches the other from itself by means of a projection of consciousness so that subject and object originate simultaneously, in one and the same act, in which there is neither prototype nor system of reference. The Self, that is to say the ego "as" reflected, has exactly the same content as the ego, and it differs from this ego merely through its position; and yet the Self is not identical with the ego, for it expresses in an abstract form what is substantive and personal life in the ego. If this were not the case, how would the relationship of consciousness be possible? There is relationship only when there is encounter and alterity. Now, the ego has relationships with the self, relationships without relations, as it were; for if the ego is absolutely and intransitively ego, in other words if the ego is what it is without any *quatenus*, the ego is not a self, and the ego, in turn, would not be ego except in certain respects or from certain points of view. I am I, but the I *is* not the ego, precisely because it becomes ego; therefore the copula that attributes the self to the ego always has a synthetic meaning. That is why to know oneself and to possess oneself constitutes a problem: How can one *have* what one *is*, and how can one *become* what one is? In other words, how can one materialize oneself? Now, this paradoxical relationship between the ego and the self is made possible through the very profundity of the psyche, which is completely organized vertically into superimposed levels; because of its duration and memory, the psyche is actually never what it can be, but it is an other at the same time to a greater and to a lesser extent: less great than the self if it is the I, greater than the ego if it is all that the self can be, it is what it is not and is not what it is; it does not coincide with itself; the self surpasses the ego, which in turn surpasses the self by always being beyond its own present. The present is never at the tympanic point of our highest aims: in this dimension of duration, which is the shadow in which the perspective relief of each instant soon fleets away, in this overcoming of ourselves by our ipseity which is too great, we find the ever-renewed occasion to become conscious and to relate to ourselves. In this way, the ego and what is mine, the ipseity and all that belongs to it make themselves unequal to one another; it is in this way that the minute distance without which it is not self-consciousness gapes between these two presents that are but one (for I am the only one to be myself.)

If all self-consciousness is consciousness of Self as thing, that is to say in the sense of a passive past participle, consciousness of a thing, in turn, is always in a certain sense self-consciousness; for the object in a relative way participates in the constituting egoity. Thus each consciousness is to a certain degree bad consciousness: for it experiences itself at the same time as it experiences its thing, finds itself back in its thing, deplores the subjectivity of its representation; and there is no absolutely good and happy consciousness except that of the creator who is unconscious of himself, because this innocent consciousness has transcended the unhappy intelligence of the one who is conscious in a sterile way; this happy innocence is paradoxically the "super-consciousness" of the unhappy self-consciousness. Our body more than anything else favors this happy form of becoming conscious: our body which is, if not the subject-object of the identity philosophy, at least the object-subject, the place of half consciousness and the seat of pain, the materialization of our intermediate situation. For pain is the thought of the body, *noesis sōmatos*, and the amphiboly of our sensory and motor aspects. Is it not true that *sōma*, this privileged object that is we ourselves, is at the same time the reflecting surface on which the centripetal excitations bounce back into movements, and the absorbing surface on which the centrifugal impulses of activity smash and linger in the form of sensations, feelings, and resentments? *Matière et mémoire* has said the last word about this. The "double sensation of the same order" produces itself on the level of the body; the afferent process folds itself, as it were, back over the efferent just as the passion folds itself back over the action; is passion not the reverberation, or the pathic rebound, of all centrifugal action? For only the *Actus purissimus* is exonerated from all expenses and costs, the only one who does not "undergo" what he "does." Such is the strangeness of the body where, for us, as one could say, is concentrated the wonder itself of existing, of hearing ourselves naming ourselves through a third, and of seeing ourselves suddenly publicly in a mirror: to realize that one is he for the others, that is to say, a responsible person, and that, at the same time, one is I for oneself; that is the discovery of which we become aware each minute of the demi-alienation of the body: for this having is our being, for this possession is we ourselves. In this way, all sensation is at the same time presentative and felt. I see what I feel, and I touch what I see, and these multiple paths furrowing the object in all senses recomplete the dimensions that envelop the self-feeling. But, taken by itself, the body would not superimpose these different spaces without the resistance of the non-ego, which forces to flow back toward the center an effort that was ready to emerge into the world; one does not make out of the other what one wishes; and the inert solid bodies, they too, show themselves little manipulable, disobedient, and rebellious in regard to my enterprises. That is why consciousness originates as differential function or as the feeling of a difference in potential between myself and the world; consciousness is the tension between the half success of a problematic objectivation and the half failure of an emotion that is action-on-the-spot, frustrated action, that is to say, agitation.

II HALF CONSCIOUSNESS

Self-consciousness, as being always halfway, finds itself caught between its vocation and its nostalgia: the nostalgia of the nightly unconsciousness in which it would like to be swallowed up, and the vocation of the space far away where the reason of its being is to insert itself in that space and in so doing to forget itself. On the one hand, there is in it, as it were, a tendency to complete the happy movement of generation to its end, which culminates in the detachment and emancipation of the offspring; but inversely one reads in the motherly anxiety a tendency to revoke the emancipation of the ungrateful offspring: just as Kronos swallowed his own offspring, consciousness in the same way would like to absorb the "other self which one can see with his own two eyes, oneself and something else, an intruder, consciousness outside you which animates and agitates arms and legs, a living consciousness over which you do not have any power. . . ."[2] Such tendency is exhibited in Tolstoi by the wonder of the Countess Rostova before Nicholas, the adult to which she had given birth. Is not Eros itself, in which Aristophanes of the *Symposium* recognizes a nostalgia of the androgyne, torn between the coincidence in Being and the alienation in Having? Diotyma, too, declares it synthetic or demonic, that is, impure, because it is at the same time want and opulence, and intermediating between humans and gods. Kierkegaard tells us about this anxiety of the mind which projects its own reality, its own my-self, outside itself, but anxiety would no longer be anxiety if consciousness were to succeed in its movement of extroversion, were to go to the end of the slope, were to finally detach itself from the adhesiveness of subjectivity. Depending upon whether or not self-consciousness finds the exit and the way out, does or does not emerge into exteriority, we call it either more intellectual or more moral; but just as all consciousness that retains the aftertaste of its own

[2] Paul Claudel, *Le Pain dur*, p. 121. Tolstoi, *Guerre et Paix*, I, iii, 6.

intimacy, remains to a certain degree conscious of self, all intellectual consciousness, too, remains to a certain extent moral consciousness or, what amounts to the same thing, bad conscience; for because it is sensible, impure, and carnal, the thinking reed never has a good conscience. That is to say, all conscious creatures are also conscientious creatures that experience themselves as caught on all sides by life, and tear themselves on all the thorns along the road; everything keeps touching them "to the heart." And from this flows that conscientious pain which is the bad conscience of all joy and the bad conscience of all happiness, which is not the current from one pole to the other, but the short circuit.[3] It is far from true that an agent "without conscience" is always unconscious: on the contrary, he is too conscious, and this lucidity is precisely the aggravating circumstance that redoubles his sin. For the distance of consciousness, such as one acquires through movements, action, theory, art, or irony, cures us of unhappiness as well as scruples. To suffer is to fold oneself back over oneself and retrace one's steps; pain therefore begins with becoming aware, at the moment when the ego for the first time tears off the surgical bandage, the adhesive tape that kept it back in the sweet euphoria of the unconscious. There is no longer a protecting dissociation and distance. It is thus that half consciousness, that is to say, the newly born pain, is well linked to our corporality, which imposes upon us the "come-back"—for the agent always implies the "patient," not only as the expiatory justice of the *Gorgias*[4] would have it, of one subject in regard to another, but within one and the same subject. It is human not to accomplish the thing one has started and simply to achieve nothing. This state of mixing leaves us a choice between three kinds of fevers: the infinite undoubling, frantic exaggeration, and paralyzing fascination. Let us call "undoubling" the feverish proliferation of a consciousness that, unable to flee its own shadow, to climb up from the depths of life, divides and subdivides it-

---

[3] Louis Lavelle, *Observation sur le Mal et sur la Souffrance*, p. 38.
[4] Plato, *Gorgias* 476 b: ἆρα εἴ τίς τι ποιεῖ, ἀνάγκη τι εἶναι καὶ πάσχον ὑπὸ τούτου τοῦ ποιοῦντος [when a man performs any act, there must be something to be operated upon by the agent].

self within itself: this consciousness believes it detaches it-self from its own center, but it labors on itself and escapes from the interior without succeeding in finding a genuine evasion; such is the despair of the incurably immanent sub-jectivity, the ironic rarefaction of an always mobile and al-ways more-tenuous spirit which becomes infinitely more com-plicated without ever finding rest. In the "quintessenced" civilizations, is not this subtilization of the exponent of con-sciousness an indubitable symptom of decadence? Extremism is another consequence of our intermediate situation; the creature that is captive of its own impurity remains faithful to its vocation of purity; whereas the morality of the right means (*meson*) installs itself most comfortably within a me-diocrity that it calls moderation, the radicalisms of youth champ at the bit. Logical radicalism, social radicalism, ex-tremism of faith, and dogmatism of pure affirmation, all yield to the dizzying temptation of the absolute; they teach that the true and the good must be taken superlatively or at the limit; they wish themselves to be intransigent, maxi-malists, and extreme purists. But one must add here that in our amphibious state these excesses, and following them the contempt of the psychosomatic complex, and all the excesses of angelism do not represent more than a caricature of catharsis; consciousness, instead of attaining extreme objec-tivity, lets itself be carried away downstream by its weight and inertia. Bad conscience is no longer here, as was the case in the first two fevers, the bewilderment of a consciousness that has lost its orientation; rather, it is a consciousness that has been stopped and, as it were, nailed to its place; a con-sciousness that is petrified by this gorgon of object-subject, by this fascinating body which hypnotizes it; this conscious-ness cannot succeed in any of the two liberating movements, neither the flight into the depths of the night, nor the evasion toward the great meridian day of knowledge and the pure air of vast plains: rather, it immobilizes itself in a kind of dim ambiguity that is halfway between broad daylight and the unconscious of midnight. Such is the penumbra of half consciousness, of that consciousness that is almost conscious and bound to its unhappiness: instead of whirling around while undoubling itself, bad conscience, stupified and petrified by remorse, takes up its position between what is beyond and what is on this side.

In the presentation we have given of it, moral consciousness should be held to be an unsuccessful consciousness, just as emotion is held by biologists to be a "failure" of the instincts; but this is tantamount to admitting the following presupposition: a successful consciousness is a consciousness that leads to, if not lasting work, then at least to the complete manageability and the full availability of its body. In fact, such indeed appears to be the activist and progressive vocation of the demiurge who was very occupied with replacing the solid bodies, piling up the freestones, modifying the figures and forms by actions of labor: intermediate between the two angelisms, that of original innocence and that of good conscience, the master of energy leaned toward the second, not toward the dreaming angels, but toward the angels who are builders of cities, colonizers, and soldiers. Thus moral consciousness is like an abortive action, which instead of ending in effective movements, holds still next to the body, becomes saltation, dance, and stationary agitation. To change into sensation energy made to discharge itself in effective gestures and efferent movements, is the whole monstrosity of the pain, the whole failure of bad conscience. And just as narcissism is that kind of love contrary to nature which employs a charitative movement, which is normally oriented toward the Other, in order to love itself, just so is unhappy consciousness a work that labors upon itself; unhappy consciousness, in this regard perverted and narcissistic, finds itself referred to the self of its ego through a kind of autophagous (self-devouring) and contradictory reflection; that is why there is a painful and unhappy element in all self-love, and a little narcissism in pain. Certainly the law of interchange valid for all creatures requires that all activity have as ransom its correlative passivity, that is to say, its elementary pain; that which touches is *ipso facto* touched by what it touches; and each mover is moved. But usually it is not our entire motricity that flows back in this way to the periphery, it is merely a small portion of it, a simple aftertaste. Pain itself is the complete confusion of the motor and the sensitive aspects, the one folded over the other. "A kind of motor tendency on a sensible nerve,"[5] says Bergson. In this case, one and the same thing is active and passive in its entirety. And yet is there not a kind of utilitarian finalism in this measuring of the failure or the success of consciousness on the basis of action, and in treating all bad conscience as an "action that failed"? One can understand that a philosophy of energy, the pragmatism of businessmen or pioneers, believes a sentiment to be a secondary rebound of the act and, literally, a resentment (re-sentiment). But what would happen if our reference system were that which is sensed, instead of being the act? If action were an ineffective result of sentiment? A diversion and a derivative for dried-up people? And even this half success, considered in its esoteric aspect, that is, as a positive fact and no longer as a slip, becomes in turn a relative triumph over unconsciousness. However, it is not the practical utility that is at stake here, but merely ethical absurdity. Sterile, supernatural, absurd, bad conscience did not promise to build hospitals and to clear up the swamps; and it is in vain that optimism exerts itself to give a kind of teleological rationality to pain. Do we not say: there are no "works" of duty?

Or would there perhaps have been room for distinguishing two degrees of moral consciousness according to the distance consciousness succeeds in keeping: bad conscience, which is "consequent," and the "antecedent," which is perhaps moral, ethical, or, better, practical sense by means of its content but intellectual sense because of the success of its undoubling. The rear guard and the advance guard, as Kierkegaard says.[6] The one is retrospective, the other prospective. The latter could be defined as the perception of the human in all ethical situations; a concrete situation being a complex of innumerable circumstances, the semelfactive intersection of a date, a place, a person; the meaning we have for it must be considered to be a kind of subtlety of mind that is simultaneously in harmony with the multiplicity of the variables

[5] *Matière et mémoire*, p. 56.
[6] *Pureté du coeur*, trad. Tissot, p. 23.

through its pluralist delicateness and with the irreversible historicity of all conjunctures through the subtlety of its tact. But it is not only this moral "taste," this sharp discrimination of values: it is also the premonitory technique, the guardian *daimōn* who infallibly unravels the Gordian knot of the cases of conscience; and it is not merely clinical intuition that establishes the diagnosis from the inextricable maze of the symptoms, but it is the good advice and the instantaneously discovered solution at the intersection of our duties. Consequent conscience, which intervenes after the act is accomplished, is not a helpful consciousness, but rather a useless and posthumous consciousness, a belated consciousness; and when one arrives too late, what else can one do but suffer? Pain is this ineffective reaction of a living being that can no longer repair the damage that has been done and now compensates for it fictively: unhappiness is neither consolation nor medication, but rather, desperate sanction. However, even here there should be room for distinguishing between a retrospective consciousness, which repairs to a certain extent, albeit *post rem*, the harm done, and a consciousness that is radically incapable of eradicating its fault. Corrective consciousness, which is nothing other than repentance, looks toward the past, just as preventive consciousness looks toward the future; remorse, on the other hand, because it is pure pain and inconsolable despair, receives its healing from a sudden and radically unprepared-for grace. Remorse is a repentance that does not know that it is penitent. In fact, two clearly distinguished types of scrupulous people correspond to the two moral consciousnesses: the scrupulists who are scrupulous "in advance," and deliberate at the threshold of the decision and are barely more than hesitating people, and the scrupulists "after the event," who only know how to suffer. On the one hand, consciousnesses that are perplexed by too much imagination, and on the other, consciousnesses that suffer from too great a memory. The helplessness, the inability to take into account the lessons of experience, are without a doubt not the distinctive traits of moral consciousness, but they designate the most characteristic consciousness, namely that which is not the firm resolution to do better, but useless suffering; it is not the robust shoulder breadth of a project oriented toward the future,[7] but the silent affliction of a desolate heart.

III MORAL CONSCIOUSNESS

In order to understand how highly theology and emotionalist innatism estimate the oracular authority of the *vox conscientiae*, one supposes that conscience represents the principle of living intimacy and, as it were, the inside, itself, of the law for all morality. There is no higher instance than a profound, serious, and attentive conviction; and just as the Cartesian analysis invites all intelligence to think again and to comprehend by itself, so the moralist Renouvier honors this interior tribunal, which the Protestant theologian Auguste Sabatier calls faith and which is the free, immanent inspiration of a sovereign consciousness. What transcends conscience transcends us. Consciousness certainly *is* in the case of thought: doubt does not deny thought except by thinking, that is to say, by positing, itself, what it denies; it cannot not affirm it; and just as this circle of the *Cogito* (never cursed but always blessed) verifies the impossibility of a total skepticism, so in the same way does the summit of moral intimacy represent the ultimate instance for which appeal is impossible, except in the case of bad faith; the strong spirit contests this unimpeachable testimony without conviction and faintly; in spite of itself, it must listen to these silent reproaches of reason of which Malebranche[8] speaks and which bad faith itself continues to hear after having closed its ears; the silent reproach of conscience still whispers and murmurs again and again in the ear of the skeptic, notwithstanding his desperate denials, just as the eye of remorse sees in the grave the fugitive who has chosen the shadows of the night. Nothing replaces this intimate consent of the whole soul—neither the superficial consent that adheres to words, nor a transcendent authority which demands that

[7] Kierkegaard, *La Pureté du coeur*, p. 22. Lavelle, op. cit., p. 64.
[8] *Entretiens sur la Métaphysique*, 3e entretien.

it, itself, be relived by conscience in order to make itself be admitted.[9] Our belief cannot be forced, it wishes to be "convinced"; for it is the first and the last word; irony, if not violence, will perhaps enter this invincible fortress of the mental restriction, love, and unconquerable will. Must we comprehend this instance without appeal as the insurmountable barrier that necessarily poses a limit to the infinite regression of our doubts? Dogmatism, which is always searching for criteriologies and absolutist canons, voluntarily yields to the need to objectify the authority of conscience: it is in this way that the myth of the infallible *magisterium* forms itself, criterion of good and evil, "inter bonum et malum discernens," as Calvin says. It is the destination of each *cogitatio* to turn one day into a *res cogitans*: dynamism turns over into substantialism: *scintilla conscientiae*, which should be the principle of our autonomy, imposes upon us the authority of God by universalizing itself. But inflexibility calls for inflexibility: a skepticism echoes this dogmatism and contests it; if there is a question of pleading immutability and finality of the instinct in the fact, does one on the contrary not have an easy game to describe its relativity and to enumerate its peculiar aberrations? Heteronomy which ignores exactness, particularity, the precision of personal experiences, makes us accustomed to probabilism, that is to say, the spirit of approximation. Above all, the spiritual automatism of infallibility expresses in man the need for a half certitude, which is an opaque certitude, for it is certain about the fact but not about the how: one invokes the infallible as he would an article of faith, that is, as something either impossible to be understood or concerning which an explanation is useless. Infallibility, a negative attribute, would suit, rather than the intelligible and diaphanous evidence of Descartes, Pascal's undemonstrable truths of the "heart," which are "fere absconditae"—that is, obscure in their principle and their goal, their properties and circumstances, and clear in their effective or quoddi-

---

[9] P.-J. Proudhon, *De la Justice dans la Révolution et dans l'Église*, 1re étude, chap. IV, sec. 19: ". . . chacun se trouve juge en dernier ressort du bien et du mal." [. . . everyone finds himself passing judgment without appeal about good and evil.]

tative existence; and this is the very formula of chiaroscuro. He who *cannot make a mistake* is thus for us a source of dim, perhaps more drastic than gnostic, certitudes. In opposition to the uncertain certitude of which we spoke at the beginning, the half-certain certitude, which is merely the experience of the *anangkē stēnai,* would not know how to be a certitude of conscience: it resembles those *probationes per absurdum,* which by skipping the itinerary of the refutation, convince without persuading, and in sum are (according to the rationalists of the sixteenth century) no more than sophisms. Thus, to make mistakes is a double characteristic of creatures: first, because of the margin of indeterminateness that results from the innumerable circumstances and factors of all mental verification, and then because, as Aristotle knew, one is wrong in claiming to be right when one is right without knowing why. In our finitude there is no other infallibility than that of the computer, which does not know what it does, nor how it does it. The automaton is right blindly, and thus it is wrong. For the manner in which something is done is what counts! No, the fallen angel, the repenting sinner we are, does not content himself with authoritative certitudes: without a consciousness to bring it to life again, blind certitude will never be more than a dead letter. That conscience which we want is certainly the term beyond which one cannot rise, but, even more, it is the positive beginning that makes everything understood, the fact as well as its why, and it develops its consequences infinitely. A fallible, too human, conscience. Because conscience is the "event" and the incontestable lived truth that is always *index sui,* and because pain is pre-eminently the event, the indubitable evidence of all distress, it becomes understandable that unhappy consciousness must be the summit of conscience. Those who speak of a "Stellungnahme," or the taking of a position,[10] certainly allude to this spiritual event, an event that is always initial and effective in an always sincere subject. Under the condition that the "heart" is in it, conscience is something that one is forced to *take seriously,* which is not participated in but completely endorsed, lived,

[10] Willy Bremi, *Was ist das Gewissen?* (Dissertation, Zurich, 1934, pp. 19 ff.).

and taken up; not just known superficially, or with a small portion of the intellect, but lived by the entire soul. One must say that the subject, far from being the neutral spectator, the judge or the witness of his act, is personally engaged through his pain, precisely in the moral destiny of which he himself is at the same time the author, the accuser, and the real victim. Such is the presence of the present, which appears in remorse as the past present: in fact, remorse is not, as is memory, an image that is dissociated from the real, a semblance and, in a certain sense, a pellicle detached from the thing; remorse is the act "in person," and as it were in the flesh and bones. Regret is the evil of a memory that has maintained the taste of the past while losing the presence of it; but remorse is a bad conscience, which, if it succeeds in *undoing the thing done*, cannot annihilate *the fact of having done it*; remorse suffers from its being unable to make what has been done undone, from being unable to make from a *factum* an *infectum*; regret is the nostalgic melancholia of the irreversible, that is to say, of the past that is too much past; but remorse is the despair of the irrevocable and is thus the irreparable fault, *culpa ipsa*, the sin itself literally present. For to have remorse over one's mistake, means to relive it, and, literally, to do it again, that is to say, to do it in the sense in which Max Scheler says of sympathy that it is "reproduction": such is the "re-creation" that is initial creation,[11] such is iteration in general that is not repetition but a continued first time. Thus bad conscience at each moment renews its sin just as the Christian sinner at each minute recrucifies his Saviour. In this respect conscience resembles Erōs, the old novelty, which stands at its beginning. In the *Symposium*, Agathon, objecting to Phaedrus, says that Love is the youngest of the gods, *neōtatos theōn*, and Pascal writes for his part that it is "always being born": that is why (the *Discourse on the Passions of Love* continues) one generally represents it with the characteristics of a child. In conscience one retrieves this youthful newness of love. A kind of onto-

---

[11] This is the meaning that Philippe Fauré-Fremiet gives to this word in his books *Pensée et ré-création* and *La Récréation du réel et l'équivoque*.

logic and tautegoric realism that is characteristic of conscience brings us immediately from the image to the truth:
the realm of moral consciousness is thus not the allegory, but
the literal sense; each agent manifests himself autodidactically in it; each student is at the same time the master; each
imitator is an inventor. That is the authentic, original, and
pre-eminently primary situation, the foundation of all good
faith, which all affectation of simulators is unable to suppress.

This anxious half consciousness does not leave us unarmed,
for the same cause that constitutes its care also founds its
power. My conscience, says Kierkegaard,[12] knows all *that* I
know, and it knows *that* I know it; thus it is the knowledge
of the *quid*, and the *quod* of this *quid*, and once more of the
quod of this *quod*, and so on *ad infinitum*; each form becomes
content or matter for it, whereas this matter requires being
surpassed in turn by the quodditative effectivity of a more
subtle form. For example, idealism says that the object exists
exclusively as thought, but it becomes dogmatic if it limits
itself to that: thus idealism's consciousness is the consciousness of the *fact* of thinking, for thought is in turn something
that is, from the moment it thinks; thought is above all a
thinking being! Descartes, too, discovers the *Cogito* and *Esse*
together, and the *Esse* in the *Cogito*. Thought is, thus it
thinks; consciousness, in so far as it is, exists, becomes therefore the unconscious and innocent object of another consciousness, of a superconsciousness that would be its subject.
This *fact-that* (*hoti*) to the second power, this effectiveness
of an effectiveness, this quoddity with exponent, this is the
object of an infinite becoming-conscious: for Socrates is conscious of his own nescience *xunoida emautōi hoti ouk oida*;
for Socrates is the shame of Alcibiades;[13] for Socrates puts
the impudents and augurs to shame through the confusion
that his exponent of conscience causes their Credo; and
everyone knows that Plato compares this perplexity (*aporia*)
of the impudent to the fecund, erotic, and maieutic discomfort of childbirth. By seeing you, the impudent exclaims,

[12] *La Pureté du coeur*, p. 201. Cf. Epictetus, *Discourses*, I, 1, 4,
and 6.
[13] *Symposium*, 216 a, b; 218 d; 213 b-c.

apostrophizing his bad conscience, I am ashamed to live the way I do. He who has swallowed all shame begins to doubt the reasons he has to live. It is conscience that thus puts into question the radical origin of existence and contests the fact that the *quid* is a matter of course, and that in interrogating itself about being, asks not only *quid sit* but also *an sit*. Being, shaken in its possibility by the categorical absolutism of this instance, becomes contingent and arbitrary. "I know that I know only one thing," Pascal says in his *Prière pour le bon usage des maladies*;[14] in so saying, he intended to uproot the evidence of good and evil and all the eternal truths. Supreme consciousness finds itself thus sent back without delay from the essence of the existence to the existence of this essence, and then to the existence of this existence; from the truth of the real to the reality of that which is true; from the relativity of being to the being of the relation. And this is the characteristic mark of an intelligence that is sovereignly complex, indirect, and ironic, namely this refusal to adhere to a reference system and to weigh heavily upon one of the moments of the regression: for example the indifferent arbitrator is fooled if he wills according to his freedom as well as according to his nature, and if he is not free of his own freedom. But if one does not wish to admit the infinite undoubling of the *idea ideae*, nor invoke the irrational decree of a will that is creative in regard to the *quod*, consciousness must be considered a gnostic intuition or the enveloping lucidity that places what is mostly conscious beyond what is relatively unconscious: for instance, the liar beyond the naïve, and maturity beyond the naïve youth. Consciousness *a fortiori* comprises the satisfied complacency; and conscious consciousness comprises so much the more the unconscious consciousness that installs itself as ordinary people do (*bourgeoisement*) in a hypothetic and notional knowledge: superconsciousness comprises consciousness, and extreme superconsciousness comprises superconsciousness. Consciousness that is more than conscious restores *ad infinitum* this quodditative order that constitutes the effectiveness of all that exists.

[14] Sec. 14.

Static complacency makes itself at home in the accomplished act just as the inspiring inspiration congeals in the inspired works, and just as the vital force, whirling in its place, immobilizes itself in the organisms: but is there not also a dynamic complacency, complacency not of standstill but of movement, which is found in the refusal of all naïveté and the insatiable thirst for knowledge? The innocent wishes to taste himself in order to enjoy himself, to feel himself in all his dimensions, to experience himself at the same time as spectator and spectacle, witness and actor: it is in this way that vision, because of its spatializing vocation, incessantly reconstitutes the voluminous and concrete body; it is in this way, also, that the rational *logos*, through the intervention of a medium, that is to say, a third party, offers its arbitration to the difference between the extremes and tends toward the undistinguished "whatever it may be," that is, to the concept, the virtual predicate, the formal and impersonal predicate of an indeterminate number of subjects in any judgment. These complications, subdivisions, and undoubling of the consciousness of consciousness are at the root of the complacency and the quintessenced affectation: for example, there is a fastidious refinement which one would like to call the good bad-taste and which is consciousness simultaneously of bad taste and of the good: good taste, conscious of what is bad, becomes unconscious in regard to the superconsciousness of the two; in this infinite distillation, extreme superconsciousness, playing with this danger, turns from "for" to "against," and then again to the "for," and always goes further away from the original simplicity and innocence. In this sense, all virtue can be changed into vice through the conscious grasp one takes of it. Indeed, this is the curse of the alternative and of the finitude characteristic of us creatures, namely that all primary sentiment leaves behind it an aftertaste, a secondary resonance, a vibration of resentment which echoes it. But through a dialectic that is ironically contradictory, the intention must take taste in itself, and know itself a little, in order to be really intended, just as happiness must know itself as happy in order to be complete happiness. Taken in this sense, nothing knows its own happiness. The same reason that in

Kierkegaard's view constitutes the "anxiety" of happiness explains the pharisaic rapture: "Nothing hinders happiness more than the memory of happiness," says André Gide:[15] and likewise, good conscience, which is content and enjoys with satisfaction its own virtue, acts and composes itself as a virtual witness, a lenient spectator in turn arousing pity and praise, whose presence transforms the innocent movement into a theatrical representation. This disinterested third, which the logical mediation charges with the care of the reconciliation of the extremes, is, in the intimacy of confidence, no more than someone who embarrasses indiscretely. The interior tribunal resembles the private conversation of a loving couple that is a direct discourse and an immediate relation of the I to the Thou; the duo is here that of subject and object. The indifferent medium that changes the duo into a trio sometimes freezes our dialogued monologue, sometimes makes virtue a role to be played, and the person into a character. That is where the obsession of the "gallery" and all good bad-faith of mannerism come from. Complacency is absurd self-pity. Innocence is like those qualities of which Schelling[16] speaks: one cannot be *pure* except under the condition of not *having* purity, that is to say of not possessing it knowingly. For example: one cannot be intelligent and say so; nor can one make it a profession to be spiritual. And that is also true of modesty, remorse, irony, grace, and all those fragile, deceptive, and contradictory qualities that exist only in the nescience of themselves; according to Tolstoi,[17] it is for this reason that the plain face of Princess Mary lights up when she does not think of herself; it is the light of innocence that shines from this face without sin, erasing the grimness of anxious lies. And inversely, it is a consciousness too well informed that makes a charming man into a professional charmer. "What I am," says Angelus Silesius, "I do not know; and that which I know, I am not." But where, then, will consciousness find lodging? La Rochefoucauld's dialectic occupies

---

[15] *L'Immoraliste*, p. 101.

[16] *Zur Geschichte der neueren Philosophie, Naturphilosophie* (Werke, vol. X, pp. 100–1.

[17] *Guerre et Paix*, 1re partie, chap. xxii.

itself in this way with upsetting the demon of complacency in our good movements, in humility and pure intentions. What is true for altruist spontaneity and devotion is not less true for aesthetic sincerity; consciousness of style is the worst enemy of style; and music, in turn, will never express anything except under the condition of not having willed to do so. This not-planned-for expression is without a doubt the true mystery of Fauré. Schelling and Rilke, speaking of God, say with Tauler: Who wants to obtain Him will lose Him. And Pascal, in the language of negative theology, says: God hides Himself from him who entices Him, and reveals Himself to him who searches for Him.[18] Is this not what made us have doubts about the ethical perfection and capitalization of duty? And yet, the subject must become aware of himself in order to exist completely, and you know that Schelling saw in this first alienation of innocence the beginning or *prōton existamenon*, the primordial upsurge of what exists; but on the other hand, the existing thing turns into its opposite if it knows itself; and thus the misfortune of existence, which is also the tragedy of all culture, demands from us this inevitable ransom: the existent *will be someone under the condition of becoming another*; an alternative where our finitude makes itself felt imposes upon us this necessary sacrifice, this denial of consciousness of oneself. The alternative gives with one hand what it takes back with the other: for it is said that no advantage will be pure and unpaid-for. On the one hand there is having without knowing it, or what amounts to the same thing, being without having it; then there is the comedy of virtue, that is to say glorious foolishness, professional and yet beautiful holiness. What

---

[18] Brunschvicg, section VIII, 557. Rilke, *Das Stundenbuch:* "Alle, welche dich suchen, versuchen dich, Und die so dich finden, binden dich. . . ." Tauler: "Doch dieses Verlieren, dies Entschwinden ist eben das echte und rechte Finden." Schelling, IV, p. 357; VI, p. 19: "Es ist . . . nur da, inwiefern man es nicht hat, und indem man es hat, verschwindet es." IX, p. 217. "Wer es erhalten wird, der wird es verlieren, und wer es aufgibt, der wird es finden." Tauler, *Les Institutions divines* (trad. des Pères minimes de l'Oratoire, Paris, 1587), chap. XIV: ". . . ils s'empêchent eux-même aux choses lorsque d'amour désordonné ils les poursuivent."

does one have to do to accumulate being and knowing? In other words, is there a reflective innocence that would be innocent *gnosis* and *docta ignorantia*? Certainly the *Actus purissimus* is the only one capable of thinking himself without there being any aftertaste of complacency that skims the pure outpouring of this charity, without there being that knowledge of knowledge (*noēseōs noēsis*) which goes to his head; God is the only one who each night, and particularly on the sixth night of the Hexameron, enjoys Himself in His work without experiencing any intoxication; God alone can admire the work of His own hands. But a creature who is satisfied with himself is in mortal danger; it is also necessary to imagine here less-transcendent solutions: the first one is the unilateral consciousness of sin, which is lucid for everything that constitutes our abjection, and naïve and ignorant in regard to everything that constitutes our dignity; it is in this sense that Newman says: prose which knows itself to be prose is already poetry, and the reproach which one makes to oneself of not loving is already love; the most frivolous Christian ceases to be despicable as soon as he scorns himself. That is why grace will not visit remorse unless remorse has sincerely despaired, and finds itself in the total unconsciousness of a salvation that was nevertheless well deserved; on the other hand, grace will refuse itself, also, to a repentance that is too conscious of its own rights. Thus Spinoza is correct: joy is not the recompense for virtue, but it must flow spontaneously from the very center of our good will—for we have sufficiently shown how this capricious will is independent of the efforts that one puts forth to obtain it; and Aristotle is correct, too, when he seems to say the opposite—for although pleasure adds itself to the actualization of a function, it crowns it as its natural efflorescence and its organic full bloom (*hoion tois akmaiois hē hōra*), but not as a mercenary goal. Let all our sentiments forget themselves, Gabriel Marcel demands, and let them never turn to their Eurydice. And Vallier expresses himself in the same vein: happiness emerges without our searching after it,[19] not like our salary, but under

19 Cf. Kierkegaard, *Le Concept d'angoisse*, p. 78; *La Pureté du coeur*, pp. 61, 64.

favor of an undeserved grace. One knows, on the other hand, Claudel's parable on *Animus* and *Anima* and the trick of pure intuition, as explained by Henri Bremond: "The soul keeps silent as soon as the mind looks at it";[20] but we can talk about it thanks to the subterfuge of *Animus*, which makes us believe in its absence during the presence of the divine lover. The will that is assured of its impunity or is condemned to be anonymous, the will that is deprived of the cheers from the pit, finds again in the incognito itself the spontaneity and the authenticity of its disposition. Thus we will sometimes be sincere by surprise. Fortunately, these surprises are made possible by the relative simplicity, the partial innocence and intermittent naïveté of the most smartened consciousness. A consciousness that would be conscious of everything and perpetually so would condemn us to insomnia. This exhausting tension, this vigilance continuing each moment, this meticulous lucidity in the undoubling of self would be strictly unlivable; and just as sleep is made possible by a kind of complete and essential naïveté of all consciousness, so our natural ingenuity in the manner of lapses deceives the surveillance that our theatric mind exercises without relaxation; in order to escape, our truth profits from a moment of inadvertence, from a break in the wall of insomnia, from a chronic barnstorming and an extralucid autoscopia. These are local and partitive naïvetés, passing distractions of the "poseur," but how revealing they are! The most conscious of all consciousnesses is still relatively unconscious in regard to the superconsciousness that includes it. One would not be able to pay attention to everything; and the insomniac consciousness does not stand guard in us so well that one would not be able to sleep somehow while being completely awake. Oblivion is that short and unilateral sleep, this innocence of the bottom of the soul, the beneficial sleepiness. And it occurs also that the poseur believes he is alone, not having to compose himself in regard to the

[20] *Prière et poésie*, pp. 112–13. Cf. p. 221: "Il est incomparablement plus facile d'aimer en se taisant que non pas en parlant." [It is incomparably much easier to love while keeping silent than it is to do so without talking about it.]

other, and finds himself natural and relaxed; for he is merely awake with one eye. La Rochefoucauld[21] says that nothing hinders us so much in being natural than the desire to appear that way. But when this desire fades away, the will finds again, without twisting or sham, this simplicity of the first movement, which Fénelon defends against the vicissitudes of reflection. And yet, it is not the vegetable innocence to which quietism invites us, but that amorous and gnostic innocence that constitutes the limit of a truly dynamic consciousness, one that is truly infinite—infinite and not indefinite! It does not have anything in common with that undoubling of the reflection which in Renouvier's view is merely a relationship of relationships and whose effect is static complacency. All consciousness that proclaims itself consciousness is literally stupid, a comfortable sufficiency and satisfaction of egoism. Thus the first word about virtue consists in systematically adopting its "manners," and the second, which has the name of Irony, consists, on the contrary, in avoiding all its appearances; and the third in avoiding all affectation of humility in which pride would find suspicious revenges. For if the good man is he who does not look like it, then genuine humility cannot always be distinguished from humble vanity which accepts honors in all gratitude and in all simplicity of consciousness. Let us finally acknowledge it: the last and final word about virtue is without a doubt to consent to just foolishly appear as that which one is: that is the superhumility that is not "false modesty," but more-than-true modesty and, in a word, love; for love *is* not, except in movement.

IV SORROWFUL CONSCIOUSNESS

Consciousness that is without complacency is at the same time both conscious, because it knows itself to be wrong, and not-conscious, because it does not know that this sentiment will redeem it: this consciousness becomes familiar to us in the equation of Feeling and Suffering and in the sorrowful positivity of all feeling. It is misfortune that gives to con-

21 *Maxime* 431.

sciousness the "pathic" resentment of its own existence. One can examine oneself about the nature of this ethical relationship which relates this suffering and this fault. Four dolorist superstitions offer themselves to justify the "good use" of our miseries: the first attributes to the posthumous grief of our repentance the same healing finality as is attributed to the antecedent griefs that work as admonition, cry of alarm, and signaling of danger to come; it is "the divine remedy for our impurities," the purgation of our inner injustice. This superstition rests on several verbal analogies, first, that which compares the teleological pain of the cure to the useless pain of a bad conscience; on the other hand, that which confuses Healing and Suffering; from the fact that the iatric, or healing, process is generally accompanied by pain, it does not follow that one recovers *because* one suffers, nor that this grief precisely is the therapy itself. One loses one's temper with those who remove the poultice too soon and who, impatient of a premature recovery, want to gain by burning out every wound. Pascal and Kierkegaard[22] have recognized in insensibility the symptom of a mortal disease; and likewise pagan ignorance was for Schelling the depths of despair: are not the deep-rooted impudence and the impenitence of a hardened sinner in some sense despairing? However, those who are able to recover without suffering would be wrong to deprive themselves of anesthesia: or what other purpose would it serve? It is not the bitterness that makes a medicine a remedy: for what is bitter, just as the surgical pain, is merely an epiphenomenon, an accidental aspect or a secondary quality of medication. Pain, this necessary evil, is always indispensable, generally speaking, but it is always dispensable in each particular case: in this respect pain resembles death, which one can always delay but is never able to avoid; the date of death can almost be postponed indefinitely, although the fact of dying (one day or the other, sooner or later) is in the long run unavoidable. One will then try to see in pain —and this is the second superstition—a means of getting rid

[22] *Traité du désespoir*, passim; *La Pureté du coeur*, p. 22. Pascal, *Prière pour demander à Dieu le bon usage des maladies*, Sec. 7.

of Nemesis and warding off one's fate: one offers one's own bad luck as a gift to the jealous divinity. Above all, do not laugh too loud, try not to be too happy, nor too noisy. Good luck brings bad luck! The belief according to which our good luck gives umbrage to the gods explains without a doubt this inclination toward penitence, narrowness, meanness, and death, which is as fundamental in man as the instinct to live; and the desire for war, which summarizes in itself all mediocrity and all penitence, has the same origin; and just as the iconoclastic mortification of Savonarola wished to atone for man's pleasures during the Renaissance, so the austerity of the rigorists and ascetics imposes the sweet torture of remorse on the sinner. This superstitious phobia in regard to triumph implies the idea that pain is a finite quantity, a certain totality that one has to pay off as a kind of credit of fate over man: the pain already *suffered* must be charged to the pain that is still *to be suffered*; in a manner of speaking, pain would be drawn on the debt we must pay, as an alternative, like a tax due to bad luck. The impersonal and anonymous character of pain, and the "vicariate" that follows from it, are the consequences of this dolorist dogmatism: it is not necessary that it is I who suffer; from the moment pain represents the debt of man in general anyone else could have done the job equally well; sacrifice, for instance, is the spontaneous substitution of the emissary patient who suffers for us in person; and in view of the fact that egos are interchangeable among one another in regard to pain, so, in the interior of my own self, pain reveals itself as negotiable; it is the sinner who chooses his torture, asks to endure his punishment immediately in order to relieve himself of it, or he redeems at one time and in advance all his eventual sins. It is as if our misfortune would be because of a certain bill of bad luck that we would have together with our fortune! Alas, the rain of the month of June does not give us any lien on the good weather of the month of August. On the contrary, lack of success attracts failure, in virtue of that ridiculous and scandalous law of avalanche, which governs immanent injustice and amplifies all inequality here on earth. We know already that duty is not a quantum on which the work of us humans, capitalizing merit, would have to draw. No, disease does not relieve us of death (although the latter relieves us of everything), and in this sense one may well have all bad things at the same time. Success does not go to unhappy people to compensate for their bad luck as if it were equitable; success goes to the happy ones who do not need it in order to shamefully and monstrously amplify their good luck; the thankfulness of the privileged is thus as anthropomorphic as the rancor of the deprived; for if the crescendo of this instability refutes a stupid theodicy, it does not justify pessimism. The mystery of undeserved suffering, the torture of the innocent, the hell of the children who died in Auschwitz—these revolting paradoxes would undoubtedly have tortured Ivan Feodorovich Karamazov. To what demoniac temptation do the perverse and violent people of the movies of Buñuel yield, or the wicked one who in the manner of Stavroguin makes the beggar suffer? In Dostoievski, there is neither sadistic cruelty nor cynic defiance in regard to bourgeois justice, as is the case in the most provoking forms of surrealist scandal: no, these Karamazoves are inspired, rather, by the passionate expectation of an absurd, supernatural, ateleological grace that alone is capable of redeeming in one moment infinite pain and injustice. Thus let us not bother to break a precious object to compensate for chance; our acts of penitence will not ward off this umbrageous fate. From this, one sees what he must think of the third dolorist superstition, which is the one of atonement, that is to say, that of magic compensation. In the relation of the ego to the self, as well as in its relation with the others, in its passionate need for penitence as well as in its justice, one reads the same thought of reversibility and re-established equilibrium. In order to restore this status quo of our purity, we use purifying fire, lustral water, rituals of honor, and also pain, which is the privileged lustration, the most burning disinfection, and the sharpest antiseptic; pain offers to the irritated god the honor of our own body, the honor of the suffering object-subject, and offers him even, in Sacrifice, the

death of this body as expiatory victim. This allopathy heals
the contrary with the contrary. And just as Hippocrates'
medicine nurses fever, that is, the *thermon*, with cold,[23] so
in the same way are afflictions the medication of the soul.
The sanctifying surgery of the *Gorgias* is quite Hippocratic
in this regard. These metaphors of atonement, redemption,
and contrition suppose as a clandestine postulate the polar
symmetry of pain and pleasure, and consequently their fundamental homogeneity: pain is reversed pleasure, just as hell
is an inverted world; there is thus a neutral substrate that is
indifferent in regard to the one as well as to the other, and
spaced out, so to speak, according to a scalar gradation similar to that which, at both sides of the zero, divides the positive and negative magnitudes. In this way pain becomes the
reparative procedure that serves to travel, in an inverse direction, the road of pleasure, that undoes what has been
done, and does again what has been undone. Now, the
polarity of pain and pleasure, with the just mean between
the two (*metaxu*), does not make more sense than those of
induction and deduction, duty and right, analysis and synthesis, good and evil, space and time: these are antitheses
of rhetoric that belie the qualitative heterogeneity and irreducible originality of our feelings. Future and past, too, are
not symmetric on both sides of the present; they do not form
a pair. That would mean to say, Lalande says ironically, that
description is the contrary of inscription, or depression of impression. Pain is not a pleasure upside down, nor the negative
contrast or inverse of this positive, and no more than the
past is future topsy-turvy or the future a past on the wrong
side, but it is an irreducible specificity (*poion ti*). Given these
conditions, what meaning could expiation have, the Platonic
tisis, the helpful wound whose task it is to acquit us of the
ransom of our joys? One will insist that the proof that all
culpability proceeds from pleasure is that one balances it by
pain. But who tells us that pain, being *sui generis*, could
ever compensate for that which does not have a common
measure with it? What remains is that pain should have in

23 *Peri Archeias Iatrikos*, aphorism 22, sec. 2.

itself an ethical signification that is independent of all healing or compensating finality. But it is here, surrounding the
idea of sanction, that the swarm of apories arises which thick-
ens the insoluble mysteries of "pathology": what relationship,
what resemblance, what common measure is there between
pain, which is an affective event, and evil behavior, which
is of the order of action, between a fact that one undergoes,
and moral values, and why is it that I must suffer as a price
for my faults? Yes indeed, why two evils instead of only one?
One will suggest that, after all, this enigma is no more enig-
matic than the union of soul and body in general: the relationships between volition and movement, between intention and act, or between quantitative excitation and
qualitative sensation are facts; furthermore, the infringement
of the laws of physics are followed by misfortunes that no
more resemble the laws than the fire in the flame "resembles"
the visual image of fire. Aristotle noted that the relation
between *aretē* (virtue) and *pathos* (affection), that is to say
the duo pleasure-pain (*hēdonē-lupē*),[24] is a fact. But even
more: since sin is an act, that is to say, is an irrational effectiveness, the gulf between fault and pain is perhaps not as
deep as that between idea and movement. Are not sin, and
pain because of sin, one and the same spiritual organism?
But aside from the fact that one does not explain a mystery
by doubling it with another, the union of thought and
brain precisely is *a fact*; now, punishment is not something
that is given, but something that one "inflicts"; and as far as
moral pain is concerned, it is essentially synthetic in regard
to the fault, that is to say, no pathology will ever be derived
from evil action: sanction, says Durkheim, is not found in
the act as malady is found in imprudence. Even pleasure,
however naturally it seems to radiate from the center of the
act as its efflorescence, or *akmē*, is to be superadded to the
sensation; pleasure is the epigenesis of the sensible quality
(*epigennēma*), the gracious and adventitious gift, the
milligram of approval that is granted to us in the bargain,
over and above the blue, red, and yellow, and for which we

[24] *Nich. Ethics*, II, 3, 1104 b15.

thank God in our prayers; bless the Creator for this gift. All the more reason why pain, which is irrational and punitive, becomes added to the moral drama as the "milligram extra" (that is to say *too much*) and not like grace, which as given for nothing, asks for our gratitude, but as inverse luxury, which one can save; pain, that is, the cinder in the eye, the splinter in the flesh, the opaque calculation in plain transparency: for pain, even "normal" pain, never pre-exists in its causes; for according to all our experience, pain is the arbitrary coefficient that one has to think of separately, and that breaks the immanence of duration. Regardless of the application that theodicy has provided in order to make evil an ingredient of the cosmic economy, to normalize and naturalize its relationships of good neighborship with all phenomena, evil will never be more than an *allogenos*, a foreign body. And pain, for all that it, too, contrasts sharply and "stands out" as a useless accident in regard to the whole of intravital relations, is an intruder, an importunate and undesirable guest who has invited himself and whom one never foresaw to be at the banquet. It is always parasitical and always exceptional, notwithstanding the citizenship and juridical legality dolorism has given it. From this it follows first that an old punishment is soon forgotten, because life takes up its rights again as soon as bad luck turns its back. On the other hand, pain, even if it is deserved a thousand times, always appears as a scandal and as something that is unexpectedly and artificially added. . . . Pain is a disease we have caught through contamination and exogenic infection. One sometimes says that pain as well as sacrifice is an agogic mediation, because it represents the necessity of a justifying proof that is nothing but antithesis. But this is still just a manner of speaking: for if the dialectic means and the instrumental means both have in common that they are deviations and intermediating moments between extremes, the dialectic means is the third concept, identical at the same time to two others between which no resemblance immediately manifests itself. The mournful mediation is, instead, the contrary of goal, namely the suspended goal. It is this inversion *a contrario* that, according to Pascal and Kierkegaard, constitutes the whole paradox of the Christologic divine irony: at least faith allows the believer to find the mysterious and consoling finality behind this sterile punishment; here pain in its own way misleads man, because it pretends to delay the final outcome. Isolated from this mystery, pain does not serve the purpose of re-establishing the continuity of the discourse, but rather of breaking it. It resembles nothing, exhausts the impetus of confidence, breaks the harmony of the self with the universe and the peace of the self with the self; incommunicable and incoherent, it cuts off the ego from itself, it makes us uncommunicative, unsociable, and lonely. The means is that which does not resemble its goal, but denies and contradicts it: and precisely pain itself does not resemble sin, for which it makes us pay (for the evil of guilt, or the ethical evil, does not always coincide with *malum physicum*, as the distress of the just and the scandalous triumph of evil as well as unexpiated injustice prove), nor the happy peace that is promised to us. Pent up, irreducible, and unsociable pain constitutes a problem; just as, inversely, any problematical situation is to some extent painful. And it is not only the case that pain resembles nothing, but my personal pain, in turn, does not resemble any other pain. For such is the double paradox of pain. It must suffice that "one" pays *in general*. . . . one, that is to say, someone, it does not matter who, I or another, provided the debt be payed off and account of it be made. But no, the essential part is not that the thing itself takes place (that a certain result be obtained), but that it is precisely I! The essential element is precisely this useless and ridiculous clause, this mysterious and profoundly misleading clause of the first-person-for-himself; the essential part is the necessity of my absurd, personal pain, of my irreplaceable pain! For it *does* matter, and it does not amount to the *same* thing whether it is my pain or that of any one deputy, if it is not precisely the pain of the wrongdoer. That someone else pays in my place by no means substitutes for my irreplaceable pain: to suffer is like dying, a thing one has to do oneself, solitarily, in one's heart of hearts. Even if another person can sacrifice himself for me under this or that determinate circumstance, in the final analysis moral man is never dispensed from the personal test; earlier or later, he has to go through it. You will ask: why me? First, why a new distress after the distress of the fault, and then *why mine?* Such is indeed the absurdity of a mediation that, just as love and death, is compelled to a detour via ipseity.

It is time now to admit that pain is the necessary disgrace, the essential accident, or better formulated, the mystery— for it constitutes a unity with the internal antagonism of the creaturely condition. Its incentive, thus, is Conflict. For this laborious pain is not only the irreducible and undeducible paradox, but also the most strained and the most incandescent degree of effort. It is the threefold meaning of Pain: *ponos,* which is sorrow, punishment, and work: pain is *our work.* Finally there is in this unjustifiable thing a secret teleology. Mournful consciousness works and painstakingly labors at his good and fructifying penitence in which the "old" man becomes consumed. Yes, it is the second Adam who gets a new skin in this moral histogenesis and organogenesis. The ardent labor that metamorphoses us is thus the evil of giving birth; the change of form comes about in inexpressible suffering. And yet, the pain remains Enigma, visitor; and glowing coals of the suffering will purify only those who in their innocence have expected nothing from it. As a matter of fact it is pain in general that is necessary without any pain taken in particular being necessary; just as there must be evil in general without this or that evil ever being necessary; just as the *fact* of death in general is unavoidable although its date can be postponed indefinitely, quoddity is an evil following from our destiny and an incurable disease, but its *quando,* that is to say the hour and day, is undetermined and depends upon our efforts. Immortality is an idle dream, but longevity is our human affair. Thus if an unlimited career opens up for an activist, a doctor, a pioneer, an engineer, and all those philanthropists specialized in the extermination of monsters, the great period in which one will have done away with pain is one of those "illusions of progress" that, just as the victory over death, will be registered among the

chimeras of indefinite improvement, or even better, among
the spells of magicians; that would be tantamount to believing that one can make angels, evade the law of alternatives, and arrive at goals without going through the means.
One can relieve pain, but one cannot annihilate *dolorousness*; delay death, but not evade *mortality*; accelerate or moderate the rhythms of time, but not nihilate *temporality*; by
means of technique have an influence on categorical circumstances, the when, how many, how, but never quiddify *quoddity*. On the one hand, pain is an evil that we protest:
also, let us take sides with the battle of Prometheus and
Heracles, who are the knights willing to help the threatened
man; the improvement of the fate of man and the transformation of nature are the parts to be played by St. Vincent
de Paul, Descartes, and Marx. On the other hand, we accept
the metaphysical legitimacy of discord if we, just like hu-
manitarianism, contest all its empirical forms; resignation,
however, does exactly the opposite of what one should do,
clinging to the circumstantial modalities that nonetheless can
be modified *ad infinitum*, and foolishly protesting their possibility. It is to the *quod* that one must consent, but against
the *quid* that one must keep one's head high. Elasticity, that
is the destiny of man! We evade this destiny through all
kinds of palliatives and alibis; we minimize evil *ad infinitum*,
braving through our chivalrous challenge the toilsome labor
and repugnant tasks: but in so doing we also lay the rock
bare of the pain flowing from our destination. Just as civilization alleviates our sufferings by generating new diseases, so
in the same way pain moves about without disappearing:
medication transforms the boil into migraine; upon the remorse of the fault that is the retrospective pain of *having-
done-it*, follows the effort that is the pain of *having-to-do-it*
and the toilsomeness of a task to be accomplished. The pain
of a future that is incumbent on me remains wholly in the
fecundity and disagreeable tension of the will; the pain of a
past that overpowers me, on the contrary, remains in the
fertile restoration one calls penitence, and in the sterile despair of a bad conscience. Well, if there is not always something to be undone, we have shown that there is always

something to be done. A purely redemptive pain would be unessential—for there is nothing to be undone if one does not first do something. To do and to undo erect from their intermittent leaps the ontic continuity of our destiny; it is in this immanent continuity that Christianity searches for pain when it somehow metaphorically brings forward a congenital sin, that is to say a fault that one did not commit, a fault of being born, and a perpetual repentance. I am faulty before being guilty—this is the very paradox of tragedy. The just man, thus, will be less scrupulous than *conscientious*; that is to say that his pain, instead of scattering itself in discontinuous moments and detailed remorses, rather assumes the continuity of a legato.

V   SANCTION

Pain is the "sanction"; formulated otherwise, the point of insertion of the law in the irrational and historical world of events; without it, consciousness would be nothing but an ideological and conceptual abstraction instead of being something for our good, and morality in general would not have enough force to go as far as the real. Although pain, indeed, is a mediator, it is nonetheless perfect immediacy; being a consciousness not at a distance but near, it leaves us head to head and face to face with danger and without spacing out in depth the intermediate planes that give to our wisdom the distance and room necessary for having some perspective. And here we are, literally in the first line and in the outposts, at the same time spectators and actors, that is to say personally engaged through the effective and incontestable truth of our suffering. The enemy is in front of us. Pain, which even happens to the body, our object-subject, excludes all those cushioning pads and plasters that the *logos* places between the danger and us. To take part in the object is thus no longer being partial, that is to say passionate, as he who is both judge and party, but on the contrary it is to test the quoddity of the pure fact. In this way one understands why pain "sanctions," and in sanctioning sanctifies. Because it is the ceremony of a crisis that, just as all other terminations do, cuts out the form and silhouette of the act. Because it is the transition from concept to effectiveness, and consequently the true consecration or validation of that which was without value. Finally, because it is the initiation to supernaturalness and the baptism of moral man. One will say that the act of a sinner who does not feel sorry would already be a way of existing *de facto*: but as for his being fixated in exteriority and letting himself be absorbed by the world without rebounding on the ego, one cannot say that the act engages the destiny of this ego with the figure of this world: only pain, the effect of a rebound, manifests the cosmic solidarity of the Other and the ego; pain is thus naturally ethical. In pain the physical perspective of action and the egocentric autism of the patient coincide. Why should we be astonished that it reforms the one who suffers it? It is the action suffered that reforms itself as effected action. In this respect pain is the accession or the promotion of primary effectiveness to secondary legality, to existence *de jure*, to the order of values, of what has-to-be; it obtains that the will *feels* or *experiences* what it *does* and thus takes seriously the consequences of its decision by undergoing their rebound, that is to say at the same time their physical repercussion and their moral reverberation; it bestows upon us, together with the feeling of our responsibility, the bitter stamp of the test. Injustice was found in the dissociation of pain and evil, that is, in fault without suffering; "to have pain" when it is another who "does the wrong thing" was the disorder of impunity. Does the Bible not build up a charge of scandal by opposing to the Greek idea the optimistic idea of the sage who is happy and rewarded here on earth, that of the unhappy just man who awaits the supernatural revenges from the other side? Job, who is unjustly punished, does not despair. The deserved expiation prevents the guilty one from cheating with an alternative or escaping the rebound of his own act; expiation re-establishes the equilibrium and restores the alternative to its rights and brings together again on one single head what injustice had divided between actor and victim; it makes pain coincide with sin, the guilty one must also be the victim of his own fault: the one who undergoes will be the same one who has "committed" or "inflicted."[25] Expiation levels the disparity that repeatedly emerges between virtue and happiness. And yet, pain could not have the last word; it is a conclusion that is a beginning: it liquidates and inaugurates, paving the way for the work of restoration, in which the "new" man edifies himself. In pain, finally, the incontestable evidence of consciousness bursts forth. Against the too-good faith of resignation, which plays the game of the devil by letting itself be defeated, and against the heroic, bad faith of the stoic derealization, which denies the evidence, pain imposes its undeniable presence on good faith without qualification. There certainly is an "ideology" of pain, but it consists in the idols of localization, rhythm, degree, or manner of being; the very Being of pain is independent of all hallucination; "believing" one suffers is still suffering, because it is believing in it, and the illusion itself is still perception.

Thus there is not much sense in asking whether one suffers; everyone knows what that means and the problem is solved in advance; one suffers already because one asks oneself about it. Let us say that the painful evidence makes manifest the personal solitude of all consciousness and the soliloquy of the mind alone with itself, *monos pros monon*; pain essentializes ipseity, and consequently lays bare the uniqueness, of my moral destiny and the impossibility of confusing the ego with the Thou, mine with yours, the one with the other. The indifferent and neutral *logos* interchanges the I and the Thou in a world of approximation in which there is no more than the "anyone whoever," that is to say, it does not matter who. Pain is the living proof of nominalism, the exact, pitiless, and incontestable precision that decisively differentiates ipseity without equivocation. It is not so, that pain brings a "message," that it signifies or symbolizes values that would express themselves through the allegory of our torture; pain is in-

---

[25] Epictetus, *Discourses*, I, 28, 10: οὐ δύναται ἄλλος μὲν εἶναι ὁ πεπλανημένος, ἄλλος δὲ ὁ βλαπτόμενος [for it is impossible that he who is deceived can be one person, and he who suffers another person].

teriority without inner life, superficial profundity which holds wholly to its appearing; strictly speaking, one does not find in it the principle of synthesis and deep contemplation: about the naked fact (*hoti*) there is nothing to be told, neither through story nor through historic narration; the pure event of pain defies all thorough analysis and all dialectical progress: there is only the everlasting Now haunted by the mournful tautology and, in the face of this *Nunc*, there is the analytic lucidity of the patient: the absolute in stagnation. Who speaks of wallowing in pain? But this does not prevent us from having to go to the end of the mediation and finally drink the whole bitter cup. Pain is the opaque and massive present that one cannot radiograph, but suffering conjugates itself; and it is here that the invertebrate and inflated present takes form, this shapeless present that is as a monster; it is here that the amorphous obsession becomes populated with hope. In this meditation on pain, *meletēma tou algous*, there was barely more to think about than in that meditation on death that the *Phaedo* makes the constant occupation of the sages; but in suffering is the seed of our salvation. Despair holds the modalities themselves to be fatal although they can be modified *ad infinitum*; foolish hope, holding the quoddity itself as dispensable and contrary to all probability, pretended to derealize the dolorousness of the pain. Pain is neither as redoubtable as despair fears it to be, nor as negligible as illusionist frivolity hopes it to be. Thus one must take it neither too tragically, nor too lightly, but simply seriously.

SELECTIVE BIBLIOGRAPHY

L'Odyssée de la conscience dans la dernière philosophie de Schelling (Paris: Alcan, 1932)
La mauvaise conscience (Paris: Alcan, 1933)
L'Ironie (Paris: Alcan, 1935)
L'Alternative (Paris: Alcan, 1938)
Du mensonge (Paris: Arthaud, 1947)

Traité des vertus (Paris: Bordas, 1949)
Philosophie première (Paris: Presses Universitaires de France, 1954)
L'Austérité et la vie morale (Paris: Flammarion, 1956)
Le Je-ne-sais-quoi (Paris: Presses Universitaires de France, 1957)
Le pur et l'impur (Paris: Flammarion, 1960)

Colin Smith, *Contemporary French Philosophy* (London: Methuen, 1964), pp. 181–201, and passim.

Chapter 3

INTRODUCTION

GABRIEL MARCEL (1889–   ) is one of the leading
contemporary French philosophers, dramatists, and critics. He
refers to his own philosophy by the term "neo-Socratism,"
but it is generally referred to by such ambiguous labels as
"existentialism" or "Christian existentialism." Although the
term existentialism certainly does not point to what is essential to Marcel's philosophy, he certainly has made a great
contribution to existential philosophy in many respects.

Marcel is opposed to a systematic philosophy, since it almost necessarily leads to abstractions and a kind of conceptual
sclerosis. Nonetheless, underlying all his investigations there
is the basic and all-encompassing idea that within the temporal and transient order, man as *viator* is already given a
foretaste of eternal reality. That is why Marcel's philosophy
as a whole is a philosophy of faith and hope.

From a methodological point of view, one could say that
Marcel uses a kind of phenomenological method, but this
method cannot be identified with the phenomenology of
either Hegel or Husserl. Marcel himself distinguishes between two different types of reflection: Primary reflection is
characterized by abstraction, analysis, objectification, and
verification. It is found in the sciences in a systematic way.
It is oriented toward problems, which it tries to solve. Secondary reflection is oriented toward mysteries; it is concrete,
individual, heuristic, and open. It is not concerned with objects, but with presences, and its contemplation does not
begin with doubt or curiosity, but with astonishment and
wonder. Rather than searching for information about the

other and dealing with it abstractly by means of classifying labels, secondary reflection tries to reveal the total presence, whether this be the presence of my body, the world, the other person, or God.

In Marcel's thought, the question concerning man himself occupies an important place. Man cannot be understood by means of universal and abstract labels or concepts, because man has to "form" himself in spontaneous freedom. However, man is not pure interiority; he is basically a being-toward-the-world (être-au-monde). In his orientation toward the world, man always finds himself in a concrete situation that is determined through his body (incarnation). This situation codetermines man's choice, but does not necessitate his freedom. Furthermore, the situation is not given to man as something that is intrinsically unchangeable; it becomes precisely altered through man's action. In his world, man encounters other human beings. He can adopt two attitudes in regard to them: I can look upon another human being as an object or a thing, and then he is merely a "he" for me (un lui); if I encounter him as presence, he is a "Thou" for me. The ego becomes mainly constituted in the "I-Thou" relationships. At the basis of these relationships is faithfulness, or fidelity: If I am faithful to the other and trust him, then I create my own Being (fidélité créatrice). At the root of our fidelity toward the other we find our participation in the absolute "Thou." Our creating fidelity itself is a participation in the creating activity of God.

Although mainly interested in an "ontology of man," Marcel has had great interest in moral problems since the time of his Philosophical Fragments (1904–14). Here, too, Marcel opposes any form of systematization. He is in favor of a "morality of love," which has its ultimate roots in our faithfulness to God. Without an Absolute, obligation and moral responsibility are nothing; without God, all values lose their meaning. From this it is understandable why Marcel strongly objects to the rationalist ethics of enlightenment, to any form of naturalist ethics, to Sartre's conception of ethics, and to all value theories that take "life" as their supreme value.

In the Introduction to Homo Viator Marcel explains that

the essential idea underlying the various essays contained in the book is to be found in a seemingly irrational attempt to connect the existence of a stable, earthly order with the consciousness of our being travelers. On his journey, man is guided by values that transcend the natural order. It is important, however, to clearly realize that asserting the transcendent character of the standards to which the true man recognizes he must conform his life is not tantamount to saying that one could ever be satisfied with a purely abstract set of rules. In other words, in this book "it is not a question of resting on anything like the postulates of Kant, since these have to do only with pure subjectivity, considered as far as this is possible, apart from the conditions of its insertion in concrete experience, experience which involves an element of specificity in a sense infinite. These postulates cannot be conceived apart from a moral formalism which seems precisely to miss what is irreducible in the human drama and in the very fact that all human life develops in the manner of a drama" (Introduction to *Homo Viator*, pp. 9–10). The book seeks to show that in this human drama there is room for hope, provided one does not lock himself up in the realm opened up by primary reflection.

In Marcel's view there is a very close connection between hope and the soul. "I almost think that hope is for the soul what breathing is for the living organism. . . . It is precisely the soul that is the traveller; it is of the soul and of the soul alone that we can say with supreme truth that 'being' necessarily means 'being on the way'" (*Ibid.*, pp. 10–11).

The two selections that follow illustrate precisely how Marcel sees the relationship between value and soul.

I VALUE AND IMMORTALITY

Gabriel Marcel

In reply to the invitation you so kindly gave me I have naturally been led to examine the nature of my journey ever since that far-off time where I first fearlessly addressed myself to the struggle which in the end all philosophy must involve. A journey implies both a starting point and a point of arrival. Now, although upon reflection I may to some extent manage to reconstitute the conditions under which my quest began and thus to mark the approximate point of my departure, I find on the other hand that it is absolutely impossible for me to state precisely, not only to others, but to myself, where I hope to arrive. There is nothing in my case which can be at all compared with that of a scholar whose researches follow a fixed line, who has drawn up a programme and is conscious of having reached a definite point in it. The truth is that the words *point of arrival* have no longer any meaning for me, and moreover it would probably be possible to show that there is also an illusion in picturing a point of departure. The really important thing is to rediscover what means one had at one's disposal, what equipment, and also what "the idea at the back of one's mind" was on setting out: but how can this be accomplished?

In reality here, as indeed everywhere, we have to get free from the claims and pretensions of an imagination which views everything in terms of space, and to recognize that on the philosophic plane at any rate (though probably wherever

Originally given in 1943 as a lecture to the members of the *Enseignement Catholique* of Lyons, this essay is from *Homo Viator*, by Gabriel Marcel, translated by Emma Craufurd (Chicago, 1957), pp. 135–65. Copyright © 1957 Henry Regnery Company.

we have to do with creation) we must regard the image of a journey as misleading. Since we can hardly dispense with an introductory metaphor, I greatly prefer to ask you to imagine a certain clearing of the ground which takes place on the spot, which is indeed only effective on that condition, but of which the successful results can never be considered as finally consolidated. There is always a risk that weeds will spread in the furrows which have been so laboriously ploughed, there will always be swarms of pestilent insects to threaten future harvests. Hence comes the necessity for constant vigilance which cannot be relaxed without compromising everything. I do not claim that this comparison takes us very far, but, in my eyes, it does at least have the obvious advantage of not substituting a pseudo-idea for what is really at issue. We can never eradicate pseudo-ideas too resolutely or too methodically. It is extraordinary to see with what regularity, and I should be prepared to say with what cynicism, they take possession of the field every time that research of genuine profundity reaches the perilous second stage—that of publication, which only too often involves exploitation and vulgarisation. I am thinking here, for instance, of the very confused notion of existential philosophy which has become current.

I was saying that I can manage to form a retrospective idea of the initial conditions under which I began my inquiries. There are two points about which my memory is specially precise. I remember very clearly my exasperation when, in studying the thought of Fichte, I came to the conclusion that the German philosopher was claiming to deduce the empirical self from the transcendental self. "What an illusion", I thought, "or what a lie! Perhaps at a pinch it might be possible to establish that the self should figure as the empirical self in its own eyes, but in this case it could only stand for the empirical self *in general*. Now the empirical self in general is a fiction. What exists and what counts is such and such an individual, the real individual that I am, with the unbelievably minute details of my experience, with all the special features of the concrete adventure, assigned to me and to no one else as my particular life. How can all this be arrived at by deduction? It is not enough to say that the attempt would be impracticable, it would be absurd in principle. The reason is that this deduction which seemed to promise so much, stops just short of the essential, of the thing which alone matters for each one of us." By this, of course, I was definitely taking up my position against formalism of any kind, and moreover I went so far as to think that to apply methods of deduction in such a realm is arbitrary and even false, that it is the unlawful transposition into the metaphysical order of a requirement which only has value and meaning in certain definite departments of scientific thought.

Now, here is the second point. I remember having listened to the controversy which started in about 1906 or 1908 between Mr. Brunschvicg and Mr. Edouard Le Roy on the relations of science and religion, and having been somewhat shocked by the immoderate use which each of them seemed to make of a certain principle of immanence, which both showed to be an irrefutable law of the mind and for that very reason of reality. I remember saying to one of my companions —it may have been to Michel Alexandre: "That is a principle which I am prepared to attack directly and which ought at least to be subjected to a very thorough examination." In reality, from that time I tended to dispute the validity of this principle, rather in the same way as Chestov opposed the principle of identity.

I am therefore able to say that from the beginning my researches were explicitly directed towards what might be called the concrete examination of the individual and of the transcendent, as opposed to all idealism based on the impersonal or the immanent. We should doubtless mark, immediately afterwards, the valuable impetus given to me in my quest by experience of the tragic element in the universal drama, successively brought home to me in my private life and, of course, in the tremendous event which laid waste or maimed our existence from the year 1914.

It is not possible within the limits of this lecture for me to deal as fully as necessary with the part which the consciousness of tragedy played in the development of my thought. But it is quite evident that it was, for instance, at the root of the dispute (friendly, if one may say so) which brought me to grips with Léon Brunschvicg, and ended in our discussions in the *Société Philosophique*, the *Union pour la Verité* and the Congress of 1937. I shall actually be returning later to the last-mentioned debate and to the particularly serious question with which we dealt, far too briefly as a matter of fact. It is, however, possible to say in quite a general way that a consciousness of tragedy is bound up with a sharp sense of human plurality, a sense that is to say of communication and conflict at one and the same time, but above all of the irreducible element which no rational settlement can remove.

I have come across a note on a slightly different plane which, if I am not mistaken, has never been published in the *Journal Métaphysique*, though I do not quite know why.

"Metaphysical uneasiness.—It seems to me probable that metaphysics amounts to nothing else but the activity by which we define an uneasiness and manage partially (and, moreover, mysteriously) if not to remove it at least to transpose and transmute it, so that far from paralysing the higher life of the spirit it tends rather to strengthen and maintain it." What are we to understand, then, by this uneasiness? First of all, it is not a form of curiosity. To be curious is to start from a particular fixed centre, it is to strive to grasp or lay hold of an object of which one has only a confused or partial idea. In this sense all curiosity is turned towards the periphery. To be uneasy, on the contrary, is to be uncertain of one's centre, it is to be in search of one's own equilibrium. This is true in every case. If I am uneasy about the health of one of my relatives it means that the apprehension I feel on their account tends to destroy my inward stability. My curiosity is the more liable to become uneasiness the more the object which arouses it forms a part of myself, the more closely this object is incorporated into my own interior edifice. At the same time uneasiness is the more metaphysical the more it concerns anything which cannot be separated from myself without the annihilation of this very self. It is probably true to say that the only metaphysical problem is that of "What am I?" for all the others lead back to this one. Even the problem of the existence of other consciousnesses is reducible to it in the last analysis. A secret voice which I cannot silence assures me in fact that if others are not there, I am not there either. I cannot grant to myself an existence of which I suppose others are deprived; and here "I cannot" does not mean "I have not the right", but rather "It is impossible for me". If others vanish from me, I vanish from myself.

Can I say that I feel this metaphysical uneasiness as a state with a direct cause—such as the uneasiness one feels when waiting for a beloved being who is late? I do not think so; I should say rather that circumstances can, and even must, inevitably arise when I shall be conscious of an uneasiness which on reflection seems to me to reach infinitely beyond these circumstances in themselves. It is of a permanent character inasmuch as it is not connected with such and such a *now*. Still more, as soon as I formulate it, I extend it to all whom it is possible for me to look upon as sharing in my own experience. It is an anxiety for all of us, and this amounts to saying that it is in no way concerned with man in general (a pure fiction invented by a particular form of rationalism) but rather with my brothers and myself.

Like all true uneasiness (that is to say uneasiness which is not merely the indistinct consciousness of a functional disorder) metaphysical uneasiness can only find peace in knowledge. But of what knowledge is there a question here? The metaphysician seems to deny his own vocation if he does not proclaim that he is seeking "truth"; but what is truth?

Perhaps we should first point out very distinctly that *the truth* with which we are concerned here has nothing in common with the *truths* which it is given to the scholar to bring to light as a result of his patient investigations.

The property of a particular truth, of whatever order it may be, is not only to be strictly definable, but furthermore to tend to identify itself with the statement in which it is formulated, or at least not to make such an identification in any way difficult. In so far as it is taken in itself, that is to say without reference to the previous researches of which its discovery is the crown, it tends to appear as independent of whoever proclaims it. This means to say that it is of the essence of particular truths to have nothing personal about them, to lay claim to an intrinsic value of their own. In this respect there is a remarkable analogy between particular truths and things. The thing is there, ready to be observed by anyone, the particular truth gives itself also, as though offered to whomever wants to recognise and proclaim it. This undoubtedly is the origin of a certain illusion of scientists. We can amass or collect particular truths as one collects pebbles or shells. But it should naturally be noted that by the very fact of our doing so, these truths are devitalised and degraded. To realise this, we only have to think of those lists of historical or physiological facts drawn up for the purpose of enabling a candidate to face such and such an ordeal of school or university examinations.

Is it, as I have appeared to imply, truth in general which we have to contrast with particular truths? On reflection the expression "truth in general" is in danger of appearing vague and meaningless. For my part, I should prefer to speak here of *the spirit of truth*. Whatever we may sometimes say about it in language which is far too inexact, it is not against truth, but against the spirit of truth that we are all constantly liable to sin. Moreover, the spirit of truth can totally inhabit a being who in the whole course of his existence has only had the chance of learning a very few particular truths, and for whom these truths have never been even formulated in terms which would make it possible to pass them on or *a fortiori* to teach them.

What then is this spirit of truth which sometimes takes possession of us and which opposes the "spirit of imprudence and error", spoken of by the tragic poet? Here the philosopher must repossess himself of a principle which he has been leaving to the care of religious thinkers and even preachers to turn to account.

It seems clear to me that it is best to define the spirit of truth in relation to our condition, and here again there is a notion to re-establish. The idealist philosophers in particular have been far too much inclined to think of the condition of man as of certain contingent limits which thought could legitimately, and even ought to, ignore whenever it was fully exercised. Thus with such men as Brunschvicg or the thinkers of the Marbourg school everything which could not be reduced to mathematics lost all value. So a fatal duality is introduced into man's essence, and the idealist is always ready to hand over any residuary elements which do not seem to him to fit in with the essential pattern of all truth to a psychology which is nothing but a department of physiology or sociology.

The spirit of truth should be subjected to a phenomenological description. We should then see fairly easily that it cannot be confined within the limits of what is generally called the intelligence, or even the reason, in so far as the latter is fatally prone to become entirely divorced from reality. The spirit of truth is essentially incarnated in the act which terminates a game I can play with myself under any circumstances—a game always springing from a certain complacency. In relation to this game the spirit of truth appears to be transcendent, and yet its proper function might well be to restore me to myself. By its light I discover that in my vanity I have really been betraying myself. Here, surely enough, the words "more deep within me than myself", find their full meaning.

We might at first be tempted to identify the spirit of truth with liberty itself. But we have to be careful not to simplify our terribly complicated situation arbitrarily. We might say that we are comparable with people whose goods are nearly all mortgaged and therefore not really at our disposal. To deny that we cannot dispose of them is once more to play with oneself, it is once more to violate the claims of the spirit of truth. What it is always within the power of each of us to accomplish is to draw up a balance sheet which is at least an approximation of our situation: it must further be added that we are, and always should be, much clearer about our debts than our assets. In drawing up this balance sheet it seems as though we should place ourselves in such a position that the spirit of truth which is certainly akin to inspiration would be able to pierce us as a pencil of light. What depends on us is in short to dispose ourselves favourably in relation to a possible grace. I use this word purposely here in the very same sense as Mauriac gives it in an admirable passage of *Ce qui*

Etait Perdu: "Madame de Blénauge said, as though it was the most obvious thing, that he, Hervé, her son, had received among others one very great grace. 'I have?'—'Yes, the greatest grace of all; you see yourself for what you are; you know yourself; you call mud, mud; you know that mud is mud.'" This knowledge, however, if we can call it that, is at the same time a valuation; in this realm, truth and value cannot really be separated.

It is indeed of the nature of value to take on a special function in relation to life and, as it were, to set its seal upon it. An incontestable experiment, which can scarcely be recorded in objective documents, here brings us the most definite proof: if I dedicate my life to serve some cause where a supreme value is involved, by this fact my life receives from the value itself a consecration which delivers it from the vicissitudes of history. We must, however, be on our guard against illusions of all kinds which swarm round the word "value". Pseudo-values are as full of vitality as pseudo-ideas. The dauber who works to please a clientele, even if he persuades himself that he is engaged in the service of art, is in no way "consecrated"; his tangible successes will not deceive us. Perhaps, in a general way, the artist can only receive the one consecration that counts on condition that he submits to a severe test. This does not necessarily take the form of the judgment of others, for it may happen that for a long time the artist is not understood by those around him—but it means at least that with lucid sincerity he compares what he is really doing with what he aspires to do—a mortifying comparison more often than not. This amounts to saying that value never becomes reality in a life except by means of a perpetual struggle against easiness. This is quite as true in our moral life as in scientific research or æsthetic creation. We always come back to the spirit of truth, and that eternal enemy which has to be fought against without remission: our self-complacency. To return to our first example, the artist may even have to admit at a given moment either that he is incapable of achieving anything and that he would do better to give up a struggle in which he is wearing himself out in vain, or that he is condemned to remain an amateur, and that, if it is granted him to give pleasure to himself, he should have no illusions about the importance of this amusement.

It certainly does not follow from this that we should be justified in simply identifying value and truth, but only that the spirit of truth and the spirit of falsehood penetrate very far into a sphere from which a superficial analysis would at first be tempted to exclude them.

"Value", I said in a lecture given in May, 1938, at the *Cité Universitaire*, "is the very substance of exaltation, or more exactly it is the reality that we have to evoke when we try to understand how exaltation can change into creative force." In expressing myself thus I was making use of and expanding a passage of Charles du Bois: "For as long as it lasts", he said, "exaltation sustains us in our race, affording the strongest of spring-boards to increase our impetus: we feel its presence both in and around us at the same time, like the presence of a being greater and vaster but not of an essentially different nature from those other guardian presences which we could not do without. . . ." I must own, however, that it seems to me now that the word exaltation could lead to grievous confusion. What we are really aiming at is not an emotional paroxysm, it is an upward rising of the very being which may be expressed, and indeed most frequently is expressed, in an absolute self-possession, a calm in some way supernatural. This calm can only be established in the presence of ultimate realities, particularly of death. But let us take care not to deal only with words. What are we to understand by ultimate realities? Surely they are our limits.

A new discrimination has still to be made, however, and there is no doubt that this time it will be necessary to introduce the category of the existential in spite of the care which it is well to take in bringing it into any philosophical enquiry. The notion of limits is indeed ambiguous in itself. Our life considered from outside as a particular phenomenon, or as the ensemble of observable manifestations whose nature is not directly known to us, can obviously only subsist within certain limits (of temperature, atmospheric pressure, etc.). It is not, of course, such limits that we have in mind when we speak of ultimate realities. What interests us is at bottom the act by which what, objectively speaking, is only a certain given stopping place, is encountered by a being who at one and the same time recognises it and positively refuses to take any notice of it. Perhaps in this case we can use the verb *néantiser* which Mr. Sartre has recourse to so persistently and even injudiciously. You may, perhaps, object that the being does not really recognise the limit since he refuses to take any notice of it, but it must be answered that not to recognise it would mean that he was purely and simply blind; yet here there is perfect lucidity; risk is taken on, and this risk can in an extreme case, such as absolute sacrifice, be the complete acceptance of annihilation, this being considered as of no importance with regard to some special end. The word "sacrifice" is the one we have to keep above all; value is probably always related to a sacrifice which is at least possible; value is, however, only authentic when something incommensurable is not only granted but established, something beside which all the rest, at least for the time being, sinks into non-existence—all the rest, including myself, that is, if by myself I mean a being who appears to himself to have begun and to be going to end.

In the light of these remarks, we see clearly that value can only be incarnate: if indeed it is reduced to an abstract definition we fall back once more into our game and consequently into falsehood, for here the game does not know itself to be a game. The truth is that we do not consent to die for beauty in general, or even for liberty in general: all that means absolutely nothing. We accept death in order to save our country, or perhaps more truly for our enslaved brothers. Again, it would be as well to ask ourselves exactly what we mean by *dying for*. Death must be an act, it must be felt as a positive mode of sharing in a certain good which is itself bound up with history. From this point of view it seems likely that it would be absurd to say that anyone died for an idea, because an idea has no need of such a death, it cannot even know about it, it is self-sufficient. On the other hand, my brothers do need me, and it is very possible that I cannot answer their call to me except by consenting to die. Here, to be sure, the consent is everything, but on condition that it is not abstractly isolated from the extremity, the limit to which it obliges us.

It seems probable then that a fundamental relationship is established between value and courage by the facts these reflections have disclosed and by the mediation of sacrifice. We find here transposed on to a different plane the implication of the terminology in use in the seventeenth century.

The conclusion seems, I admit, to conflict with the realism concerning values that a great many contemporary thinkers have claimed to establish. Furthermore, it is somewhat difficult to see how it can be applied to purely æsthetic values. Is not gracefulness a value for instance? And what relationship could ever be discovered between gracefulness and courage? Perhaps the answer is that we establish a category of the graceful and then set it up as a value by virtue of an illusion. What really exist are graceful human beings, there are also works of art that are graceful, and besides these there is a spiritual attitude to which these beings and works correspond. This attitude, however, cannot be considered by itself either as a value or as something creative of value. Must we not then in some way identify value and merit, in other words must we localise the value in the effort at the price of which the work of art was achieved? This interpretation is obviously absurd. All that we have to remember from our foregoing analyses is that there can certainly be no value in the precise meaning of the word without vigilance on the part of a consciousness exposed to the temptation of surrendering to a facile and complacent system which is springing up around us. Only it is quite clear that we have so far only succeeded in formulating a quite negative condition which cannot be conceived of without an opposite—and perhaps this opposite is not absolutely definable. I am inclined to think that it can only become clear by a consideration of the working consciousness (*conscience œuvrante*).

There is no doubt that we must proceed *a contrario* here, that is to say we must get to the root of the nature of unemployment. Unemployment is first seen from outside as a fact. It tends to become boredom or tedium as it becomes more conscious. The unemployed appears to himself to be unat-

tached and even cast away by what is real, as it were on some
desert shore; it seems to him that life has no more use for
him. He tries to invent interests for himself; to form habits,
but he does not manage to dupe himself with them. The
wife of the man on the retired list busies herself in punctu-
ating his life, in making sure that he has regular amusements,
which means in reality that she creates different forms of slavery for him, but the result of it all is only to provide a very
imperfect disguise for his unemployment. What eats into
him is the more or less distinct sense of life's almost inconceivable cruelty. Why should it persist within him, since he
has no further interest in anything, since no one needs him
any more? The only unknown element he can still look for
is that of sickness and death. All this, of course, only applies
to the lonely unemployed, or the one who has felt the loosen-
ing of the vital bonds which united him to his friends and
relations. Here unemployment borders on despair; despair is
nothing but unemployment which has attained the most
acute self-consciousness, or again, to put it rather bluntly,
it is the breaking of an engagement, the desertion of a consciousness which has no further part in reality.

To be at work, on the other hand, is to be possessed by
the real in such a way that we no longer know exactly
whether it is we who are fashioning it, or it which fashions
us. In any case, difficult as it is to form a perfectly intelligible
idea of this operation, we can say that it involves the reciprocal movement by which man and reality embrace each other,
which is none the less effective in the artist and the scholar
than in the artisan, for instance, or the labourer. All that
varies is the manner in which the real is present to man or,
correlatively, the manner by which man is present to the
real. One thing becomes apparent in all cases—to the confusion of a superficial logic which only applies to the world
of things and Having (here these terms are synonymous)—
it is that wherever the operating consciousness is effectively
at work, a mysterious inversion takes place and in the end an
identification is established between giving and receiving. It
is not, indeed, enough to say that we receive in proportion
to what we give; the truth is far more paradoxical and more

subtle: we receive in giving, or to put it still better, giving is already a way of receiving. The unemployed or the man without hope of whom I spoke just now is not only someone who no longer gives anything, he is someone who has lost the power of animating the world into which he feels he has been thrown, and where he is superfluous. But this animating power should not be understood in a purely subjectivistic sense, like the faculty of making fantastic shadows move across a lifeless screen: the power of animating is the power of using to the full, or, to go more deeply, of lending ourselves, that is to say of allowing ourselves to be used to the full, of offering ourselves in some way to those *kairoi*, or life-giving opportunities which the being, who is really available (*disponible*), discovers all around him like so many switches controlling the inexhaustible current flowing through our universe.

And yet is there not something deep down in us which protests against this optimism? Not by an abstract opposition or a sneering denial drawn from our pride: no: but does not the spirit of truth itself force us to face those extreme cases— those cases where all sources of help seem really to have dried up, where everything seems to have failed—the case of the prisoner, alone in the depths of his cell, of the exile, lost in a strange land, or, finally, of the incurable invalid who day by day feels the flickering flame die down and remains helpless while life, continuing its relentless and purposeless game, slowly deserts him.

It seems to me that a philosopher worthy of the name can never consider these extreme cases with too great anxiety and insistence, and it is indeed the spirit of truth that requires him not to turn away from them in order to establish some well-adjusted, harmonious, soothing system where they are all omitted. We are here at the exact point where honest thought changes into a *De profundis* and by the very fact of so doing opens to transcendence. I am speaking of the one authentic transcendence and ask you to be good enough to ignore or rather to refuse to accept the often vague and most certainly injudicious use which so many contemporary thinkers, for the most part existentialists, have made of this word.

Yes, it is indeed here that invocation arises, that an appeal for help to the absolute Thou is articulated. I have never ceased repeating this many and many a time. But I should like to be much more explicit on a point which, to tell the truth, has always seemed to me essential and upon which there should be no possible uncertainty. The spirit of truth bears another name which is even more revealing; it is also the spirit of fidelity, and I am more and more convinced that what this spirit demands of us is an explicit refusal, a definite negation of death. The death here in question is neither death in general, which is only a fiction, nor my own death in so far as it is mine, as Mr. Brunschvicg admitted in the course of the debate which brought us to grips at the *Congrès Descartes;* it is the death of those we love. They alone in fact are within reach of our spiritual sight, it is they only whom it is given us to apprehend and to long for as beings, even if our religion, in the widest sense of the word, not only allows us but even encourages us and enjoins us to extrapolate and proclaim that light is everywhere, that love is everywhere, that Being is everywhere. "To love a being," says one of my characters, "is to say you, you in particular, will never die." For me this is not merely a sentence in a play, it is an affirmation which it is not given to us to transcend. To consent to the death of a being is in a sense to give him up to death. Moreover, I should like to be able to show that again here it is the spirit of truth which forbids us to make this surrender, this betrayal.

Yet nothing could at first sight seem more arbitrary or even more iniquitous than to compare what appears to be the pure and simple recognition of a fact to a betrayal. Is it not, on the contrary, unreasonable and almost blameworthy to refuse to accept this fact, and ought we not to say that those who, silencing their longings and even their aspirations, admit and proclaim it, are the more truly courageous? Is it not the unbeliever who refuses all fallacious consolation who is the real representative of the spirit of truth? In addition, it might be asked what does this active negation of death amount to? Is it anything but a purely verbal negation, the refusal made by minds all aureoled with infantile sentimentality to accept the reality which they have not the courage to face? There we have in my view one of the most important problems with which the existential philosopher has to deal, and the solution which I am inclined to propose is in direct opposition to the positions adopted in our own time by such men as Heidegger and Jaspers.

It seems to me that we should begin by observing that there can be no question of treating the absolute cessation of consciousness as a fact, and this is a sufficient answer to the supposed objectivity on which he who is hardened in his denial prides himself. In the first place, in fact, we have no sort of possibility or right to speak of a consciousness in the same way as we speak of an object which can be defined as "this particular thing", which first appeared at a given moment of time and will come to an end (will break, for instance, or dissolve) at another equally fixed moment. I should also be quite ready to say that consciousness cannot be defined ostensively; what can be designated is never it itself, it is something (the particular body) which perhaps keeps up and doubtless tends to impair a whole set of relationships with it, which are inextricable to the point of contradicting themselves as relations. Moreover, we must remark that if we admit that consciousness is a manifestation there can be no question of observing anything but the more or less prolonged eclipses of consciousness. We are, however, unable to go to the extreme limit and to speak of a final eclipse or an absolute disappearance, for unless we fall into an indefensible materialism, we can neither apprehend nor even imagine the principle of which consciousness is the manifestation. From this point of view we might say very simply that if death is a silence we cannot mark its boundaries, for we neither know what it is veiling, what it is protecting, nor what it is preparing. The fallacy, the treason, consists in interpreting this silence as non-existence, as a decline into non-being.

Perhaps it may be objected that such considerations do not take us beyond an agnosticism which many of the poets of the end of the nineteenth century, from Tennyson to Sully Prudhomme, expressed, with pathos, no doubt, but with very unsound philosophy. Only I do not in the least think that agnosticism is the last word here. The active negation of death,

which I was advocating a moment ago, has in it both something of a challenge and of piety; more exactly, it is piety
which from our mode of insertion in the world is bound to
appear as a challenge. The world seems to assure me cynically
that this tenderly loved being no longer exists on its lists,
that he has been struck off the universal register—and I for
my part claim that he exists all the same and that he cannot
help existing. I am thus caught in the toils of an agonising
contradiction. Can I free myself from it?

First, I have to remind myself that the departed being of
whom they now want me to believe that there is nothing left
but a past, who is altogether past, was at the beginning nothing but a future. A loving conspiracy had at first to be formed
around him, at a time when nothing was as yet known of what
he would or could be. The essence of this being was still only
the prophetic hopes he awakened in his relatives. And I have
to ask myself in the presence of this death, which is perhaps
only a birth or an ascension, if the conspiracy is not to be
reproduced on a higher plane. This time it is round a sleep
that the conspiracy must be centred—a sleep which must not
be disturbed by intruders. But against what intrusion except
that of infidelity and negation have we to guard?

There is still a serious ambiguity, however. You may say
that this infidelity is simply forgetfulness; it is a *memory*
which we have to respect, and we are guilty of a veritable
paralogism in fraudulently changing this *memory* into an
existence, to be protected and promoted. We have then to
choose between two interpretations, the one modest and in
strict conformity with the given facts of experience, the other
arbitrary and almost delirious.

But if this divergence is possible, it is because we are no
longer in the realm of practical existence, where it is always
possible, at least in theory, to investigate what we seek to
verify. To return to the simile of sleep, everything happens
as though we were watching from the other side of a trans-
parent partition; we cannot make sure of the exact state of
the sleeper; the very meaning of the words "real state" is no
longer quite clear. The sleeper has been taken beyond our
reach, we are no longer permitted to proceed to any sort of

examination by manipulation which would give us some way of pronouncing upon his state. If a manipulation is still possible it can only be carried out upon a thing which, because it is a thing, is no longer *he*, and which, moreover, is in process of disappearing. It is required of us, whatever the circumstances, to triumph over the obsessions which cling to this thing, whether it be to preserve a memory or to dwell upon a presence.

Nevertheless, it appears upon reflection that he who limits himself to respecting a memory is at bottom still sufficiently in awe of the "thing" to consider it as the remains of what we can no longer preserve within ourselves except as an image. Moreover, this image grows fainter each day, like a badly printed photograph which we vainly keep on dusting. But would it not here be as well to destroy an illusion. Supposing that I really do cherish a materialised or purely mental image, it is not for itself that I do so, but out of love for the being this image evokes. This being himself, then, should not and cannot be created as an image, otherwise we shall fall into an absurdity, the image being referred back to another image, and so on and so on for as far as we can see. Our fidelity can only be founded on an unfailing attachment to an existence which it is impossible to relegate to the world of images. If our thought here tends to be confused, it is really because some image, rudimentary as it must be, and consequently a mere shadow, is necessary for this unfailing attachment to become conscious of itself. This shadow, which may be only a name still impregnated with affection, is the mode by which a presence makes itself known to me.

It does not seem as though all this can be seriously disputed. It may certainly be objected, however, that the existence seen through the image is only something from the past; we shall therefore speak of a "still existing" (*un exister encore*), of that which "no longer exists" (*n'existe plus*), if we want to define what we are here considering. But if we break away from this abstract jargon, we shall without a doubt be forced to recognise that the question is always and ever concerned with the image; yet it is precisely from this that we want to free ourselves, it is a non-shadow that we are striving to grasp, that is to say something *indefectible*. There is not and cannot be piety except where relations are maintained with what is indefectible. But we must at the same time emphasise the paradox that as a matter of fact the memories, or more exactly the images, can very well tend to stifle the indefectible essence which it is their business to evoke. There is no piety which is not in danger of degenerating into idolatry.

Let us penetrate further: indefectibility is that which cannot fail where deep-rooted fidelity is preserved, and this amounts to saying that it is a reply. Only this reply could not be automatic without fidelity becoming weakened in its very essence (for it would degenerate into a process or technique). It must therefore be well understood that the faithful soul is destined to experience darkness and that it must even be familiar with the temptation to let itself be inwardly blinded by the night through which it has to pass. Moreover, this is saying too little and the language I have used here is not courageous enough. Fidelity is not a preliminary *datum*, it is revealed and established as fidelity by this very crossing of the darkness, by this trial combined with everyday life, the experience of "day after day". So then the Indefectible is not the permanence of an essence, or, more exactly, it is not in the mode of such a permanence that it can be given to us. The essence is in fact made known to thought as it advances, by way of a law definable only in universal terms. This law is not conceivable where relations between one being and another are in question. Consequently, there is room for every sort of error, false move and deception on the side of the subject. It is through these errors and vicissitudes that we are allowed to behold the intermittent gleaming of the indefectible fire. I will not try to disguise, but emphasise rather, the contradiction which these words contain; it seems to me to be bound up with our human condition.

Such I think are the preliminary data concerning what is really somewhat improperly called the problem of personal immortality. I am actually very far from hazarding any conjectures on the mode of existence of the departed and the nature of the palingenesis for which they are no doubt destined. Moreover, it does not matter that I refuse to be interested in such speculations. It must, however, be recognised that those who do indulge in them are generally quite unprovided with any equipment for reflection, hence their theories are in danger of degenerating into pure fantasies. On the other hand, theological interdicts, of which it would be well to examine the foundations very closely, help in great measure to paralyse all independent research in this realm.

I should like now to go back briefly in order to bring out the unity, admittedly hard to grasp at first, which underlies the preceding considerations. The fundamental connection seems to me to be as follows: whatever the Stoics or idealists say (we will not here consider the less elevated doctrines), if death is the ultimate reality, value is annihilated in mere scandal, reality is pierced to the heart. This we cannot disguise from ourselves unless we enclose ourselves in a system of pleasure. Simply to admit or accept this scandal is not only to bow before an objective fact, for here we are outside the order of fact; it is rather to destroy human communion itself at its very centre. The spirit of truth here identifies itself with the spirit of fidelity and love. We should really go further: value can only be thought of as reality—and by that I mean saved from a verbalism which destroys while thinking to proclaim it—if it is related to the consciousness of an immortal destiny. We have seen clearly that it is not separated from courage and sacrifice: but whatever the being who sacrifices himself may think about himself and his metaphysical chances, reflection cannot accept this annihilation, even if he is himself resigned to it. Do not let us be the dupes of words: reflection, as an abstract entity, is nothing; what is real is I myself, meditating about the destiny of my brother.

I do not in the least disguise from myself the numberless questions which arise here—particularly concerning the part played in this realm by the appeal to absolute transcendence. Is it possible to conceive of a real personal survival independently of this transcendence? I think that my reply would be as follows: there is no human love worthy of the name which does not represent for him who exercises it both a pledge and a seed of immortality: but, on the other hand, it is really not possible to exercise this love without discovering that it cannot constitute a closed system, that it passes beyond itself in every direction, that it really demands for its complete realisation a universal communion outside which it cannot be satisfied and is destined to be corrupted and lost in the end. Moreover, this universal communion itself can only be centred upon an absolute Thou. It is time to do away once and for all with the positivist illusions on this subject.

There is another point on which I should like briefly to explain myself. What real relation can be established between value and immortality? There is, for instance, no doubt that the beautiful work of art is uncorrupted and untouched by time. "A thing of beauty is a joy forever", as the poet says. But is it true that this is in any way connected with what we understand by a real survival, by the soul's or the person's actual victory over death? Perhaps we could reply as follows: in a world of scandal where absurdity had gained the upper hand, that is to say where what is best and highest was at the mercy of blind forces, where "because a little piece of iron had passed through their heads, it had become for ever impossible to get on with people like Péguy or like Alain Fournier" (Jacques Rivière, *A la Trace de Dieu*)—there would not perhaps be a single value which was not in danger of appearing ludicrous and suspect. We are thus led to wonder whether the essence of value—independently of what we have seen to be its function—is not to be found in its translucency. This amounts to saying that value is the mirror wherein it is given us to discern, always imperfectly and always through a distorting mist, the real face of our destiny, the "truer than ourselves". What it shows us certainly reaches its full development in another world—a world which it seems to be the property of our earthly experience to open or half open to us, or in extreme cases, to prevent us from entering.

Thus to make the other world the axis of our life is, of course, to take the opposite position from that of nearly all contemporary philosophers, and I do not deny that, at the bottom of my mind, there is an anxious voice protesting and persistently arguing in favour of the metaphysicians of Earth. It is, however, to be wondered whether the systematic re-

fusal to accept this other world is not at the origin of the
convulsions which have reached their paroxysm at the present
time. Perhaps a stable order can only be established if man is
acutely aware of his condition as a traveller, that is to say, if
he perpetually reminds himself that he is required to cut
himself a dangerous path across the unsteady blocks of a universe which has collapsed and seems to be crumbling in every
direction. This path leads to a world more firmly established
in Being, a world whose changing and uncertain gleams are
all that we can discern here below. Does not everything happen as though this ruined universe turned relentlessly upon
whomever claimed that he could settle down in it to the extent of erecting a permanent dwelling there for himself? It is
not to be denied, of course, that the affirmation of the other
world entails risk, it is the "noble venture" of which the ancient philosopher spoke, but the whole question is to know
whether in refusing to make this venture we are not starting
upon a road which sooner or later leads to perdition.

II DANGEROUS SITUATION OF
ETHICAL VALUES

From an abstract point of view, which has been that of most of the philosophers up till now, it may seem ridiculous to speak of a situation of values: and if values are considered as ideas there is no sense in saying they are situated. It is quite otherwise if one admits, as I do not hesitate to do, that a value is nothing if it is not incarnated. Moreover, the word incarnated must be defined. What does it mean for a value to be embodied? To simplify matters let us only consider what are properly speaking ethical values here. The property of a value, as I said recently, is to assume a certain function in relation to life and, as it were, to mark it with its seal. For that, it is still necessary for the value to be incorporated in some cause. It seems to me, in fact, that in its general lines we can adopt the theory which was presented with such force by the American philosopher, Royce, in his fine book, *Philosophy of Loyalty*. A cause is neither an individual nor a collection of individuals, nor an abstract principle. A cause is not impersonal, but rather supra-personal; it is a particular type of unity which holds together a number of persons within a life which they share. Hence a relationship of a special kind, which we can call loyalty, is established between the individual and the cause; it is not a mystical renunciation, but a fully conscious attachment which presupposes the free subordination of the self to a superior principle. "My loyalty", Royce says, "means nothing theoretically or practically if I am not the member of a community. No success I can achieve will be valid if it is not also the success of the community to which I essentially belong, in virtue of the real relations which bind me to the whole of the universe." This last detail is extremely important. If we only took the first definition we might indeed fear that it justified allegiance to a party, for instance, with all the servitudes which can go with it. But, for Royce, if loyalty is a supreme good, conflict between varying loyalties is the greatest of evils. It must be recognised that some causes are favourable and others contrary to the development of loyalty in the world. "A cause is good not only for us but for humanity—that is to say, in itself—according to the measure in which it serves the spirit of loyalty, that is to say that it helps us in our loyalty to our fellows and fosters it."[1] This amounts to saying that there is a universal cause which is that of loyalty in the world. Loyalty is infectious, it is a good which spreads wide, it is a ferment of extraordinary potency. Such is indeed the cause to which I should consecrate myself. When I speak the truth I do not only serve the supra-personal community which I form with my interlocutor, I help to make man's faith in man grow in this world, I help to strengthen the bonds which make a universal community possible.

I do not think all this can be seriously disputed, and the effort of the American philosopher to save universality without becoming separated from the realm of concrete action is to be admired. But at the same time we should most certainly be giving way to baleful illusions if we made any mistake about the opposition this idealism is bound, in fact, to meet with to-day, even if it obtains a theoretical and lifeless assent from many minds. And it is precisely here that we are obliged to introduce the notion of situation. It is probable that at no time the faith of man in man, not only faith in his fellows, but in himself, has been subjected to a more harsh and formidable test. What is in danger of death to-day is man himself in his unity, and this is just as true of the individual considered as a concrete whole as of the human race considered as the flowing out or expansion of an essence. Hence there is a great risk that Royce's idea of the spirit of loyalty will be felt as an empty aspiration, as an inconsistent dream, as a fiction.

[1] Royce, *Philosophy of Loyalty* (Macmillan), p. 118.

It is evident that a metaphysic of faith can be built on the ruins of humanism: and here there develops an impassioned dialectic. For if it is possible to say that the death of God in the Nietzschean sense preceded and made possible the agony of man which we are now witnessing, it is legitimate in a certain sense to say that it is from the ashes of man that God can and must rise again. Am I mistaken in presuming that the ideas of Barth in particular draw part of their strength from the radical pessimism to which events have brought us on the purely human level?

But here the particularly serious problem arises which I want to consider now. Have we the right, even from a strictly Christian point of view, in a certain sense to sacrifice the ethical? What in reality would such a sacrifice amount to? To put it briefly, it would consist in sanctioning an actual division which we are tending to create between those on the one hand who establish their existence on a mystical basis and those on the other who try simply to get along with as little harm as possible in this adventure, so incomprehensible and in the end so frightful, this adventure into which they have a sense of having been hurled by chance, or by inhuman and uncontrollable forces, which comes to the same thing. In thus imagining the fissure which is tending to develop at the centre of the human mass, we are however in danger of excessively over-simplifying and even of misrepresenting a situation which is infinitely more complex and which it is probably scarcely possible to schematise.

When we speak of existences seeking to base themselves on mysticism we are in great danger of letting ourselves be taken in simply by a word and of grouping realities which have nothing in common under one head. The very term of mysticism, so abused, so emptied of all value but nevertheless so difficult to avoid, calls for serious reservations. What is really in question is, on the one hand, fidelity to "God's Word"—and, from this point of view, differences of denomination should be treated as of relatively secondary importance; and on the other a phenomenon of magnetic attraction or we might say of crystallisation. The announcement of an order to be set up in accordance with what the masses are vaguely awaiting is here embodied in some leader or group of leaders. In both cases we can say with certainty that the individual is required to make the sacrifice, not only of his immediate interests but eventually even of his life, to a suprapersonal end. In the first case this end is found in an eternity which envelops and transcends the present, and in the second case in a more or less near future. But between these ends which, if one may so put it, are not situated in the same metaphysical dimension, it seems to me very difficult to establish either a definite connection or a radical opposition. One point, however, is clear: in so far as the terrestrial order to be established allows the domination of some and the subjection of others, it must be stated without hesitation that it can only be set up in defiance of all the values converging towards the inaccessible centre for which we reserve the name of eternity. On the other hand, in so far as the terrestrial order is conceived of as effectively excluding all privilege and all slavery, it is just possible to see in it a symbol, imperfect, no doubt, and perhaps even inconsistent in the main, of a reality which can only be effectively established under conditions incompatible with the fragile, ephemeral and contradictory structure of our actual experience. These simple observations will be enough to show the equivocal and even dangerous character of certain momentary alliances which at a time of crisis may be entered into between Christianity or some Christian confession on the one hand and on the other the most active form of earthly mysticism—the only one which stands a real chance of still surviving to-morrow after the nameless tempest we are passing through to-day. On the strictly tellurian plane, that is, in an order where given concrete dynamisms are at work, it is difficult to see how anything but a more and more powerfully organised systematised plutocracy can oppose this earthly mysticism to-morrow. Such a plutocracy would, moreover, be inevitably tempted to mobilise in its service, not so much genuine spiritual forces, as some of the feeblest interpreters—those most open to suggestion and seduction—whom the spiritual forces must call upon to represent them in visible form before the eyes of the majority. Hence there will be a danger that a situation may develop which will be all the more inextricable because, in such a struggle, what might originally have still figured as mysticism will have inevitably degenerated into a pure system of spite and gratification.

Under these conditions it may seem as though the Christian were condemned simply to retire from a conflict in which the stake appears to him to be more and more futile, since this stake amounts to nothing but the possession of the world, in other words the seizure of the unseizable. At the end of this dialectic, which it would be only too easy to illustrate with concrete examples, we are apparently faced with what was already given us at the start; an irreparable rent in the very stuff of which our humanity is made.

But at the same time, as we have already suggested, it is clear that the Christian cannot rest content to observe and accept this rent without denying his own Christianity and without emptying the very notion of salvation of its substantial content.

Does this mean that in order to preserve the meaning and value of this notion, the Christian has to arrogate to himself a sort of right or duty of guardianship over the non-Christian? Briefly, must we subscribe to the establishment of a spiritual paternalism which will be both at the cost and to the advantage of the Christian? I am sure that such a position is impossible from every point of view. On the one hand, indeed, it would give the Christian an essentially pharisaical sense of superiority; on the other hand it would none the less fatally cause in the nonbeliever a sort of bitterness, or *invidia*, which is probably the root of anti-religious passion. The Christian in fact cannot in any way think of himself as possessing either a power or even an advantage which has been denied to the unbeliever. There we have one of the most paradoxical aspects of his situation, for in another sense, he is obliged to recognise that grace has been bestowed upon him. This, however, only remains true on condition that the grace should inhabit him, not only as radiance, but as humility. From the moment that he begins to be proud of it as a possession it changes its nature, and I should be tempted to say it becomes a malediction.

Philosophers as a whole have taken little trouble to scruti-
nise the nature of this humility. Yet it is essentially in its
name that the Christian must constantly be on his guard
against the temptation to paternalism. At its root there is an
assurance, or I should be ready to say a knowledge that, in his
quality of a Christian, he acts neither on his own account
nor through the power of a virtue which is his property, or
even which having been infused into him has become authentically his own. Under these conditions he cannot in any
way claim to be worth more than the disinherited brother
to whom he is speaking. It would moreover be unlawfully
pretentious on his part should he glory in having a good
leader, or a good master, whilst the unbeliever has no one,
for this would mean that he was putting himself once more on
the plane of Having, the plane where one boasts about what
one possesses. It would not be difficult to show how this paradoxical humility tends at first to strike the unbeliever as unbearable hypocrisy. This has given rise to a tragic misunderstanding, especially as the sincere Christian can always
wonder whether the humility he is practising is any better
than an attitude adopted in conformity with something he
has been taught.

If this is the case, to come to the help of the unbeliever
spiritually can scarcely mean claiming literally to bring him
something of which he has been deprived. Such a claim would
in fact always be in danger of annulling or making sterile the
good which we set out to do. All that we can propose to ourselves is, in the last analysis, to awaken within another the
consciousness of what he is, or, more precisely, of his divine
filiation; to teach him to see himself as the child of God
through the love which is shown him. From this point of
view, I should be rather tempted to say that, contrary to what
Kierkegaard proclaimed, there is probably a Christian maieutic, of which, however, the essence is naturally very different from what we know of the Platonic maieutic. It is in
treating the other as a child of God that it seems to me to be
within the limits of possibility for me to awaken within him
a consciousness of his divine filiation. But in reality I do not
give or bring him anything. I merely direct the adoration of

which God is the unique object on to the divine life as seen
in this creature, who from the beginning has been unaware
of his true nature and is all the more unaware of it the greater
his self-complacent vanity may be.

These considerations may at first seem rather far removed
from the problem we have set ourselves, but they are not
really so. We shall, however, have to apply what we have been
saying about any Christian, to the Christian thinker.

I am going to strive to put the question in as distinct terms
as possible. We shall get a better idea of its immense range
if we remember that it does not only concern the relations
of the Christian with the non-Christian, but also the relations
of the Christian with himself, in so far as he discovers within
himself "immense regions where the Gospel has not been
preached". Moreover, it is in the depths of these regions that
a greater part of his existence develops; the most important
part, perhaps, often the most visible and sometimes the only
visible part.

In the light of the preceding remarks what would the theory
of a Christian philosopher amount to if he set out to deny
the specific and authentic character of the ethical values, that
is in fact to say if he set out to crush them to nothing between revelation on one side and undiluted sociology on the
other? Let us get away here from pure abstractions. A theory
is absolutely nothing apart from the subject who propounds
it, there is no affirmation without someone who affirms. But
who is making an affirmation here? It is I as a philosopher,
it is I, consequently, in a special definite capacity, as I address "you others," or, which comes to very much the same
thing, as I take counsel with myself concerning those others
on whom I am going to give judgment. From the position
which I occupy, I declare that what you consider good is not
truly good, or again that the reasons you think you have for
adhering to it are without solidity or truth, and that, in the
last analysis, you only act in conformity with impulses of
which the temporal and impure origins are to be found somewhere in the social structures which control your existence.
As for me, on the other hand, I claim to see the light which
is actually hidden from you and which alone could illuminate

the darkness in which you are groping—you who do not even know that you are surrounded with gloom, so complete is your blindness. It is only too clear that an assertion of such a kind, a judgment so summary, must be regarded as contrary to the Christian, and particularly to the Catholic tradition, which has always granted so large a place to the natural virtues.

But all these reflections are precisely concerned with the phenomenon of the eclipsing of the idea of natural virtue, and this phenomenon is itself bound up with another very genuine fact which it seems to me has been the chief feature in the evolution of western humanity for the last century and a half: the disappearance of a certain confidence which is both spontaneous and metaphysical in the order which frames our existence, or again what I have elsewhere called the severance of the nuptial bond between man and life. We shall be able to show without any difficulty, I think, that the optimistic humanism of the eighteenth century or of the middle of the nineteenth, paradoxically as it may seem, marked the first stage in this tragic disintegration. "Everything leads us to think", I said recently, "that the giving way of religious beliefs which has been going on for five hundred years in large sections of the civilised world has brought as its consequence a weakening of the natural foundations on which those beliefs were built. If this be so it means that what we need to reawaken within and around us is this piety, not Christian but pre-Christian, or more exactly peri-Christian. Each one of us probably knows Christians who are over supernaturalised and who have lost the sense, we will not say of nature but of the nascent grace which stirs at the heart of nature. I am strongly inclined to think that, apart from Revelation, this piety is the only true *vinculum* which can bind men together, and that all abstract universalism which claims to do without it, however upright its intention, really serves only to prepare the way for a nihilism whose devastating action we can discern on all sides."

I should express very clearly what I mean if I formed the hypothesis that the forces of destruction which are let loose everywhere around us and tend to sweep away all the embodied values, whether they are incorporated in the life of a family, a school, a hospital, a museum or a church, have only been able to develop beyond all limits because they started from a way of thinking which, if we may say so, denied the real by deconsecrating it. But of course there can be no more fatal error than to imagine that anything with which to reconsecrate it can be found in these forces themselves. There is no possible doubt that to seek to return to paganism under any form whatever, is to sink even lower into delirium and abjection. The Christian philosopher who wants to do positive work in the field of ethics to-day should, it seems to me, start by acquiring on his own account an increasingly concrete and extensive consciousness of the underground connections which unite the peri-Christian to what may strictly be called revelation. These connections are not of a strictly logical order, but they depend on a metaphysical anthropology of which for the last fifty years or so thinkers as different as Scheler, Peter Wust or Theodor Haecker, as Chesterton, Péguy, or to-day Thibon, have begun to trace the features. To undertake this, perhaps the most delicate of all tasks, requires an analytical effort of the utmost patience and severity, but also a most ardent faithfulness to the human element which is of the order of love and without which the analysis will become dry and barren. To tell the truth it is only the counterpart on the plane of intelligence or human creation of the mysterious work by which a tissue is re-formed or an organ regains its power. I do not think I can convey my thought to you more explicitly than by here introducing this reference of which the implications go far beyond those of a simple metaphor in my eyes.

I am indeed very far from under-estimating the dangers which there can be in introducing biological categories into the spiritual. And on this point it may be permissible to think that Bergson, the Bergson of *Deux Sources*, is not altogether beyond reproach. But is it not a fact that in reality the biologist as such, by a fatality of which it is not impossible to discover the principles, tends increasingly to lose all consciousness of what life is, and, I should say (though of course this does not apply to Bergson) that he does this in so far as he has managed to persuade himself that he will one day be able to produce it himself. Here again we have to recognise a sense of proportion which it is the function of humility to preserve. It seems clear that when biology claims to grant itself rights comparable with those belonging to physics and chemistry in the realm of inanimate nature, it is inevitably guilty of the disastrous intrusions that we have seen becoming widespread in our time. Actually I am quite prepared to recognise that it is difficult, and perhaps even impossible, to trace a precise line of demarcation between what is lawful and not lawful in this field; on its boundaries there are questions and species about which one can only speak with knowledge after the most minute examination of each case and all the principles which it involves. The thing, however, that we can assert— and it is what matters from the point of view I am taking—is that all demarcation disappears and man gives an irreparable opening to the Monstrous from the moment when he weakens in that piety in his relations to life which can alone guide his steps in an order where murder seems to be so easy, so indiscernible, so tempting, that it is not even recognised as such by him who accomplishes it.

A serious objection, or at the very least a delicate question, can scarcely fail to occur to our minds at the point we have now reached. If we put a sort of pre-Christian or peri-Christian piety at the basis of ethics are we not either making them depend on an irrational feeling over which we have no control, or else embarking upon the paradoxical or even hopeless undertaking of trying to resuscitate natural religion which the philosophy of enlightenment tried vainly to establish? Are we not in any case ruining the specific quality of ethical values which we meant on the contrary to safeguard?

It is certainly difficult to reply to this question in a completely satisfactory way within the limits of a brief exposition such as this. It could only be done, I think, by first of all attacking the classic and arbitrary distinction which it presupposes between feeling and reason. As an illustration of my objective at the moment, we might call to mind the beautiful analysis which Soloviev, for example, has given of modesty, pity and reverence, in his *Justification du Bien*. There we have principles expressing the human quality as such, this human quality which we mutilate and betray when we claim to reduce its essence to a mere faculty of association, a faculty, moreover, which the higher animals are far from lacking.

The real and most agonising problem seems to me much rather to concern the extent of our control of these principles. How far does it depend on us to revivify them? It is impossible to be too sceptical about the efficacy of philosophic preaching in this field—and I am not even thinking, of course, about the vulgarised expressions which such preaching is liable to adopt. As Thibon has so admirably pointed out, it is above all a question of moral renewal. It is conceivable that it will be the task of small communities coming together like swarms one after the other to form what we might call centres of example, that is to say nuclei of life around which the lacerated tissues of true moral existence can be reconstituted. It is not here a question of fleeting dreams. The most actual and immediate experience shows that men can relearn how to live, when they are placed in conditions which are real and when a light illuminates the group they form (with each other and with the things supporting them) at its summit. There is every reason to think that the guarantee of the success of such undertakings is bound up with the humility in which they originate and which shapes their first objectives. Levelling, in the ambitious forms under which it was conceived before the war, characterised by a titanism which was its original defect, has every chance of being wrecked in a nameless cataclysm. In any case, on ethical grounds it can be asserted that it is not only doomed but that it is complete nonsense.

I have no illusions about the disappointment which may accompany such a conclusion. What I really want to stress is that it is urgent in all departments to carry out clearing operations which will make it possible to find once more the lost springs for lack of whose values men would be condemned to an infra-animal existence, an existence of which our generation will have had the painful privilege of witnessing the first apocalyptic symptoms.

SELECTIVE BIBLIOGRAPHY

Journal métaphysique (Paris: Gallimard, 1927). English: *Metaphysical Journal*, trans. Bernard Wall (Chicago: Regnery, 1952)

Être et Avoir (Paris: Aubier, 1935). English: *Being and Having*, trans. K. Farrer (New York: Harper and Row, 1965)

Du refus à l'invocation (Paris: Gallimard, 1940). English: *Creative Fidelity*, trans. Robert Rosthal (New York: Farrar and Straus, 1964)

Homo Viator (Paris: Aubier, 1945). English: *Homo Viator*, trans. Emma Craufurd (New York: Harper and Row, 1962)

Le mystère de l'être, 2 vols. (Paris: Aubier, 1951). English: *The Mystery of Being*, trans. G. S. Fraser and René Hague (London: Harill Press, 1950–51)

Les hommes contre l'humain (Paris: Vieux Colombier, 1951). English: *Man Against Humanity* (also: *Man Against Mass Society*) (London: Harill Press, 1952; Chicago: Regnery, 1962)

L'homme problématique (Paris: Flammarion, 1955). English: *Problematic Man*, trans. B. Thompson (New York: Herder and Herder, 1967)

Présence et immortalité (Paris: Flammarion, 1959). English: *Presence and Immortality*, trans. M. A. Machado and H. J. Koren (Pittsburgh: Duquesne University Press, 1967)

The Existential Background of Human Dignity (Cambridge, Mass.: Harvard University Press, 1963)

Seymour Cain, *Gabriel Marcel* (London: Bowes and Bowes, 1963)

Pietro Prini, *Gabriel Marcel et la méthodologie de l'invérifiable* (Paris: Desclée et de Brouwer, 1953)

Paul Ricoeur, *Gabriel Marcel et Karl Jaspers* (Paris: Seuil, 1947)

Roger Troisfontaines, *De l'existence à l'être*, 2 vols. (Paris: Vrin, 1953)

Chapter 4

INTRODUCTION

PAUL RICOEUR (1913–) is one of France's most influential philosophers today. He has been very prolific in his writing; some of his books deal with the work of other contemporary philosophers, such as Husserl, Jaspers, Marcel, and Heidegger, while others contain Ricoeur's own contribution to contemporary philosophy. Ricoeur's philosophy is greatly influenced by the ideas of Kant, Hegel, Husserl, Heidegger, Marcel, Jaspers, Sartre, Merleau-Ponty, Nabert, Mounier, and Eliade. The final conception to which he has come, however, is by no means eclectic in nature. Ricoeur's philosophy certainly belongs to what has often been called "existential phenomenology," but like Sartre and Merleau-Ponty he has come to a philosophical position typically his own.

Ricoeur's most important work, *Philosophie de la volonté*, was originally set up as a work in two volumes. Ricoeur later decided to add a third volume, but it had already appeared necessary to publish the second volume in two parts. The first volume, *The Voluntary and Involuntary*, appeared in 1950, and the second volume, *Fallible Man* and *Symbolism of Evil*, appeared ten years later. The third volume will be entitled *Poetics of the Will*.

In this monumental work, Ricoeur tries to show concretely, different but related approaches to an understanding of man's will and of his being in general. Ricoeur labels these approaches by the substantive terms eidetics, empirics, symbolics, mythics, and finally poetics. The first volume (*The Voluntary and Involuntary*) contains an initial approach that Ricoeur calls the *eidetic* approach. Here Ricoeur tries to describe very accurately invariable and essential, intentional structures of man's practical and affective life. The label *eidetics* refers to what Husserl called "the regional ontology of man's psychic life" and also "phenomenological psychology," and which he defined as the aprioric, eidetic, intuitive, purely descriptive science of man's intentional experiences. The important point in this context is not the question of whether or not Ricoeur is faithful to Husserl's original ideas, but to localize the source of Ricoeur's inspiration. In an essay, "Méthodes et tâches d'une phénoménologie de la volonté" (in *Problèmes actuels de la phénoménologie*, ed. H. L. Van Breda [Paris: de Brouwer, 1952], pp. 115–23, pp. 115–16), Ricoeur explained his major concern as follows: If for every problem one goes immediately to the "existential project" and the "movement of ek-sistence," which entails all authentically human conduct in the way Sartre conceives of it, one takes the risk of missing the specificity of the problems and of pushing the contours of the different modes of orientation toward the world in a kind of indistinct existentialist monism which repeatedly tells the same story when speaking about emotions, sexuality, speech, imagination, perception, etc. What is necessary is first and foremost an accurate description of the invariable structures (*eidos*) of man's intentional experiences.

But although Ricoeur found his inspiration in Husserl, and Merleau-Ponty's interpretation of Husserl's phenomenology, as far as the method used is concerned, for the content of this work he was largely inspired by Marcel's ideas, mainly the latter's conception of the "mystery" of man's body as subject: "meditation on the works of Gabriel Marcel is in fact at the root of the analysis of this book" (*The Voluntary and Involuntary*, p. 18).

Pure, eidetic description of intentional experiences cannot be accomplished without a reduction, that is, without leaving out a great number of aspects that cannot be adequately dealt with by a mere description of essential features. That is why the description is to be completed by other approaches which are reflective, hermeneutical, and "dialectical" in nature, and focus precisely on those aspects which were left out of consideration in a pure description. Among those aspects, the basically human phenomena of "fault" and "transcendence" occupy the predominant place. They constitute the immediate subject matter of the second and third volumes of the work.

In *Fallible Man*, Ricoeur focuses on man's fallibility, which in his view constitutes man's fundamental basic condition. Fallibility as the capacity for evil is an integral part of the explanation of man's fault. The word "fault" means originally a break, breach (*faille*), gap (*écart*), rift (*fêlure*), tearing (*déchirement*); there is in man essentially a kind of break, which makes him go astray, deviate, err, become divided against himself, and thus to become a "flawed" creature. In the realm of the will, this "break" refers to the same phenomenon as that to which Heidegger refers with the expressions "temporality" and "historicity" and the fallenness that flows from them (= finitude). The method used in this part of the second volume, devoted to a "phenomenology of fallibility," has many aspects in common with Nabert's reflexive method. The second part, *Symbolism of Evil*, is hermeneutical in character. Ricoeur turns here from fallibility to fault, and in trying to understand it concretely, turns to the "fullness of language," which leads to a hermeneutics of symbols and myths. Instead of engaging in pure reflection or description, the author now turns to an interpretation of the fundamental symbols in terms of which man avows his *actual* fallen condition.

The selection that follows here is the last section of *Fallible Man*, in which Ricoeur attempts to answer the question of how "ontological" fallibility is related to moral evil in man.

THE CONCEPT OF FALLIBILITY

Paul Ricoeur

LIMITATION AND FALLIBILITY
FALLIBILITY AND THE POSSIBILITY OF FAITH

What is meant by calling man fallible? Essentially this: that the *possibility* of moral evil is inherent in man's constitution. This reply calls for two kinds of clarifications. It may be asked, indeed, in what features of this primordial constitution the possibility of failing resides more particularly. On the other hand, one may ask about the nature of this possibility itself. Let us consider these two aspects of the problem in succession.

1 LIMITATION AND FALLIBILITY

A long philosophic tradition, which attained its most perfect expression in Leibniz, would maintain that the limitation proper to creatures is the occasion of moral evil. Considered as the occasion of moral evil, this limitation would even merit the name of metaphysical evil. Our whole preceding analysis tends to rectify this ancient proposition in a precise way: the idea of limitation as such cannot bring us to the threshold of moral evil. Not just any limitation constitutes the possibility of failing, but *that* specific limitation which consists, for human reality, in not coinciding with itself. Nor would it be of any use to define limitation as a participation in nothingness or not-being: we remember that Descartes, *before* elucidating

This essay is from *Fallible Man*, by Paul Ricoeur, translated by Ch. Kelbley (Chicago, 1965), pp. 203-24. Copyright © 1965 Henry Regnery Company.

the relation of the will to the understanding, elaborated a brief ontology of human reality which consisted in combining the idea of being or perfection with "a certain negative idea of nothingness, i.e. of what is infinitely far removed from every kind of perfection." Thus he could say "I am a something intermediate between God and nothingness." But any combination of being and nothingness does not constitute the occasion of failing, for every reality which is not being as such is, in a quite general sense, "intermediate between God and nothingness." We can understand how Descartes could be satisfied with that brief outline: he did not intend to set forth an ontology of human reality but merely to brush aside the hypothesis that man is endowed with a positive power of erring which would argue against divine perfection. In showing that man is composed of being and nothingness, he left room only for the idea of a default in being and ascribed the privative factor which is conjoined to this simple default to the bad use of the will. And so a brief ontology of the creature in general was enough to acquit God, and a philosophy of the faculties enough to indict man. Descartes' purpose here is purely apologetic; he makes no claim whatsoever of determining the mode or the degree of being peculiar to man. But if we undertake to formulate such an ontology, the idea of limitation as such can no longer account for the idea of fallibility: what we need is a concept of human limitation which is not a particular instance of the limitation of the something-in-general. As Kant showed with respect to the categories of quality, there is nothing more in the idea of limitation than the synthesis of the positing and negating of something. Now we have need of a concept of limitation which is straightway one of human limitation.

The idea of "disproportion" seemed to us to satisfy this demand for a direct ontology of human reality which unfolds its particular categories against the background of a formal ontology of the something-in-general. The general concept of limitation belongs to such a formal ontology; but we cannot pass from the *specification* of the limitation of something to man's limitation. We must put in the particular categories of human reality.

These categories peculiar to human limitation must be disengaged directly from the disproportionate relation of finitude to infinitude. It is this relation which constitutes the ontological "locus" which is "between" being and nothingness, or in other words, man's "degree of being," his "quantity of being." *It is this relation which makes human limitation synonymous with fallibility.*

Let us try to disengage those specific categories of human limitation by initiating a kind of "transcendental deduction," that is, a justification of concepts through their power of making a certain domain of objectivity possible. If we could show that these categories are the condition of possibility of a certain discourse on man, these categories would receive all the legitimation that one could require.

Accordingly, we shall complete our enterprise of total reflection on the *pathétique* of misery by elucidating those conditions of possibility of a discourse on man. Moreover, the myth of melange and the rhetoric of misery include an implicit understanding, in the mode of "right opinion," of these categories themselves. The concepts of "melange" and "intermediacy," characteristics of the great rhetoric on the human condition, are already existential categories, but adumbrated in the pathetic mode. That reflection can recapture them as categories, Plato himself assures us when he passes from the myth of "melange" to the idea of μεταξύ [metaxu] and "mixture." The etymological continuity from the rhetorical theme of "melange" to the dialectical notion of "mixture" assures us that the grace of language is with us in this enterprise.

Our guide in this deduction of the categories of fallibility will be the Kantian triad of the categories of quality: reality, negation, limitation. Why privilege this triad at the expense of those of quantity, relation and modality? Because nowhere else does the transcendental deduction so clearly go beyond a strictly epistemological reflection bearing on the *a priori* constitution of the physical object, to bring itself nearer to a transcendental phenomenology centered on the manifestation or the appearance of the object in general. What Kant says of the schemata of quality suggests of itself the free use we propose to make of the corresponding categories: "Reality," he says, "in the pure concept of understanding, is that which corresponds to a sensation in general; it is that, therefore, the concept of which in itself points to being [*ein Sein*] (in time). Negation is that the concept of which represents not-being [*ein Nichtsein*] (in time). The opposition of these two thus rests upon the distinction of one and the same time as filled and empty." In this way, there arises the schema of degree or a quantum of reality which is nothing other than the "quantity of something insofar as it fills time."[1] Disregarding Kantian orthodoxy, we will not seek to transcribe this triad into a *science* of the degrees of sensation.[2] Rather, we shall transpose it onto the level of a philosophical anthropology so as to systematize the language employed throughout the course of this book.

In passing from an axiomatics of physics to a philosophical anthropology, the triad of reality, negation and limitation may be expressed in the following three terms: *originating affirmation, existential difference, human mediation.* Our study expresses the progression of this triad through knowing, acting and feeling. What is in play in this dialectic is a more and more concrete determination of the third term which truly represents man's humanity.

Rather than recapitulating this concrete dialectic such as we have set it forth, we shall elucidate its founding concepts so as to show how they *make possible* an anthropology worthy of being called philosophical.[3]

First, it turns out that the initial guiding concept of such an anthropology is not and cannot be that of finitude. In this dialectic finitude is the result and not the origin. In this sense we must admit that Kant is right when he posits first the idea of a rational being in general, then restricts this idea by the difference of a sensibility to bring forth that of a *finite rational* being. This explains why the first crest in our own anal-

[1] *Critique of Pure Reason*, A 143 (N. K. Smith, 184).
[2] J. Vuillemin, *Physique et métaphysique kantiennes*, Paris, 1955.
[3] With regard to this, cf. "*Négativité et affirmation originaire*," in *Aspects de la dialectique* (Paris: Desclée de Brouwer, 1956), pp. 101–24.

ysis is the one which passes through the three moments of originating affirmation, namely the Verb, the practical to-tality or the idea of happiness, and Eros or the happiness of the heart. From the first of these moments to the second, from the second to the third, originating affirmation becomes progressively richer and more inward: at first it is only the vehemence of the Yes, which has for a correlate the "is" that is signified—or to be more precise, supra-signified—by the Verb. This is the "transcendental" moment of originating affirmation. This moment is necessary but not sufficient; it is necessary to make the power of existing pass from the register of "living" to that of "thinking"; it is insufficient to assure us that we *are* that thinking. It is ourselves that we affirm next in the practical idea of a totality which we approach through the understanding, always in process but never completed, of all the projects of all men and against which the enclosure of our character stands out. This essential openness or accessibility to the ἔργον [ergon], to the "function" or the "project" of man as such, grounds the person in giving him a horizon of humanity which is neither I nor you but the task of treating the person, in me and in you, as an end and not as a means. The person is not decipherable directly without the guide of the idea of humanity which gives the person a goal. In this sense, humanity, understood as a totality to-be-made-to-be, is the condition of possibility of the person. But if the idea of humanity is capable of leading from the transcendental to the practical, it does not yet tell us that we *are* this humanity of thinking. It is Eros, it is Love that shows that this aim, which is immanent to the function of man, is happiness anticipated in a consciousness of direction and of belonging. Feeling alone, through its pole of infinitude, assures me that I can *"continue my existence in"* the openness of thinking and of acting; the originating affirmation is felt here as the Joy of "existing in" the very thing which allows me to think and to act; then reason is no longer an other: I am it, you are it, because we are what it is.

But the originating affirmation *becomes* man only by going through the existential *negation* that we called perspective, character and vital feeling. Before Descartes and ever since the Platonic myth of Poros and Penia, we have known that man is intelligible only through participation "in a certain negative idea of nothingness." From Hegel to Sartre we have been told that man is this very negation. But what has been lost in the course of this victorious march of negation is its true relation to the power of affirmation which constitutes us. The problem of the "for-itself" of *man* is by no means resolved in its opposition to the "in-itself" of *things*. Such an opposition of a nihilizing "for-itself" and a reified "in-itself" still leaves the two terms external to each other and leads less to a dialectic than to a dichotomy between a stable "being" and a "nothingness" which uproots and isolates itself. The description of "nihilizing acts"—from absence to refusal, to doubt and to anguish—certainly accounts for the promotion of man as non-thing; but the thing's being that man nihilizes is not the whole of being. And even when the "in-itself" represents my own dead past, my evolved being, the "having-been" (*gewesen*) of my existence, hardened into essence (*Wesen*), it is still external being that I rise up against. If contemporary philosophy has overvalued the nothingness of rupture and isolation to such a degree, it is through a disavowal of the originating affirmation or, as Spinoza says, of the effort to exist, identical to actual essence, which is wholly power to *posit* (*ponere*) and not to *do away with* (*tollere*). This is the being in question in man's being. Being is here affirmation, yes, joy. I do not thrust this being aside as the already transpired and dead; I am it and I participate in it.

Existential negation is a negation of this affirmation. No negation is more inward to being than this one. It is no longer a question of a nihilizing retreat from the having-been, but from the manifestation of the Verb in a perspective which denies it, of the totality of ends in a character which denies it, of love in an attachment to living which denies it. If we follow the course of this existential negation from the exterior toward the interior, it first appears as a difference between me and the other, then as a differing of myself from myself, and finally interiorizes itself in the sadness of the finite.

The most elementary reflection on perspective contains

this whole process of thought in epitome; for I know perspective as perspective only as transgressed by the truth-intention; but I verify this transgression only through the opposition of perspectives other than mine. Thus when we speak of "several" consciousnesses, this is not to be taken as a simple arithmetical plurality; the otherness of consciousnesses is relative to a primordial identity and unity which make possible the understanding of language, the communication of culture and the communion of persons. Thereby another is not only an other, but my like. Conversely, this fundamental unity of λόγος [logos] is relative to the difference of λέγειν [legein].[4] This difference signifies that the unity of humanity is realized nowhere else than in the movement of communication. Thus, difference is not absolute, as if the multiplicity of consciousnesses were purely numerical and their coexistence merely contingent, nor is the unity of the being man absolute, as if the impure causality of bad will alone would generate the splintering of consciousnesses. Man is this plural and collective unity in which the unity of destination and the difference of destinies are to be understood through each other.

By becoming interiorized, the difference between myself and the other becomes a difference of myself from myself; it is no longer a difference between destinies but, in the center of an individual destiny, between its need and its own contingency. The need, in Kantian terms, is the totality that reason "demands" (verlangen); in Aristotelian terms, it is the happiness man "pursues" (ἐφίεσθαι) in his action. The contingency of character is what expresses this need. This consciousness of contingency is more inward to the primordial affirmation than was the consciousness of my difference from others; the latter still rested on the feeling that the quantity of reality that I am excludes the immense possibilities of humanity realized by others and not by myself. The feeling of difference left the otherness outside of me, but the feeling of contingency interiorizes it; in it the need reverses into its contrary. That which I am to be is denied in the feeling that it

---

[4] λόγος, logos or the faculty of reason. λέγειν [legein], the verb to talk, which can mean speaking, exhibiting, recounting, setting forth, etc. (Translator's note).

was not necessary that I be such as I am, nor even that I exist, that it was possible for me to have been another and even not to have been. This feeling cannot be stated without absurdity since the imagination of my being-other stands out against the background of the unquestionable presence of this body and of this life which excludes *ipso facto* all other possibilities; but the brute fact of existing in such a way, here and now, when it is measured against the demand for totality, emerges as existence that I do not produce, that I do not posit. Existence is discovered to be *only* existence, *default of being-through-self*. The imagination which forms the possibility there was of not being is, as it were, the revealer of that default of being-through-self. I did not choose to exist, existence is a given situation: that is what language brings out in the rational sign of non-necessity or contingency. I am here, and it was not necessary; a contingent being who reflects on his existence in the categories of modality must think of it as non-necessary; and this non-necessity exhibits the negativity shrouded in all the feelings of precariousness, of dependence, of default of subsistence, of existential dizziness, which come of the meditation on birth and death. In this way there arises a kind of coalescence between this lived dizziness and the language of modality: I am the living non-necessity of existing.

It is this non-necessity of existing that I live in the affective mode of sadness. "By sadness," says Spinoza in the *Ethics*, "I mean a passion by which the soul moves to a lesser perfection." Besides the sadness which expresses the intermittent character of my effort to exist, there is a ground of sadness that may be called the sadness of the finite. This sadness is nourished by all the primitive experiences which, to express themselves, have recourse to negation: lack, loss, dread, regret, deception, dispersion and irrevocability of duration. Negation is so obviously mixed in with them that we can indeed hold this experience of finitude for one of the roots of negation.[5] It must be admitted as a primary fact that some feel-

[5] I do not say that the negation of finitude is the sole root of negation. No doubt one must give up the idea of unifying the origin of negation. The idea of otherness, such as Plato first elaborated it,

ings have a certain affinity for negation in language because they are negatives. Negative language, such as it is formed in the objective sphere, principally through the operation of discrimination or distinction which separates the same from the other, offers itself for the expression of these lived moods. Need is expressed in an "I do not have," regret in a "no longer," impatient desire in a "not yet." But spoken negation would not suit these affects if it did not manifest a negative lying deeper than all language and which we may epitomize, following Spinoza, in the excellent word "sadness." This lessening of existence affects the very effort through which the soul endeavors to persevere in its being, and so it may well be called a primitive affection. Sufferance in all its forms exalts this negative moment implied in many affects; in suffering, consciousness isolates itself, retires into itself and feels denied.

If such is the dialectic of originating affirmation and existential difference, it becomes understandable that "limitation"—Kant's third category of quality—is immediately synonymous with human fragility. *This* limitation is man himself. I do not think man directly, but I think him through composition, as the "mixture" of originating affirmation and existential negation. Man is the Joy of Yes in the sadness of the finite.

This "mixture" has appeared to us as the progressive manifestation of the *fault*[6] which makes of man, mediator of the reality outside of himself, a fragile mediation for himself.

The synthesis of the object is the silent synthesis of Saying and of Appearing, but *in* the thing itself, on the object. If this synthesis can be called consciousness, it is not self-consciousness. The transcendental imagination which makes

---

is linked to the operation of "distinguishing" which belongs to objectifying thought: the constitution of the perceived thing, of living individuality, of the individual psyche, presupposes the distinction of the something and another thing. The objective distinction is just as primitive a root of negation as the negative affects which make up the sadness of the finite. We shall come back to this in the third volume of this work.

[6] Fault (*faille*) in the geological sense (Translator's note).

it possible remains an art concealed in the depths of nature. The synthesis of the person endows the mixture with a practical sense and no longer a theoretical one; but this mixture remains a task. Mediation is sought through the varieties of the "mean" (μεσότης) which Aristotle worked out in the *Nichomachean Ethics* and which are not so much the golden mean of virtue as the difficult path of practical conciliation which threads its way between the opposed abysses, represented by the diverse, disconnected forms of acting. Man even projects these "means" outside of himself. He projects them in works—the works of the artisan, the works of the artist, of the legislator, of the educator. These monuments and institutions extend the synthesis of the thing. The thing was *understood* in the unity of Saying and Seeing; the work is *made* in the unity of Sense and Matter, of Worth and Work. Man, artisan, artist, legislator, educator, is for himself incarnated because the Idea is in itself materialized. In particular, the work of art *endures* because the Idea it incarnates is saved from oblivion by the *durable* elements of the cosmos. But the discipline of the finite, dear to Goethe, effects the synthesis of need and contingency only in a new correlate of man, and this is precisely the "task." In himself and for himself man remains torn.[7]

It is this secret rift, this non-coincidence of self to self that feeling reveals. Feeling is *conflict* and reveals man as primordial conflict. It shows that mediation or limitation is only intentional, aimed at in a thing or in a task, and that for himself man suffers disunion. But this discord that man lives and suffers approaches the truth of language only at the end of a concrete dialectic which discloses the fragile synthesis of man as the *becoming of an opposition:* the opposition of originating affirmation and of existential difference.

2 FALLIBILITY AND THE POSSIBILITY OF FAULT

If the capacity to fail consists in the fragility of the mediation that man effects in the object, in his idea of humanity

[7] *Déchirement* (Translator's note).

and in his own heart, the question arises concerning the sense in which this fragility is a capacity to fail. What capacity is this?

Weakness makes evil possible in several senses which may be classified in an increasing order of complexity from the *occasion* to the *origin* and from the origin to the *capacity*.

In a first sense, it may be said that man's specific limitation makes evil merely possible; in this case fallibility designates the *occasion*, the point of least resistance through which evil can enter into man; the fragile mediation appears then as the mere space of the appearance of evil. Man, center of reality, man, reconciler of the extreme poles of the real, man, microcosm, is also the weak link of the real. But between this possibility and the reality of evil, there is a gap, a leap: it is the whole riddle of fault. In the language of Scholasticism, which was still common to Descartes, there is no unbroken path from "default" to "privation." In the terms of Kant's *Essay to Introduce into Philosophy the Concept of Negative Grandeur*, evil is "a nothing of privation" which implies real opposition, actual repugnance, something the idea of fragility could not account for.

This gap between the possibility and the reality is reflected in a similar gap between the mere anthropological description of fallibility and an ethic. The first is prior to evil, the second finds the real opposition of good and evil. The most fundamental presupposition of every ethic is indeed that there is already a cleavage between the valid and the non-valid and that man is already capable of the dual: of the true and the false, of good and evil, of the beautiful and the ugly. Objectivity itself, which in the transcendental perspective was merely the unity of sense and presence, becomes, in an ethical perspective, a goal which may or may *not* be attained. Objectivity, which is synthesis *par excellence*, splits, as truth-value, between the valid and the non-valid. The same holds true for action. We have seen that man is by destination a mediation between the demand for happiness and the contingency of character and of death. But for ethics this mediation is a task, the task of working out a "mean," as Aristotle says, between the bad extremes. Taste itself, in the aesthetic realm, likewise implies a bad taste as opposed to it, although the idea of taste *can* be constituted, as in the *Critique of Judgment*, without reference to this contrary through the mere consideration of the free play of representations and of "pleasure without concept." Thus, ethics, taken in the broadest sense of the word, which takes in the whole realm of normativity, always presupposes man as having already missed the synthesis of the object, the synthesis of humanity in itself and its own synthesis of finitude and infinitude; that is why ethics would fain "educate him" by means of a scientific methodology, a moral pedagogy, a culture of taste: "to educate him," that is, to draw him out of the sphere where the essential has already been missed. Accordingly, philosophy conceived as ethics not only presupposes the abstract polarity of the valid and the non-valid, but a concrete man who has already missed the mark. Such is man as philosophy finds him at the beginning of its route: the man that Parmenides drags along on his journey beyond the gates of Night and Day, the one that Plato draws out of the cave onto the precipitous road of the Sun, the one Descartes rouses from prejudice and leads to truth by way of hyperbolic doubt. Man, such as philosophy takes him at the beginning of its route, is bewildered and lost; he has forgotten the origin.

The enigma thenceforward is the "leap" itself from fallibility to the already fallen. Our anthropological reflection remained short of this leap, but ethics arrives too late. To catch sight of that leap we must make a fresh start and enter upon a new type of reflection bearing on the *avowal* that consciousness makes of it and on the *symbols* of evil in which this avowal is expressed. The hiatus of method between the phenomenology of fallibility and the symbolics of evil only gives expression, therefore, to the hiatus between fallibility and fault in man himself. The symbolics of evil, then, will make a long detour at the end of which it will perhaps be possible to resume the interrupted discourse and reintegrate the findings of that symbolics into a truly *philosophical* anthropology. In this first sense, then, fallibility is *only* the possibility of evil: it indicates the region and the structure of the reality which, through its point of least resistance, offers a "locus" to evil.

But in this first sense the possibility of evil and its actual reality remain external to each other. Now, the very "leap," the very "positing" of evil can in a certain sense be understood starting from the notion of fallibility. Invoking a second sense of the word "possible," we may say that man's disproportion is the possibility of evil: in the sense where every defection of man remains within the line of his perfection, where all destitution refers back to man's constitution, where all degeneration is founded on a "generation into existence" —on a γένεσις εἰς οὐσίαν [genesis eis ousian]—to go back to the words of Plato's *Philebus*. Man can only invent human disorders and evils. Thus, because speech is his destination, the evils of idle talk, lying and flattery are possible. I can only imagine the sophist as a mere semblance of the philosopher; as Plato said, an "image-maker"; and Baal can only be the "idol" of Yahweh. Thus the primordial is the original, the pattern, the paradigm starting from which I can generate all evils, through a kind of *pseudo* genesis (in the sense in which pathology speaks of disorders as hyper-, as hypo- or as para-). Man can be evil only in accordance with the lines of force and weakness of his functions and his destination.

No doubt it will be objected, in the style of the Bergsonian critique of the possible, that evil is possible only because it is real and that the concept of fallibility merely records the repercussion of the avowal of the evil that is already in the description of human limitation. That is true, fault carves out behind itself its own possibility and projects it as its shadow onto man's primordial limitation and thus makes it appear fallible. It is undeniable that it is only *through* the presently evil condition of man's heart that one can detect a condition more primordial than any evil: it is through hate and strife that one can perceive the intersubjective structure of the respect which constitutes the difference of consciousnesses; it is through misunderstanding and lying that the primordial structure of speech reveals the identity and otherness of minds. The same holds true for the triple quest of having, power and worth, perceived through avarice, tyranny and vainglory. In short, it is always *"through"* the fallen that the primordial shines through. But what does "through" mean? The trans-parency of the primordial through the fallen signifies that avarice, tyranny and vainglory, first in the order of discovery, of themselves designate having, power and worth as first in the order of existence. And these "passions," in manifesting the "quests" in which they are enrooted, receive from them in return what might be called their mark of downfall. Thus the evil of fault refers intentionally to the primordial; but in return, this reference to the primordial constitutes evil as fault, that is, as digression,[8] as de-viation. I can think of evil as evil only "starting from" that from which it falls. The "through" is therefore the correlate of a "starting from"; and it is this "starting from" that allows us to say that fallibility is the *condition* of evil, although evil is the revealer of fallibility.

Can we, then, isolate this representation of the primordial from the description of evil through which the primordial was perceived? Yes, but only in an *imaginary* mode. The imagination of innocence is nothing but the representation of a human life that would realize all its fundamental possibilities without any discrepancy between its primordial destination and its historical manifestation. Innocence would be fallibility without fault, and this fallibility would be only fragility, only weakness, but by no means downfall. It matters little that I can only depict innocence by way of myth, as a state realized "elsewhere" and "formerly" in localities and in times which have no place in the rational man's geography and history. The essence of the myth of innocence is in giving a symbol of the primordial which shows through in the fallen and which exposes it as fallen. My innocence is my primordial constitution projected in a fanciful history. There is nothing scandalous in this imagination for philosophy. Imagination is an indispensable mode of the investigation of the possible. It might be said, in the style of the Husserlian eidetics, that innocence is the imaginative variation that makes the essence

---

[8] *E-cart* (Translator's note).

of the primordial constitution stand out, in making it appear *on* another existential modality. At that moment, fallibility is shown as pure possibility without the fallen condition through which it ordinarily appears. Consequently, to say that man is so evil that we no longer know what his goodness would be is really to say nothing at all; for if I do not understand "good," neither do I understand "evil." I need to understand the primordial destination of "goodness" and its historical manifestation in badness together, as a superimpression, so to speak. However primordial badness may be, goodness is yet more primordial. That is why, as we shall see, a myth of fall is possible only within the context of a myth of creation and innocence. If that had been understood, one would not have wondered whether "the image of God" may be lost, as if man stopped being man by becoming bad. Nor would Rousseau have been accused of inconsistency when he obstinately professed man's natural goodness *and* his historical and cultural perversity.

But the concept of fallibility includes the possibility of evil in a still more positive sense: man's disproportion is a *power* to fail, in the sense that it makes man *capable* of failing. As Descartes says: "If I think of myself as participating in nothingness or not-being, in other words, insofar as I am not myself the sovereign Being, I find myself subject to an infinity of imperfections, so that I should not be surprised if I err."[9] *I find myself subject to. . . .* What does this mean? Is it not necessary at the same time to affirm the "leap," the "positing" of evil, the "passage" or "transition" from fallibility to fault?

As we shall see, the myths of fall which most stressed the character of rupture, of the abrupt positing of evil, at the same time relate the subtle sliding, the obscure sag from innocence to evil, as if I could only depict evil as welling up in the Instant, without thinking of it at the same time as intruding and progressing in Duration. It is posited, and it moves ahead. Indeed, beginning from evil as a positing, the contrary aspect of evil as an *Accomplishment of weakness* is uncovered. But this movement of yielding weakness, sym-

[9] *Meditations*, IV.

bolized in the biblical myth by the figure of Eve, is coexten-
sive with the act by which evil happens. There is something
like a dizziness which leads from weakness to temptation and
from temptation to fall. Thus evil, in the very moment when
"I admit" that I posit it, seems to arise from man's very
limitation through the unbroken transition from dizziness. It
is this transition from innocence to fault, discovered in the
very positing of evil, which gives the concept of fallibility
all its equivocal profundity. Fragility is not merely the
"locus," the point of insertion of evil, nor even the "origin"
starting from which man falls; it is the "capacity" for evil.
To say that man is fallible is to say that the limitation peculiar to a being who does not coincide with himself is the primordial weakness from which evil arises. And yet evil *arises*
from this weakness only because it is *posited*. This last paradox will be at the center of the symbolics of evil.

SELECTIVE BIBLIOGRAPHY

Gabriel Marcel et Karl Jaspers (Paris: Seuil, 1947)
Philosophie de la volonté
  Vol. I: *Le volontaire et l'involontaire* (Paris: Aubier, 1950).
    English: *The Voluntary and Involuntary*, trans. Erazin V.
    Kohak (Evanston, Ill.: Northwestern University Press, 1966)
  Vol. II: *Finitude et culpabilité*: 1. *L'homme faillible*; 2. *La sym-
    bolique du mal* (Paris: Aubier, 1960). English: *Fallible Man*,
    trans. Charles Kelbley (Chicago: Regnery, 1965); *Symbolism of
    Evil*, trans. Emerson Buchanan (New York: Harper and Row,
    1967)
Histoire et vérité (Paris: Seuil, 1955). English: *History and Truth*
    trans. Charles Kelbley (Evanston, Ill.: Northwestern Uni-
    versity Press, 1965)
De l'interprétation: Essai sur Freud (Paris: Seuil, 1965). English:
    Freud and Philosophy: An Essay on Interpretation, trans. Denis
    Savage (New Haven: Yale University Press, 1970)

Part II: AXIOLOGICAL ETHICS

Since the time of Plato, many philosophers have focused their attention on various problems connected with what we call the "good," "right," "true," "beautiful," "holy," and so on. Several post-Kantian philosophers have suggested the idea that all these problems somehow belong together, since all are concerned with "value." This term, a word from our ordinary language, first received a technical meaning in mathematics, then later in economics and aesthetics. As a philosophical technical term the word was first used by Lotze, who defined a value as something that man emotionally recognizes as transcending him, and to which he can relate himself by means of intuition, appreciation, veneration, or aspiration. Since the middle of the nineteenth century, the word has been used in many ways in philosophy, but most of its uses are specifications of one of the two usages that are also found in ordinary language: 1) a value is a principle, an entity, or a quality that is intrinsically desirable, worth while, or good; 2) value is the relative worth, utility, or importance of something in regard to something else.

Axiology is the philosophical discipline that focuses on values. Two major domains of investigation were originally clearly distinguished in such a general theory of values: an epistemological domain, mainly concerned with the question of our "knowledge" of values; and an ontological realm, which was to explain the ontological status of values. In their attempts to solve the pertinent epistemological and ontological problems, the philosophers have come to quite different solutions. But all these differences notwithstanding, all the philosophers who have explicitly dealt with values have defended the view that the realm of values is to be distinguished from the realm of facts. Whereas metaphysics is concerned with "what-is," axiology must deal with "what-ought-to-be." Most philosophers have defended the thesis that axiology must lay the foundation for ethics, whereas others have felt that axiology is identical with a part of ethics, or even with ethics as a whole.

The following philosophers have played an important part in the history of axiology: Hermann Lotze (1817–81), Friedrich Nietzsche (1844–1900), Franz Brentano (1838–1917), Alexius Meinong (1853–1920), Christian von Ehrenfels (1859–1932), Wilhelm Windelband (1848–1915), Hugo Münsterberg (1863–1916), and Heinrich Rickert (1863–1938). In contemporary philosophy a great number of philosophers in Europe have defended axiological views. Among these the following must be mentioned: Edmund Husserl (1859–1938), Max Scheler (1874–1928), Nicolai Hartmann (1882–1950), René Le Senne (1882–1954), Louis Lavelle (1883–1953), Raymond Polin (1910–   ), Georges Gusdorf (1912–   ), Jean Nabert (1881–1960), Hans Reiner (1896–   ), and Dietrich von Hildebrand (1889–   ). In England, Canada, and the United States, many philosophers have written on values, among them John Dewey, C. I. Lewis, Ralph Perry, Wilbur M. Urban, D. H. Parker, John N. Findley, Richard Hare, Patrick N. Howell-Smith, George H. von Wright, William Werkmeister, and Paul W. Taylor.

It is interesting to note that many philosophers who belong to the phenomenological movement and have written on moral issues have been axiologists. Husserl himself was the first. Between 1891 and 1924 he devoted fifteen courses to moral issues, and in all of them tried to apply his phenomenology to the realm of values. At first he was influenced by Brentano and Theodore Lessing; in his later reflections, the influence of Scheler is noticeable. Husserl has made a few very important contributions to axiology. However, since not all his manuscripts dealing with moral issues have yet been published, I have decided not to include Husserl in this anthology. For anyone interested in his views, the study by Alois

Roth, *Edmund Husserls ethische Untersuchungen* (The Hague: Nijhoff, 1960), is perhaps the best introduction.

Today many philosophers are of the opinion that axiological theories in ethics are on the way out. Vernon Bourke describes this view as follows: "In a sense value ethics has been too successful. Practically all ethicians now talk about values and mean many different things when they use the term. As a result, the notion of value has become so diluted that it is almost a transcendental term in contemporary ethics. Value enabled people to discuss the possibility of a rather ill-defined realm of moral standards without - too clearly committing themselves on their status of being. And so, except for its usefulness as a general term, value is no longer a major item in strictly contemporary ethics" (*History of Ethics*, p. 248). If we refrain from all "value judgment" we may say that Bourke may be right for the English-speaking philosophers. It seems to me that axiology in ethics still has a very great influence in Europe, particularly in France.[1]

In choosing the selections for this anthology, I have assumed that the ideas of Max Scheler, Nicolai Hartmann, and Dietrich von Hildebrand are relatively well-known in the United States, and that anyone interested in their views has easy access to the original works as well as to excellent secondary sources. I have included a selection from the works of Lavelle in the first part of the anthology, because I feel that although Lavelle has written on axiology, his view is nevertheless better characterized by the label "spiritualism." As for Nabert, I would like very much to have included a selection from his remarkable *Elements of an Ethic*. I have finally decided not to do so, because I came to the conclusion that it is impossible to isolate a chapter from the rest of this rich book without doing a grave injustice to Nabert and the views for which he stands. This is due not only to the fact that Nabert occupies a rather unique position in contemporary philosophy, but mainly to the fact that his book on ethics constitutes a unity from which one cannot isolate parts without making them incomprehensible.

[1] Cf. Raymond Polin, "Philosophy of Values in France," in *Philosophical Thought in France and the United States* (Albany: State University of New York Press, 1968), pp. 203–18.

Chapter 5

INTRODUCTION

RENÉ LE SENNE (1882–1954) was deeply influenced by Bergson and Hamelin, and, in the field of psychology, by Heymans and Wiersma. Le Senne has made a substantial contribution to contemporary characterology. In philosophy his main interest seems to have been ethics. His principal works in this area are *Le Devoir* (1931), *Traité de morale générale* (1942), *Obstacle et valeur* (1934), *La destinée personelle* (1951), and *La découverte de Dieu* (1955).

Le Senne characterized his own philosophical position by the term "ideo-existentialism." He used this term to indicate that, although in many instances he is close to existentialism, he nonetheless maintains that consciousness is the essential element in man. This consciousness is not something one receives or has once and for all, but is to be fought for and gained in the face of a fundamental obstacle, which is reality as man finds it. Each time a man wishes to accomplish something because he thinks it to be of value, he encounters obstacles. Value and resistance are inseparable in man. Man wishes what is valuable; what is valuable can be reached only by conquering unavoidable obstacles. In materializing what is valuable, man therefore encounters resistance. That is why suffering is "essential" to man also. Suffering and resistance are found in all of man's experiences. Formulated differently, man's life is never without contradiction. It is this contradiction, which is, but should not be, that leads man to reflection as well as to action, which are inseparable. It is the task of the philosopher, therefore, not only to comprehend the world, but also to change it. Duty is nothing but the task of each man, who in harmony with his fellow men, must give meaning to the contradiction inherent in his situation. In so doing, man can either succeed or fail. If he succeeds he finds himself in authenticity. Only a philosopher who helps man in this task is a genuine philosopher.

The human personality is conceived of by Le Senne as "existence as it is formed by the double *cogito*: hindered by obstacles, elevating itself by and toward value." In this attempt, man participates in an absolute and transcendent Value. Man's task, thus, is not to create values, but rather to "concretize" the absolute Value by making it determinate in a given, concrete situation.

Reality is at the same time the vehicle of self-creation and the determination of values as well as an obstacle to all of this. In a sense it degrades value, but on the other hand it actualizes and concretizes value by making it determinate. Furthermore, it is precisely reality that reminds us of the value-creating Source in which all of us participate.

The selection that follows was chosen from Le Senne's *Traité de morale générale*.

ETHICS AND METAPHYSICS

René Le Senne

1 [INTRODUCTION]

[After having given a detailed sketch of man's moral life, in the final chapter of his book Le Senne asks the question concerning the relationship between morality and its contents on the one hand, and the principle of reality in which these contents materialize on the other. In his view this question is a metaethical problem. The appropriate question to be asked here is, strictly speaking, the following: Are the morals, goods, and duties they determine, and the life they recommend, mere phenomena or even illusions, or on the contrary do they concern the Absolute so as to find in Him, if not their foundation (which would mean to confuse morals with knowledge), then at least the highest authority, of which all their rules and goals are merely expressions, further determinations, and restrictions? (606)

Le Senne argues that it is not right in this connection to reduce morals to metaphysics, and to argue that metaphysics constitutes the foundation of morals. Once it is shown that metaphysics does *not* constitute the foundation of morals, one must draw the conclusion that morals are equally independent of science, art, and religion. Morality constitutes an autonomous realm, which cannot be reduced to any one other realm, be this metaphysics, science, religion, or art. (688)

Following Kant, and in agreement with suggestions of

This essay is from *Traité de morale générale* by René Le Senne (Paris, 1961), pp. 692–711 and 724–34. Copyright © 1961 by Presses Universitaires de France. The present essay was translated into English expressly for this edition by Joseph J. Kockelmans.

Bradley, Le Senne states that, in his view, adopting such a point of view does not exclude all relationships between morals and the Absolute. On the basis of a kind of faith (*croyance*), as associated with Kant's postulates, and a live feeling (*sentiment vivant*), one must subscribe to the view that the Absolute constitutes the absolute Value, in that it manifests itself as the source of all that constitutes the price of our experience and of all possible experience.]

2 VALUE AND VALUES

But let us now disengage ourselves from these historical considerations and come to the framework of the theses that will allow us to draw some conclusions concerning the relation between metaphysical reality and moral life. We will do no more here than indicate them, because value is not of interest to this work except in so far as it is moral value.

1. Our minds are animated by two undeniable and uncontrollable exigencies—one for unity and one for transcendence. For example, "to comprehend" means "to unify," but also "to aim beyond." If one denies either one of these exigencies, then experience, in so far as it pertains to man, gives way either to despair or to routine, that is to say, quite soon to failure. On the other hand, if one decides to take inspiration from them, one implies that the one and infinite Absolute which they must express and at which they make us aim, is worthy of being sought by us in the course of all the approaches of which we are capable: knowledge, action, desire, and feeling. *That which is worthy of being sought after* is what everyone calls value. Thus the Absolute must be conceived as the absolute value. In fact, it is impossible that value, if it is not merely phenomenal, that is to say, if it has validity (*vaut*), depends upon something no one knows what, which could be behind it and before it; for that other thing, taken as something other than value, would then be without value, and value itself would be stricken by a radical contingency.

2. The unity and the infinity of the supreme Value must manifest themselves in our experience by means of a reconcil-

able and renewable multiplicity of humanized values. The Absolute must "found" knowledge through truth, "warrant" action through the good, "charm" our receptive sensibility through the beautiful, and "delight" our dynamic sensibility through love. These cardinal values become diffracted or connected in such a way that they generate infinitely more-abstract or more-concrete values.

3. In so far as the absolute Value must eminently possess personality, which we know to be the highest value and the heart of the mind, the Absolute must be called God; but we know Him only through the participations in value that He gives us in proportion to our searching for it. It is through these participations in value that we accede to personality. . . .

4. Because of this opposition between absolute Value and each one of the values that are determined and tested by some finite consciousness, each value appears as *a relation between a transcendent source*, the Absolute considered in Himself and unknowable in His superabundant plenitude, *and an immanence*, that is, this particular value which this subject tests in this historical situation, and through which he obtains a certain contact with the Absolute (a contact that otherwise cannot be exhausted by analysis and consequently transcends all definition), in proportion, so to speak, to the degree to which it condenses the Absolute. In fact the determinations are as many mediations which (in that they lead to an immediation or through their transparence) allow us to penetrate a value that was unknown to us until then, but also as many obstacles which place an opaqueness between the supreme Value and us. Using the word "appearance" in Bradley's sense, we may say that the appearances are more or less important finitudes that never annihilate themselves in unreality, because the positive Infinite grants them, through their value, more or less reality and suggestiveness.

5. The unity of the values must not be sought in the guiding principle of a unilateral hierarchy of determinate values that are distinct from one another and according to which they would be subordinated to any one among them in order of progressive excellence. One must understand this unity as

a unity of radiation: the absolute Value is at the center of the values, as the mind is in the bosom, and constitutes the origin of their content; and the values emanate from it as the flames from a fireplace, which create light and heat.

3 MORAL VALUE

These principles suffice to allow us to deal now with a proper consideration of moral values.

Moral value is a determinate value among others. We must first stress the fact that moral value is not the absolute Value; it is a certain determinate value with an originality that is different from that of the others, but it does not have any right to substitute itself for them. It is not entitled to order either disrespect of the truth, which is an intellectual value, or contempt for beauty, which is an artistic value, or depreciation of love, which is a religious value. Each one of these values is an expression of the absolute Value; moral value, too, manifests the absolute Value in so far as the latter must be willing, in this particular case must make itself, the will of the divine Mind, which is the source of and the model for all freedom that materializes value. But whereas the absolute Value must concentrate all values in itself, human life, because of the inalienable limitation of the subject, is always more or less condemned to move in abstraction and to choose, so that moral value as we know it in our experience must be determined by separating it more or less profoundly from the others. From this it results that the absolute Value remains and will definitely remain for our experience as above the moral values, that is, as an ideal, that supraterrestrial condition in which all values immediately abandon themselves to morality, which in this instance has become absolute holiness, "Paradise"; that is, the place where at the same time and definitively we would possess complete truth, pure joy, accomplished virtue, and infinite love.

We cannot reach that perfection in the sense in which this would mean that we would become confused with it; but we would have been unable even to reach its idea had we been unable to partake of it somehow, participate in it, obtain something from it; that is to say, in a limited and provisional way experience the union of merit and the good. That happens each time sacrifice is rewarded and in addition, through success, leads to courage, so that in retrospect sacrifice no longer appears to be anything but mediation of the good. If this harmony is not effected visibly, moral consciousness gives evidence of an act of faith in the absolute primacy of the Value, hoping that, via another way and perhaps after death, the good will be the reward of virtue. It must be that way, because there must be enough finality and even enough appearing finality in our world in order to guarantee that morality does not appear as absurd, and it is also necessary for us not to approach that level on which all morality would be excluded because it is superfluous.

Moral value is the value of the ego taken as will. Let us therefore place ourselves on the level of those values that man is able to know, and try to define the most important ones among them, namely the cardinal values. Their list originates from the double operation by means of which the ego opposes itself spatially to existence and its determinations, and temporally to past and future.

In this way we obtain as main values:

a) The value of natural determination, truth. Truth is that value in virtue of which the determinations given to us as prior to the act through which we think them, distinguish themselves from those that are false, illusory, fictitious, merely subjective, and thus not worthy to remain in our knowledge, and are incapable of giving to our action that solidity in which it finds security. Truth founds: it is the value of our knowledge: its absence is ignorance, and its perversion is error. Just as nature exists only through and for the plurality of subjects, and subjects cannot communicate except through the object, truth in so far as it is given, is by far the highest foundation of society. But this communication is insufficient to assure the unity of souls, because one can make an identity of communication into a wall in order to separate one from the other, or an army to combat one another, as well as a bridge to join one another.

b) The value of intimatized determination, beauty. Beauty is that value by virtue of which determinations that are given to us as constitutive, and which as such belong to nature, are also worthy not only of being agreed upon but also admired by consciousness, whose intimate sensibility they shake in a harmonious way. In truth and beauty, reason becomes concept, proportion; but reason is poor and analytically thought in truth, and rich and qualitatively experienced in beauty.

Truth and beauty are the values of retroversion; they constitute the framework and surface of being, which is the value of the past as it results from the action of the Spirit and mind. We must now turn to the values of "proversion," the future, of the *quaerendum* in so far as it is an *agendum*.

c) It is here that we find moral value, that is, the value of ideal determination, legitimacy, which through its actualization, becomes the guide of virtue. Thus, moral value can be defined as having-to-do, in which "to do" means "to do something." It is the value of action; and since action, taken in the sense in which it takes place according to a determination that serves as a paradigm of a goal or ideal, proceeds from the ego which has determined itself into will, moral value must be conceived as the *value of the will*, just as truth is the value of knowledge, just as beauty is the value of imagination, and just as love is the value of the heart. The domain of the will is also the domain of moral value. One does not will what is true, nor what is beautiful, whereas love transcends the will; but, on the contrary, one must will the good. When virtue comes into science, art, or religion, for instance, in order to command the scientist to be conscientious, the artist to work, the faithful to love, this is always by way of subordinate aid to bring us to a condition of favorable receptivity; in morals, the opposite is the case: where nature, artistic delicacy, and love are of interest to morals, it is because they favor virtue.

d) Finally, there must be another value of having-to-be which instead of being concerned with determinate, objective goals, and manifested action, is related to psychic energy itself, a value that changes the mental into the spiritual either in that it creates the feelings that are indispensable for good action, or, above all, in that it, beyond all action, establishes the concurrence of the feelings and the union of the souls; this value, which is the most intimate of them all, is love. It is oriented toward the future, just as virtue is, but what it intends is not to affect the object, but to procreate, taken in the sense in which "to procreate" means to awaken a soul.

So placed within the framework of the other cardinal values, moral value, and we mean, in the same sense, virtue, manifests its originality. It is not the value of an intelligent witness for whom it suffices to understand what takes place without his intervention; moral value requires on the part of the ego that it engage itself in the production of things. The neutral person who, standing before two belligerents, asks himself who is going to win, adopts the attitude of a historian; his reflection taken in itself is by no means moral. It becomes so only the moment he decides to help that one of the two who fights for justice. Moral value supposes the undeniable feeling that the future depends upon my ego, that within the limits of its powers, it bears the responsibility for it, and that to dissociate oneself from it still means to bring about that future, but now contemptible where it could have been noble. Moral value is neither the delicate and happy enjoyment of nature by the ego, which derives from it joy and approval for being the way it is, nor communion with life on the way to blossom out. On the contrary, it is a protest against the insufficiency of what is, a protest that is always incipient, but without bitterness, and full of confidence in the future; it is the demand of a having-to-be that is superior to that which already has had to be, the service of an *ideale Forschung* similar to that which Ibsen's drama has so often proclaimed. And finally, if courage, just like love, abandons itself, spreads, counts on its own power, virtue opposes itself to charity in that it still supposes obstacles, efforts, and pain: love does not have to will any longer and is no longer in need of the will's tension; strictly speaking it is suprahuman, it soars above the difficulties; the moral will, on the contrary, is required precisely when man is at the level at which he is still in need of courage. Love is a superior spontaneity: at its perfection it is a sovereign ease that is diametrically opposite to the ease of lethargy; and the ego that love makes all-powerful in regard to itself and things is at the same time profoundly humble, for it no longer thinks of itself. Virtue is not the value of the triumphing ego that indulges itself in the *glory of love*, but it is that of the threatened and militant ego. However consolidated it may be, it must still maintain itself. Briefly, moral value is the value of freedom in so far as it is will, that is, all peculiarity aside, the value of desire or of love.

Merging of courage and the good in moral value. After situating moral value among the other cardinal values, we must now return to its intrinsic originality. In view of the fact that, as we have indicated above, all value emerges from the encounter of a human quest and a gift that localizes the transcendence of absolute Value, we must now consider moral value as the merging of a movement toward value, a mode of our quest, and a movement toward us, an inspiration expressing its conformity with that which transcends us, that is to say, almost everything; thus a merging of a *sursum* and a *deorsum*. Thus, knowledge already presupposes the *curiosity* of the scientist; it is this curiosity that gives him the power to search, to sound out the facts, to formulate and criticize hypotheses, to verify them; this curiosity, however, does not suffice if he is to discover some new truth, for it can come to nothing, and he is in need of the inspiration of a true idea which precisely constitutes the transcendent value of our knowledge. In the same way, too, the artist is pushed toward beauty by the desire that the need for quality awakens in him, but he knows very well that he has to find it and that the discovery of beauty is difficult and rare. Finally, in religious intimacy, prayer invokes grace, but it is still necessary for grace to come and fulfill it.

It cannot be otherwise in the case of moral value or, as we have already said more simply, of virtue. That is why we must express it with two words: we define it as *the courage of the good*.

Let us go now from courage to the good, from the ego of the value to the value of the ego. We have already recognized that courage is the essence of moral feeling, that no feeling will ever become moral except at the rate of, and in proportion to, the part that courage takes in it. This is the contribution of man himself to morality. Courage, which is often called value, is not yet virtue, but it is already a psychological, ideo-energetic value, because it combines the representation of a project, and of its means, with the mobilization of bodily and physical energy. In fact, it is indeed a value, for if there is no courage without will, neither is there courage without organic and other conditions that are independent of the will, and without a fortunate but risky merging of these conditions.

As value, then, courage must imply a being-extrinsic-to; and in so far as this being-extrinsic-to is such that it has to be, transcendence of nature is implied also, not only in a downward direction, but also upward. However, this transcendence is, as it were, granted, conceded, immanentized: it is placed and kept at the disposal of man for action; it has become natural for him, and through exercise he becomes more and more natural, too.

However, it is impossible to limit oneself to this: moral value cannot be reduced to courage. A criminal can be courageous; he is not virtuous; energy considered in itself is indifferent in regard to the value of the use made of it. Thus, a second element must have as its essence the power to connect the action not only with its author, but also with the unity of the world into which he directs it. This world transcends him on all sides: if in its very principle the world is delivered to pure contingency, morality can be nothing but absurdity; on the contrary, if its course obeys a design, or rather initiates it, then conformity of our action to this design constitutes the significance of our moral action, and thus is indispensable for it. *This reference of an action to a universal source of actions-of-value is the good.* In so far as this source, the absolute Value, authorizes the action, it is the sovereign good; in so far as here or there our courage materializes one of its expressions, it becomes a good. Virtue must thus appear at the intersection of our search (in so far as the latter, seen morally, takes the form of courage) and a universal inspiration, which at its moment of encounter materializes itself as the idea of a good.

Unless one is thoughtless, one cannot doubt that the good must come to us from no other thing than us ourselves and thus by degrees from a universal source that constitutes it as good. Pure voluntarism is as scandalous in morals as it is in knowledge. The truth cannot be the pure creation of the arbitrariness of a man or men. It is not itself that the ego, in so far as it would separate itself from the absolute Spirit, can search for in the truth; for that means that it would then be free to make truth according to its own taste, today in this way, tomorrow in another way, at its whim. And it cannot be itself, either, that it discovers in the good, for the ego would then be its own legislature; without reference to a value that inspires it, it would be nothing but a tyrant, entitled to define the just and the unjust as it would see fit. We know quite well that it is not so, for at the moment that the good appears as being most violently opposed to what our pleasure would like it to be, we feel most sharply its right to guide us. From that moment on, it is related to courage, as courage caused it to search for it.

Thus courage and the good call for one another and determine one another. Each one without the other comes to nothing: for without the good, courage becomes destructive, which is the greatest impotence, the double powerlessness of being unable to create and even to maintain; on the other hand, without courage the good would remain without effect, a pious dream. All creation supposes a power; but this power leaves it to us to determine it within the limits of that which is worthy of being. It is the mission of courage to bring forth the good; but it is the good that constitutes the dignity of courage. Courage is the premoral value, whereas the good is the supramoral value: moral values emerge from their reciprocal conformity. Through courage, man prays to have the good; he receives it if he is worthy of receiving it; but when he obtains it, this good is not his good except at the rate of the courage through which he deserved it for himself and appropriated it; for, on the one hand, the good is a good for someone only under the condition that he assimilate it for himself and, on the other, the good does become his only because he has contributed something to it. Moral value is a form of spiritual relation: this relation may not be carved up on a cutting board, but within it, its extremes become anastomosed and they lose their determined independence of being separate terms. The relation becomes pure spirituality by devouring its terms.

Thus, one must never ignore either one of the two aspects of moral value. From above, moral value is a condescension, a grace. One cannot separate the consideration of the human effort and that of the inspiration that gives it its orientation and permits one to overcome the obstacles. As Maine de Biran has shown, higher than the relation between the ego and the non-ego as found in this effort, another relationship is exerted between this first relation and a supplementary aid from which the ego will draw in order to overcome the resistance. At each moment, the resistance is overcome only through the voluntary mobilization of some surplus of energy. Whatever this help may be, a physical energy, other tendencies, the support of someone else, this help points toward the consideration of a spiritual and universal source, which must have a moral value in order to aid morality by attracting it. This surplus energy, which is liberated by the will and courageously employed by it, is thus the vehicle, the support of moral value, its excipient; or, if you prefer, it localizes and situates the value that it makes moral by investing it with energy oriented toward the objective realization of a project.

On the other hand, if one were to forget the voluntary and courageous intervention of the ego in this actualization, one would replace the scrupulous and exact description of moral life by an Edenic utopia.

Well, the characteristic of an Edenic utopia is that it suppresses merit. Man no longer has to endure or to show courage; he merely has to receive. Risk and sacrifice are eliminated and soon discredited: at the end, action is replaced by contemplation, as if the latter could exist without action and as if responsibility could be dispensed with here. (One more case in which a term at the end overshadows the operative relation that is the suggestive trajectory of our lives and is eternally heuristic. There is no longer any obstacle between departure and arrival: one has arrived before departing, the result is independent of each road one might have taken; human life is devoid of all contribution toward the actualization of value, God does not associate us with Him; the future is fictive, for everything is preformed.) What makes this conception, in turn, scandalous is that, conjuring our freedom away, it entails the assimilation of the noble and the base, the hero and the thief. The relation of correspondence between virtue and the good is severed. The criminal and his victim are identified; and it even becomes evident that, in so far as the criminal reaches his well-calculated goals, he must appear as superior to his victim: contrary to justice, he obtains the advantage. One cannot deny that one could think along these lines; it is true that we are all tempted to think this way when history shows us that the just are persecuted; but whoever admits that morality is metaphysically warranted, refuses to accept this capitulation and avoids indifference toward good and evil, just as he in general avoids indifference toward all value, toward truth and falsehood, the beautiful and the base, the detestable and the lovable.

The irradiation of moral value. By admitting that the absolute unity of all values is similar to the unity of a fireplace, which can be compared to the mind at the center of its operations, we have come to see that all values irradiate from the absolute Value. Because of the original identity of values, we must conclude from this that each one of them is equally radiant. This explains that around virtue, understood as the good courage, a cluster of other moral values spreads out, in the heart of which courage is connected with different intimate modes of the good.

Thus one will admire nobleness, which is the courage of the good that has become the soul itself of a man who renounces his subjectivity, in so far as it has something mean and greedy in it, in such a way as to form a unity with generosity. This is spiritual aristocracy. If one connects virtue with the perpetuity that translates eternity into time, one obtains *fidelity*. Thus it is advisable to distinguish between the fidelity that one generally can call contractual, by extending to a determination the meaning of the word that designates fidelity, and *spiritual* fidelity, which is indestructible adherence to spirituality, as such, beyond all determinations. Faithfulness to an appointment is of the first kind, fidelity in regard to a friend is of the second.

Purity manifests that aspect of moral consciousness through which at some point it succeeds in making itself identical with the ego of the value, its ideal; but here, too, one must distinguish between the essential purity of a concept, of a determination, and thus of morals, in so far as rules become consubstantial with the ego, and pure spirituality, which does not come from something in the mind to which it gives itself, but from the spirit itself, in so far as nothing coarse or false becomes mixed up with it. One speaks of *purity* when one thinks of the spirit in its content, whether this be particular or total; one speaks of *sincerity* when one thinks of someone in so far as he does not intervene to change this content. The morality of the one as well as of the other results from the courage one needs to avoid what would corrupt them; but courage is disguised here because it succeeds as in a supreme form of art.

Fullness of being is the union of a full harmony of active elements of consciousness and a tension that is felt as a superabundance. It could be presented as the highest virtue if the absolute Value were not transcendent to all values; their names alone are sufficient to distinguish and consequently to limit this highest value.

Moral strength, which is the supreme value for Descartes, unfolds itself in generosity: it consists in "causing us to esteem very little all the good things that may be taken away . . . and on the other hand to esteem highly liberty and absolute dominion over self. . . ." (*Passions of the Soul*, art. CCIII) It is easy to see that moral strength is essentially an energetic power whose tension is superior to all the perturbations we can receive from things. At its source it is courage, and in its intention it is the good. . . .

4 THE MERGING OF VALUES IN THE LIGHT OF ABSOLUTE VALUE

In order to make the insufficiency of each value in regard to the others evident, it suffices to show that each one of the cardinal values requires another one, and so on, until all of them appear as indispensable powers of the Spirit, the value from which all determined values emerge and originate.

a. The Solidarity of Values

Let us suppose that knowledge is the only available step consciousness can take and truth the only value; then action would be superfluous. Even then, man's life would not have to search for anything except to double the universe with its copy. If one were to materialize the identity of the model and its copy, then there would be no real double and knowledge would consist in returning to what one has already; on the contrary, if knowledge were in some sense different from the model, it would be false: in both these hypotheses it would be superfluous: "to double" is to do nothing or it is to betray. In fact, knowledge is only one special manner of apprehending a part of the contents of consciousness; it bears only upon what is already accomplished and determined; and what has been done, the past, cannot be thought and understood except in relation to the future, which it is not. Together with the future, the good offers itself as a value that is transcendent in regard to action. In its turn, does morality appear as the queen of the mind? One could defend this idea if the determinations that moral action must imprint on existence could be conceived of without it. But existence must be experienced, and actual in order to be experienced. One thinks laws and ideals; but one enjoys existence. It is where the object is experienced so as to enjoy consciousness without baseness, in short in beauty, that morals find their actual end. The connection of the good and beauty has always been familiar to thought. But whereas the good makes the condition of its objectivity prevail against its subjectivity, the opposite is the case of beauty. Furthermore, beauty remains more or less spectacular, and the experience of sexual life suffices to show us that beauty is destined to revoke love. Love leads the mind to what is most intimate, to the energy that moves the mind and is spiritualized by love! In this way we are led back to determinations and their values. We move in a circle.

From this movement it follows that values have solidarity and that, consequently, if one is neglected, all of them will indirectly be affected. All of us are aware that in each one of us the man is superior to the scientist, the artist, the man of action, the believer. It may be that a scientist is great because of the discoveries he has made, but his greatness, which evokes our admiration, will not sustain this admiration if we know from other sources that he is tactless or greedy. A determinate baseness entails complete unworthiness. We expect spontaneously that the one value calls for the other, for, after all, if the search for a determinate value is put into the service of a betrayal of the total value, the obtained value becomes negative value and corrupt. Thus science in the service of hatred is without honor. Beauty in the service of vice prostitutes itself, religion in the service of immorality blasphemes, and finally, morality in the service of lies, rudeness, and brutality turns into the spirit of domination.

From the solidarity of the values, which does not annihilate their originality, it follows that each determinate value comprises two instances; the one belongs to it in so far as it is by itself, the other in so far as it is with the others. According to the first instance, it receives its positivity from that which, coming from what is outside itself, composes itself from it. Such is the case for truth in regard to the data and principles it constructs; for beauty in regard to the harmony of the qualities that are its parts; for the good in regard to the coherence of the means; and finally for love in regard to the convergence of the tendencies that it orientates. This is what one could call their internal positivity. But this is not enough, for from the fact alone that one distinguishes between internal and external, one implies that what comes to a value from itself must be completed by what it receives from elsewhere, through an extrinsic positivity. No value by itself would be more than an iridescent bubble without a content which constitutes its reality and its power. Just as the most pure ego must be filled up by what it receives from the outside, so all value leaves a trace of its originality, but supposes that with which the others (that is, what is better in the rest of consciousness) furnish it.

In this way, a truth is a truth concerning the world; that which we estimate in it is that which it expresses, provided we realize that what it enounces has bearing on the universe of truths through an infinity of relations that are known or not yet known. Behind each truth there is the world of thought simultaneously total and unfinished. In a similar way, can beauty remain without relations to the rest of man's life? What furnishes it with its matter is the body, landscapes, the tragedy of action. Were it to attempt to confine itself to what it proposes to our admiration, it would remove itself from the multiplicities of the bonds that tie it to the events of life's history. And what is true concerning its relationship with the empirical is true also of its relationship with that which transcends experience. If beauty were to detach itself from a reality from which it would proceed in no respect, if it were just a deviating phenomenon, if it did not have behind it a propitious infinity capable of indefinitely supplying our needs for quality and artistic emotion, then nothing would distinguish it from the agreeable taste of a poisoned dish, that is to say, a lie. It is necessary that beauty, in addition to the proportions that constitute its skeleton, contain a secret reference to an infinity of beauty, or it would be without charm; for all that comes to a standstill will stop us, and therefore deceive us. Must there not be equally, in man's courage, confidence that reaches beyond all particular enterprises and courage itself? Courage for the sake of courage would be to the discredit of courage. For then it would be necessary that the will be for the will, whereas it is evident that all volition under penalty of being absurd intends beyond itself. One turns the switch in order to have light, one wishes to have light in order to set aside ignorance concerning a place, one makes an inventory of this place in order to serve oneself with it, and so on indefinitely; in short one lives to live, that is to say, to draw from a supposed infinity of life more goods and action. The will, just as does love, rushes toward the infinite; or it would be the pure and simple desire to die. In fact, does love attach itself to a skeleton or a mannequin? If it loves someone who is alive, then the entire reality concentrates itself in him or radiates from him, thus intends beyond what it sees.

Are we then to understand this plural solidarity of the values as an incoherent totality in which each one is absolutely heterogeneous in regard to the others? It is impossible to admit this: this would mean to deliver the mind to heartbreak. It is war that is the turmoil of opposite values: values to live, in so far as excluding ideals oppose the belligerents; living values, in so far as they themselves oppose their egoist or generous interests. If one does not wish to make war the ideal of consciousness, one must conclude that the harmony of values is a value also; or rather, that this harmony in itself, to the degree to which we are able to attain it (that is to say, through a greater or less-extensive participation) is the absolute and first Value from which all values radiate. First and central value, and harmony of values, are synonymous expressions. The absolute Value is beyond all determination; but we must materialize it, and in materializing it we impose upon it our own limitations, which will determine it, be it under the form of a special value or under that of a nuance that colors the concurrence of the values. In the latter case, at the moment we grasp several values in the concrete unity of their source, the indetermination that originates from the absolute Value becomes one with the active indetermination of our mind. There results from this a conversion of our identity with the Absolute. Until then, for instance in the good, there was only a contact; but a contact leaves the feeling of otherness in the one who receives it; but at the moment in which our partial identification with the first Value comes about, in which It blends with us so as to consubstantialize itself in us; then all that is left of externality in a contact, even in a spiritual one, vanishes: and there emerges a cooperation in which the Absolute reveals its Spirituality through its identity with us, which now is no longer lived, but living. The intuition of the spiritual is fulfilled herein through the intuition of the Spirit. If it has ever happened that we have arrived at that experience (which is always new in its quality) through the mediation of morals and the good, then morals have led us to knowledge of the Absolute, or rather, beyond knowledge, to our identification with Him, within the limits that are compatible with our condition and, as it were, in proportion to the height of our consciousness. Time will soon tear it away from us; but it depends upon us to search for it more often and at a higher level.

b. *Compensation and Composition*

Can this merging of value be obtained under one single form? It is obvious that one would return, then, to giving a privileged position to one of the two terms of the antinomy between rest and movement. In fact, harmony and the emulsion of values alternate in our life. Thus there must be two ways in which the concurrence of values can take place. The one is *composition*: no derivative value occupies the center in regard to the others; all are at the same level, but they harmonize with one another; the other is *compensation*: in this case, one value dominates, and consciousness is happy through its deepening or sharpening, but this predilection, which remains praiseworthy as long as the service of one value does not turn against the others, requires that somewhere compensatory movements take place that bring each one of the other values to a comparable level. Compensation searches for the absolute Value by expanding a determinate value: this is the way a specialist approaches the matter. Composition obtains this through an equilibrium between the values; it favors tactfulness rather than force: this is the manner of the philosopher.

In order to justify the distinction between these manners, to support their duality, one must end in philosophy, for philosophy itself has as its value the thought of value. Now philosophy argues about two possible options. The one has been that of classical thought: it has manifested respect for the sovereignty of the One. This respect implies the privileged position of spatiality and tends toward systematicness. This preference is sufficiently explained by the fact that knowledge is that stage of consciousness to which it is most easy for a philosopher to reduce it, as soon as one begins in perception, continues through science, and ends with intellectual metaphysics. Spinoza has shown with the greatest clarity what one comes to think if one radically subordinates life to knowledge and knowledge to its object: one deifies the systematization and swallows man up in the whole as an indistinguishable fragment of nature.

In the course of the nineteenth century, particularly under the influence of the feeling that the mind would lose its initiative in the idolatry of the eternal necessity, thought had little by little rehabilitated Time under a number of forms and then given it a privileged position, as being the aiming toward the other. Through this revolution, the mind has found itself in a position of becoming more and more aware of itself, in opposition to the object and its abstract eternity. The criticism of the ontological usage of the concept of substance, empiricism, Kant's criticism of the idea of totality, history, Hegel's dialectic, Bergson's duration, and a number of other intellectual events have co-operated with the movement that has led things back to life and to the mind. Becoming is no longer sacrificed to Being; and both are now subordinated to a more and more vivid feeling of freedom and spiritual responsibility.

Let us try to make abstraction from the bias of our own epoch. It will become easier for us to recognize the fact that neither space nor time is made to have the upper hand over the other. The simultaneity of two points for the mind supposes that the mind circulates between them, and this circulation would mean the alternate oblivion of the one and the other, if simultaneity had not to a certain degree persisted in the heart of succession. Space without time, and time without space, are limit-fictions. It is the mind that plays with them in itself, and consequently its freedom is equally superior to space (the condition of systematization) and to time (the condition of innovation). The antinomy of the One and the Infinite is an antinomy for the Spirit, whose existence transcends them. The spirit is always more than all that one is able to do, than all that one can think and say about one's self.

It follows from this that the merging of the values must oscillate between two limits—the one in which the supreme Value would manifest only its unity by the harmony of determined values, at the risk of crystallizing itself in them; the other in which this unity would be its infinity through a process not only uninterrupted, but even immediate and without pauses. Beyond these limits, our life unites the peace and war of values, a peace that cannot be perfect and definitive, a war that cannot become total; and accordingly as our mind is inclined toward the one or the other, two modes of participation that are related to the two modes of concurrence will offer themselves to it.

The one is the *participation of preference*; it is that participation searched for by those consciousnesses who are dedicated to the service of one favorite value. The artist, the scientist, the believer are oriented by their desire, curiosity, faith, toward the proper value; but if they obtain the salvation that is suitable to them in the human condition, that is to say, to some degree and for some time, then it is because their value appears to them in depth and scope to imply all the other values. In this way, the highest works of art make of art an expression of the whole mind; the most penetrating thoughts seem to imply the whole creation; love by divinizing itself sanctions all activities. In the same way, the hero attains through his action a proper perfection in which all the other values, as it were, begin to gather together: its act is the most intelligent, it has the beauty of a work of art, it radiates love. The concurrence of values is obtained here by interpenetration. But the preference for one value gains for it a special tonality and greater intensity.

The other participation, this time in harmony with systematization, is a *participation of embracement*. One may call it philosophical, for it is characteristic of the philosopher to search less for the intensity of life than for that breadth of vision that allows him to recognize in it all its aspects and, so to speak, to taste all the principal sources of values. The maxim of a man of action and of anyone who searches for a participation of intensity is *Semper plus ultra*; that of the sage, in opposition to the hero, is *Ne quid nimis*. Philosophy, morals, have had some martyrs; they have not brought forth heroes. In his relationship with action, the philosopher as philosopher can be nothing but a moralist; but this moralist remains a philosopher to the extent to which he combines morals with all other emanations of the spirit. By placing action in its proper place through thought, by showing and celebrating its value, by marking its limits in order to safeguard our other powers, he obtains this concurrence of values that one can attain only by means of a harmonious composition. He loses in this the intensity of the life of the hero; but he gains in so doing that refined and purified joy that is granted by the representation of order and by our sympathy with the genesis of the first possibles, namely wisdom.

Through either one of these two participations, human consciousness unifies itself mysteriously with absolute Value, the undetermined source of values and minds. Such a mind takes part in the activity of the Spirit, co-operates with His operation, either in the participation of preference by grasping it as a creation, or, on the contrary, in the participation of synthesis by conceiving of it as an organization. Thus the honest man, the hero, the conscientious worker, the soldier who fights for the freedom and security of his country, the woman who gives birth to a child and takes care of it, the explorer who reaches new lands and fortunes unknown to civilization, take part through their action in the divine design of history, which the moralist serves by disengaging from it the moral destination and the directions implied in it. One may ask oneself whether he should prefer noble actions or noble maxims: if progress provokes reflection and the will, and if the latter work for progress, then one cannot separate morals from life; and consequently there must be good maxims in order that life may become more and more moral, and noble actions in order to avoid having morals replace morality. Who would ask man to sacrifice lucidity for generosity, or generosity for lucidity? Lucidity, intelligence, gives satisfaction to the *exigence of the One*, whose ideal term would be a complete determination, where necessity would reach its completion in harmony. Humanity gives free rein to that ideal when it gears toward organization, proposes itself as the promised land, a society so precisely organized that the order necessary for the satisfactions of life would correspond to the order in which desires awaken, in such a way that the latter would not arise except in order to be fulfilled by the former. One cannot doubt that there is a value in organization, that the exigence of determination must incessantly bring forth new fragments of order. But it is equally impossible to believe that order could suffice for mankind, for determination taken by itself is the condition of boredom, which is one of our undeniable limits. Then generosity appears as the moral mode of the other exigence of our life: *the exigence of the Infinite*. Try as one may to protest the danger, the evil spells, to exorcise imperialism, romanticism, feeling; one could not do it so often and so vividly, if the exigence of infinity did not manifest everywhere its inexorable power and inexhaustibility. It is at that moment that one recognizes the profound value of morality. If the exigence of infinity must never abandon us, then the only thing left to us is to recognize it and to spiritualize it. When it torments us, we begin to desire boredom; but the moment boredom strikes, we throw ourselves into action, which, the moment it becomes unsuccessful, brings forth torture. This means that we always can verify that above the exigence of unity which should give us rest, and that above the renewed exigence of the *other* which awakes unrest; the task of morality consists in manifesting the art of the will which alternates between composition and compensation. The most precious thing we can attain through them in moral life is in turn an oasis in which a provisional and limited contemplation temporarily gives us the One in the good, or on the contrary gladness over a trustful enterprise, even, and particularly, if it is a difficult one, where the momentum to counterbalance, promoted by the representation of more or less remote opposites, has for us the value, not only of satisfaction of the good that is accomplished, but also of joy in accomplishing it.

SELECTIVE BIBLIOGRAPHY

Introduction à la philosophie (Paris: Presses Universitaires de France, 1925)

Le Devoir (Paris: Presses Universitaires de France, 1931)

Traité de morale générale (Paris: Presses Universitaires de France, 1942)

Obstacle et valeur (Paris: Aubier, 1934)

La destinée personnelle (Paris: Flammarion, 1950)

La découverte de Dieu (Paris: Aubier, 1951)

Chapter 6

INTRODUCTION

HANS REINER (1896–   ) studied philosophy, classical
philology, theology, and natural economy at the Universities
of Freiburg, Munich, and Marburg between 1919 and 1928.
He graduated from the University of Freiburg in 1926. Subsequently, he taught at Halle, and in Freiburg im Breisgau
from 1947. Reiner's interest has always been in the realm
of ethics and the philosophy of religion. His first publication
was *Freiheit, Wollen und Aktivität* (1927). Other publications include: *Das Phänomen des Glaubens* (1934), *Pflicht
und Neigung* (1951), *Die Ehre* (1956), and *Der Sinn unseres Daseins* (1960).

Generally speaking, one may say that Reiner is a phenomenologist. In his essay *Das Prinzip von Gut und Böse* (1948),
he has tried to determine his own position in regard to other
leading phenomenologists such as Scheler and Hartmann.
Reiner comes to a new conception of ethics in this essay, but
gives only a schematic survey of it in the study. His view was
later explained in detail in *Pflicht und Neigung: Die Grundlagen der Sittlichkeit erörtert und neu bestimmt mit beson-
derem Bezug auf Kant und Schiller* (1951). According to
Reiner's own statement, he came to a final view concerning
ethics in 1961. This view was published in Spanish under
the title *Fundamentos y rasgos fundamentales de la ética*
(1964), which was included in an anthology also containing
older publications, *Vieja y nueva ética* (Madrid: Revista de
Occidente, 1964). In 1965 the author gave two television
lectures during which he explained his final view in an elementary form. These lectures were subsequently published
under the title *Gut und Böse*. The following selection is an
English translation of this entire essay.

GOOD AND EVIL

Origin and Essence of the
Basic Moral Distinctions

Hans Reiner

I

Generally we human beings first learn about good and evil
from our parents when we are children. They in turn received
their knowledge on the subject in a Western, Christian world,
usually through the teachings of Christianity, that is to say,
through God's commandments as they are preached to us.
However, when we conceive of these commandments of God
as binding, we presuppose that this God is a *good* God. Therefore, before we ever hear about God's commandments, we
must already somehow have a certain knowledge of what good
and evil means. In this case the question is not so much what
good and evil is in particular, but rather, primarily upon what
the distinction between good and evil ultimately rests; thus,
what constitutes the essence of good and evil. How do we
human beings know about this distinction? How do we come
to make it?

Finding the answer to these questions is not only of theoretical interest, but it is also important from a practical point
of view. For in our private life as well as in our public life
we repeatedly encounter questions that originate in doubt
about a certain way of doing something, whether it is re-

This essay is from *Gut und Böse*, by Hans Reiner (Freiburg im
Breisgau, 1965), pp. 7–41. Copyright © 1965 by L. Bielefelds Verlag. The present essay was translated into English expressly for this
edition by Joseph J. Kockelmans.

sponsible and thus morally good, or whether it is objection-able and therefore evil. It is more likely that such questions can be answered adequately after the origin of our knowledge of good and evil has been explained, and with it the essence of the distinction.

As can be shown, mankind has known the distinction be-tween good and evil for at least forty-five hundred years; the oldest certain testimonials we have for this are Egyptian epi-taphs dating from the third millennium before Christ. The investigation of this distinction began in Greek philosophy over two thousand years ago. At that time, Aristotle founded ethics as the special science concerned with this distinction. We wish now to see what this science has to say today about our question.

To do so, it is necessary to start by taking another deter-minate point into consideration at the same time; namely, the fact that for us a consciousness of the ought (*Sollens*) is connected with the distinction between good and evil. Actu-ally this consciousness is primarily connected with evil, for it always appears to us as something we ought *not* to do. True, the good, on the other hand, is also connected with a certain consciousness that we ought to do it. But this having-to-do does not have the character of such a stringently binding demand as that connected with the having-not-to-do of evil. We must try to explain here how this consciousness of ought originates, if we wish to determine adequately the essence and foundations of the difference between good and evil.

In order to accomplish this goal, we shall take our point of departure in a universal fact I should like to describe in the following way: All we encounter in our world, be they things or plants, animals or human beings, be they human institu-tions, activities, or attitudes, be they facts or events in nature or in history, or in both at the same time, all these and every-thing else that perhaps may be in the world, we encounter either as *enjoyable* (*erfreulich*) or *unenjoyable* (*unerfreu-lich*) or in the third place as *indifferent* in the sense of neu-tral and standing between these two opposites. The character-istic properties of what is enjoyable and unenjoyable possess, furthermore, special forms and "shades" of varying kinds. They appear for instance in the special forms of the beautiful or the ugly, the agreeable or the disagreeable, the useful or the detrimental, the good or the bad, the pleasurable or the distressing, the lovable or the abominable, the inspiring or that which calls for indignation, that which asks for high esteem or the contemptible. Indeed, even the holy and the unholy belong to this, although it is true that in the case of the holy its characterization as agreeable is much too weak and insufficient to express the affirmation and recognition we show in its regard. And yet, in all these oppositions there is a common universal trait that can be identified as the characteristic of the enjoyable on the one hand and the unenjoyable, or deplorable, on the other.

It seems that the enjoyableness or unenjoyableness of something, as such, is a matter of feeling. However, in the experience or representation of the enjoyableness or unenjoyableness of what we encounter, we have in the final analysis an objective quality of it in mind. For it always depends somehow upon the objective quality of a fact, whether or not it appears to us as enjoyable or unenjoyable. It is obvious that so-called subjective moments play a part also; for our disposition or our attitude, or perhaps even our momentary mood, apparently matters somehow in this context. And yet we always find something enjoyable precisely because the situation itself *is* in this or that way. Had it been different as far as an objective quality is concerned, opposite to the one it has, then in many cases we would have found it unenjoyable or perhaps neutral.

Thus the enjoyableness of the fact so experienced is something secondary, something that only plays a part in the second place. What really matters in these cases is the quality of the relevant thing, or more precisely the relevant being; for persons, or other beings as well, can be enjoyable or unenjoyable in the way they are. It is because the relevant being is such and such that we meet it with a certain esteem; and that is also the reason it appears to be enjoyable to us. However, the fact that we meet it with esteem is founded in the fact that it appears to us to be worthy on the basis of its typical qualities. And this, namely the fact that something appears to us to be worthy of esteem, is what matters to us as far as its enjoyableness is concerned.

In our language there is a concept that designates this genuine objective core and ground of the enjoyableness of what is enjoyable taken in its general form. This is the concept of *value*. A value is that quality in a thing which lets this thing appear to us as being worthy of our esteem and thus as being enjoyable. The philosophy of our time, and ethics in particular, has correctly taken up this concept of value as found in ordinary language usage and made it one of its basic concepts. It has posited non-value (*Unwert*) opposite to value as its counterpart; here we must understand by non-value, then, something unenjoyable and worthy of our disdain. In ethics, non-value is often designated as negative value, which is then opposed to the enjoyable as a positive value. The concept of value thereby acquires a broader meaning and includes both positive and negative values.

The experience of positive and negative values in their enjoyableness and unenjoyableness is obviously of great importance for our entire human existence (*Dasein*). Our wishing, willing, and doing are above all determined by positive and negative values. For the goal of our desiring and acting is always found in this, that we either achieve or secure the reality of (positive) values or prevent or remove the reality of negative values. Often, however, both coincide, in that the avoidance or removal of something that is unenjoyable (thus of a negative value) itself is always enjoyable and thus constitutes a (positive) value.

But what is meant here by achievement of the reality of value? A more careful consideration will show that we must make a distinction between two essentially different cases, because the reality upon which the enjoyableness of value finally depends can be of two different kinds, and because, correlatively, the values themselves that are at stake here, appear to be of two different kinds.

In the one case, what really matters to us is that we acquire something, possess or enjoy something, or bring it into another, similar, real relation to ourselves; in this case the reality that is at stake here is thus, strictly speaking, a possession or enjoyment or a similar kind of having-something-at-one's-disposal. We designate something as a *good* that is of the longer-lasting durability characteristic of a value of this kind and thus can become the object of a possession; and one can further distinguish here between material goods such as money, bodily goods such as health, and spiritual goods such as honor and fame. Knowledge, too, is a good, and thus a bearer of a value of this kind. But in addition to such lasting value objects, all kinds of activities and acts of experience that immediately bring with them pleasure or joy, such as dancing, making music, listening to music, are also bearers of values in the sense in which we have them in mind here.

From what has been said, we can now derive what is characteristic of the values in question. In the case of these values, their agreeableness originates finally and properly only when they (as we say) *are in the benefit* of one or more determinate human beings (or of other beings that perhaps may be capable of enjoyment). This means that these values, in order to receive their meaning as values fully and properly, are brought into a determinate, real relation to a being, similar to the relation of possession or enjoyment, for instance. Thus the reality we strive for in these values ultimately consists in the establishment of such a relation in regard to ourselves, namely, that we possess or enjoy them. Because of this peculiarity, one has designated these kinds of values as *relative* values. However, this does *not* mean that these values would be "merely relative" values; that is, values not for all men in the same way. After these present explanations, we shall return to this question concerning the so-called relativity of values as such, which we touched upon earlier. Here a completely different issue is at stake, namely that determinate kinds of values receive their genuine reality only when they are "in the benefit of someone." In order to avoid all misunderstanding and at the same time use a clear English expression, we wish, rather, to call these kinds of values, values that are need-fulfilling, or conditioned by need. For the relation with reality in which the enjoyableness of these values becomes finally fulfilled consists precisely in the fact that they always satisfy a need of him for whose benefit they are.

We must first note that in the case of these need-fulfilling values, there are two different and even opposite directions in which we can strive after realization. For we can aim either to let such a value be to the benefit of ourselves, in that we attempt to attain or even to enjoy the relevant good for ourselves, or we can let such a value be to the benefit of one or a number of others. Thus, in the first case we bring one of our own needs to its fulfillment through a kind of appropriation of such a value, whereas in the other case the need of one or more others is fulfilled. In this way, such a value receives either the function of being a value that fulfills one's own need, or a value that fulfills someone else's need. If we now fall back on the old label taken from the Latin language and call these values relative values, we could also speak of values that are relative to oneself and relative to someone else.

We must now distinguish a completely different class of values from these values whose enjoyableness in the final analysis presupposes a determinate, real relation to a human or perhaps another being that is gratified by it. In the case of these other values, their enjoyableness consists in the fact that they are simply there as that which they are; thus, in their mode of being, or character, in their essence (*Sosein*). A real relation, through which they should first be to someone's benefit, does not play a role here; the reality of such values is fulfilled merely through the fact that a certain state of affairs just happens to be the case. We encounter values of this kind, for example, in the personal character attitudes of people: we experience, for instance, attitudes such as diligence, perseverance, patience, sincerity, courage, generosity, and the spirit of sacrifice, just as we meet them, as enjoyable, even though they are in no way for our personal benefit. Even the courage of the enemy and the diligence of the competitor, which certainly are not to our own benefit, but rather do us harm, can compel respect from us and thus be recognized by us as enjoyable in themselves. And the same thing is true also for the courage and the diligence that, because of unfavorable circumstances, will not reach their goals and thus are to nobody's benefit at all; the attitude as such remains enjoyable nonetheless. It is in the same way that we, in-versely, experience the opposite attitudes, such as laziness, insincerity, cowardice, stinginess, etc., as unenjoyable in them-selves, even where we ourselves do not suffer any detriment from such characteristics of others, and even where no detri-ment for anyone arises.

One has labeled as *absolute values* these values which con-sist in the fact that the reality of something, taken in its proper characteristic, appears as enjoyable in itself. This label expresses the idea that these values in a certain sense rest upon themselves; not in the fact that they find their essence in being to someone's benefit, but rather in the fact that their existence in itself is experienced as enjoyable. However, it belongs also to the typical character of these "absolute values" that they refer beyond themselves to the metaphysi-cal, in that they let us anticipate a ground of being that lies in their depth but cannot be understood by us, and that in-spires us with a high esteem of a special kind, a high esteem that at the same time brings with it deep respect or rever-ence for the bearers of these values.

Among these absolute values, the value of life itself is a very important one. True, we encounter a value of life first as a value conditioned by need in our own life: we shrink back from the possibility of an early death, and this means that while we are standing in life we wish to continue to live, we would like to possess further life for ourselves. But there is still a completely different way of looking at this: it is when we focus our attention objectively, in a certain sense, on life and what is living in the world in general, completely aside from our own desire to continue to live; it is when we see life as something that mysteriously arouses respect, and this means as something holy, which we should not destroy with-out momentous grounds. This holds first and foremost for the life of each man. However, one can, in addition to this (as Albert Schweitzer has shown), also recognize something that demands respect, and thus something holy, about life in general, the lives of animals and plants included. And thus, here too, we have, generally speaking, an absolute value be-fore us.

Still another absolute value is to be mentioned here, a value that indeed is also somehow connected with a value conditioned by need, but that nonetheless itself is not a value determined by need. This is the value of right, provided we do not understand here by right the so-called positive right, which is definitely formulated in state laws, but law taken in the original sense as it is found among men before there was any political organization. What is here called "right" has as its counterpart what in English is called injustice (*Unrecht*). Injustice in this original sense is found, for instance, in the case when a man is punished although he is not guilty, or when someone is murdered. Everyone has a right that something like that never be inflicted upon him.

However, just as in the case with legal right, here, too, one must make a distinction between two meanings of right, namely right taken as title, or legal claim, which is also labeled subjective right, and right as legal order taken in its entirety, which is called objective right. Subjective right is always to the benefit of the one who possesses it; thus it contains a value that is conditioned by need. But it has its foundation in the legal order, in objective right. The latter, objective right, is something that requires respect in itself and thus is an "absolute" value. (One may find a more elaborated reflection on right, in the sense meant here, in my booklet on natural right.[1])

Finally, as other kinds of absolute values we have yet to mention the values of beauty and art.[2]

---

[1] *Grundlagen, Grundzüge und Einzelnormen des Naturrechts* (Freiburg i. Br.: Karl Alber, 1965).

[2] The distinction between "absolute" and "relative" (by-need-conditioned) values does not coincide with that between "value in itself" and "value in function of something else" (values that have the character of means or of usefulness in regard to something), but must strictly be distinguished from it. There are values that are conditioned by needs that are values in themselves, as for instance the agreeableness of moderate warmth of the sun. On the other hand, among the values in function of something else are those which serve absolute values as well as those which serve values conditioned by needs. The value of a book about education or about ethics, for instance, is of the first category, whereas the value of a warming

Thus we have seen that "absolute" values are essentially different from relative values, which fulfill a need. The character of absolute values according to which they are very different from values conditioned by needs, as we have just described them here, notwithstanding our *relationship* to them, can nonetheless be similar. And this is mainly the case where values conditioned by need are considered not as being to our own benefit but rather to the benefit of other people. In these instances as well as in our relationship to absolute values, we find something enjoyable and will it not because of ourselves, but rather by rising above the point of view determined by self-interest to a higher and, in a certain sense objective, standpoint.[3] That is why we can include the absolute values together with the values that are relative to someone else or fulfill someone else's needs, and call all these *objectively significant values*. In opposition to these, the values that are relative to ourselves or fulfill our own needs must then be characterized as *merely subjectively significant values*.

The division of values we have reached in this manner can be shown in the scheme below.

Through the distinctions we have just gained, we are now very close to the state of affairs that forms the distinction between good and evil. In order to comprehend this distinction, the only thing still to be done is to focus our attention more closely on the relationship of these different kinds of values to our wishing and willing.

When we encounter in our lives values that fulfill needs, be this in reality or merely in the order of thought, these values, because of their enjoyableness, easily arouse our desire to possess and enjoy them, so that we most eagerly grasp each opportunity to acquire them that offers itself, and even

---

stove is of the second. The service value (*Dienstwert*) of money can be placed in the service of absolute as well as of by-need-conditioned values.

[3] Moreover, the values that fulfill the needs of someone else, and the absolute values, are in their significance for us closely related to one another in so far as some of the forms of personal behavior that we evaluate as bearers of absolute values consist in the readiness to stand up for values that fulfill the needs of others.

VALUES

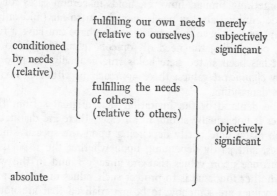

search for these opportunities. And in so far as we are not exactly indolent and lazy, we are also even prepared to take pains and stresses upon ourselves in order to achieve or secure their possession. Thus our will is, as it were, *enticed* by these values as they stand before us as offering a fulfillment of our own needs. To that extent they are "subjectively significant," that is to say, meaningful for the relevantly acting man or for the one who finds himself still faced with a decision. But we can and may withdraw from the enticement of such a subjectively significant value also, at least in so far as it is *merely* subjectively significant and not connected with an objectively significant value; thus we are allowed to renounce such a value without further ado.

The *absolute* values are completely different in this regard. Their enjoyableness has an influence on our wishing and willing, too. Generally speaking, however, they do not attract us, but encounter us rather as a *demand*, or at least as an *invitation*, an appeal addressed to us. The demand or invitation is (in so far as these values encounter us as existing in reality) oriented toward their not being infringed upon; where their existence appears to be threatened, we are invited to protect them in so far as we are able to do so. Finally, where we observe that such values are lacking in reality, we see ourselves invited to provide for their reality, if possible.

Something similar, however, holds in certain cases for values determined also by needs; namely, in so far (and only in so far) as they have the function, or perhaps can have a function, of fulfilling the need of *someone else*. That is to say, what has been stated here holds true generally for all *objectively significant* values; these approach us either as inviting or as demanding.

The demand or the invitation that originates from these values is not equally strong in all cases; there are distinctions to be made here partly depending upon the special kind of values, and partly depending upon whether the issue is not to infringe upon values that are already found in the world or whether the issue is to protect such values or whether perhaps values are somehow to be materialized that are not yet real at all. Taken from the viewpoint of the kind of values involved, the strongest demands originate from the absolute values, and among these, first and foremost, from those of right and life. Taken from the viewpoint of the reality status of the values, the demand that, generally speaking, is the strongest is the one that requires that there be no infringement upon values that really exist or are found in someone else's possession. We find not so much a demand as an invitation or appeal when the issue is about protecting values that exist but are threatened in their continuance. Generally speaking, the invitation is still not as strong when there is a question of somewhere materializing values that are still lacking, thus of an invitation to an active engagement toward the realization of a value. It is only in certain cases, as for instance in regard to one's relations or where a debt of gratitude is to be paid, that the invitation becomes stronger and could even develop into a demand. Generally speaking, however, an active engagement can be required only to a limited extent, namely within the framework of what is possible for someone. The negative demand not to infringe upon existing values, on the other hand, is also stronger, because anyone can fulfill this demand to a great extent, precisely because he does not have to do anything, but merely omit various things.

After these clarifications we have now come so far that we can grasp and determine the distinction between good and evil. The *morally* good consists precisely in nothing other than the fact that any time in some life situation or other that the reality of an objectively significant value is put into our hands, in that we have to act or to omit something in its regard, *we comply with* the demands or invitations to maintain or to materialize that value which approaches us in this way. For in many cases, although by no means in all, it is necessary that at the same time we renounce a merely subjectively significant value; and in the cases in which this necessity does exist, the moral demand of such a renunciation originates at once. Inversely, evil consists in the fact that we do *not* respond to such a demand to maintain or materialize an objectively valid value. In this case, when we are not willing to do so, the ground for it is usually to be found in the fact that we do not wish to renounce a merely subjectively significant value, which we should have to give up in that case. This means that the common ground of evil is to be found in the predominance of selfishness and egoism. In addition to this there is certainly yet another, less frequent form of evil, namely the genuine so-called *wickedness* that consists in the fact that an activity is directed toward the destruction of an objectively significant value for its own sake. For the rest, there are *differences of degree* in good and evil that correspond to the various forms of strictness of the moral demands or invitation; but here evil taken in its lowest degree is usually no longer designated by that name; one says then merely that a form of behavior is "not very fine."

After this discussion, and in concluding the first part of our explanations, we are now able to return to the question of the so-called *relativity of values*, which we touched upon in the beginning, and to make an essential statement in this regard. We see now that the determination of the essence of good and evil, as we have gained it, is independent of the fact that various values in particular may be relative. For the distinction between good and evil, according to our determination, by no means depends upon particular values, but merely on the distinction of the general value *forms* we have explained in our discussions. These value forms, however, are forms of *conceptions* of values (we may say *value-categories*), which are independent of the manner in which we experience the individual values. For in the case of good and evil, in the final analysis, everything depends upon what we *will*: whether we will something *for ourselves*, which would be to our own benefit, or whether we will something we experience as full of value in itself, for its own sake. All relativity of values taken in particular cannot change anything in regard to this basic determination.

It seems to us that what is basically essential in the distinction between good and evil has been captured and explained in these preceding determinations and observations.

II

In the first part of our investigation we heard about values; we made a distinction between objectively significant values and merely subjectively significant values, and we came to the conclusion that moral good consists in the fact that we comply with the demands of objectively significant values we encounter, whereas moral evil consists in that we act contrary to these demands. And yet, notwithstanding the determinations we have gained in this way, there are still several *objections and questions*, which make further complementary considerations necessary.

The first of these objections is the following: from the explanation we have gained, it seems to follow that in order to act right we may never follow *egoism*. For we are very well able to let each possession of a subjectively significant value, and for that matter a value conditioned also by need, be to the benefit of another human being; and according to the principle we have established, in order to act right we should always give preference to this respect for the other above our self-interest. But this cannot possibly be true, for it would mean that complete self-sacrifice would be demanded of us. However, one also speaks of a justified and sound egoism, and this manner of speaking surely has on its part a certain justification. The question, however, is one of whether and how this conception can be founded from our determination of good and evil, and how and where thereby the precise line is to be drawn at which egoism loses its justification.

One will say first that everyone has a certain *right* to let values that fulfill a need and are at his disposal also be to his own benefit, that is, to materialize them as subjectively significant values. Everyone seems to have such a right specifically in so far as he has honestly earned the means personally to enjoy these values through his own work. One will say that claiming the right to satisfy one's own needs cannot be evil, but that at least it is morally unobjectionable, or formulated differently, that it is without a doubt morally *permissible*.

Generally speaking, this view is certainly correct, in so far as in morality the issue is about real *demands*. That is to say, if we do not take into consideration relationships that are obligatory because of special reasons, then generally speaking there can be no question of a strict demand (instead of one's own personal enjoyment of a value at his disposal) to let this value go to the benefit of someone else. However, in many cases a certain invitation to do so can nevertheless arise; and one must say that the moral good then becomes materialized precisely through the fact that we comply with this invitation, although on the other hand not-to-do-that is not yet to be labeled as evil (in the normal sense of the term). It is here that the distinction between moral demand in the strict sense and mere invitation, that is, the *appeal* made to us without strictly obligating us, a subject we touched upon in the first part of our essay, receives its full significance. However, our point here is not yet sufficiently clarified by merely referring to that.

In order to reach full clarity here we must first focus our attention on a matter of a completely different nature. An example may serve to make this clear.

Let us assume that a councilman of a town that is destroyed by war has to codecide whether a certain amount of available money should be used for building a *school*, or for building *houses*. In such a case, there is obviously no question of a decision between merely a subjectively significant and an objectively significant value, but there are here on *both* sides objectively significant values from which to choose. In our private life it is not rare that we have to make decisions of this kind also. For instance, consider parents who have to decide upon a question concerning the education of a child; let us assume that the issue concerns the school to which a child is to be sent, in which case each school that comes under consideration has its particular advantages and disadvantages for the education of the child. Such decisions, too, have moral significance, for they are obviously connected with an essentially moral *responsibility*.

However, we have to realize here first—and it is of importance to see this clearly—that decisions of this kind are, strictly speaking, no longer decisions between good and evil, but have a fundamentally different meaning. This follows from the fact that in such decisions, we normally will what is good from the outset, and whoever acts in such an attitude, that he wills what is good, can in so doing never act in an evil way; the question is then merely this: from among various things that appear as good in themselves, which is the right thing to choose? But in a decision between good and evil, I know what is good and thus to be done, but often I have not yet decided to do it; rather, a kind of inner battle of the will is going on in me, in which I must make a decision between that which presents itself to me as something that objectively ought to be, and that in which I merely have a subjective interest of agreeableness or something similar and that I know I must renounce. On the other hand, whoever finds himself in a position in which he has to decide between *two objectively* significant values, has to that extent already decided to do what is good, and thus there is *no inner battle of the will* taking place in him; he is merely uncertain in his knowledge about what is the right thing to be done here. In this case the decision therefore has a completely different character from that of the choice between good and evil. The latter decision must be characterized rather as a decision between what is *right* and *wrong*;[4] and in such a case the question is, what in a given case is the right thing to do. However, since—as we have noted already—it is a matter of moral responsibility that we do not only what is good, but rather what is right, we must now face the question of how one is to decide between what is right and what is wrong. That is to say: how are we to decide which one of two or more objectively significant values between which we must choose, deserves preference?

In regard to this we must note first that here there is not such an obvious and encompassing solution as there was for the question concerning the distinction between good and evil. After all, we have here a series of principles of which, depending upon the situation of the case, sometimes this, sometimes that could help us to ascertain what is right.

First we have to establish that, within the value of life in so far as it constitutes an "absolute" value, we discover a distinction between higher and lower values. Thus we recognize, for instance, in a noble animal such as a horse an essentially higher value than in a worm. And we are accustomed to correctly considering the life of man, in which reason and the capacity for moral action concomitant with it, holds sway, as standing above all animal life.

The appreciation of right, in turn, is intimately connected with *reason*. And since, as we have seen, right equally constitutes a high, objectively significant value, it follows that in the human realm the value of the highest rank is found where the demand of respect for man's life is connected with the demand of respect for right. Next in the hierarchy of

[4] Here, as well as in what follows, Reiner's expressions *sittlich richtig* and *sittlich falsch* are translated by "right" and "wrong," respectively. It is important to note that both these expressions, in Reiner's view, merely refer to a mode of behavior that purely and objectively manifests itself as appropriate or inappropriate and in this sense as correct or incorrect, in such a way, however, that a possible personal advantage or disadvantage does not play any part therein. Thus the meaning of moral praise or blame, which in English is usually more or less cosuggested by the expressions "right" and "wrong," should be excluded from the significations that these two expressions have here.—Ed.

objectively significant values we then find those which make life possible as *social life* by means of the legal order: namely the right to outer *freedom* and to the safety (*Unverletztheit*) of one's own body, as well as the right to properly earned *property*. In moral action, all these values occupy a privileged position in regard to all other values precisely in so far as their *non-violation* is demanded. And as we have seen as a general rule, such negative demands always precede the positive ones.

As far as the *positive* engagement of our action is concerned, there is a whole series of principles that establish the preference between objectively significant values (and thus what is right), and values to which, depending upon the nature of the case, sometimes this, sometimes that is to be applied. Such a principle is, for instance, the principle of the greater *number*, or *quantity*. This principle is applicable to cases in which we find *equal* values on both sides of the decision, but a different number, or quantity, as far as its realization is concerned. For example, according to this principle a doctor who is simultaneously called to one individual sick person and to a large traffic accident involving many wounded people, will (assuming that he has no additional information in regard to either one of the cases) rush first to the traffic accident. According to the same principle, the preservation of a certain good for a whole *community* occupies in the event of conflict a privileged position in regard to the preservation of the same good for one other *individual*.

It is impossible here to enter into the further principles of preference that play a part in the positive realization of objectively significant values. One will find a whole series of these principles described in my book *Pflicht und Neigung* (*Duty and Inclination*). Merely by way of indication, it may suffice here to say in this regard that in such cases it is often of importance to see in which value engagement we shall have more *chance of success*, and also on what side we find the greater or more pressing *need* that is to be removed. Thus the establishment of the objective relationships (*Wirklichkeitsverhältnisse*), and not a distinction between the order of precedence between the values in themselves, is decisive here.

As has been indicated already, from what has been said it follows that a certain knowledge of what is ethically right is not always possible. Specifically, where a judgment concerning a reality to be expected in the future plays a part, obviously a certain knowledge often cannot be acquired.

However, in these decisions, which aim at hitting upon what is right, there can be no moral guilt either, if taken merely as such, except in cases in which the mistake originated in a guilty way. For when, standing between two objective significant values, we choose the one that is not preferable, then taken in this respect, we do not have any ground for doing what is wrong instead of what is right. Here Socrates' statement that no one does consciously what is evil, holds true. And yet, in *one* case this is different, as we shall see.

We wish to clarify this matter for ourselves using the example (given earlier) of the councilman who has to choose between the building of houses and the building of a school. A councilman who finds himself in this position will first have grounds to make no other decision than an impartial objective one in favor of that which he, considering all available data, believes to be the more necessary and the better; thus, for instance, for the building of houses, when the need for houses is still essentially greater and more urgent in that town than the need for school space. However, it can occur also that such a councilman has a personal interest in one project or the other; for instance, if a piece of land he owns were suitable and its sale would bring him great profit. In this case, a subjectively significant value, on the one hand, interferes in the decision involving two objectively significant values on the other. And there we have grounds to do, instead of what is right, what is wrong. This means that the councilman can be tempted to advocate the building of the school even when he has to say to himself that in the given situation the building of houses is more urgent. If the councilman now yields to this temptation, the choice is not only wrong, but also evil. And the choice is evil precisely because here, too, a decision against the reality of an objectively significant value is made in favor of a merely subjectively significant value. The fact that in this instance an objectively significant value is connected with the chosen subjectively significant value is, for ethical evaluation, insignificant, since this objectively significant value appeared to be considered inferior.

On the other hand, in the case of our councilman obviously it could equally well happen that his subjective interest coincide with that one of the two objectively significant values that appeared to be the more important one. Then there is again no grounds for choosing the less important of the two, and thus what is wrong. But the choice of what is right in that case is not yet always also morally good. Rather it is without a moral value when it is made merely because of the subjectively significant value. It is even the case that if the choice is based exclusively and decisively on this latter value, so that because of it even what is wrong would have been chosen if necessary, then, its moral correctness notwithstanding, the choice is still evil. (Kant speaks of mere "legality" in such actions.)

These cases, in which a merely subjectively significant value is connected with one of the two objectively significant values, between which one must make a choice, are not rare in our lives. There are even typical cases in which a decision always has to be made between two or more objectively significant values and at the same time at least one subjectively significant value, too, since we also have a subjective interest in the relevant action or its goal. Cases concerning various questions that to some extent are often discussed, are of this nature, such as for instance, the question of whether marriage is dissolvable, and if so under what circumstances; of whether birth control is allowed or even should be demanded, and under what conditions and with the help of what means; of whether atomic weapons and generally our modern warfare, even in the case of self-defense, can be morally justified, etc.

After these clarifications, we are now able to return once again to the question concerning the moral justification of *egoistic* action, which did not receive its adequate solution in the preceding. However, the insights we have just gained should also shed new light on this question.

In the foregoing, the evaluation of egoistic actions was presented in such a way that it would mean the choice of a value that merely fulfills one's own needs, and thus of a merely subjectively significant value, although instead of this an objectively significant value could always be materialized. However, such a conception of the question, upon closer consideration appears not always to be adequate in regard to the state of affairs under consideration.

In order to see the matter with clarity, we must subject to a more accurate consideration the values that are conditioned by a need. These values, as well as our striving after them, have a characteristic function in our lives. By and large, these needs, which form the reason why we seek to acquire these values, serve, in the order of nature, the purpose of encouraging and assuring the preservation of our own being. That is, they serve partly the preservation of the individual existence of the one who experiences these needs, but partly also the preservation of the race, and thus, in the case of us human beings, the preservation of our human mode of being, or mankind in its entirety. That is why one speaks here, also, of the *drive for self-preservation* and of a *drive for preservation of the species* from which these needs arise and which they serve.

But in this context we must note the following: When we carefully consider the needs that originate from our so-called drive for self-preservation, then generally speaking we are by no means, on this account, also focused on our self-preservation as the goal of our corresponding actions. Thus, for instance, when we feel hungry, generally speaking, by no means do we aim at protecting ourselves against death by starvation, we just wish to get rid of the disagreeableness of that feeling of hunger. If just once we do *not* appease our hunger, we are under ordinary circumstances not immediately threatened by death from starvation. And this is all the more so when we desire to eat something not because of our being hungry, or to drink something not because we are thirsty, but when we just feel tempted to eat or drink something in particular, something we just happen to see somewhere or that just happened to enter our mind, and of which we know that it tastes particularly good; thus, for instance, when we long for a good piece of roast, or for a piece of Black Forest cherry pie, or a good glass of wine, etc; in these instances, we certainly do not think of self-preservation. Similar and even clearer cases are found in the needs that serve the preservation of our species: in sexual desires we do not first and foremost aim at the procreation of a child; in fact this is even quite often feared and prevented in so far as possible.

Generally speaking, we must establish that there is no one-to-one correspondence between the goals of which we are consciously aware in our needs, and the *natural goals* connected with these needs. The difference between the goal of a need, and an end aimed at by nature, reaches even further: for in concrete cases it is very often so that, even objectively and taken as such, the fulfillment of a need does not precisely serve the goal intended by nature, although it, generally speaking, serves to reach this goal. Thus we often eat and drink even when we no longer feel hungry or thirsty; we continue to eat and drink because it tastes so good. The enjoyment of the pleasant taste and our desire for it drive us frequently so far that giving in to it is detrimental to our health and thus our self-preservation, although we are clearly aware of the detrimental effect. Thus, in order to achieve its goals, nature has provided us not only with the exactly necessary number of needs, but as it were even with an excess of them. There are even needs that according to their entire *nature* are detrimental. The needs that, strictly speaking, do not originate from nature, but to which we have just accustomed ourselves, are of this type; for instance the smoking of cigarettes, from which many people can no longer escape, so that time and again they experience a desire in this regard.

From these findings, it follows that, within the realm of our needs, we must make a *distinction* between different groups of them. A first group comprises needs whose fulfillment is necessary for the preservation of our existence. The necessary nourishment, the necessary sleep, the necessary protection against cold and wetness, and so on, belong to this group. A second group of needs is constituted by those whose fulfillment, although not unconditionally necessary for our existence, yet is somehow required. Those needs which serve the purpose of developing our force and power, and not only just bodily forces but also the development of our mental powers, belong to this second group. Thus, for instance, our desire for knowledge (in so far as it is not merely a question of curiosity), and for everything that serves our education, is of this type. A third group of needs is constituted by those whose fulfillment is not demanded or required by our existence, but merely by our agreeableness or pleasure, and at the same time not harmful to our health; here we must certainly take into account that for the preservation of our health a certain minimum amount of joy and recreation are necessary, too. Fourth and finally, there are needs whose fulfillment is detrimental to our bodily or mental health, but that nonetheless are clearly experienced as needs. Of this kind is the desire for food and beverages that transcends the measure of what is wholesome, or a need for cigarettes, as we find in people who smoke just from habit.

On the basis of the distinction between these four types of needs, the principle concerning good and evil which we have established in part, receives another meaning than it seemed to have at first sight. For we see now that indeed the fulfillment of many of our own needs serves the purpose of materializing merely subjectively significant values, but on the other hand, that there also are needs whose fulfillment, although at first we equally have a merely subjectively significant value of them in mind, in fact also demand the realization of an objectively significant value. This holds true, for example, in the fulfillment of needs of the first two types as we have distinguished them here. For our own life has, just as does the life of any man, an "absolute" and "objectively significant" value. The same thing holds also for the abilities that stimulate and increase our life. This shows that we not only are entitled to satisfy our own needs in so far as they serve these values and thus that such action is not only morally permitted, but that the satisfaction of one's own needs receives, to that extent, a morally positive meaning, also; that is to say, receives thereby the character of what is right, and even the character of what is morally good, in so far as we recognize it, and for this reason we act accordingly. Thus in this case ethics correctly speaks of "duties" that man has "in regard to himself."

On the other hand, however, the relationships we have just explained in part even sharpen the demand to *renounce merely* subjectively valid values. For as far as needs whose fulfillment is detrimental to our health are concerned, it follows that we have to renounce their fulfillment for our own sake, thus without even taking respect for other people into consideration, and that this means the realization of a morally negative value (*Unwert*) if we do not achieve this renunciation. Thus these sacrifices, too, belong to the duties we have in regard to ourselves. However, the demand for such a renunciation follows more than ever when we can thereby fulfill the needs that are vital for *other* people.

Considered in a general way, egoistic actions appear to be a case in which the question concerning rightness becomes connected with a decision between good and evil. As far as the decision is concerned, the situation is thus similar to that of the councilman in our example. Yet the situation there was such that first, and as it were *in the foreground*, a decision was to be made between *two objectively* significant values, one with which *under certain circumstances*, and as it were *in the background*, a merely subjectively significant value was connected. On the other hand, in our question concerning the justification of egoistic action as such, it is the case that, first and foremost, a decision must be made between a merely subjectively significant value (for fulfilling one's own needs) and an objectively significant value (for fulfilling the needs of someone else). But if we take the background into consideration, it appears that here in many cases an objectively significant value is connected with the one that is merely subjectively significant.

A further distinction between the two cases is found, in addition, in the fact that the councilman knows at the very heart of his conscience that he is not permitted to decide according to his personal interest. On the other hand, in the case of an action that even in the foreground clearly appears to be egoistic, the boundaries between what is morally imperative and what is merely permissible, and for which we no longer bear responsibility, are not so clear. These boundaries become readily clear only when, for instance, the care of a family becomes connected with the care of myself. Otherwise, the double reflection that in the preceding pages was performed, on the absolute value of life as it manifests itself in an objective consideration, as well as the equally objective value of one's own life, is a presupposition for achieving such clarity. To perform such a double reflection, however, is, generally speaking, no longer a matter for the average man in his everyday life, but requires that one have started to reflect philosophically. And even ethics itself until now has not been able to reach complete clarity in this matter. If my explanations in this regard have brought some new clarity to a broader audience, then part of their function has already been fulfilled.

This partial finding, however, must be inserted into the main findings we have accomplished here. Thus I hope that I may list a clarification of the essence of good and evil, and the recognition that these are different from what is ethically right and wrong, as well as the insight that is connected with this, namely, the fact that doubt concerning what is right, which indeed cannot always be solved, can by no means annul and overrule the clear distinction between good and evil.

SELECTIVE BIBLIOGRAPHY

Freiheit, Wollen und Aktivität (Halle: Niemeyer, 1927)
Das Phänomen des Glaubens (Halle: Niemeyer, 1934)
Pflicht und Neigung (Meisenheim am Gl.: Hain, 1951)
Die Ehre (Frankfurt a.M.: Mittler, 1956)
Der Sinn unseres Daseins (Tübingen: Niemeyer, 1960)
Das Prinzip von Gut und Böse (1948) (Freiburg: Karl Alber, 1960)
Die philosophische Ethik (Heidelberg: Quelle und Meyer, 1964)
Gut und Böse (Freiburg: Bielefelds Verlag, 1965)
Grundlagen, Grundzüge und Einzelnormen des Naturrechts (Freiburg im Br.: Karl Alber, 1965)

Chapter 7

INTRODUCTION

RAYMOND POLIN (1910–   ) has devoted the great-
est part of his philosophical investigations to ethical and political problems. His most important publications are: *La
création des valeurs* (1944), *La compréhension des valeurs*
(1945), and *Du laid, du mal, du faux* (1948). His political
treatises are, among others, *Politique et philosophie chez
Thomas Hobbes* (1952) and *La politique morale de John
Locke* (1960).

According to Polin, philosophy faces grave problems the
moment it conceives of man in terms of freedom but nevertheless wishes to develop an ethics as a practical theory of
man. As Polin sees it, every ethics is intimately connected
with a theory of man. But whereas most philosophers have
first developed a philosophical anthropology in order to found
their ethical view upon that basis, for Polin ethical philosophy
is a philosophy of man, and its basic principles should determine the meaning of what is human.

In developing his view, Polin rejects the idea that one can
attribute to man once and for all an invariable structure
which determines his essence. In this regard Polin defends
a position similar to that held by Sartre. He disagrees with
Sartre where the latter defends an "absolute" freedom in
man. According to Polin, man's freedom is intimately interwoven with what is given, and the given is somehow preserved and transcended in man's free decision at the same
time. In other words, man's freedom comprises both "nothingness" and "creativity." This view gives Polin the possibility
of developing a *functional* definition of man's nature in which

what is given and that which is universally definable in man is man's function of freedom, the ability to become on the basis of what is, and the power to create.

From this it follows that to determine the meaning of man is to assign a specific end each time to his function as man, and thus to treat him as a value around which the world of men should be ordered in relation to him. To every definition of man there is a corresponding conception of the world and an effort to make it come true. In this way, man is defined by his vocation; his function as man takes on a meaning in relation to the value he proposes to realize and to which he feels bound by an obligation. In other words, a definition of man is essentially a moral definition, because it is affirmed as a value and imposed as a duty.

Most philosophers have tried to define man by appealing to one or more of his characteristic traits: consciousness of self, consciousness of the future, the ability to speak, freedom, reason. All these definitions of man remain inadequate as long as one does not take into account the elements of "meaning" and "value." The reason for this is that all man's characteristic traits are merely means to the creation of meaning and value by man. Among these "means," freedom is the "means of all means." Freedom can take on meaning only in relation to a given situation and in relation to an order that is to be established, on the basis of the order that is already inherent in the given. Most philosophers who have thought along similar lines have made the mistake of taking the given order as something unquestionable and definitive: an order established by a divine Absolute, or an order essentially inherent in nature and in man, an order prescribed by a historical determination. And they have done so because otherwise it seems to be impossible to justify the obligatory character of our moral standards, regardless of what these may be concretely. Polin thinks he can justify the obligatory character of moral imperatives by pointing to the fact that the order that man's freedom establishes on the basis of an already given order consists essentially in a system of comprehensible relationships, because order and meaning are mutually inclusive. Thus one can develop an intelligible theory of such an order, and from this theory one can derive the universally valid moral imperative: "Act in such a way that there can be an intelligible theory of your actions."

In order to understand values and to arrive at an ethics of action, we must thus not start with a divine Absolute, nor from a static ontology based on eternal and invariable essences, but from values, that is, "from evaluation understood as the dialectic unity of value, action, and achievement" ("The Philosophy of Values in France," p. 214). Values are nothing if they are not potential actions. We find in each man a creative process by which consciousness raises itself beyond the given reality, invents values, then, according to this evaluation, attempts to act on the given and to impose upon it an order that should be its own work. This process arises from the dialectical succession of transcendencies by means of which consciousness transcends itself and the given reality, enabling it to invent the order by intentionally creating a hierarchical relationship between the imagined order and the real, and in an act of efficient and effective transcendence, transforming the given reality in harmony with the chosen imaginary project.

Consciousness has the tendency to conceive of these created values as stable and communicable *goods* from which one can derive intersubjectively valid *norms*. Our interpersonal relationships are very often dictated by such goods and norms; this leads to a crude communication between consciousnesses, in which each one tends to impose on the other his own transcendence and values. In this form of goods and norms, values gradually lose all their axiological virtue, power, and originality. The genuine task of each man, however, is to transcend the given situation and all "goods" and "norms" by creating personal values on the basis of this situation. Values are inherently subjective and "unreal." However, as we said before, such a subjectivistic "unrealism" of values does not preclude the possibility of developing an intersubjectively valid theory of values, and thus an ethical theory (Ibid., pp. 214–16).

The selection that follows is a translation of the last chapter of *La création des valeurs*.

VALUES AND TRUTHS

Raymond Polin

I EVALUATION AND TRUTH

Anyone who is no longer satisfied with a morals of obedience renounces the universal, the eternal, the one, a transcendent datum; all these are appeasing witnesses and guarantors of a supreme value, a final goal, a completion of history. There is no longer even as a last resort the possibility of joining up with Nietzsche's imprecations against a "morals of the herd." In virtue of what dogma would he do so, since in his view the dogma of the will to power is no more than one myth among many others concerning the transcendent? If there is no longer any reason to obey, why should anyone be granted the right to command? And so, deprived of all possibility of axiological agreement or communication with the other, is one not forced to a doctrine of isolation, of solitary finitude? The axiological reflection, as an expression of the principle of transcendence, seems to condemn man to a perpetual discovery of values, to a continuous and indefinite creation of himself and the world of values. But does the negation not outweigh the creation, and does man not lose himself in this ceaseless pursuit of the other than himself? Do values not disappear, are they not continuously transcended and reinvented? By refuting an axiology of the transcendent in favor of an axiology of transcendence, one denies that there is an ideal norm for the activity of transcendence and, therefore,

This essay is from *La création des valeurs*, by Raymond Polin (Paris, 1944), pp. 271–99. Copyright © 1944 by Presses Universitaires de France. The present essay was translated into English expressly for this edition by Joseph J. Kockelmans.

that one could assign limits to arbitrariness in the evaluation. Is this not the nihilism that Nietzsche defined and pretended to overcome?

1 OUTLINE OF A NIHILIST SOLUTION

The principle of nihilism consists in the negation of all given, transcendent reality. By denying the existence of transcendent beings, nihilism makes the appearance of any hierarchy of values impossible. It separates the axiological meaning and essence from ontological reality and concludes from this that there is no being to which a value should be linked in an intrinsic manner. The first nihilist thesis thus denies the ontological reality of values. Nihilism passes from this thesis to a radical negation of all values, just as one passes from a principle to its consequence. And it is not only true that there is no axiological reality, but there is no axiological essence, either. Nothing has value. For the nihilist, everything is neutral, amorphous, indifferent; his preferences and his choices are devoid of signification and even of meaning. Nothing deserves to be called beautiful or ugly, good or bad, sacred or profane. Each evaluation is an invention without real foundation and without constant law. Each value must be reduced to a subjective illusion, to an insignificant game of the mind, to an arbitrary combination of words. Since the nihilist does not allow for a creative moment which brings about a hierarchy, he is unable to recognize a coherent axiological order. As Nietzsche observed, the categories of unity and totality have lost their signification for him. This elusive chaos resists any effort to bring about an order systematically, and particularly a teleological interpretation. The axiological incoherence is such that even the useful and the useless can no longer be defined. For the nihilist there are no more goals and norms than there are values. That is why he is forced to renounce action and lock himself up in a contemplative attitude, as does a Buddhist nihilist; action has no more creative power than it has teleological significance. Everything is in vain, because nothing has value. Thus, axiological nihilism is on the way to total, ontological nihilism in that man successively renounces evaluating and acting. But in doing so, in fact he refuses existence to himself as well as to all things.

By defining values in terms of activities that bring about a hierarchy and reflect transcendence, we have affirmed at the same time their unreality and their indetermination. Can unrealism and indeterminism of values not be shown to constitute the two sufficient principles of any axiological nihilism? In fact, one would like to deduce from their unrealism the negation of values as far as their existence as well as their essence are concerned. Value is nothing, much less a stable datum, because it is unreal. It becomes blurred with an unrealizing consciousness, a hierarchizing invention, a flash of transcendence between the obscure reality of the given and the obscure reality of the completed work. One cannot even talk about it without immobilizing and extinguishing it. Is axiology more than something imaginary, a free and vain play of the imagination? In fact, is that not the best interpretation of that indeterminism we have made into a doctrine? But if values are indeterminate, then they do not participate in any order that could found them; the relationships between them are thus marked by transcendence, each one of them is isolated and unique and stands opposite to all the others. How could this incoherent pluralism of axiological monads create goals and provide us with motives for a practical decision? In the invention of values, one would let himself be led by a kind of absurd dream that would not even reach its completion in his contemplation. For no one contemplates chaos.

Under these conditions, our axiological reflection would not lead to any other result than a tragic one. Man's essence would impose upon him a self-contradictory and insoluble destiny: man could not be, except by denying himself; nor reach his completion, except by renouncing existence. The tragedy of man would find its origin in the principle of transcendence. Man's destiny would not be to exist, but to annihilate himself in order to exist as a human person. This overcoming, this annihilation of each instant, would be a prefiguration of death. Man would not be the way he is except in so far as he would have consciousness of his own impending death; for in order to transcend himself he cannot annihilate himself except by becoming aware of his own nothingness. It is out of a need for eternity, the nihilist declares, that man creates for himself a provisional existence, here and now, in time. And it is because he is in time, that he will never be eternal. It is out of a need for immutability that man strives for the transcendent, and creates by transcending himself. And because he transcends himself, man changes from transformation to transformation. In order to be, he must become different, and because he becomes something else, he is not. It is precisely being, the static datum that shows a semblance of immutable and eternal permanence, that seduces the philosopher defending an immanent position; it would constitute the foundation of universal values to be received from simple knowledge. But by immerging into the given, man receives death, or ceases to live as a man. Taken as such, man is never a static datum, a simple being. This tragic conflict is identical to that of the necessary particularity of the person who has the power to transcend and to create the other, and thus the desire for universality, which is the essence of man. It expresses itself in thought as well as in man's work. It animates both and entails their precariousness.

In thought, the impetus to transcend is expressed through the evaluating reflection. And this reflection is tragic, because it presupposes and searches for absolute values and ultimate goals while denying any hope of them in each new movement of evaluation. Man reflects in order to find the truth; because he reflects, he cannot be satisfied with an immutable and definitive truth. Neither a solution nor a compromise is possible between the desire for an immanent truth and the impetus that negates, and thus transforms and creates, the reflective transcendence, between the adequate, conscious grasp of the given and the creation by consciousness. But this creation, in turn, reveals its tragedy. For at each moment, the action without which man does not exist as a man, destroys and transcends its own work, or destroys itself by establishing the work through which he reaches his completion, annihilating himself at the same time. The result of the action comes to an end and turns into defeat. Moved by a power to transcend, which is kept in balance by a desire for immanence (both being at the same time contradictory as well as essential), man carries along in their dialectical progress not only the abstract images of his axiological universe, but also the realities he creates through his action, and above all others, the reality of his own personality. This self-concern would translate into existential terms the tragic contradiction that is essential to man; he would have a clear consciousness of it each time he would comprehend his essential self-concern, and would decide to act anyway, without foundation, without hope, without friendship, in what is uncertain.

There is no doubt that nihilism appears as the simplest interpretative system of indeterminist unrealism, that system on which we focused our attention in the beginning. It even constitutes a necessary step for all reflection on values; for by showing that all values, and even value as such, can be put into question and denied, it proves their unreality and reveals that no value can be demonstrated or is necessary, that no value possesses a foundation that is objective and sufficient. But methodological nihilism is not merely a necessary stage for the elaboration of new values, as Nietzsche would have it; for Nietzsche's doctrine of values falls in turn under the nihilist negations. Nihilism prepares a new comprehension of the essence of values which allows us to transcend it after having understood it. In fact, the nihilist system of interpretation implies the postulates of the classical axiologies whose futility it pretends to demonstrate. It remains faithful to the demand for an axiological realism as well as to that for a theoretical knowledge of values. It originates in the desperate and vain search for an axiological reality.

This is precisely the reason why it conceives of the unrealizing and indeterministic transcendence of axiological reflection as the source, as well as the proof, of a radical nihilism. In this realist perspective, the doctrine concerning the unreality of values is confused here with a pure and simple negation of values, because nihilism requires values that are ontologically real, on the one hand, and because only the presence of real values would in its view make theoretical knowledge of them possible, on the other. It agrees to believe only in values that it can know by immanence and organize into a system that can be deduced by starting with supreme values. The possibility of a theory of values that can be logically demonstrated is taken to be the condition of the reality of, and even of our having coherent thoughts of, values. In a word, the nihilist longs for a truth of values, a unique, eternal truth concerning the highest value, a truth that can be systematically deduced from secondary values. He conceives of the refusal of any supreme value and of the renunciation to speak of the truth of values as a double failure and as the mark and proof of axiological nihilism.

But what is left of these accusations if one disengages himself from the realist, as well as from the theoretical, prejudice, something we have shown it possible to do? It is precisely thanks to the unrealism of value that we hope to safeguard and confirm what is serious in axiological thought against the blows of the insoluble plurality of realist axiologies. For this permits us to understand the atomist individualism of axiological inventions without taking away anything of its importance in regard to the evaluating transcendence, because, on the contrary, we make this the very principle of man's existence. Each human person is defined by the constellation of his own values and is situated in regard to them in a factual, subjective certitude. The arbitrariness and possible vanity of each particular value does not affect the primordial, essential characteristic of our axiological consciousness. Is it not true that it is the source of all transcendence *in actu* and of all genuine human existence? Axiological reflection serves as a preliminary condition for our practical decision and creative action. Far from deriving from this a renunciation of all action, axiological unrealism is completely oriented toward the effective accomplishment of the act of transcendence, to the point where we have been able to ask ourselves the question of whether action for action's sake in its form does not constitute the final goal of all axiological reflection, as well as that of man's existence. That is why the restlessness of the self, which when taken in isolation is always insufficient, is dialectically related to self-esteem; axiological unrealism oscillates necessarily from the one to the other without ever coming to a standstill in anxiety and self-negation. Only the problem of the truth of values would remain open to the accusations of nihilism, if one were to declare that there is no truth of values. But does this mean that values that are essentially inadequate in regard to all reality, are false? Is it possible to apply the concept of truth to that of values? Is truth itself a value? This is the double problem that we must now try to elucidate.

Is it true that a double negative answer will still take us back to nihilism? Let us note that the nihilist interpretation of axiological unrealism derives its principal argument from the negation contained in the act of transcendence. But the negation, as we have defined it, is not exclusively destructive and nihilating; it is the most indeterminate form of transcendence and the most preliminary phase of creation to which it leads. The negation, just as the nihilist attitude itself, is merely a phase and does not constitute a goal in itself. Far from reducing the given order to nothingness, the negation through transcendence transforms it, invents imaginary hierarchies, creates through its very action a new order that preserves and overcomes the precedent order. In view of the fact that, through transcendence, negation is the condition for axiological existence as well as man's existence, it could never serve as the principle of nihilism. Furthermore, in the mind of one who becomes aware of the transcendence he brings about, self-esteem vies with anxiety, and prevails over it each time he comes to a creative act. Self-esteem is necessary for the accomplishment of transcendence; it expresses subjectively, in its personal certitude with respect to values, the defeat of nihilism, whereas the created work marks its objective defeat.

2 CREATION AND FOUNDATION OF VALUES

Does not the rejection of nihilism, which gives back their meaning and importance to values, imply that they essentially require an objective foundation, which again urgently imposes itself upon us as something to be examined? By pushing aside nihilism, and with it all realist and theoretical axiologies, we have meanwhile pushed aside, and in so doing even neglected and overcome, indeed maintained in the realm of nothingness, all axiologies that presuppose a datum to be accepted. Thus, in an axiological unrealism, the notion of foundation must lose its classical significations; the foundation for which we are searching cannot consist in an objective reality, which is exterior to us, self-sufficient, and capable of serving as guarantee and support for a value; neither can it be a real motive, which, within the perspective of an objectively recognized order, would be capable of simultaneously determining and legitimating the invention as well as the certitude of a value and thus capable of a practical decision-making. Axiological unrealism as a philosophy of creation stands in opposition to the philosophies of the given.

But from the moment one renounces the metaphysics of the given and rational universes of values that define reason as a creative instrument, if not as the demiurge of the real universe, can one not then precisely identify the act that founds with the act that creates and innovates? When the issue concerns values, to know a foundation does not yet mean to give a foundation. The relation that founds is the one that unites the creator and his creature, for the creator contains in himself the sufficient reason of the creation; the creative action serves as law for the development of the creature; the creator constitutes the principle and the responsible guarantor of what he creates and that cannot not depend upon him. In an axiology of creation, the search for the foundation of values leads progressively toward the definition of the creator who is responsible for them.

However intimate the links that unite creator and creature may be, and however harmonious their natures may be, they are not identical. For in fact, without the radical irreducibility to his own work of the one who creates, one would understand neither his action nor the guarantee he gives to it. The relations of exteriority and dependence that unite the creator and his work are not reciprocal; they bear witness to an oriented, descending relation of transcendence of one in regard to the other. The creator founds his work because he is transcendent to it and because he maintains himself in it; he guarantees it to the extent that he is responsible for it.

In the unfolding of transcendence, the three significations of the concept of foundation are found again, and legitimate one another reciprocally; first of all, the original meaning, which insures the effective reality of the other two: to found means to build, to create a value that has value in itself, which is founded by the very fact that one creates it by means of transcendence. The second meaning must be understood in regard to the value and no longer in connection with its creator: to found means to found itself upon the creator, to receive support from his exterior, objective, and transcendent reality, which support is thus incommensurably valid and valuable. Finally, the merely phenomenological meaning constitutes the synthesis of the other two: to found a value, an intention, means to found to the extent that one knows that he is its inventor, creator, and responsible guarantor.[1]

Consequently, one sees that this foundation does not assert itself except for the subject who creates and founds it. At the root of all action that creates foundations, one finds thus the creation of the self by the self. Man is first his own responsible author and his unique guarantor, for he can deliver himself from everything except himself, under pain of annihilating himself. In fact, the act of transcendence, which is the principle of all creation, is an act carried out by a subject. To transcend is a subjective activity, as Heidegger observed when he reciprocally wrote that the subjectivity has transcendence as its basic structure.[2] Now, the action of the subject, contained between an invention and an actualization of transcendence, is free. He who says "transcending creation" says "freedom,"[3] for it rises above all present data and cuts off all determining bounds it has with it. Transcendence founds and innovates because it is free. The creator constitutes a first beginning, and in regard to his own work he plays the part of an "absolute." Freedom assures the primacy of the creator at the same time that it assures his origi-

[1] Martin Heidegger, *Vom Wesen des Grundes—The Essence of Reasons*, trans. Terrence Malick (Evanston, Ill.: Northwestern University Press, 1969), Part III, pp. 100 ff.

[2] Ibid., pp. 34–37.

[3] Ibid., pp. 100–5.

nality. For one who thinks and reflects on his freedom, the free invention or the free action alone can serve as a foundation.[4]

However, the freedom of man, of the subject, shows no less the limits of his institution of values, for no foundation holds out against his dissolving power. No foundation can maintain itself for man, who can free himself from all given foundation. The only essence from which he cannot escape is his own, his function of transcendence and the reflexive consciousness he has of it. But this is precisely the principle of his own indetermination. Whereas the antinomy between the concept of freedom and the concept of foundation of values maintains itself on the ontological level, on the phenomenological level the foundation of values manifests itself in their free creation. There is no foundation except in one's self-esteem, that is to say, in the subjective certitude of one's own values, in the consciousness of one's own free creative power and one's own work. Self-esteem is at the same time the principle and the consequence of creation, for one would not create if one did not have self-esteem, and one does not have self-esteem except for the fact that one founds and creates himself.

Unrealist axiology in regard to creation of values makes the latter's institution and foundation a function of man and of the human subject.[5] For each man who creates them and accepts their guarantee and the responsibility for them, values are founded by right but they are not universal. They are in fact common, that is to say socially universal, but deprived

[4] Ibid., pp. 128–31.

[5] Besides, one could make the remark here that from a phenomenological point of view the subjectivity of axiological thought entails neither its limitation nor its illegality. All values receive meaning only with respect to a subjective, transcendental consciousness, because all essences are in a necessary correlation with transcendental subjectivity. Every object is an object of a consciousness. (*Ideas*, sec. 125). Does the phenomenological reduction not let the necessary character of the subject appear? (*Cartesian Meditations*, pp. 27 ff.) The fact that in phenomenology it is always true that "a person addresses another person" (*Philosophie als strenge Wissenschaft*, Logos, p. 338) does not deprive an axiology of its intelligibility.

of reflexive foundation. We can limit ourselves to this formula on a phenomenological level to the extent that it permits us to comprehend the individual action by discovering the certitude in each consciousness, and at the same time to explain the axiological communities and collective actions by recognizing the effective community of accepted values. But the creative activity is gifted with the power to found and establish values only and exclusively for the creative subject. Can one content oneself with a foundation that is only subjectively sufficient? Under what conditions and at what cost?

3   THE OBJECTIVITY OF VALUES AND THEIR "OBJECTIFICATION"

The notion of objectivity adds nothing to the concept of axiological foundation defined as the free activity of a creative transcendence. Only a realist and theoretical philosophy can search for a foundation of values in their objective, ontological, or essential exteriority. If, on the contrary, value is an activity of transcendence that brings about a hierarchy, how could it be in harmony with an objective reality of which it is the negation as well as the overcoming? Upon what could a knowledge of an objective reality that is adequate through immanence found an evaluation if one defines the latter as an invention of transcendence? The very idea of objectivity belongs to theoretical reflection, and in the final analysis reveals itself as having no common measure with axiological reflection. And objective presence cannot play the part of a foundation in an unrealist axiology: it cannot even have a place there, except in order to mark the disappearance of values.

In a purely subjective attitude, to invent values means to transcend oneself as well as all things. In so doing, the subject transcends itself by inventing the other than self, which is outside itself, beyond itself. The transcendence that negates the object, by taking place, makes the project of its creation objective. Transcendence is the subjective, the merely subjective, positing of an objective existence. In the interior of a personal constellation, transcendence carries with it a progressive objectification of which the subjective creation constitutes the law and marks the rhythm. The created object constitutes its result and its residue when the subject abandons it by ceasing to posit it as the correlate of its invention and action. In what does this objectivation consist, or rather, if it were possible to use this expression, this "objectification"? How can man as a subject place himself opposite himself, expel from himself any thought that he withdraws from his own grasp, from his own domination? By inventing the unreal, by attributing a transcendence to it that grants it a form of exteriority. The transcendent unreal is, albeit not objective, at least "objectified." As we have shown, even the imaginary ceased to be completely at the disposal of its creator the moment he had invented it. The unreal, imaginary object resists; but the axiological unreal comprises a kind of internal coherence that is still-more profound, for in virtue of its essence it tends to constitute itself as norm and order. Its unreality bestows upon it a kind of immutability, permanence, and independence, in regard to whose reality even the person does not cease to be the law.

The process of "objectification" becomes confused with the progressive elaboration of the value into a goal, and then from goal into norm. The attraction to transcendence that is in harmony with the invented goal, and then the exigency of transcendence that imposes the norm, constitute the different phases of the formation of the axiological object. That which one understands by objective value is therefore nothing but the norm that is established and deprived of its axiological signification: it manifests itself then as a transcendent datum; its imperative force expresses its "objectivity." Thus one cannot speak of the objectivity of values, just as one cannot speak of norms, except on the social level, within the framework of axiological communities that have been formed around orders of norms. The norms are accepted in the interior of a society that constitutes the geometrical place of the reciprocal actions of domination performed by all its members. The axiological communities they bring forth constitute limited axiological universalities (which reason extrapolates *ad infinitum* on the conceptual level) that serve not as criterion but as second cause in regard to the seemingly objective character of the norms. Indeed, they assure their permanence because the social time serves as a durable framework for the variations in human convictions. They make the norms independent of each particular subject, because they depend upon the reciprocal transcendence of the totality of the members of the society. In short, everything takes place as if the transcendence of the others in regard to oneself, *in fact*, provides the norms with an objective foundation.

The subjective position of an "objectified" existence can originate either from the transcendence of the subject, which imposes upon itself its own transcendent product, or from the transcendence of the other, which is subjectively accepted and undergone as such. Obviously it gives rise to a false semblance of objectivity that provides us with neither a guarantee nor a foundation of values. We have already outlined the boundaries of the power that is able to impose norms, limits that become intermingled with the boundaries of their objectivity. They are those of the individual human person which are defined by his power to transcend, projecting a constellation of values up to the confines of his universe. Man is contained in the interior of his own axiological reflection and does not have any guarantor for his own values than himself to the extent that he attributes the responsibility for them to himself. Values can have no other foundation than their own creator. But if man's self-esteem is high enough, he may affirm that the values have a foundation that is absolutely satisfactory.

II   ACTION AND TRUTH

One must renounce the attempt to found a value *de jure* except on the certitude that the human person acquires in the act by means of which he creates it, to the extent that each creator of values is for himself the sufficient and first principle of this creation and of this value: creation and certitude, which go hand in hand without transcending the boundaries of the subject that transcends and creates; a foundation that does not receive a signification *de jure* except through the creator's renouncing the right to discuss its principle, that is to say himself, because each man is for himself his own creator and his own guarantor.

Now, all axiological, reflexive certitude is free and subjective. It emerges from a decision, that is to say, from an action that puts an end to the uncertainty by concluding a free axiological reflection. The certitude that itself is the product of an evaluation by transcendence, does not find any other foundation except its own advent. But in view of the fact that the action from which it springs precedes the certitude and necessarily comes about in the uncertain, it can never serve as a legitimate foundation for another evaluation except by renouncing each attempt to transcendence, which contradicts the very essence of man. The certitude grows in proportion to the taking place of the action; taken at its limit, it marks the completion of the action, but also the vanishing of the values. Axiological certitude exists only in fact; it is all the more perfect as it is less axiological. And even more, man invents values and creates them only because he is anxious and uncertain; the novelty of the creation originates from a repudiation of the real, from an overcoming of the given, which presupposes the acceptance of the uncertainty. Action in the full sense of the term is subjectively uncertain and objectively free. As Lagneau describes it, ". . . it is an adventure that begins."[6]

Under these conditions, do ethical conduct, that is, conduct that is coherent with respect to its values, and social life, remain possible for a man who is aware of the subjective and arbitrary character of thought and the certitude of values? Or is he, rather, condemned to fall back into a nihilist skepticism or into isolation? Are there limits to the arbitrary in the process of creation?

1 INVENTION OF VALUES AND CYNICISM

We can offer a classical answer to this question which can serve as a solution for all the conflicts and all the ethical incoherences because it is purely formal. Does it indeed not suffice to take, as a goal for man's activity and as the principle of hierarchy, the ethical coherence, the harmony between the values, as the harmony between consciousnesses?

[6] J. Lagneau, De l'existence de Dieu, p. 146.

Indeed, all conflicts cease as soon as the antagonists agree to take their harmony as more desirable than their particular goals. Under the name of the *good will* has Kant ever celebrated anything other than an ethical will which establishes coherence between its proper values and harmony with the values of the other? But he substitutes for the search for material harmony the concern for the universality of the harmony, which has the advantage of determining the form of this harmony and binding it to reason, which is the power to think universally. Such a solution transcends the goals for which it was searching, for it finds itself condemned to the vanity and emptiness of the formalism it employed. If a value holds only in virtue of its harmony with another one, then this latter value, and not the value of the harmony as such, constitutes the real principle of the choice. The coherence between the values has meaning only with respect to value as such, a purely formal value, with which formally all other values are in agreement. The search for a formal harmony does not exclude the need for a choice of fundamental values with which one will decide to remain in harmony.[7]

As soon as the ethical value of coherence is intentionally directed to a well-defined axiological hierarchy, it implies an attitude of obedience and of submission. It becomes reduced to a search for a social harmony that conforms to an order of norms. Such is the axiology of conformism, which serves as an axiomatic system for all social axiologies. Either it founds the value of social harmony on the pre-eminence of an order of norms and then ceases to be a philosophy of social harmony, or it subordinates obedience to norms to the search for social harmony, and this entails the relativity of these norms in regard to the primacy of the harmony as such. Under these conditions, why should one decide to agree with

[7] "Loyalty for Loyalty," preached by Josiah Royce in his *Philosophy of Loyalty* (chap. *iii*), does not escape from these difficulties. It attempts in vain to deduce the unique, concrete "cause" with respect to which a universal loyalty should be possible from this *ideally teleological behavior* that defines the pure form of loyalty. It is only the divine intervention to which he appeals that is capable of solving this problem.

such an order of norms rather than with another one, which can be chosen from among the infinity of possible orders? Not only would man be bound to an inhuman attitude of renouncement, but he would renounce all values in favor of norms in which he could not have sincere faith. On the contrary, the morals of obedience imply faith without limits in norms that are identified with the transcendent. Now, the idea of social harmony that is incapable of conforming to the transcendent always appears as a means with respect to the construction of real situations, or to the triumph of certain values. In other words, no one would search for a social harmony without conditions.

Otherwise, he would have to limit social harmony to the reciprocal respect of the personal values of everyone and profess the kind of optimism that leads to anarchy. One supposes, then, that harmony between values would naturally follow not from the choice between this and that particular value but from their axiological essence. But this would amount to considering the formal harmony of values as sufficient, or to admitting that the values that are obviously so different can be grouped into a hierarchy that is at the same time unique, absolute, and true. Kant's good will of treating each man as a moral person and recognizing dignity in him is thus very close to Descartes's generosity, which is defined by the legitimate esteem of one's own value as well as of the value of others. Generosity, which follows each conscious awareness of the self, prevents us from scorning the others and tends to assure the reciprocal recognition of the values of everyone in a kind of factual universality, upon which one reflects, to which one agrees, and which one loves.

In these different attitudes, the taste for the universal reveals the common rationalist inspiration that leads sometimes to a rational theory of values, sometimes to a rational axiological formalism. The one as well as the other are contrary to all our conclusions. They merely express a "reasonable" point of view, and, on the fringe of all specifically axiological considerations and by means of a secret and avowed negation of the originality of the values, they evoke that which (as, theoretically, it would be desirable) they should be. The renouncement of the objectivity of values entails the renouncement of its criterion, universality, which rightly appears as a theoretical demand independent of the essential coherence of values and, in fact, under the form of a community of normative orders, as a situation that results from their progressive degradation.

What possible attitude remains, then, for an isolated man who has taken refuge in axiological certitude that he knows he owes to a decision he has consciously made in an arbitrary and uncertain way, when he has chosen to evaluate, and to act, in order to exist? Historically one calls a philosophy of action that is combined with contempt for all theoretical speculation, *cynicism*. In addition, everything being equal, this term could as well be used for a doctrine that disengages evaluation from all theoretical and immanent definition in order to make it an operation of transcendence and a beginning of action. However, it would suit this view only if one were to divert from cynicism its traditional insolence and effrontery, and eliminate all hedonist and egoist deviation, frequently found in the antique doctrine, as well as all skeptical inclination toward passivity.

Under these conditions it would be excessive to call a cruel and evil man who acts out of cruelty and wickedness a cynic. In our view the cynical man is not he who systematically searches for something evil (which with certainty he holds for evil) to be accomplished, but rather he who beyond all ethical concern for coherence with the good and the evil, brings everything into play to accomplish the goals he has chosen for himself. Can cynicism, taken in this sense, be called immoral? However, the transcendence of all ethical perspective does not necessarily imply the systematic renunciation of all values, whatever they may be; for cynicism would, through indifference, cease to be cynicism to the extent that it would make action impossible, even that form of action that is found in ascetic passivity. For the hedonist cynic, the indifference in regard to values was accompanied by the affirmation of certain among them, or rather by the affirmation of certain goods to which the cynic was attached without discrimination. On the contrary, if this indifference is total, it gives rise to a passivity that can be the same as that of the dilettante, of the man who attaches so little importance to values that he, without any attempt at discrimination, accepts all those of which he happens to think. The dilettante lives frivolously and finds it more in harmony with his contempt for values (and human beings) to disperse himself in frivolous and provisional desires. The cynical intention remains to the extent that the dilettante maintains his freedom of indifference, or let us rather say, his freedom of indecision. On the contrary, we call a cynic the one who affirms values and acts in clear consciousness while admitting that he no longer affirms values and acts in regard to an absolute good, or in regard to values of which he is legitimately certain. The cynic philosopher posits values, knowing that their certitude has meaning only for him and is relative to him. But he knows, also, that the essence of his existence as well as of his condition consists in inventing value, that is, that *other* with respect to everything that is already given, and in creating the other that as *other* is transcendent. He must be a cynic in order to perform an act of transcendence. And he must be so even more in order to carry out this transcendence, to act in uncertainty, and to build up his work teleologically, radically against all values.

This attitude of retreat, beyond all preoccupation, in regard to a foundation of values, contains two implicit postulates, which it expresses just by the fact that it exists: self-esteem and freedom. The free man alone can found values and decide to consider himself as their genuine and first foundation. The free act, however, is, in virtue of its very essence, a cynical act. Indeed, it is not bound to values that are sufficiently founded, without which the latter would be transformed into realities and become the determining cause of actions that, by that very fact, would cease to be free. Is cynicism not the free affirmation of uncertain values? This freedom of the creator, which at the same time is responsible and guaranteeing, can on the other hand serve as a foundation only if it is conscious and gives rise to legitimate self-esteem. However, this self-esteem, inheritor of Descartes's generosity, and adversary of pride, consists in appreciating oneself at one's true value. To estimate oneself as man is tantamount to recognizing one's power to transcend and create, but also to recognizing one's limits: man does not create anything except himself. Now, value is already the *other*, which still remains the self to the extent to which one creates it, but which becomes the *other* because one has created it transcendent. Thus self-esteem does not suffice, even if one is subjectively certain of his values, for being certain of values in the absolute. That is why the creator of values cannot escape cynicism: either he lives on illusions, and then he is a cynic without knowing it; or he is aware of his cynicism, and then he wishes to establish values, justify them through his action, and impose them upon the other, thus mastering his anxiety only by means of an action whose arbitrariness he accepts.

Cynicism thus reveals its conformity with the essence of evaluation to the extent that axiological consciousness spontaneously exercises a cynical function. To invent values is tantamount to inventing the *other* as such, giving credit to no particular, given, axiological content. By creating a value, the inventor provokes a process of overcoming, accomplishes a transcendence in which the form and order surpass the vivid content in importance. Cynicism maintains merely the form of values and affirms the gratuitousness of their content. That is why there is no cynical hierarchy of values, not even a hierarchy that would be attached to the pure form of transcendence as to its supreme value, and to action as to its sovereign good. Cynicism is first conscious of itself, thus conscious of the arbitrariness of the decision that founds its own axiological certitude. It reaches its summit when in the refusal of a supreme value or of a sovereign good, it finds a supplementary motive to will to transcend, deny, act, create.

2 ACTION AND CYNICISM

Finally, to the extent to which the power to transcend forms its principle, cynicism conforms to the existence of man. The latter would escape cynicism only if he could come to a certitude that is consciously legitimate and if, although powerful enough to transcend himself, he would not lack all power to bring his own self-creation to an end. Man is inventor and creator in regard to his real works, in regard to his values. Now, all limited creation is cynical, because all creation is at the same time subservience to one's work, crystallization and solidification of one's self in that work, as well as liberation and freeing in regard to the work that is already accomplished. The creative exercise of transcendence is therefore cynical because it implies the surpassing of one's values and one's work. To be oneself is at each moment tantamount to creating oneself, not in order to maintain oneself, but to transform oneself. Man is cynical because he exists and maintains himself only by becoming other.

Cynicism thus does not lead to contemplation. It is not the theoretical contemplation of values, which is always realistic and appeasing, which discovers at what point the values are empty, uncertain, negligible when one takes them one by one and each in itself. Man comes to cynicism in the same way as he maintains himself in it, namely through the clear comprehension of his power and the transcendence he brings about by means of conscious and reflexive action. Does this mean that cynicism gives back to the action a value for itself, and that it is thus reduced to an axiology of "action for action"? Previously we have discovered that action is not a value and that no determinate value can be attached to it in an essential way. Action as such, which is a pure form (namely conformity to transcendence at the moment it is brought about), has no axiological meaning: it is not capable of functioning in a hierarchy and even less of constituting the keystone of a hierarchy. In full awareness of his responsibility, the cynic opts for creative action as such not because it constitutes a supreme value which would determine his action axiologically, but because it represents the condition of his own existence. He does not make it the principle of a hierarchy (for all values have validity in regard to action), but the principle of an existential attitude. And yet, even if action is a condition of human existence, this does not necessarily imply for the cynic any demand for action, whatever it may be. To say that action is necessary is not tantamount for that reason to being indifferent to the nature of actions. On the contrary, the cynical attitude implies a choice, a decision that breaks the uncertainty or the indifference. If this decision is arbitrary, then it simply means that it is without legitimate and sufficient motive. It does not mean that it is without any motive. Cynicism consists in choosing in favor of certain motives although one is completely aware of their insufficiency. Nothing is further away from skepticism than cynicism, because the former pretends to deduce the renunciation of all action from the vanity of axiological illusions.

The cynic does not renounce anything. He has decided to create, and exerts himself to be the master of his own creation. The cynic's self-mastery in no respect resembles ascetic mastery, which in the final analysis, consists in being master of nothing, however much the ego finds itself constricted and reduced by asceticism. Self-mastery presupposes the purification of oneself to a point that tends toward annihilation. The only thing respected here is the principle of purification, which is held to be essential for man, and of which one claims to be the master. But what signifies the mastery of the principle of the self when one has renounced oneself? One not only renounces what one is, but one also annihilates what one can be; for one deprives oneself of all possibility of creation. Indeed, to act means to affirm and to create the *other*, thus to create that of which one will cease to be the master, to the extent to which one creates it as *other*. Thus it is not possible to preserve a pure, ascetic mastery of the self in action.

Cynical self-mastery, on the contrary, extends to the limits of the work for which the ego holds itself responsible. By defining man by means of a dialectic of transcendence and desire, we have, indeed, enlarged the ego so as to include the objects of our desires and the products of our creation. To be master of oneself thus does not consist in eliminating one's power to transcend and to desire, but to make the best possible use of it, to make a "good use" of it. To be master of oneself means to be master of one's entire personality, not in order to purify and exhaust it through asceticism, but in order to create it. Self-mastery receives its meaning only through the work over whose creation it presides and for which it accepts the responsibility. That is why on the theoretical level it implies a clear consciousness of self, and on the axiological level an action of transcendence that is creative as well as reflective. Creation constitutes the principle of self-mastery, but it also marks its limits, for the mastery does not last longer than the creation. One ceases to be the master of one's work the moment it has become the *other*, and because of that, independent of its creator. Man can remain the master of one single work to the extent to which it, in virtue of its own essence, remains unfinished: that is, the continuous creation of his own self. Because the ego can always transform itself, because the ego has never completely become the other, nothing is entirely lost, except in death. The mastery remains perfect only as long as the identity of the creator with his creature lasts.

Cynicism makes possible the realization of the only ethics that is in harmony with the creative activity of transcendence, the ethics of responsibility. A creative action is, indeed, possible only for a man who takes the responsibility for it; and he estimates his responsibility in so far as it is in his creative power. A circle establishes itself between creation and responsibility in such a way that the one becomes the necessary condition for the existence of the other. The cynical man manifests himself as responsible master and founder, first because he is aware of the essential certainty of his axiological decision and the anxiety concerning his self that he must overcome; and then because he is aware of not being the master of all the consequences of his decisions, and of being unable to act, either individually or socially, without axiological incoherence. In the presence of his work, the cynical man believes in his responsibility all the more as he believes it to be more arbitrary and more freely chosen in more complete uncertainty. He is responsible for it because he considers himself his first and sufficient foundation. He could naïvely hold himself responsible for it, if he took himself to be the creator of a coherent and teleological world. On the other hand, he will cynically accept an equivalent responsibility the moment he admits that (however true it may be that a man is master of himself) his work, nevertheless, depends not upon him alone, but on his situation in the world and the given structure of the world as well. Thus, to decide to act means to take responsibility for a work that never integrally depends upon oneself, but that also reveals the world and the others. Man is never the master of the totality of the results of his action, for his action always becomes collective. It is here that the cynic's ethics of responsibility receives its full signification, which is a social signification: a man who holds himself responsible imposes his values upon others under the form of norms, and decides for them. He plays the part of a master or a leader. In so doing he accepts responsibility for the entire work created by him and by those who, in obeying him, offer him their work.

By taking responsibility for his own work, the master not only founds it in his own eyes, but by obtaining voluntary obedience and work from the others, he transforms his values into norms for the others. And in the final analysis, would he not grant objectivity to them and a foundation in the eyes of the others, if he were to obtain their co-operation not through force, but through a spontaneous and cynical decision of obedience? Does not the work, taken in its purity, indeed represent an activity of transcendence that is conceived of and accomplished in common? In a community of work that materializes itself in this way, technically speaking, there would be leaders and executives, but axiologically all of them would, in virtue of their work, participate in one identical responsibility and one unique mastery. The ethics of responsibility would then make possible self-mastery, as well as the foundation, the institution, and the cynical basis of values not only for the isolated individual, but even for our collective life. It would define the ideal type of collective action in regard to an order that is consciously objective and true.

III TRUTH AND VALUE

If it is true that there is neither a foundation nor an objectivity of values, if they escape all reality as well as all determination, what relationships are there, then, between truths and values? The very idea of truth, indeed, calls attention to an attitude that is simultaneously realistic and theoretical. No doctrine succeeds in disengaging itself entirely from the traditional definition: *adaequatio rei et intellectus*. There is truth only where knowledge is concerned. Truth can be conceived as *noesis* and an act of consciousness, as the revelation of a reality; or as *noema* and the result of this act, as revealed reality. In the one case, as well as in the other, it expresses a certain theoretical immanence that is to be established or found again in regard to a given reality. We have been able to establish thus far that formal axiology permits us neither to give an axiological signification to truth, nor to appreciate a truth of values. The idea of an axiological truth would be limited to an ethical coherence of an invented value and of an axiological hierarchy that is conventionally accepted: the idea of truth, realistic and theoretical though it is, becomes reduced to a formal but axiological concept of an ethics. Another indication is no less remarkable: the definition of the great types of values has not given rise to classifying truths among values, nor to determining what one commonly understands by logical values. Does this mean that we are led to set down these findings as a doctrine and deny explicitly that there is truth in values? Are truths, or are they not, values?

1 IRREDUCIBILITY OF VALUES AND TRUTHS

In order to determine the extent to which truths and values can be reduced to one another and can be expressed each by the other, we shall attempt to answer these two questions successively.

Is there a truth of values? The truth of a value should reveal its reality. Now, a value is not a real thing which is given; it is essentially imaginary and unreal; it does not contain any reality that is susceptible to being revealed. And yet, does it, itself, not reveal reality? It certainly does not reveal the object it evaluates. But, nevertheless, can one not say that value as such reveals the reality from which it proceeds, that is to say, man's axiological consciousness, the existence of a deliberate transcendence conscious of itself, which would constitute the revealed truth of the pure value? But then one would play with the word "revelation": through its very presence, the value witnesses the essential principle of axiological consciousness, but it does not reveal it as a real knowledge would, which is a conscious grasp, by means of integral immanence in the object and adequation with it. The evaluation constitutes a deliberate transcendence that brings about a hierarchy and creates, but that does not reveal any data.

However, can one not say that each particular metaphoric value reveals the work it creates? Does the work not constitute the truth of the axiological process of which it is the product? But true knowledge rests on the given work; nothing allows us to say that this work would be the objective reality that corresponds to the value. On the contrary, the transcendent action that creates the work provokes a surpassing of the value, and makes the work essentially irreducible and inadequate to preliminary axiological reflection. The work is axiologically neutral and reveals nothing of axiological intention. One will be able to evaluate, without arbitrariness, only the technical result of the project of the work contained in the value. But one will then discover, in the work, only a technical and pragmatic truth of the value, and not its axiological truth. That is why we have been able to draw an *a posteriori* foundation for the value from the work.

How would it otherwise be possible to apply the act of immanence of true knowledge to transcendence, taken in the process of discovery and constituting the value? The truth of the value blends with the value itself by identifying itself with the movement of the transcendence of this value. It becomes reduced to a repetition of the value, to a simple axiological tautology without theoretical signification. Just as does the value, it overcomes the given and becomes intermingled with it no more than it reveals it. It is founded no more and no less than the original value. It depends upon the same decision and gives rise to the same uncertainty. To affirm the truth of a value is tantamount to proclaiming that one believes in it, that one is certain of it. Thus one can speak neither of the truth of a transcendence nor of the truth of a value.

The fact that the concept of axiological truth is incomprehensible furnishes us with the first proof of the irreducible heterogeneity of values and truths. Does this heterogeneity express the plurality of values of the one in regard to the other, or rather an even more irreducible, essential incompatibility? Do we have to conclude from this that truths are no values?

The classical, eclectic attitude was accustomed to classifying truths among values under the name of logical values. This thesis remained valid as long as one subscribed to the ontological realism of values, and assimilated evaluation to an operation of knowledge. The true, the good, and the beautiful become identical in being, and in our knowledge of being. This identity complies with a philosophy of the transcendent that, in the hierarchy of values, granted the primacy to the beautiful or to the good, as well as with a philosophy of immanence that granted this primacy to truth.

As soon as one denies the ontological reality of values, one is led to make the evaluation a discovery that is specifically distinct from knowledge, so much so that one makes the axiological essence of truth questionable. And yet, by interchanging the terms of the problem and by attempting to reduce knowledge to evaluation, Rickert pretends at the same time to maintain the truths among the values and to distinguish theoretical values from other axiological domains, which can be defined within the framework of an "open system" of values. Only in this way can one avoid the insufficiencies of the purely theoretical philosophies that resorb all human activities in knowledge, as well as those of the anti-theoretical and mystical philosophies. According to Rickert, the theoretical values correspond to an impersonal contemplative activity; they can be logically demonstrated and deduced, and can be organized into an "infinite totality" in a monistic framework. As values, the theoretical values stand irreducibly opposite to being and do not participate in it. They do not exist, either really or ideally: they have *validity*;[8] their mode of being is that validity. The value "truth" thus

---

[8] H. Rickert, *Der Gegenstand der Erkenntnis*, p. 260.

cannot be defined by the conformity of judgment with being; neither is it the conformity with the act of judging, without which it would have no more meaning than in a subjectivist psychologism. Rickert pretends that each cognitive judgment expresses a preference, depends upon an intuition, a feeling of validity, and can be reduced to a value judgment. Indeed, the truth of a judgment does not rest on this judgment, but on the affirmation of its validity. To say that a judgment is true is tantamount to saying that this judgment has validity. For Rickert, all truth is a value, because all truth is known and evaluated as a value. It possesses an objective, intemporal validity that manifests the objective and absolute character of true values, their transcendence in regard to all relations, and makes it the foundation of all validity.

The logic that is inherent in Rickert's doctrine entails its consequence; the progressive identification of knowledge and evaluation, just as much as that of evaluation and knowledge, provokes an objectivity, whatever it may be, that is correlative to theoretical thinking. It is particularly in Rickert's later philosophy that the eternal value of truth tends to signify an ontological reality. This return to realism shows quite well that corresponding to pure theory, pure contemplation, are only real objects, and not values that belong to a conscious activity of transcendence. In other words, either values do not have any ontological reality but have validity, and then the notion of truth loses all its meaning; or the only reality is the validity of values, and then their truth would consist in the fact that they are grasped by an effective intuition that is expressed in value judgments. But then, values would be value-truths, and Rickert would see, his value system notwithstanding, that all values become absorbed in truths. Now, the concept of value-truth unites verbally two essences that are irreducible, for truth cannot be conceived of without immanence in regard to a reality, whatever it may be, where on the contrary, evaluation entails the overcoming of transcendent reality. The idea of a true value is absurd and contradictory: it would mean the idea of a value that is in conformity to reality and that thus would cease to be transcendent, or inversely, the idea of a truth, or a revealed reality, that would become transcendent in regard to reality, and then at once cease to reveal it.

Rickert's criticism allows us to affirm that values and truths are essentially irreducible in regard to one another. Is this not Husserl's thesis? Whereas values are essences that are correlative to acts of the desiring soul or of the will, truths are for him the correlate of the theoretical attitude in its primitive character: "Truth is manifestly the correlate of the perfectly rational character of the primitive *Doxa*, or a certain belief."[9] Truth is the essence that specifically corresponds to the act of knowing reason. There is no question of evaluating the truth of a cognitive act, of a *noesis*; the noetic proposition has its foundation *de jure* in itself and carries its truth within itself.[10] At the very moment that such a *noesis* is intentionally directed to the *noema* it posits, it is directed to the truth just as *noesis* and pure act of knowledge. All intuitive thought is true, for its essence consists in having the truth as its correlate. Thus, the problem of truth would then become dissolved in the phenomenological analysis of intuitive evidence.

But, for Husserl, theoretical and axiological truths are parallel to one another because both become resolved in an evidence. Values belong to a region of essences; they are the fully intentional correlates of the evaluating act; they are essences that differ from other essences no more and no less than the other essences differ among one another. Truth is thus not a value, because it belongs to another region than values; but it is, just as are the values, a real essence. The act that posits the axiological essences, just as the act that posits the noetic essences, is deprived of all active and creative character; it is actual and actualizing. Thus, truth is not posited by the one and only act of the primitive *Doxa*, but is posited as a real essence beyond all split between subject and object. Rational consciousness, which constitutes a certain truth, blends the intentional positing of a heterogeneous correlate with that correlate, and immanent intuition with the same essential correlate. This intuition, which posits an

9 Edmund Husserl, *Ideas*, sec. 121.
10 Ibid., sec. 139.

infinity of essences that are all heterogeneous with one another while participating in a same "essentiality," does not distinguish between the different products of the acts of consciousness. That is why Husserl can define a truth of values, although truths are not values.[11]

2   TRUTH, THE WORK OF THE CREATING MAN

On the contrary, by accepting all the consequences of the phenomenological position, we have irreducibly opposed to the act that invents values and conforms to the principle of transcendence, the act that knows real objects and conforms to the principle of immanence. Whereas noetic consciousness, by means of an act of immanence, is lost in the object, and, by becoming aware of it, expresses its truth and reveals it, there axiological consciousness, by means of the act of transcendence, overcomes the given, invents the unreal, and creates. The act that is completely full of transcendence pursues its creation from value to work without any gap in continuity. Under these conditions there is no parallelism whatsoever, not even a formal one, between values and truths. Truth is not a value; and decidedly there is no truth of values. But there is a truth of action.

We have attributed to the intentional act that posits the essences (taken as Husserl defines it) a meaning that is effectively active and creative; the act of creation prevails over the simple, evident intuition with which, for the latter, it becomes identified. The truth of action does not reside in intuition, but in creation; the true is the reality that is created, beginning with the axiological reflection taken as it appears to its creator. The adequation comes about not through harmony between thought and reality, but through harmony between the created reality and the axiological project and intention; it expresses a second intention of ethical coherence or of technical result. Axiological reflection becomes true to the exact extent that creative action transforms the given reality in conformity to the axiological project. The created work completes the action and makes the value true

[11] Ibid., sec. 147.

by suppressing it. All hierarchical, axiological structure is eliminated from the work, which becomes neutral. It need not be interpreted as if it were intrinsically axiological in order that one could know its truth. It, itself, reveals the truth to the extent to which it is known theoretically. The axiological neutrality of the work confirms the fact that it cannot reveal the truth of a value. There is no truth except the truth of action and truth with respect to the technical creation it brings about. The work is the truth of action and not the truth of a value.

Does this thesis not lead us back to the pragmatism of a James, who considers the world as a given chaos in the midst of which man maintains himself through action, in which each successful work takes the place of a provisional truth? Taken in the strict sense, the pragmatist conception of truth is absurd, for it pretends to apply to the real world while at the same time ignoring it; the result does not reveal reality; it is no more than a consequence of the concept of truth, which is first taken as criterion, and then for the concept itself. If, on the contrary, one admits that action is effectively creative, its work becomes the only truth, because it is reality, and for axiological consciousness, the only reality. But it is not a truth because it is a result that can be known theoretically, for otherwise there would be no truth; for the result is never integral, neither with respect to a project nor with respect to an intention. The truth is the product of our action, and not that of knowledge. And since truth is the product of an activity of transcendence, one comprehends why it has so often been assimilated to a value. Indeed, it takes place in the axiological process, whose internal coherence it assures, so to speak, because action tends to transform the given reality and to recreate it in function of the imaginary project and the axiological intention. Here one has confused the reality that was held to be true with the axiological process that leads to it.

In his action, man creates himself at the same time that he creates his work. That is why the truth of action encompasses the totality of the work and its creator. It is at the same time the work and the man who accomplishes this work. Each particular human creation constitutes and reveals the truth of each creating human being. Taken as creation in the passive and active senses, each work is for its creator simultaneously revealed and revealing. This personal truth joins a common truth to the extent to which a work is executed jointly and originates in a collective work. For the group, there is a truth that, if not universal, is at least collective, namely that truth which the work, accomplished by a common, creative act, reveals. But there are no eternal truths, because there are no eternal works. All reality that has been brought about by work, and thus is historical, can at each moment again be put on the stocks, either by its creator, or by other people to come. In the final analysis there would be a universal and eternal truth only at the end of history, in an immobile world, without values and without action, a world of total immanence.

But truth is only a reality *de facto*, in which axiological reflection is completed and disappears, a given reality that axiological transcendence creates, but that also exhausts it. It founds neither the one nor the other; it is founded by them, that is to say, by man as man. Creative man thus appears at the beginning as well as at the end of the axiological activity; he reveals his principle and his essence through his work. If the reality he creates is his truth, if he is completely one with it, it expresses power, that source of transcendent creation which determines man's essence. The circle of our investigation closes, then, in the definition we have taken as our principle: namely that of man's consciousness. But this truth of the human reality is purely formal; it reveals the conformity of his work with the creative principle of transcendence. One can derive from it neither the laws nor the foundation of a concrete human truth.

It belongs to each man to choose the orientation and scope of his own transcendence, and to decide in an essential uncertainty, beyond all determination, on his values and actions. Now, the structure of the act of transcendence is essentially subjective. Man, the power to transcend who invents its unreal values and creates its works, depends at each moment only upon himself. In this creation of the self by the self, he founds himself. With respect to the certainty he acquires and the work he creates, he is a god who is responsible and sufficient. Values and actions are founded *de jure* only within the framework of the subjective human person, and also only for him. What more could the search for a truth, which always remains useless because it is revealed only by the accomplishment of the work one plans to undertake, or the discovery of an objectivity, which remains ever fallacious or conventional because it is essentially relative to the subject that defines it, give him? The human person who is subjective, but by no means isolated, because he is dedicated to a collective action, can evaluate and comprehend himself sufficiently cynically in order to be self-sufficient, and to assume at the same time the responsibility as well as the guarantee of his own thought and conduct. The subjective human action of transcendence, both imaginary evaluation and real transcendence, is founded only upon itself. It exists inevitably accompanied by decisions and sacrifices; thus it is sufficient unto itself.

SELECTIVE BIBLIOGRAPHY

La création des valeurs (Paris: Presses Universitaires de France, 1944)
La compréhension des valeurs (Paris: Presses Universitaires de France, 1945)
Du laid, du mal, du faux (Paris: Presses Universitaires de France, 1948)
Du bonheur considéré comme l'un des Beaux-Arts (Paris: Presses Universitaires de France, 1965)
"The Philosophy of Values in France," in *Philosophic Thought in France and the United States* (Albany: State Univ. of New York Press, 1968), pp. 204–18.

Chapter 8

INTRODUCTION

GEORGES GUSDORF (1912–   ) is mainly known for his contributions to the history and the philosophy of the human sciences, as well as for his investigations in the realm of ethics. Although the author has come to quite personal views in philosophy, generally speaking one could say that he has been influenced by the existential phenomenological movement, and mainly by Husserl and Marcel. In his *Traité de l'existence morale*, Gusdorf stresses the immanence of moral values within the ek-sisting man, rather than the fact that values come originally from a transcendent source. He certainly does not exclude this transcendent source, and it is basic to his position that he keeps trying to make a transition from the immanence of values to some form of transcendence. But in Gusdorf's view, a philosopher must try to do so without ever going beyond the realm of man's experience. As he sees it, we must try to elucidate the mystery of reason "in the direction of the immanence of man to his own experience" (p. 96 in Gaston Berger, "Experience and Transcendence," pp. 87–102, in *Philosophical Thought in France and the United States*). In other words, in his view, metaphysics can no longer rest on transcendence; rather, it must develop from anthropology.

As far as ethics is concerned, Gusdorf argues that the task of the moralist consists in explaining the near and remote conditions of the action of man, who finds himself at each moment in a concrete situation in the universe. In considering man's action, the moralist must take action within the perspective of the particular mode of ek-sistence in which he finds it and in which each particular action is preceded by a "personal history" and will be followed by other actions. Thus it is impossible to isolate one particular act from this personal history and to pass judgment on it. Each action is to be considered within a horizon, and this particular horizon is part of some more-remote horizon. Thus, if the moralist is to do justice to man's activities, he must try to understand them within the unity of that man's life taken as a whole. In other words, the moralist is not so much interested in activities as in human beings, whose integrity he must respect. This is not to say that the particular activities do not count; rather, it is important to realize that each concrete situation is to be understood on the basis of the meaning of man's moral ek-sistence taken as a whole. Man's ek-sistence, taken as a unity, then, gradually constitutes itself within a universe that is characteristic of him. Each particular activity of man must be understood as an attempt to come to grips with himself in mastering the world. In this attempt man sees as his ideal an equilibrium between the exigencies of his individuality and the possibilities of satisfaction that are offered to him by the world that surrounds him. That world, in turn, is constituted in function of the personal aspirations that become incarnated in it, whereas it, itself, grants to these aspirations forms of intelligibility and their indispensable consistency.

This equilibrium cannot be immediately established, once and for all; because of difficulties that continually arise, it is to be re-established time and again. Ethics, therefore, must be defined as a certain manner of considering the attempt of man to express himself in the world. That is why our study of man's moral experience must take its point of departure in a careful analysis of the general conditions of man's self-affirmation in the world. And in so doing, we must try to go back to the very origin of this attempt at self-realization and self-expression. On this level, the basic exigencies must be defined in terms of values that justify man's basic intentions and actions, because in the final analysis, moral consciousness and the feeling of duty derive their meaning and obligatory character from these values. Once these basic values are brought to light, it will be possible to understand the dominant life styles as functions of a particular category of values taken as predominant, and to comprehend how the attitude characteristic of moral affirmation originates in each particular style from this privileged category of values.

Traité de l'existence morale consists of an introduction, two major parts, and a conclusion. The first part of the book is devoted to a careful investigation of the basic structures of man's moral ek-sistence, whereas the second describes the various concrete engagements and commitments of our moral being. The selection that follows is a translation of the major section of the first chapter of the book's first part, and contains what I consider to be essential to Gusdorf's conception of values taken as principles of moral action.

VALUES AS PRINCIPLES OF ACTION

Georges Gusdorf

1 THE CONCEPT OF VALUE

The personal activity of man, taken in its entirety, can be considered an attempt at expression. The presence of man leaves its mark on the universe in the form of a multiplicity of more or less urgent questions to which the individual searches for answers. Thus there is a continuous change from intention and aspiration to realization. Man never keeps himself before the world in an objective and disinterested attitude. The human reality does not respect the universe. It overthrows it in order to establish it again. It organizes it and constitutes it. It establishes a new kingdom, wherein all things take on a new meaning. It is impossible to refuse to recognize this shifting from nature toward man—thus to ignore the fact that for man nature represents merely a framework in which his action will develop, an ensemble of elements he will put to work in virtue of a right of sovereign recovery. This cosmological advent of man corresponds to the affirmation of values by man.

The concept of value must here be understood in its most general sense. The human person solicits from his surroundings the satisfaction of extremely diverse exigencies, from the most primitive to the most refined. The organic needs of food and drink must be satisfied. A minimum of comfort in his existence must be secured. But loftier claims are to be added

This essay is from *Traité de l'existence morale*, by Georges Gusdorf (Paris: Colin, 1949), pp. 48–88. Copyright © 1949 by the author. The present essay was translated into English expressly for this edition by Joseph J. Kockelmans.

to these unwieldy ones. The education of our needs shows itself in their growing complexity, in man's search for luxury. Even moral, aesthetic, and religious aspirations complicate the first and apparently simple affirmation of his being in the world. An animal, too, constitutes its universe in function of its needs. But in the animal the values, apparently closely connected with the organism, remain brute and do not possess the sublimations with which they become enriched in man's consciousness.

Thus it appears that value is found to be present everywhere in man's conduct. It is value that determines its orientation and its structures. In each situation, regardless of what it may be, man's freedom will never be an undifferentiated freedom. The world of objects seems to offer itself to us flatly, in extended order, and in a way that is completely objective. But our view of the world adds a new and invisible dimension to it that imposes a discrimination, an order of urgency, upon it and grants the scene its concrete signification of the moment.

Thus, the most general definition of value would characterize it as a reality structure that is immanent to our action, as a manner of meeting the world and of qualifying it as a function of our constant or momentary exigencies. All of the ambiguity of value consists in its immateriality, in that characteristic of being the condition of all existence without itself being existence. It grants itself to us incessantly under the guise of an object to be desired, a goal to be reached, an equilibrium to be materialized. But it is never identified with the object or the moment that incarnates it. Once the goal it proposes to us is reached, it often happens that the value eludes, disappears, affirms itself, in turn, in the form of a new demand. Pleasure, happiness, joy, which are so enduring in our hope, lose the best part of their power while we possess them. Another aspiration comes to the surface and polarizes our personal life in its benefit. Value is situated at the horizon, rather than near at hand.

Values thus intervene in our concrete existence as instigators of action, a prospect of engagement, as the reason for our behavior and our expression in the universe, as the key of

intelligibility, although it cannot be directly understood by
our intelligence. It is important to note at this point this
transcendence of values in regard to the norms of our intellect. Intellectualist philosophy has misunderstood the universality of value; it was doomed to commit an error in this
domain because it refused to admit values except as projected
within the framework of a universe of discourse, in the form
of judgment. Once it was decided that the primacy of reflection is to be maintained at all cost, one had to deny all philosophical dignity and all moral signification to everything that
affirms itself in our conduct without passing through the intermediary of rational consciousness. Value was then found to
be reduced to discursive appreciations, which it indeed sometimes inspires. One spoke about value judgments, whose logic
philosophy tried to compare with the logic of judgments concerning reality.

However, values do not assure the unity of man's conduct
except through the universality of their influence. But in order to affirm themselves, values do not wait for a rational
ratification. In fact, in that case animal existence, which does
not know of an intervention of consciousness, could not be
interpreted in terms of values, and thus, in addition, would
remain unintelligible to us by virtue of the same reason as
the entire non-reflective part of our own behavior. . . .
(48–50)

Consciousness commonly credits acts that are manifestly
unreflective, with a moral signification, be it positive or negative. It disapproves of egoism, greediness, brutality; it ad-
mires generosity and sacrifice as they manifest themselves in
spontaneous attitudes. It even considers an unreflective form
of behavior as more significant, because the authentic reality
of the person better appears there. Also, reflection introduces
calculation, a possibility of cheating. The goodness, wickedness, and perversity of this or that man manifests itself to us
with greater certainty in a sudden initiative, in an immediate
reaction that reveals the secret and true orientation of the
concrete man. Common consciousness instinctively recognizes
the universality of values as principles of action. On that issue it joins the notion in psychoanalysis according to which

the person makes himself known more clearly in those moments in which a slip, a false movement, something that escapes his control, occurs.

If morality is not to be reduced to an ideal beyond life, if it corresponds to the rhythms that are essential to activity, it must be found in those principles of orientation that we call values, those immanent to all of our conduct. Taken in its full signification, value, thus, is not, as Le Senne would like to believe, "that which is worthy of being sought for",[1] and thus something that supposes a recognition, an authentication of reason. Rather, it is what the individual in fact searches for in an original way, what is found in us in the state of intention and what our conduct aims at making explicit; that at which our activities spontaneously aim. In this sense, values, indeed, designate the effective structures of our conduct and not an exterior and superadded organization that is imposed by an authority such as reason, social tradition, or divine order—but the order that is immanent in our existence and to which we refer when we wish to qualify or disqualify this or that man, or such and such conduct.

The entire development of morals is found in principle in the initial choice in virtue of which one situates it either in the abstract, in the domain of rational justification and as a universe of discourse outside the world, or on the contrary in the human reality, among its concrete engagements, on the level of the exigencies that affirm themselves in fact in order to orientate our activities. The concrete rootedness of our action cannot be sought and found except in a study of the conditions of all personal affirmation. There is not, and there cannot be, a rupture between the values that are immanent to man's conduct taken in its totality and the indications of morals. Or rather, if morals indeed presuppose a divorce between the being of man and his having-to-be, as it all too often happens, they are condemned to a definitive extraterritoriality. The morals of that rational moral being in general, such as Kant conceives of it, perhaps hold for living species outside the human race that may exist on other planets. It

[1] René Le Senne, *Traité de morale générale* (Paris: Presses Universitaires de France, 1942), p. 693. [Supra, p. 130]

is too bad that they do not apply sufficiently, do not apply really, to the concrete man because they do not accept him in his authentic reality. The hypothetical advantage of Kant's morals in the order of extension unfortunately does not mean much if one compares it with the certain disadvantage with respect to the comprehension of man's being in a situation in the human world, which in any case remains the only thing that counts for a morals that is conscious of its own mission.

By determining and adhering to its original place in the world of values, concrete morals bring about a conversion that implies for its proper domain the conversion of contemporary philosophy. The philosophy of values in fact asserts itself as a renewal of thought at the end of the nineteenth century. It becomes connected with the philosophy of action and existential philosophies, which equally insist on presence to the world, engagement, and on the destiny of man in his immanence in the world. . . . (51–52)

2 VALUE AND REALITY

The traditional reflective attitude that tries to grasp a value in the judgment is inclined to oppose value and reality. The real is a datum, the value is an appreciation of this datum. Polin writes, "Value is not a real given thing, it is essentially imaginary and unreal."[2] Thus one could make a distinction between a knowledge of the given, a positive knowledge without engagement; and a knowledge according to values, which entails the intervention of a new form of affirmation. The evaluation is here distinguished from objective knowledge in a completely categorical manner. "Value," Polin goes on to say, "through its very presence witnesses the essential principle of axiological consciousness, but it does not reveal it as a real knowledge would, which is a conscious grasp, by means of integral immanence in the object and adequation with it. The evaluation constitutes a deliberate transcendence that brings about a hierarchy and creates, but that does not

[2] Raymond Polin, *La création des valeurs* (Paris: Presses Universitaires de France, 1944), p. 292. [Supra, p. 202]

reveal any data." It seems that under these conditions one will eventually end up placing nature opposite to value, value being defined, as man himself, to be added to nature. Polin prefers to underline "the irreducible heterogeneity of values and truths."[3]

Now, this unreality of values, as well as this conception of reality, nature before any value, by no means corresponds to the concrete experience of man. If instead of considering reflective and conceptualized operations, one makes an effort to understand the spontaneity of personal affirmation, it is clear that our being in the world cannot become conscious of itself except through the incarnation of values in the lived situation. All knowledge, however humble it may be, coincides with a value experience. Thus one cannot genuinely distinguish between an axiological, or evaluating, consciousness, and an objective, or purely psychological, consciousness.

For us, value is the first and necessary revealing factor of the world. This is already clear on the level of perception. We never face a universe that is indifferent and given as flatly lying before us, in its impersonal determination. Our knowledge of the universe always remains partial and biased, demanded by the exigency of this or that need. Alain insisted on the fact that we never see the six sides of a cube at the same time. It is incompletely given to our perception and is always seen in perspective. But the true cube, said Alain, is the one that one never sees except through the eyes of the mind. In the same way for intellectualism, which tries to preserve the objective reality of nature, the real world is the world of science, visible only through the eyes of science. It is in this way that a universe of reason becomes substituted for the universe of our concrete experience.

It is this universe of the concrete that we must try to retrieve here. Our knowledge of a given landscape offers itself to us spontaneously in a signification pertaining to the lived moment of our life. Effective perception is never equivalent to the complete panorama of the moment. It omits an indefinite number of possibilities that are offered nonetheless to

[3] Ibid., p. 293. [Supra, pp. 202–3]

our sense organs. It selects from among all the sensorial possibilities the reality of the perceived. This passage from the possible to the real in the entire extension of our knowledge corresponds to the intervention of personal values. Far from being unreal, from opposing itself to nature, value, then, is the ground of all reality, the structure and climate of affirmation. Le Senne correctly says, value is "atmospherical."[4] It basks in its own presence, and magnetizes each moment of our history with its action.

Thus the universality of value is closely related to its constant presence, which is independent of all reflective judgment. The affirmation of values is immediate, it expresses the spontaneity of man's being on all the levels of his activities, beginning with the most humble. Value is tied to our sensibility. Bréhier notes that it has value "because its presence in an object is felt as the satisfaction of a need."[5] Each moment of a man's life situates itself in a universe that is oriented and polarized by momentary or constant exigencies of the person. Absolute equilibrium and perfect objectivity, which would coincide with perfect indifference, never constitute the state of a living man. Our presence to the world is defined by certain vigilances that impose their directives upon our activity. I am hungry, I am restless, I am happy, or I am unhappy—these are some of the many conscious or implicit constitutional principles of the setting of my universe at a particular instant. There is no "truth," there is no "nature" independent of this immanent orientation that makes the exterior reality pass from the state of brute and neutral presence to the state of representation in the heart of our thought. We always situate ourselves in a field of values that for the moment in question inspire our "awareness of nature."

This constant and decisive presence of value can sometimes seem to decrease, depreciate, and disqualify itself. But just as in the most immediate spontaneity there can be a value attitude before consciousness, so there can be a value affirmation when consciousness has retired. Habit, mechanical rou-

4 René Le Senne, *Obstacle et valeur* (Paris: Aubier, 1934), p. 175.
5 Émile Bréhier, "Doutes sur le philosophie des valeurs," *Revue de Métaphysique et de Morale*, 1939, p. 406.

tine, seems to empty our conduct of its real signification. But in reality, even there the value that has become unapparent continues to justify our human conduct. The most automatic gesture presupposes a consent to the world, a deliberate decision to live in a certain way that was admitted at one time: implicit affirmation, value judgment without judgment, but by no means less essential. The affirming power of the automatism comes to full light the moment a rupture occurs and we must disengage ourselves from one tradition in order to inaugurate a new tradition. Then there is the difficulty of physical, intellectual, and spiritual experiences to be "learned." The value of the automatism appears in full light when we have to abandon it. That is the drama of all renunciations. One does not give up without difficulty a group, a family, a nationality, a religion. And one discovers then how much weight these evidences, which are so familiar that one no longer notices them, bring to bear on life.

This constituting action of values thus assures the unity, the cohesion, of the universe for each given individual. One cannot define an order of truths except by situating it outside all reach of man. An order of things cannot subsist unless one disconnects it first from our appropriation of things, which precisely gives it its meaning. The moment we appropriate a truth or a thing, it enters a system of values, it takes on a value that is never completely amortized, it becomes defined in function of a reference system represented by this or that particular existence. From the first moment I intend it, each scientific truth takes on for me a certain meaning within the context of my thought and life—and this meaning necessarily differs from one man to the other. There could not be any truth without an action, a thought, a person. Someone, a being, a living being, places himself upon the immense background of natural possibilities and actualizes some of them, which are then detached from the whole and promoted from the unreal to existence. Otherwise even the activity of the animal creates a universe that the animal organizes according to the lines of force that correspond to its proper values.

It seems that values, far from opposing themselves to the

real, correspond to that complex function defined by modern psychiatry under the name of *sense of the real*, and upon which Pierre Janet has insisted so emphatically. There is a question here of a superior function of equilibrium that assures insertion of the person into the world, good contact with beings and things. The affirmation of our being in the world materializes more or less completely according to the degree of continuity and harmony attained by the way we are rooted in our milieu. Our activity really satisfies us only if we feel we have come to grips with what surrounds us, if there is really agreement between us and our environment. This superior unity of the ego and the world is like a ratification and mutual validation in which the success or failure of an existence resolves itself. Personal experience taken as a whole intervenes as a calling into question of man, as an examination of conscience, or rather of his own being, as a revelation of authenticity. Man will show himself to be capable or incapable of taking himself upon himself and of taking the world upon himself. The test of life is the test of personal validity. Beginning with confused needs, instincts, and primitive tendencies, a personal, well-ordered history will constitute itself, enter the universe via a detour of the circumstances. Or the event will find us at fault, transcend our possibilities, and finally ratify the failure of our being in the world. . . . (55–59)

[In fact there is a pathology of values whose existence confirms our conception of value as the principle of the constitution of the real. After giving some examples, Gusdorf continues:]

All these cases seem to confirm quite well that man's experience at all levels of his development must be understood as a value experience. It is the value, this or that value immanent to our action, that gives us reality and determines its meaning in our opinion. A theory of knowledge and a doctrine concerning activity must take their points of departure from an exegesis of values. To the extent that moral exigency is authentic, it must prolong this requirement of primitive spontaneity. Morals must constitute themselves in the authentic man, and not outside him or against him. It will thus have its meaning in an effort to constitute the unity of man's experience. For if values manifest themselves often in an isolated state, they organize themselves in us as an inclination toward the totality that transcends each moment and aims at a total expression of our being. Permanently, and beyond the occasional cause, beyond the particular engagements of this or that situation, a global anticipation of the complete realization of our being in the world affirms itself in us. The very meaning of our activity organizes in this manner a horizon beyond the more or less narrow circumscription of present activity.

3 JUSTIFICATION OF VALUE

Value therefore offers itself to us under the form of an orientation immanent to our conscious grasp of the real, the very form of man's affirmation under all circumstances. In this way all the structures of our activity should be defined in function of values, so that a general determination of human values would finally lead to designing an outline of action. From this, one understands the importance of the meaning of all our significations and the necessity of better clarifying its nature. Moreover, if value is found everywhere, one must regroup the intentions in which it expresses itself, in so far as this is possible, in order to avoid a pluralistic subjectivism, in which all hope of any possible reconciliation between men would be lost. For each one, value is that which anticipates and authorizes his experience; it is the project in us of the experience to come. Thus it is important to recover it once again in its origins, in its fundament, which cannot be the appanage of the individual. The very validity of value demands caution here. Beyond the human fact of the exigency of value, it is necessary to search for a right that guarantees it, and that in addition permits us to assure the convergence of individual experiences. The problem of the fundament of values thus becomes connected to the problem concerning the foundation of morals.

A first conception of value takes as its point of departure the incontestable relation between the lived value and the

fundamental tendencies of the organism. The elementary affirmation of values prolongs the vital needs. For man, just as
for the animal, the first needs are those of nourishment, shelter, and the sexual needs. These needs define in a very great
number of situations what is important in our eyes. This
explains the vast number of doctrines that see in values the
prolongation of our organic structure. Vital usefulness would
be the value whose sign could be found in the pleasure or
pain that sanctions for the individual the encounter with
this object or that circumstance. The world of values would
then be no more than the intellectualized and sublimated
expression of a biological finality. In short, this is the thesis
defended by the evolutionist thinkers, Spencer in particular,
who take all the consequences of Darwin's scientific theories
in this way. We appreciate each experience according to the
degree of satisfaction or dissatisfaction it procures for us.
And this appreciation is justified to the degree to which our
being in the world essentially corresponds to our organic equilibrium. All human activity strives to maintain the existence
of and the search for as many and as varied satisfactions as
possible. . . . (61–62)

[Such a view, which seems to be justified in a great number
of circumstances, is unacceptable, mainly because it is incapable of explaining the value experience in its entirety:
pleasure is not always a criterion of value, and it is certainly
not the only one, if pleasure is understood in the sense of
biological naturalism.]

This moral and intellectual insufficiency of biological naturalism has been clearly understood by other thinkers, who,
struck by the opposition between nature and value, have en-
deavored to constitute an order of values in a more direct
relationship to the human reality. Far from being an affirmation of nature, values appear in this case as the expression
of a right man has to recapture nature. The fundament of
value is found in the transcendence of nature, in an affirmation of ideals. On the other hand, the existing values are not
merely decisions of the subject. They assure a certain unity
among men. They are recognized, and in case of need impose
themselves upon, human collectivities with an authority that

does not take into account the immediate interests or aversions of any one individual. It is a matter of fact that values assure a certain unity among men in this way. But this unity cannot be extended to the human species in its entirety. Values become modified as time goes on. And, in the same period of time, they vary from one collectivity to another, from country to country, and from social class to social class.

Thus the foundation of values should from this point on no longer be sought in the inhuman meaning of a purely biological organization, but rather in a supra-individual will, in the promotion of individual aspirations that justify the behavior of all and each one in particular. That is the conception proposed by Durkheim in a famous study. In Durkheim's view, value judgments, which are irreducible to nature, refer to an ideal reality that itself is the work and the reflection of collective existence. It is in this way that subordination of the egoistic interest in regard to the goals that transcend it, can be explained. Society delivers us from nature. . . . (63–64)

Thus Durkheim's naturalism finally ends up by making values a kind of domain that is independent of our personal activity. Values are given to the person, who receives them ready-made and must conform to them, just as he must conform to "the laws of nature." Durkheim, like his predecessor Auguste Comte, passes directly from biology to sociology without granting any importance to the individual existence of man. But it is a fact that our experience proves that values in their social expression do not compel man with the same necessity as the law of gravitation, for instance. Furthermore, there is no experience of value nor any value attribution in the strict sense as long as the value is not recognized as such, consented to, and willed by the subject himself. Obedience to the laws of physics takes place automatically and does not implicate our merit or demerit. On the contrary, the experience of value judges us to the extent to which it requires an engagement on our part, a certain range for interpreting the nature of the data or the choice between them. Durkheim's doctrine, thus, disregards the appropriation of value, which is a decisive element of our experience. [Durkheim has felt these difficulties, but in Gusdorf's view he has not succeeded in completely overcoming them in the different attempts he has made in this regard.] (65–66)

In our opinion, the characteristic trait that all these views have in common is that they tend to deprive man of his experience. Philosophies of nature and philosophies of mind finally come to define an order of values in itself that is determined in an impersonal objectivity. What is important in these is not my body, my existence, but the species, the social group. It is not my thought, but Thought in itself that becomes mine only when I am willing to erase everything I am. The individual destiny that nonetheless is the main affirmation of man, his sharing of the world, has to move to a second level; our personal life with its uncertainties and battles seems to be disqualified. Dupréel has expressed this quite correctly: "The basic mistake of classical morals is that it reduces the explanation of morals to a transfer operation: the philosopher hopes to posit (that is to say to discover) value once and for all: God, the order of the world, the nature of the soul, happiness, in such a way that the only thing left to be done is to transfer this value to the activity of each of us, just as one cashes a check from a bank account."[6] This capitalist scheme of value thus ultimately leads to immobilizing value, to ratifying in this conception a kind of deprivation of the person, whose whole effort should strive after casting aside whatever in it constitutes an obstacle to the affirmation of universal truth. (68)

4　Values and the Measure of Man

The insufficiency of all these conceptions of values, however different they may appear in their affirmations, consists thus in fact in a common lack of appreciation of the human reality. For the defenders of sociologism, for those who defend biological naturalism, as well as for those who defend various forms of metaphysical rationalism, the experience of value

[6] E. Dupréel, "La morale et les valeurs, consistance et précarité," *Bulletin de la Société française de philosophie*, 1936, p. 71. Cf. also: *Esquisse d'une philosophie des valeurs* (Paris: Alcan, 1939).

is merely an epiphenomenon added to the very being of value. Value suffices in itself. It does not gain anything by this insertion into a personal life. Reality in the proper sense of the term is not found at the level of personal activity. The latter takes on an illusory character, and theorists endeavor much more to exorcise it than to comprehend it. The experience of value would be the one subjective side of a coin whose other side is the only real one, just as is the case in Spinoza's system.

Value theory thus does an injustice to the concrete man, and in addition, does not even try to understand him. It does not preoccupy itself at all with assuring his unity. For the evolutionists, man is above all an organism that fools consciousness; for the intellectualists, man is a consciousness who must not let himself be fooled by his body; for the sociologists, he appears to be an individual support destined to serve as the place where collective representations are to be inserted. The personal dimension in its originality appears here to be misunderstood in all cases. As we have seen, Comte and Durkheim pass from biology to sociology without making room for a psychology or an anthropology that situates the human condition at its proper place between the two disciplines that border it without being able to absorb it. Descartes was more frank when he declared the union of soul and body to be unintelligible and yet to be constitutive for personal existence. The mystery he affirmed without being able to clarify, seems to have maintained all of its opacity in his successors.

The characteristic originality of the concept of value lies precisely in the fact that it is located at the borders of body and thought, in this original penumbra from which the meaning of our entire being in the world proceeds. The philosophers who were pressed to put value into formulas in order to be able to reduce it, have brought it completely over to the order of thought. In this way, morals are subordinated to an ideal of rational transparency, where the autonomy of the intellect asserts its authority. All activity is then considered as subjected (in theory at least) to a judgment, to collective or rational representations. If it is true that only what is explicitly conscious and consciously justified, has dignity, then one can neglect the biological elements, because they are transcendent to reason, transcendent, that is, downward by means of a transcendence of a bad sort. Thought is self-sufficient. Under these conditions, there are moralists who have been able to assimilate human activity in a universe of discourse and to formulate the principles of an arithmetic of pleasure and pain in which the good activity finds its inspiration. According to Bentham, in each situation the sage measures the pleasures and discomforts for himself and for the other. Once the situation is thus put into an equation, he chooses from among the different possibilities that which represents the greatest positive advantage, to be paid for by the least discomfort. He thus acts as if in this way the entire human existence could be taken apart in pieces that are isolated and identical from one experience to another and could be reduced to a common measure. The intellectualist aberration, the lack of appreciation of the unity of man and the singularity of the existing being, has reached its fullest development here.

If one refuses to mutilate the existence of man, the concept of value appears then in its essential signification of being the intermediary between body and mind. If it assures the unity of our concrete experience, it is to the degree that it expresses an engagement of the indivisible human reality. The great biologist Monakow has shown that values are rooted in the organism, whose exigencies they prolong into the order of thought. . . . (68–70)

Value taken in the fullness of its concrete signification presents itself, therefore, not as a lucid affirmation of a thinking subject, but as the putting-to-work of the human reality as the function that regulates the whole. Our fleshy being finds itself mobilized, and consciousness clarifies only a part, and perhaps, even not the most decisive part, of the operation. That is the reason why value taken as the meaning of an engagement of a human being can never be reduced to the measure of a formula, regardless of what this may be. Our existence materializes to the same degree as does our incarnation, which must be understood in its effective signification of reciprocally symbolizing the organism and thought under the inspiration of a common finality. If one wishes to avoid a definitive lack of appreciation of man's existence, there cannot be any question of reducing one of these two orders to the other, and thus of denying what it, in fact, contributes to the composition of our life. The constitutive individuality of each personal life is defined by the reciprocal implication of body and mind, as the foundation of all presence to the world taken in its singularity. The totalitarian doctrines of value, which place it on the level of the Spirit, Society, or Reason, always fail to resolve the question concerning our individuality. Here the individual is always accounted for in function of a superior reality that is more true than he, and that alone is authentic.

Thus the individual must remain the point of departure as well as that of arrival in a satisfying doctrine concerning values. The definition of value must make it an object of personal experience, of a choice and preference in function of which the subject becomes engaged, and which he thus abandons at the same time he aspires to it. The experience of value is an experience of the person, a promotion of the individual; and one cannot speak of value in the moral sense of the term if there is still a question of passive obedience, of pure conformity to an organic or a social imperative. But this is not tantamount to saying that the determination aimed at in this way would situate itself beyond all organic and social circumstances as if it were an absolute beginning. On the contrary, the biological needs manifested by our instincts and social needs specified by collective representations, play an essential part in the value drama. It is always between them that it must make its choice, for or against their opposed complaints. To choose is to always obey them, or rather adjust oneself to this or that perspective of nature, be it personally human or social. Here as everywhere else, freedom is not an arbitrary and gratuitous creation, but choice, integration into that situation in which it must bring about, from among the possibles, the real to come.

One could obtain some clarity here from the distinction that biologists have established between social milieu and the

organic basis of our individuality. Our organic being carries
with it a certain number of structures that are constitutive
for the species and enriched by hereditary acquisitions. But
the milieu intervenes in the affirmation of the individual
position. Its influence facilitates and directs in man to a certain extent the conscious grasp and utilization of the virtual-
ities that are inscribed in the organism. The social milieu
proposes, to the individual, representations that correspond
to the possibilities he carries within himself. But these social
determinations are not imposed upon a passive being, who
would adopt them without further ado and in a certain sense
would owe to them his very existence. They are presented
to a being who in each epoch and under every climate possesses a certain biological structure. The same instincts, the
same elementary needs, govern in all regions. The individual
can speak of them in a different way, but he is by no means
less bound to satisfy them, or to come to terms with them in
one way or another. The unity of all thought therefore consists in the immanent and biologically necessary unity of
man's being, so that there cannot be any question of calling,
concerning this matter, upon an acquired universality, that
of reason.

The fundamental biological unity has imposed its form in
advance on the collective representations determined by the
milieu. The individuals recognize in it an anticipated formulation of themselves. The possibilities so offered depend,
themselves, upon the human form in function of which they
have been formulated. Thus one could defend before the
sociologists the point of view that society depends upon man
and not man upon society. But at any rate, the human dimension is the one that intervenes between the biological and
the social. The individual intervenes in order to consciously
take possession of himself in a situation in which the multiplicity of roles he can possibly make his own are already determined: a situation that above all characterizes the *superabundance of determinations*. Contrary to what sociologists
as well as biologists, each in their own domain, usually subscribe to, there is no absolute social or organic imperative. At
every moment there is the necessity of a sorting through the

possibilities that are available. It thus suffices that the person, for one reason or for another, recovers the meaning of the concrete reality of a situation distorted through habit, and that the experience of value reassumes its rights. Throughout the whole life of an existence that once has been awakened to itself, value remains man's share.

From this it is understandable that one could use two languages to define value. Two meanings and, as it were, two opposed sources offer themselves to justify the experience of value, depending upon whether or not the theorist is more particularly attentive to the organic origins of the affirmation of values and places them in the extension of our instincts beyond clear consciousness, or whether he adheres to the value judgments formulated by the milieu and made explicit by it for the education of the individual. In the first case, values are closely related to needs. In the second, they transcend the needs of the individual and together constitute a superior order that is imposed on man as a unity of goals for his aspirations, and that is often in manifest disagreement with his instinctive preferences and egoist interests.

This duality of interpretation results in a kind of divorce, which splits in two parts the philosophy of values that is disputed among these two opposed orientations. If value refers to tendencies and instincts, one will end up in the doctrine of materialist and organicist persuasion, which reduces the superior to the inferior and is incapable of justifying ideal values, contenting itself with discrediting them instead. Or, if one is attentive to the ideal character of values, if one bases oneself on their frequent opposition to the immediate exigencies of man's nature, one will develop a spiritualist but disincarnated conception in which value affirms a reality that contradicts normal experience. . . . (70–73)

In the end, one arrives at the necessity of distinguishing between a domain of organic values and a domain of spiritual values, which corresponds to a double vocation in man, the one natural and the other supernatural. Or more exactly, the human reality finds itself dissociated between two concomitant and simply juxtaposed existences. Man's nature becomes unintelligible. Thus the philosophy of values does not get beyond simply recovering the ancient difficulty of the union of soul and body. Just as is the case with the classical doctrines, it does not hesitate to formulate almost insoluble problems and the most complicated solutions, without succeeding in any way in rejoining the pure and simple affirmation of our common experience, which gives us the unity of man as a fact. The latter does not pay any attention to our difficulties in analyzing it; nor does it wait in order to affirm itself until we have given it the right to exist.

It thus seems to conform more with the reality of things to take our point of departure in this basic experience rather than in our intellectual presuppositions. In fact, man's activity taken in its entirety obeys certain rhythms. Unlike a soul that has bound a body and tries to get out of it again as much as it can—as Chateaubriand said of Joubert—man, as being of flesh and mind, affirms through his presence in the world an ensemble of aspirations and needs that will doubtlessly fail to materialize without some conflict, without for that reason usually breaking the unity of man's existence apart. It is this basic measure of man that inspires values at all levels of his experience. It is not possible to understand and justify them from their most humble emergence to their highest accomplishment, except by relating them to the concrete person as he finds himself in a situation in the universe.

Indeed, it is clear that values derive their meaning from man's structure and that in the final analysis all other interpretations refer to this basic structure. . . . (73–74)

5 ANTHROPOLOGY OF VALUES

. . . The originality of man's experience depends precisely on the interdependent unity between body and thought that it materializes. The values present at the level of the most primitive forms of behavior of the animal, which they guide toward their object, qualify not only the immediate and concrete universe of man, but also the world of his thought. It appears, for instance, to be difficult to separate from our sexual instinct the hierarchy of the forms of life that express it at all levels of man's experience. For man, as for the animal, the sexual instinct inspires forms of behavior that tend toward mating. But these forms of conduct and the experience they constitute are capable of spiritualizing themselves in man. The love between man and wife grows richer with the help of all the resources of thought. It is capable of polarizing all the energy of the person and, finally, of developing the simple organic vocation into a very complete realization of self. In this respect, if suffices to think of the immense place that love occupies in literature and art. And what is more, love can in a certain sense transcend its physiological condition and emancipate itself from it, whether this be through sacrifice or in the sublimated forms of human charity or love of God. And yet it would be absurd to deny the community of intention to which these very different aspects of our experience of value testify. It always concerns the same constitutive sector of man's nature, but little by little it is subjected to new influences which time and again renew its expression. To cut off the love of God or the love of Beauty from their organic roots would be tantamount to disembodying them and reducing them to an abstract tendency in which man could never completely engage himself. Plato himself never thought of that. But, inversely, to pretend that love of God or our passion for beauty are no more than camouflaged expressions of sexual instincts that in themselves do not present any original value, would mean to ignore the fact that the destiny of man has as its proper domain this promotion of the biological to the spiritual. It seems that certain theorists of psychoanalysis, eager to discover more or less disguised manifestations of sexuality everywhere, have sometimes believed it possible to "reduce" all our personal life to some of these biological conditions. In so doing, they have shown themselves to be incapable of understanding the specificity of the human order.

The truth about man must be found in the refusal of these attempts at dissociation, whose misapprehension will incessantly falsify our understanding of man in situation in the world. In order to discover the meaning of the difficulty, it

is necessary to go back to the very conditions of intelligibility.
Man can become aware of his presence in the world in two
different ways. Two possibilities of expression determine for
him two styles of intellectual and spiritual life.

A first form of knowledge retains from sensation the information with which it provides us about the exterior world;
openness, receptivity, and (as far as possible) forgetting of
personal implications. Here the universe appears as a totality
of objects proposed for our action, which must utilize them
to the best of our interests. From this it follows that man
makes an effort here to determine as clearly as possible the
objective panorama that surrounds him. This is the perspective of the *homo faber* anxious to assure his subsistence. It
permits the creation and development of techniques that are
inspired by a completely spontaneous pragmatism. It is a
question of mastering the world and thus first of obeying
it, that is to say, making for oneself a personal life in its
image, clearly determined and effective. This attitude prolongs itself in the order of thought that little by little formulates itself in us as a universe that must double the universe
of things in order that we may be able to manage it from
within. To the stability of the object, there corresponds the
fixedness of word and concept in the universe of discourse.
In this way the word allows us not only to conveniently put
the world into an equation, but in addition, it also assures
communication between men, good understanding, by suppressing individual variations. It is in this way that our discursive knowledge, and science (which forms its crown), become constituted little by little. Mathematics represents the
final result of this form of knowledge, which is brought here
to its highest perfection. Here is the domain of impersonality,
of truth in the third person, which eliminates the subject in
favor of the object. Man's mind hopes to universalize this
triumph, to make mathematics govern over nature, which
thus can be tamed, and over thought itself. Intellectualist
philosophy, taking as its basic elements clear and distinct
ideas that it endeavors to unify according to a geometrical
order, constitutes a generalization of this first attitude of

man-in-situation in the world. It seems that the meaning of the situation is somehow lost here. The subject that intellectualism talks about has disengaged itself from its limitations. It dominates the universe, which it has put into equations. Or rather, in view of the fact that its attempt at mathematization always suffers from some limitations, it imagines a thought more perfectly rational than its own, on which it acknowledges itself to be dependent. This triumphing thought represents for it divine Thought. The latter defines the unity of its aspirations, and the provisionally inaccessible meaning of all human values.

Thus this first attempt at intelligibility leads finally to defining a form of knowledge that is more perfect to the degree that it is more dehumanized. Individuality represents merely an arbitrary factor, an aberration factor in regard to the Truth. In fact, intellectualism guarantees the preponderance of objectivity, of exterior reality, starting from the elementary necessities of action. But the real as it is immediately lived implies not only man as subject of representation, center of all perspectives, that is to say as abstract point of view, but as real presence to the universe. The "I am" is anterior to the "I think." Intellectualism endeavors to exorcise the first person without being able to succeed completely in its enterprise. Language, and science, which is the rationalization of language, immobilize me, make of me an object in the world of objects. This is the domain of impersonality and anonymity. The identity of words presupposes the identity of the moments of my personal reality, which they designate.

The discontinuity, the solidity, of things and words disguise the fundamental dimension of our personal life, which gives itself to us first as unity, continuity, mutual interiority of the moments of our existence. . . . (77–80)

In opposition to this knowledge in the third person, which is analytic and can be formulated, there is, thus, a knowledge in the first person, according to the order of quality, intensity, and interiority. The senses disperse us in the world. Words wrest us away from ourselves. They implant in our mind the

certitudes of the other. But in our innermost self we know of
another certitude, which is without a doubt the only authentically valid one, however much it withdraws from all discursive elucidation. Our presence in the world nourishes itself
from our capacity for love, intuition, and sympathy. We
place the best part of our very being not into the rigor of
analysis, but in the communication that is beyond words, and
perhaps even in silence. It is from this knowledge of the world
that art, poetry, and religion provide more or less happy and
complete expressions, but witness the definitive powerlessness
of the objective style, of the language of the mind, to evoke
the ultimate realities. The personal style, on the contrary,
supposes the engagement of the person, who no longer distinguishes himself from his object and who no longer pretends to manipulate it as he sees fit. The object is no more
than the symbol for the integral reality of our personal life,
body, mind, intelligence, as well as of obscure influences,
unconscious roots, the entire, constant presence of the organism. . . .(80)

[Gusdorf refers then to the fact that the distinction he is
trying to describe seems to be at the basis of Dilthey's and
Weber's distinction between explaining and understanding,
and Marcel's distinction between problem and mystery.]

Thus it seems that in the distinction between the two types
of intelligibility we find again the part of man who affirmed
himself in connection with the conceptions of values. On the
one hand, there is a tendency to disembody and affirm ideal
and transcendent essences, which are objectively valid for all
and everyone. On the other hand, there is the affirmation of
an irreducible, personal singularity which in the final analysis
is intimately connected with organic existence and more particularly with the instincts. Philosophers believe that they are
forced to choose in one direction or the other. Their theories
thus endeavor to recapture the human experience by means
of a kind of passage to a limit which blocks the experience's
entire reality in this or that mode of its affirmation. This is
an attempt that in principle is doomed to failure. For the
systematization that is thus established proves to be incap-

able of accounting for the lived world in its totality. In fact it must secretly reintroduce what it had expressly excluded. Indeed there could not be any completely objective knowledge that would not take personal attitudes into consideration. I am constantly oriented by my intimate moods. The intellectualist, obstinate prejudice represents a certain engagement of the human reality. It disembodies man only seemingly. In fact, it stylizes its total expression in a particular direction. The negation of the body does not suffice to answer the question. Rationalists such as Descartes, Spinoza, and Brunschvicg are certainly forced to recover the organic existence that at first they disqualified: it intervenes again under the form of a confused, degraded, but tenacious knowledge. . . . (81–82)

[But on the other hand, it is equally true that first-person knowledge is incapable of materializing the unity of knowledge adequately. It would be meaningless to appeal exclusively to an immediate, completely instinctive, purely intuitive knowledge which closes its eyes to the world. All genuine awareness presupposes incarnation, that is, intervention of objective elements that must support the affirmation of the most subjective moments of man's experience. (82–83)]

. . . It is possible, however, to give a positive meaning to this duality of functions of man's knowledge. It is inscribed in our organism, whose anatomy and physiology determine in advance the structure of our knowledge. The central nervous system, that is to say, that system which in the course of history has almost exclusively drawn the attention of philosophers, corresponds to our sensorimotor possibilities. Through its sense organs and its muscular drives, it assures the exterior politics of man being inserted into the world. It furnishes us with the order of things, which, moreover, thanks to the support of the central functions of the brain, it allows us to redouble through the universe of discourse, that is, through our spoken and thought language. It is in this way that the order of our discursive intelligence develops, which as we have shown, tends to acquire a kind of monopoly in the eyes of scientists and philosophers.

But contemporary neurobiology has brought to light the

existence of a more primitive regulation than that of our
cerebrospinal system.[7] Whereas the sensorimotor functions
situate us in relation to the environment, our personal affirmation, our presence to ourselves, is affirmed in internal
sensations, the coenesthesic consciousness of the organism, in
our affective life and our instinctive needs. It is at this level
that the interior politics of the person is at work. It inscribes
itself in our organism under the form of regulations whose
nature appears today in a clearer way; the sympathetic system, the hormonal regulations that depend upon glands with
internal secretion, constitute a complex totality that is subordinated to the influence of the lower brain. Our vegetative
equilibrium depends upon this ancient region of our nervous
system. The great vital rhythms, for instance that of sleep,
here find the justification for their good or bad influence.

Moreover, it is clear that man's integrity demands a close
and constant correlation of the sensorimotor and the peripheral systems. Their mutual implication remains at each instant the law of our activity. Not only would it be absurd to
imagine a man who had lost one of these systems, but what is
more, the slightest alteration of one of them is reflected in
the other and entails a lack of balance about conduct in its
entirety. Our presence in the world in its full signification
depends upon a psychobiological health whose different com-
ponents must harmonize with one another at each instant of
our existence. We are in the world not only through our external senses, which tell us about its configuration, or through
our representative faculties, which further develop the data
of the senses; we are in the world on the basis of all of our
neurobiological reality. The right contact with reality, the
meaning of the real, supposes the dense affirmation of the
body, its heat, its affectivity, and its desires, to which it inspires us. The sensorimotor indications do no more than develop the primary data of our biological needs, through which
we are rooted in the universe. Their contributions symbolize
for our discursive consciousness that primary affirmation of

---

[7] I have justified these views more extensively in my book *La
découverte de soi* (Paris: Presses Universitaires de France, 1948),
pp. 301 ff.

us to ourselves. The objective knowledge of that which is not us, thus, always hides an indirect knowledge of our personal being. . . . (83–84)

[Using a distinction suggested by Von Monakov and Mourgue,[8] namely that between the sphere of our instincts and the sphere of sensation and causality, Gusdorf suggests that the former refers to the origin and the very being of values.] Values have their foundation in the sphere of our instincts. They originate in us from the primary needs. In any case, they express themselves first in our personal life as desires, unjustifiable compulsions. Needs felt, preferences, reasons of the heart, presentiments—these are the things in which that which is essential in a personality quite often expresses itself. But in order to penetrate to clear consciousness, to acquire genuine dignity in thought, values must be reassumed at the level of the sphere of the sensations and of causality. They find themselves then assumed by language, constituted into concepts, and rationally justified.

There is therefore a second intellectual birth of values when they pass from the biological order to the sensorimotor order so that they may acquire their indispensable expression. The mistake intervenes when one supposes that the second birth is in fact the first. . . . (85)

An authentic comprehension of values must try to recover in them, beyond the artificial constructions of intellectualism, the fundament of each particular experience, a kind of measure of man that is immanent in the development of his activity and alone capable of giving him its meaning. Values proceed from the biological determination of existence. But it would be useless to pretend to reduce them to those organic data in which their point of departure indeed consists—just as much as reduction to a completely conceptualized system proves to be unjustifiable. The originality of value consists, in fact, in its function of being the principle for the development of personal history. Effective value is a reality of psychobiological nature. Being the intermediary for the connec-

[8] Von Monakov and Mourgue, *Introduction à l'étude de la neurologie et de la psychopathologie* (Paris: Alcan, 1928), p. 41.

tion between the body and the mind, the person and the world, it can affirm itself on all kinds of levels according to the vicissitudes of destiny. In reality, it represents the meaning of our presence in the world and corresponds in a concrete form to that principal of individuation with which certain generations of philosophers have been preoccupied. Values underlie the irreducible unity of human expressions. From the biological to the vital, from the vital to the spiritual, these same fundamental intentions manifest themselves through a series of successive promotions.

It would thus be false to consider values as an organic *a priori*—or as an intellectual and metaphysical *a priori*. It is nonetheless true that, starting with the biological structures of the individual being, they imply all the moments of its action and all the manifestations of its thought. But it would be an insufficient schema that would distinguish an area of values before all experience, and an area of value expression in the very heart of man's conduct. One cannot dissociate concrete values from their affirmation, which permits a kind of education of their primitive exigencies. For each personal life there is a destiny of values. They are like ciphers of personal events. However, reciprocally, the events in which they become incarnated and settled, constitute, themselves, a kind of cipher of our essential values. The interpretation reacts here on the primitive intention. Intention and realization are interdependent. They form one body. That is why there is an uncertainty, the possibility of a development, progress and regression, betrayal and fidelity: the whole history of self-discovery and self-creation. The given should not be abstracted from the lived, which does not translate it but rather gives it being by bringing it up to the mark. The first and the third person symbolize mutually; they make one another fruitful, and give one another a new being which is distinct from their respective contributions, which ratifies an enrichment in regard to the one and only subjectivity as well as to pure objectivity.

This explains the ambiguity of value, and this appearance of refusal which always hides it from our grasp. It is the reason as well as the regulation of our existence. It founds our being in the world; it roots us among things and makes us have a solidarity with the beings that surround us. It materializes the effective structure of the lived universe. And thus it is the fundamental element of our moral life, a quest for the most complete equilibrium between us and ourselves, and us and the others. (86–88)

SELECTIVE BIBLIOGRAPHY

La découverte de soi (Paris: Presses Universitaires de France, 1948)
Traité de l'existence morale (Paris: Colin, 1949)
La vertu de force (Paris: Presses Universitaires de France, 1956)
Signification humaine de la liberté (Paris: Payot, 1962)

Part III: THREE CONTEMPORARY CONCEPTIONS OF HUMANISM

This part of the book constitutes an attempt to compare three different forms of humanism found in the so-called "existentialist" literature: namely, the conceptions of Sartre, Camus, and Heidegger.

I have already indicated why I think the term "existentialism" is a rather inadequate label to characterize these three conceptions; strictly speaking, it applies only to the view defended by Sartre. On the other hand I do not deny that, taken in a broader sense and provided it be interpreted differently in each case, the term could be used in this connection and extended so as to include the views of Camus and Heidegger, authors who have almost nothing in common except for the fact that, like Sartre, they have used the label "humanism" to characterize their views.

As far as Sartre is concerned, I have made a brief survey of his view on ethics as found in *Being and Nothingness* and *Existentialism Is a Humanism*. Since I feel that Sartre's view as a whole, and particularly the last section of *Being and Nothingness*, cannot be understood adequately without a good commentary, I have added a selection by Francis Jeanson that explains interpretatively and critically Sartre's basic concern, as well as a selection by Simone de Beauvoir in which Sartre's view is clarified and further developed.

As for Camus, I have decided to include an excellent article on his position in ethics because I feel it is almost impossible to give a clear idea of Camus's position merely by quoting a few selected passages from his works.

Although Heidegger has never explicitly dealt with ethical problems, it seems to me that his *Letter on Humanism* contains some very important and highly relevant suggestions in regard to the conceptions of humanism developed by Sartre and Camus.

Finally, Bollnow's essay is a critical analysis of the position of "existentialist" humanism, mainly the view of Sartre. Bollnow explains why in his opinion a "philosophy of hope" as defended by Marcel is much preferable to the views defended by Sartre, Camus, and Heidegger.

Chapter 9

INTRODUCTION

JEAN-PAUL SARTRE (1905–   ) is certainly the leading
existentialist philosopher in France today. He has promul-
gated his ideas in philosophical, critical, and literary publications. His philosophical position, which is perhaps the only
one properly referred to by the label "existentialism," has
been influenced by the philosophies of Descartes, Malebranche, Kant, Hegel, Nietzsche, Husserl, Heidegger, and
Marx. A great deal of Sartre's work consists in criticism of
the various forms of idealism and dualism that have been
characteristic of the rationalist tradition since Descartes, but
all this criticism notwithstanding, his own thought still contains the mark of its heterogeneous sources. The views to
which Sartre has finally come, first in *Being and Nothingness*
(1943) and later in *Critique de la raison dialectique* (1960),
are without a doubt highly original and personal, but this
original view takes up a tradition to which it remains faithful
in many instances, even while transcending it in many other
respects.

One can distinguish three different phases in Sartre's development. First there is the period in which his interest
focused on phenomenological psychology: *The Transcendence of the Ego* (1936), *Sketch of a Theory of Emotions*
(1939), and *L'Imaginaire* (1940). Second, there is the phase
in which Sartre was mainly interested in a philosophical ontology and its moral implications: *Being and Nothingness*
(1943), *Existentialism Is a Humanism* (1946), *Situations*,
6 vols. (1947–65), *Baudelaire* (1947), *Saint Genet* (1952),
and other publications. Finally there is the period in which

Sartre attempted an extensive restatement of Marxism: *Critique de la raison dialectique* (1960).

The two selections that follow deal exclusively with Sartre's second period. I feel that the selections, taken together, will give the reader a clear idea of Sartre's position in ethics.

SARTRE ON HUMANISM

Joseph J. Kockelmans

In his major work, *Being and Nothingness*, in which he gives an outline of a phenomenological ontology, Sartre explicitly refers (at the very end of his investigations) to the ethical implications of this new kind of ontology.[1] At that point, in 1943, he promised to develop a more systematic survey of an existentialist ethics in a later work,[2] but to date this book has not appeared. Instead, he wrote a popular lecture touching directly upon this issue,[3] and some assorted papers dealing with ethical problems.[4] According to Simone de Beauvoir, by 1950 Sartre had come to the conclusion that the project of working out a systematic ethics was irrelevant, if not completely impossible. He had reached this insight, she tells us, because of his conviction that "the ethical attitude appears in a bourgeois society when technological and social conditions render positive conduct impossible; ethics is no more than a collection of idealist devices to help you live the life that poverty of resources and lack of techniques impose upon you."[5] Sartre returned to this conviction later, but then on

[1] Jean-Paul Sartre, *Being and Nothingness. An Essay on Phenomenological Ontology*, trans. Hazel E. Barnes (New York: Philosophical Library, 1956), pp. 625–28.

[2] Ibid., p. 628.

[3] Jean-Paul Sartre, *Existentialism Is a Humanism*, trans. Philip Mairet, in Walter Kaufmann (ed.), *Existentialism from Dostoevsky to Sartre* (New York: The World Publishing Company, 1956), pp. 287–311.

[4] Jean-Paul Sartre, *Situations*, 6 vols. (Paris: Gallimard, 1947–65).

[5] Simone de Beauvoir, *Les forces des choses* (Paris: Gallimard, 1963), p. 218.

different occasions motivated his view in quite different ways.[6]

Practically, it is beyond the scope of this paper to attempt to deal with the issues connected with Sartre's later position. Whatever his actual position in regard to the topic may be, I shall limit myself here to considering a brief outline of the "existentialist ethics" he promised in *Being and Nothingness,* and some basic related ideas found in his lecture on humanism as well as in some of the papers in *Situations.* Although these ideas have never been systematically developed by Sartre himself in any of his published works, I nevertheless believe that there is sufficient evidence available for a delineation of the basic lines of his thought in the papers just referred to, as well as in the explanatory remarks to be found in the works of de Beauvoir[7] and Jeanson.[8] Some of these ideas are negative in that they explain why many former attempts to develop a systematic ethics were impossible; others are positive and indicate clearly the direction in which Sartre was looking for a new view in regard to the basic principles of morality. I shall begin with the negative elements in his view.

If one adopts Sartre's ontology and notably his conception of the human reality, it becomes immediately evident that an ethics built upon absolute values or standards is excluded in principle. For the fact of freedom means that "in the bright realm of values we have no excuse behind us, nor any justification before us."[9] There is nothing behind us that can justify our own free choice, be this God, Plato's world of Forms, a social moral system, the Freudian unconscious, or external stimuli. And, on the other hand, the values we have chosen are valid only in so far as we have chosen them; they are valu-

---

[6] Hazel E. Barnes, *An Existentialist Ethics* (New York: Knopf, 1967), p. 30.

[7] Simone de Beauvoir, *The Ethics of Ambiguity,* trans. Bernard Frechtman, (New York: The Citadel Press, 1967).

[8] Francis Jeanson, *Le problème moral et la pensée de Sartre* (Paris: Presses Universitaires de France, 1947).

[9] Jean-Paul Sartre, *Existentialism Is a Humanism,* p. 295.

able here and now, without for that reason becoming universal or absolute.[10]

Sartre's position is altogether rather simple. The starting point for his ethics is found in the conviction that God does not exist and that it is necessary to draw the conclusions of his absence right to the end.[11] The fact that God is dead is extremely embarrassing for the existentialist, for there disappears with Him all possibility of founding values upon Him, or to find them in an intelligible heaven. There can no longer be any good *a priori*, because there is no infinite and perfect consciousness to think it. Furthermore, if God does not exist, then everything is permitted and man is in consequence forlorn because he cannot find anything to depend upon, either within or without himself.[12]

Another basic issue in Sartre's conception of ethics is his view that in man, and man alone, existence precedes essence. This means that originally man is nothing; he will not be anything determinable until later, and then he will be what he has made of himself. There is no human nature, because there is no God to have a conception of it. Man is nothing else but that which he makes of himself. Primarily man is something that propels itself toward a future. He is primordially a project, and before that projection is brought about, he is nothing. There is no intelligible heaven; that is why man will be first what he has projected himself to be. But if there is no invariable human nature, then every common form of humanism is excluded, particularly in so far as such humanism is supposed to solve the basic ethical problems.[13]

There is a third insight that plays an important part in Sartre's conception of ethics. From the fact that man's existence is prior to his essence, it follows in Sartre's view that man is responsible for what he is. Existentialism puts every man in possession of himself and places the entire responsi-

[10] Norman N. Greene, *Jean-Paul Sartre. The Existentialist Ethic* (The University of Michigan Press, 1966), p. 46.
[11] Jean-Paul Sartre, op. cit., p. 294.
[12] Ibid., pp. 294–95.
[13] Ibid., pp. 290–91.

bility for his existence squarely upon his own shoulders. And man is not only responsible for himself alone; he is also responsible for all men. Every man must choose himself, but in choosing himself he chooses for all men. In creating himself, man projects an image of man such as he believes it ought to be. To choose something is to affirm the value of that which is chosen. For we can choose only what is good, and nothing can be good for us unless it is somehow good for all men. When a man commits himself to anything, fully realizing that he is not only choosing what he will be, but is thereby at the same time a legislature deciding for the whole of mankind, in such a moment no one can escape from the sense of complete and profound responsibility; at that moment, man appears to himself as anguish. Everyone who denies this fact is in bad faith.[14]

Sartre's view here has something in common with Kant's attempt to develop a purely formal ethics, but there is also an important difference between the two. For Kant does not realize the very essence of man's situation, and that is that man *is* anguish. I am nothing, and I know that no one is going to prove that I am the proper person to impose, by my own free choice, my conception of man upon mankind; and nevertheless I am obliged at every instant to perform actions that are examples. Everything happens to every man *as if* the whole of mankind has its eyes fixed upon what he is doing and will regulate their conduct accordingly; and nevertheless I know that I do not have the right to act in such a manner that humanity regulates itself by what I do. And even if the other is going to regulate his actions by what I am doing, then he still remains within the realm of the inauthentic, because he does not understand that he, too, *is* freedom,[15] and that values exist only in so far as they are freely chosen; in other words, he does not see that he, too, is left alone without excuse, condemned to be free.[16] It is certainly true, as Kant said, that one cannot regard another person as a means; but

14 Ibid., pp. 291–92.
15 Ibid., pp. 295–98.
16 Ibid., pp. 293–95.

it is also obvious that this is purely formal advice and much too abstract to determine a person's concrete behavior in a given situation.[17]

Before attempting to draw conclusions from these presuppositions, I wish first to focus briefly upon some topics that I think are essential to Sartre's position in ethics. For this I shall take my starting point in the first part of *Being and Nothingness*.

In the book, Sartre intended to deal with the question of Being. After a brief analysis, performed in the *Introduction*, he comes to the conclusion that this basic ontological problem is tantamount to the question concerning the relation between the In-itself and the For-itself, that is between world and man.[18] He agrees with Heidegger that in order to find an answer to this question one must analyze the human reality, which, as being-in-the-world, is a concrete whole in which the two poles given are united. It is within this concrete unity of man's reference to the world that concrete forms of reference can be singled out and analyzed as to the conditions of their possibility.[19]

Taking man's questioning attitude as a kind of human conduct, Sartre comes to the conclusion that non-being must be conceived as a component of the real.[20] This non-being is not the consequence of an act of negation, such as the negative judgment, nor does it depend upon negation as a category (Kant), nor can it be explained by the In-itself, which is pure positivity. On the other hand, as incapable of existing by itself, it calls for a nothingness as its origin that is a structural feature of the real.[21]

Furthermore there are a great number of realities experienced by the human reality that are inhabited by negation in their inner structure. These *négatités*, too, require that nothingness cannot be conceived of outside Being and that, although nothingness is given in the heart of Being, it cannot

[17] Ibid., pp. 296–97, 308.
[18] Jean-Paul Sartre, *Being and Nothingness*, pp. xlv–lxvii, 3–4.
[19] Ibid., p. 4.
[20] Ibid., pp. 4–6.
[21] Ibid., pp. 6–12.

have its origin in the In-itself.[22] Therefore, the question arises: where does nothingness come from, if it cannot be conceived of either outside of Being or in terms of Being, and if as non-being it cannot derive from itself the necessary force to nihilate itself?[23] The answer is that there must be a being (not the In-itself) whose property it is to nihilate nothingness. This being is man.[24] A careful analysis of man's questioning attitude as well as the *négatités* shows clearly that it is man who brings nothingness about.[25] This thesis, however, provokes another question. What must man be in his own being in order that through him nothingness can come into being? For being can generate only being. Thus man must be able to put himself outside of being. This cannot be done by annihilating things, but by putting concrete things out of circuit and by putting himself out of circuit in regard to them. Man can retire behind a nothingness. This possibility to secrete a nothingness is what Sartre calls *freedom*.[26] This freedom, taken as the source of the nothingness in the world, however, is not a property of man's actions, nor a property connected with his essence; freedom is the very being of man in so far as he conditions the appearance of nothingness in the world. Freedom taken as man's typical mode of being, which precedes his essence, means that man can detach himself from the world. This implies that man reposes *first* in the depth of being, and *then* detaches himself from it by a nihilating withdrawal.[27] But this is possible only if freedom is necessarily interwoven with *temporality*. In other words, the condition on which man can deny all or part of Being is that man carry nothingness within himself as the nothing that separates his present from all his past, and his future from his present. Freedom is the human being himself putting his own past out of play by secreting his own nothingness; and this original necessity of being his own noth-

22 Ibid., pp. 21–22.
23 Ibid., p. 22.
24 Ibid., pp. 22–23.
25 Ibid., pp. 23–24.
26 Ibid., pp. 24–25.
27 Ibid., pp. 25–26.

ingness does not belong to man's consciousness on the occasion of particular negations only, but it is his innermost mode of being. In freedom and as freedom, man is his own past and future *in the form of nihilation*.[28]

It is in anguish that man becomes conscious of himself as freedom: anguish is the mode of being of freedom as consciousness of being. Anguish is precisely my consciousness of being my own future in the mode of not-being. The self I am, depends upon the self I am not yet, to the exact extent that the self I am not yet does *not* depend upon the self I am. In other words, the freedom that reveals itself to us in anguish must be characterized by the existence of a nothing that insinuates itself between motive and act. On the other hand, anguish as the manifestation of freedom in the face of the self by means of reflection, means that man is always separated from his essence by a nothingness: essence is what has been. Essence is everything in man that we can indicate by the expression: it is. The human act is always beyond that essence, taken as what has been already. Anguish appears as an apprehension of the self inasmuch as the self exists in the perpetual mode of detachment from what is already, from what *has been*.[29]

This analysis necessarily leads to the following quite obvious objection. It was said that in anguish freedom is anguished before itself inasmuch as it is bound by nothing. On the other hand, it was said that freedom is a permanent structure of man. Thus it follows that anguish must be a permanent state of man's affectivity. This is clearly not so, since anguish is a very exceptional phenomenon in a man's life.

Sartre agrees that anguish, indeed, occurs very seldom. It only occurs when consciousness sees itself cut off from its own essence by nothing, or separated from its future by its very freedom. Most of the time, man is engaged in what he is doing, and thus transcends himself in the direction of the things in the world. Then he remains within the realm of the non-reflective consciousness. But in each case there is and

[28] Ibid., pp. 26–28.
[29] Ibid., pp. 28–35.

remains the possibility of putting this act in question and bringing man into the situation described above, by means of *reflection*.[30]

The same thing is true, Sartre continues, for the relation between ethical anguish and our everyday morality. There is ethical anguish only when I consider myself in the *original* relation to values. Then I realize that my freedom is the unique foundation of values, and that *absolutely nothing* justifies me in adopting this or that particular set of values. As a being by whom values exist, I am completely unjustifiable. My freedom is anguished at being the foundation of values, although I myself am without any foundation.

But although it is my continuous possibility to overturn the whole scale of values, ordinarily my attitude to values is eminently reassuring: I am just engaged in a world of values without putting them into question. Usually our being is *immediately* in situation. In the world of the immediate I find values that ultimately derive their meaning from an original projection of myself that stands as my choice of myself in the world. But as soon as I reflect, the possibility of anguish is there. Then I know that I do not have recourse to any value against the fact that it is I who create and sustain values, whatever they may be. Nothing can assure me against myself, cut off from the world and from my essence by this nothingness that I am. When I refuse to reflect on the undeniable datum, or when I flee into psychological determinism, or try to disarm my anguish by asserting that I am my essence in the mode of being of the In-itself, then I am in *bad faith*, for bad faith is the nihilating power that nihilates anguish in so far as I flee it and nihilates itself in so far as I *am* anguish in order to flee it.[31]

Sartre returns to the problem of values when he tries to explain in what sense consciousness as Being-for-itself is the negation of its own Being-in-itself. As such, Being-for-itself is incomplete; it is a lack of being. As such, therefore, it must reach out beyond itself and complete itself. The For-itself

[30] Ibid., pp. 35–38.
[31] Ibid., pp. 38–44.

strives for a complement to be a whole; it *transcends* itself to eliminate its lack of being. The human reality *is* its own transcendence toward what it lacks; it surpasses itself toward the particular being that it would be if it were what it is. Human reality is not something that exists first in order to lack this or that afterward; it exists as lack, and in an immediate, synthetic connection with what it lacks. Thus the pure event by which human reality rises as a presence in the world is apprehended by itself as its own lack. In its coming into existence, human reality grasps itself as an incomplete being. It apprehends itself as being in so far as it is not being; in the presence of a particular totality which it lacks and which it is in the form of not being what it is. Human reality arises as such in the presence of its own totality (self) as a lack of that totality. And this totality cannot be given by nature, since it combines in itself the incompatible characteristics of the In-itself and the For-itself, that is, because it amounts to the useless passion of trying to become God.[32]

The being of the self is essentially value. The concept of value is affected with the double character of both being unconditionally and not being. Moralists have pointed to these characteristics, but they have very inadequately explained them. As value, value certainly has being, but this normative being does not have to be as reality is. Its being precisely is to-be-value; that is to say, *not* to-be-being. And since the being of value as such is the being of what does not have being, value appears to be incomprehensible. Sociologists often make of value a requirement of fact among other facts; in this way they take value as being, and radically misunderstand its reality; in this way, the contingency of being characteristic of the fact destroys value. On the other hand, if one stresses the ideality of values too one-sidedly, one extracts being from them altogether. One can achieve an intuition of values in terms of concrete exemplifications, but this does not mean that values exist on the same level as the acts on which they confer value. Value is always given as a beyond of the acts

[32] Ibid., pp. 84–90, 615.

confronted. Value is indeed beyond being as a kind of limit, but nonetheless it possesses being in some way at least.[33]

These considerations point to the fact that it is the human reality by which values arrive in the world. But for value, the meaning of being is that it is that toward which a human being surpasses his own being. The supreme value toward which the human reality surpasses itself as consciousness is the absolute being of the self, with its characteristics of identity, purity, and permanence, in which it hopes to find its own foundation. This supreme value as the beyond of transcendence as such, provides the foundation for all my concrete acts of transcendence, but toward this supreme value itself I can never surpass myself, precisely because each concrete act of transcendence presupposes it. This enables us to understand why value can simultaneously be and not be. It is at the same time the meaning and the beyond of all surpassing; it is as the absent In-itself which haunts the For-itself. But we have seen already that the For-itself can never become the In-itself without losing *eo ipso* its most characteristic features, its consciousness, its nothingness, its freedom. Value, therefore, is in its own being the always missing totality toward which the human reality makes itself be. Value haunts being in so far as it attempts to found itself, not in so far as it is: *value haunts freedom*. Value is that being which has to be in order that the For-itself could be the foundation of its own nothingness. Yet while the For-itself has to be this being, this is not because it is somehow forced to be that way, but because in its being, it makes itself be as having to be this being. In other words the For-itself, the ideal Self, and their mutual relationship stand within the limits of an unconditioned freedom; this means that *nothing* makes value be, unless it is that freedom which by the same stroke makes me myself be; they also stand within the limits of concrete facticity, since as the foundation of its own nothingness, the For-itself cannot be the foundation of its being. There is then at the same time a total contingency of being-for-value (which will bear very heavily on morality in that it paralyzes

[33] Ibid., pp. 92–93.

and relativizes it), as well as a free and absolute necessity.[34]

In presenting this brief summary of Sartre's view on values, we incidentally touched again upon a presupposition which is of great importance for his conception of ethics, namely his atheism. In defending atheism, Sartre takes his point of departure in the conception of God as offered by Christianity and notably by scholastic philosophy and theology.[35] According to this view the proposition "God exists" is *of itself* a self-evident statement, because the subject and predicate of the proposition are the same in that God is His own existence. According to this view, therefore, God is not only his own essence, but also his own being. In other words, God is the sufficient cause of His own being.[36] In Sartre's terminology, as we have seen already, this means that God must be defined as the Being-in-and-for-itself. This expression, however, obviously contains a contradiction in that the In-itself *is*, whereas the For-itself is its own nothingness and thus refers to a lack in being.

It is a well-known fact that in *Being and Nothingness* Sartre developed various arguments to justify his atheistic position.[37] For our purpose here it is not necessary to mention all of them. It seems, however, of some importance to indicate two types of argument that are immediately connected with what has just been said. A first argument is connected with Sartre's conception of man's freedom. Here he says, for example, that if man in his inner being were not dependent upon God, then he would have no need for a Creator, whereas if man were dependent upon God, he would not be an independent being and therefore could not be free.[38] A second argument (which has some elements in common with the one Camus uses repeatedly)[39] takes its start-

[34] Ibid., pp. 93–95.
[35] Norman N. Greene, op. cit., p. 61.
[36] Thomas Aquinas, *Summa Theologica*, I, 2, 1, c; 3, 4, c.
[37] Norman N. Greene, op. cit., pp. 60–79.
[38] Jean-Paul Sartre, *Being and Nothingness*, p. 232.
[39] Albert Camus, *The Myth of Sisyphus and Other Essays*, trans. Justin O'Brien (New York: Random House, 1955), pp. 3–48.

ing point in an accurate and careful description of man's experience. Among man's experiences, absurdity, anguish, and despair occupy important places. Anyone who believes in God, and defends his existence, can never be sincere in regard to those experiences. Since those experiences are not only had by some people in certain particular circumstances, but are also immediately connected with the human situation as such, it follows that there cannot be any God, and that the idea of God cannot be more than the fruit of man's projection.[40]

In concluding this brief excursus, we may say that in Sartre's view on ethics the basic presuppositions are the following: there is no God; there are no *a priori* values; there is no invariable human nature, man is free, man is nothing else but what he purposes, he exists only in so far as he realizes himself, he is nothing but what his life is in so far as he has chosen this in freedom; purely formal ethical principles are meaningless because of their abstractness.[41]

Given these presuppositions, one can ask the question of whether an ethics is still possible. Sartre answers in the affirmative and bases his view on the following considerations.

1) Although it is impossible to find in each man a universal essence that can be called human nature, there is nevertheless a universality of the human condition. There are universal limitations that *a priori* define man's fundamental situation in the universe. This is the reason why every purpose that a human being projects is not wholly foreign to me, since it presents itself as an attempt either to surpass these limitations, or to widen them, deny them, or to accommodate oneself to them. Consequently, every purpose that man projects is, however individual it may be, of a universal value. The important point to realize here, however, is that such a value is not something given in advance. As value, it can only be understood the moment it is brought about in an actual and free decision.[42]

2) It is this universal and therefore absolute character of

---

40 Norman N. Greene, op. cit., pp. 64–73.
41 Jean-Paul Sartre, *Existentialism Is a Humanism*, pp. 299–300.
42 Ibid., pp. 303–4.

the free commitment by which every man realizes himself in realizing a type of humanity, that gives an absolute character to the existentialist ethics by means of which it can escape mere caprice,[43] and enables it to "judge" others.[44]

3) Furthermore, one must realize that freedom, with respect to concrete circumstances, can have no other end and aim but itself; and when once a man has seen that ultimate value depends upon himself, in that state of forsakenness he can will only one thing, and this is freedom as the foundation of all values. This does not mean that he wills it in the abstract; it simply means that the actions of a man of good faith have as their ultimate significance the quest of freedom itself as such.[45]

4) From this it follows that every time there is commitment on my part, I am obliged to will the freedom of others at the same time as my own. I cannot make liberty my aim unless I make that of others equally my aim. When I recognize that man is a being whose existence precedes his essence, and that he is free and cannot in any circumstances but will his freedom, at the same time I realize that I cannot *not* will the freedom of others. Thus in the name of that will to freedom which is implied in freedom itself, I can form judgments upon those who seek to hide from themselves the wholly voluntary nature of their existence and their complete freedom. The imperative obviously escapes from Kant's abstract formalism in that it is as concrete as the free decision I am going to make.[46]

5) This obviously leads in the final analysis to a morals of ambiguity. As Sartre says, my values are not really serious, because I choose them myself. He adds that he regrets it has to be this way. But, he continues, if I have excluded God the Father, there must be someone to invent values. One must take things the way they are. The real meaning of these last remarks is that in his view there is no meaning in a man's

[43] Ibid., pp. 304–5.
[44] Ibid., pp. 306–7.
[45] Ibid., p. 307.
[46] Ibid., pp. 307–8.

life *a priori*; life is nothing until it is lived. But it is up to me to make sense of it, and the value of it is nothing else but the sense that I choose.[47]

Simone de Beauvoir, referring to the "ethics of ambiguity," carefully points out that ambiguity must not be confused with absurdity. For, to say that man's existence is absurd is to deny that it can ever be given any meaning. But to say that it is ambiguous is to assert that its meaning is never determined and that it must be constantly brought about in freedom. If man's life is absurd, then all ethics is impossible. Ethics would be impossible also if the rationalization of the real were ever completed and finished. It is precisely because man's condition is ambiguous that he seeks to save his existence. But trying to save your existence implies that there will be success as well as failure. Man's moral action, as is true for his artistic and scientific endeavors, is such that in any particular case human transcendence must cope with the same problem: it has to found itself, though it is prohibited from ever fulfilling itself. In other words, man must in any event and under any circumstances assume his finiteness, not by treating it as transitory, but by reflecting the "infinitude" within it and by treating it as absolute. There is liberation of man only if, in aiming at itself, freedom is achieved absolutely in the very fact of aiming at itself. This requires that each action be considered as a finished form whose different moments, instead of fleeing toward the future in order to find their justification, reflect and confirm each other so well that there is no longer a sharp separation between present and future, between means and ends.[48]

At any rate, this kind of existentialism certainly is a humanism, though not in the sense that it subscribes to the thesis according to which man is an end-in-itself and therefore the supreme value. For man is neither an end nor the supreme value. Man is always still to be determined. This view defends a humanism in that it gives it to man, and man

[47] Ibid., pp. 308–11.
[48] Simone de Beauvoir, *The Ethics of Ambiguity*, pp. 129–31. [Infra, pp. 289–90]

alone, to decide what he is going to be. In that sense it is true that this view is nothing but an attempt to draw the full conclusions from a consistently atheistic position. God is dead. And even if God existed, that would make no difference from the viewpoint of an existentialist.[49]

[49] Jean-Paul Sartre, *Existentialism Is a Humanism*, pp. 310–11.

MORAL PERSPECTIVES IN
SARTRE'S THOUGHT

Francis Jeanson

"Ontology itself could not formulate ethical precepts. It is concerned solely with what is, and we cannot possibly derive imperatives from ontology's indicatives. It does, however, allow us to catch a glimpse of what sort of ethics will assume its responsibilities when confronted with a *human reality in situation.*"[1]

Taken from the last section of *Being and Nothingness*, this is the beginning of the answer we can find in Sartre to the questions we can been asking since the Introduction [of this book]. These few lines, and those which follow until the end of the last page, seem to be of such a nature that they definitely preclude all ambiguity; and yet it is still necessary to read them, and not just with the unique aim of extracting from them some passage or other from which one might like to derive a result that could cause a sensation.

Thus we must read these lines again and draw the greatest possible profit from this text upon which we can still rely— before trying to decipher somewhat more-remote and less-direct implications for which we alone will have to assume responsibility.

Ontology has revealed to us that "the various tasks of the

This essay is from *Le problème moral et la pensée de Sartre*, by Francis Jeanson (Paris, 1965), pp. 265–89. Copyright © 1965 by Éditions du Seuil. The present essay was translated into English expressly for this edition by Joseph J. Kockelmans.

[1] Jean-Paul Sartre, *Being and Nothingness*, trans. Hazel E. Barnes (New York: Philosophical Library, 1956), pp. 625–26.

for-itself can be made the object of an existential psychoanalysis, for they all aim at producing the missing synthesis of consciousness and being in the form of value and self-cause."[2] From a human point of view—and this is the only one that philosophy can claim for itself—a being that is its own foundation or, what amounts to the same thing, a consciousness that completely coincides with itself, is absolutely contradictory, and consequently, inconceivable. Only religious faith can say with Tertullian: *Credo quia absurdum*, I believe because it is absurd, or: "The Son of God was crucified, this is not shameful because it is shameful; and the Son of God is dead, this is even more credible because it is absurd; and buried He is risen, this is certain because it is impossible."[3] And yet faith has the right to adopt such a position only by manifesting its own power to regenerate man, by transcending the speculative contradiction, by effectively refusing to remain on the speculative level: it is precisely because it establishes itself on a level on which it breaks the laws of thought that such a faith can maintain itself through its acts alone. But, from there on, the problem concerning the very orientation of action poses itself again. And once more, one is compelled to attempt the solution on the human level, for it is only on that level that a man can act. Furthermore, it serves no purpose at all to wish to evade the problem by arguing that faith moves mountains, and dissolves all problems in order to let only mysteries subsist. A man acts only by taking his starting point in his situation: his manner of acting always refers to the choice he has made in regard to himself, and quite a number of choices are possible within the framework of a religious faith. It is much too easy just to rely on God: there are not too many signposts on the way that lead to Him; for the authentic believers, there are no specialized agencies capable of working out a travel plan for such a voyage; as far as the others are concerned, it so happens that one can never propose anything to them except excursions that, after all is said and done,

---

[2] Ibid., p. 626.

[3] Cf. Chestov, *Kierkegaard et la philosophie existentielle*, p. 152, quoted by Em. Mounier, *Introduction aux existentialismes* (Paris: Denoël, 1947), p. 39.

lead them back to their point of departure—something with which they are otherwise quite easily satisfied. Thus man is, here too, still committed to himself, abandoned, alone, free, and unjustifiable: and even if he believes that grace can suddenly illuminate his faltering course, still he does not have the right to pause under a tree waiting for grace to come; he must strive toward it through all the realities without counting on any eventual miracle. But to work out one's own course is tantamount to inventing oneself, to choosing oneself freely. Will one pretend that all choices are good and that there are a thousand and one ways to serve God?

This is certainly correct: but who will give up trying to determine that the main issue is to serve Him at least *authentically*? Indifference in regard to the absurd is no longer possible here.

Finally, nothing, not even the religious choice, exempts man from making a moral choice—one whose unique criterion consists in "the degree of consciousness in which he possesses his ideal goal." Only for the theologian is it true that God *is real*. And without a doubt the believer often gives way to the theologian: but then his faith dissipates in the absurdity of a sterile metaphysics that is worse than doubt. Indeed, it is through oneself that one believes, and faith is always the free choice of an ideal. One does not give value to this ideal just by calling it God, but through a perpetual concern for the authenticity of the practical definition that, whether one likes it or not, one gives to it, precisely in serving it. Such is the profound truth hidden behind the scientistic exaggerations of sociologists—when they pretend to demonstrate the non-existence of God by means of the anthropomorphic character of our concept of God: the God of each man is the God whom he has chosen to serve. If man could reach God and coincide with Him, then the question would perhaps be solved, because then there would no longer be a choice to be made; but in so far as he is man, such goal remains inaccessible to him: thus he must serve Him, and define Him the way he serves Him. As the case may be, I could choose to abandon all concern for this world and to spend twenty years on a wretched bed without ever getting up, or to fight in order to assure on each occasion the freedom of consciousness for all those who share my religious conviction, or to convert my fellow men, or to take care of the lepers, or even to lead a mundane life in order to manifest to the skeptics that a believer is not inhuman. . . .

But how can I assure myself of the value of the choice once I have made it, if I do not interrogate myself concerning its profound significance; if I refuse to question it; if I blindly accept the risk, under the pretext of a burning faith, of having chosen some form of abandonment, renouncement, some anticipated appropriation of my salvation, some immediate justification in order no longer to find myself unjustified?

In order to approach the question from another perspective let us note that Descartes's *Cogito* (to which we have denied the value of a point of departure for ontology) can very well serve as a point of reference in the formulation of the moral problem if one takes its reflexive character into consideration. It is a fact that this *Cogito*, indeed, is primordially a *dubito*, an "I doubt." We have seen that this cannot be found on the level of my existence, which is already confirmed and present to itself in what we have called with Sartre "the prereflexive *Cogito*." This *dubito*, which is an act of reflection, could not be doubt about my own existence, but merely doubt about the significance of my existence. In other words, on the level of the natural attitude, I, myself, am in question for myself in each one of my forms of behavior in regard to the world, and such is the initial aspect of my freedom; on the level of philosophical reflection, I question my own value in so far as I discover that I am responsible for these forms of behavior. The moral problem cannot appear except in a moment of hesitation, that is to say, within the possibility of a refusal of all moral value. From this moment of hesitation on, the moral problem appears simultaneously as one that cannot be refused: even if I choose the refusal, I manifest by that very fact an attitude that engages me morally, and as one that is undetermined: for its formulation by no means entails its solution. One knows how Descartes proves the existence of God: I doubt, thus I am an imperfect being who has the idea of the perfect; and this idea cannot have been put in me except by a Being that itself is perfect. At that moment, all possibility of a moral attitude breaks down to the exact extent to which all further possibility of doubt and refusal becomes illusory. For either I conceive of God as perfectly "transcendent," and from then on His existence is an absolute without influence upon me and I fall back upon my nothingness by having made God the total Being; or God is somehow immanent in me, I participate in His perfection, but because the latter is realized in Him, it is that which governs me and realizes me according to the True and Good, and all the rest is merely ripples on the surface, a ridiculously unimportant epiphenomenon. It is in this way that Descartes's rationalism equally opened the way to eighteenth-century atheism—which suppresses this God who is indifferent to everything human—and to a pantheism of Necessity, which Spinoza formulated with merciless logic. One can see the source of this double error: it consists in the fact that Perfection is realized either outside man, or in man. But in both cases one ignores the fact that all value is valorization.

The perfect does not grant itself to us except by refusing itself; its sole existence for us is that of being to be realized. In the idea of the perfect there is no evidence concerning a Being, but rather the experience of a vocation. "God exists" is a proposition that as *proposition* is impossible. And it would be equally impossible as theoretical *supposition*. It cannot be valid except under the form of an active position and of a practical valorization. To suppose that God exists is only profitable to the believer who engages himself in it with all his faith. But then it is he who makes God exist for him. The idea of God is not in our possession. It does not lie with us to encounter this idea once and for all, we do not *have* the idea of God: we must continually give it back to ourselves in the choice we make of this or that moral course.

The issue, thus, is not to deny the existence of God, but to refuse it as a proposition that is valid in itself. God exists to the extent to which my actions lay claim on His existence, to which my actions make Him exist for me. When the believer doubts God, he doubts himself, his power to maintain in himself this practical orientation, this intimate efficiency.

A God who exists in spite of man is a guilty God, a God who is responsible for all evil: and this would mean that man is innocent and beyond all problems and beyond all morals. Our experience of the doubt regains its place only in a human world, where man appears to be effectively capable of that transcendence of himself by himself which, when it takes place, is the only authentic position of God.

God gives Himself only to those who search for Him. To say that God exists is tantamount to speaking for oneself and affirming a faith that is sufficiently active to continually promote it.

In short, either Descartes's *dubito* is merely an artifice of metaphysics, or it means: "I hesitate, thus I can will that God exists."

From the moment this hesitation is known as such, it manifests moral freedom. Standing completely opposite to the bewilderment that submits the animal to the servitude of exterior determination, the doubt ratifies the spiritual power to pose a problem and to impose its solution upon oneself. Whether I deny this power or whether I pretend to explain it by means of the existence of God, in either case I have adopted an attitude and have manifested in this way my ability to intervene as far as my own orientation is concerned, that is to say to make my life a vocation.

This is the point to which we must always return, for it is the only point from which we can start. At any rate, one sees to what extent an authentic humanism can call itself "atheistic." All philosophy is a humanism, for the philosophical attitude is, in the final analysis, never more than a questioning of the human by man. And it is solely on the level of human vocation that the invocation of God even receives its meaning.

But most of the philosophies seem to forget that their task is to determine a question for which our existence alone can give the answer. One should read again the beautiful conclusion of Merleau-Ponty: "Shall I make this promise? Shall I risk my life for so little? Shall I give up my liberty in order to save liberty? There is no theoretical reply to these questions. But there are these *things* which stand, irrefutable, there is before you this person whom you love, there are these men whose existence around you is that of slaves, and *your* freedom cannot be willed without leaving behind its singular relevance, and without willing freedom *for all*. Whether it is a question of things or of historical situations, philosophy has no function other than to teach us once more to see them clearly, and it is correct to say that philosophy comes into being by destroying itself as separate philosophy. But what is required here is silence, for only the hero lives out his relation to men and the world. 'Your son is caught in fire; you are the one who will save him. . . . If there is an obstacle, you would be ready to lend your shoulder, provided that you could push away that obstacle. . . . Your abode is your act itself. Your act is you. . . . You give yourself in exchange. . . . Your significance shows itself, radiant. It is your duty, your hatred, your love, your steadfastness, your ingenuity. . . . Man is but a network of relationships, and these relationships alone matter to him.' "[4]

Let us now return to what Sartre tells us. "Man makes himself man in order to be God . . ."; but here the issue is not to accuse man of egoism; one must renounce all utilitarian interpretation of man's conduct in order to trace its *ideal* signification: ". . . precisely because there is no measure common to both human reality and the self-cause it wants to be, one could just as well say that man loses himself in order that the self-cause may exist. One will then consider that all human existence is a passion, the famous *self-interest* being only one of the ways freely chosen among others to realize this passion." In so far as the purifying reflection did not intervene, in so far as man still imagines that his mission, however he may conceive of it, is inscribed in things, all human activities are equivalent, all of them are in principle doomed to failure. "Thus it amounts to the same thing whether one gets drunk alone or is the leader of nations. If one of these activities takes precedence over the others, this

4 Maurice Merleau-Ponty, *Phenomenology of Perception*, trans. Colin Smith (New York: Humanities Press, 1962), p. 456 (with some minor changes). Merleau-Ponty's quotation is from A. de Saint-Exupéry, *Pilote de Guerre*, pp. 171 and 174.

will not be because of its real goal but because of the degree of consciousness that it possesses of its ideal goal; and in this case it will be the quietism of the solitary drunkard that will take precedence over the vain agitation of the leader of nations."[5]

Thus "the pure and non-abetting reflection" must intervene. Its role will be to unveil to man—by making him approach the moral level of authenticity—his very search for being and his concern for the appropriation of the in-itself *as possibilities among other possibilities*. In this way, it will allow him no longer to hold as irreducible the value that had fundamentally oriented all his choices, namely the ideal presence of the being which is self-cause. In so doing, it places man in a position to *choose* this value itself, to evaluate it—or, on the contrary, to refuse it: the one of these two attitudes is possible only because the other is equally possible. Pascal said something to this effect: it is because God exists, that He is not certain. This formula implies its reverse: it is to the extent to which God is not certain, that there is authentic value in actively holding Him as existing. The choice of the believer can be called authentic only from the moment when the believer ceases to conceive of his own faith as polarized by a God of evidence, in order to take it again in its real value —and to accept it as a "bet," in which he engages himself at each moment without reservation.

But there are not only believers. There are in fact many more atheists than one thinks. Clearly, the same question suggests itself again for this group as the one we asked above in connection with the believers. Some of them pretend to ignore their own atheism and attempt to cover up with a word the choice that their acts have long ratified; inversely, others flaunt it with cynicism—thus manifesting a bad conscience, which they reinforce in themselves rather than giving it up; still others believe they can remain neutral. . . . Finally, a small number of them have perhaps risen to the authentic choice of total absence. In this way, with the true believers, having arrived at that absolute simplicity from which one

[5] Jean-Paul Sartre, op. cit., pp. 626 and 627.

can as validly invoke the Presence as the Absence, Being as well as Nothingness—that is to say, where one can invoke or choose not to invoke—they have opted for an existence whose perpetual transcendence is not polarized by any goal that is exterior to it, as a freedom that understands itself as its own value and its own goal.

The temptation is strong here to contrast this second attitude with the first one, just as one contrasts an ethics of autonomy with an ethics of heteronomy. But it is clear that one should not yield to this: once a being has transcended the factual value through which his own choice has let itself be determined and oriented, it matters little whether he chooses this value or whether he chooses to renounce it—for in the one case as well as in the other, he has been able to disengage himself from what he was in order to choose what he has to be. The authentic attitude could not be anything other than an attitude of autonomy. But perhaps it is even more exact to say that this attitude is found beyond autonomy itself because it founds it—and thus correlatively founds heteronomy—in its initial effort to transcend all illusions, to justify its conduct by laws that pretended to make it consistent in advance.

But whatever one may think about this last point, we grasp at least the meaning of the moral conversion. Regardless of the choice that can intervene then, it consists in approaching a level on which freedom ceases to be a free pursuit of a preset goal, in order to free itself also from this goal by placing this goal itself in question. From the first pages [of this book] we have said that ethics consist in the moralization of the moral being: we could anticipate seeing "value"—which, there, was still no more than an indication of the irreducible self-transcendence that is constitutive of the human reality —in ethics going back over itself in order to evaluate itself, and man renouncing therein the impossible coincidence with himself, the inaccessible justification of himself, in order to assume that distance from himself which constitutes his humanity, and assuming that absolute responsibility which guarantees his humanization.

It seems that we are far away from Roquentin of *La Nausée*,

who was searching for the best possible way to justify his existence. And yet, did he himself not make the remark that it is
a mistake to will to be, because sooner or later one has to
recall that one exists? And the existence that flows back on
you is ambiguous; it reveals itself in Nausea as well as in Anxiety; and freedom can never be finished with itself; and to
the end, man must carry the burden of his own initiatives.

In this way, we have passed from bad faith, which factually
proceeds from non-coincidence with oneself, to a new, more-
fundamental attitude, which originates in the evaluation of
this non-coincidence by means of the free choice the subject
executes therein. We have transcended the moral *existing*
man toward the moral *agent*, and the first act through which
the latter has manifested himself has been to recognize that
the ambiguity that defines man's existence is the unique
source of values.

Such is the perspective *de jure* to which we have come.
. . . The entire problem, however, remains to know whether
it is in fact possible for man to "*live* this new aspect of being."
Only an ethics can formulate this with precision and attempt
to solve this problem by indicating the conditions of the possibility for the realization of such a choice. "In particular, will
freedom by taking itself for an end escape all *situation?* Or
on the contrary, will it remain situated? Or will it situate
itself so much the more precisely and the more individually
as it projects itself further in anguish as a conditioned freedom and accepts more fully its responsibility as an existent
being by whom the world comes into being? All these questions, which refer us to a pure and not an accessory reflection,
can find their reply on the ethical level. We shall devote a
future work to them."[6]

As a matter of act, their very formulation would already
suffice to suggest to us the direction in which Sartre intends
to answer them. It is obviously the second term of the alternative that will receive the privileged position in his following work. Actually, the most explicit confirmations are

[6] Ibid., p. 628.

not lacking in the part of his work we already know, either. It is perhaps not useless, by way of illustrating the preceding theoretical considerations, to review for the last time some of the essential themes of Sartre's view and to indicate about each of them the practical perspectives that open up from here on—beyond the discouraging walls ontology seems to have set up for us on all sides and as if with pleasure.

We must indeed return to that man whom we have abandoned on a shore line from which the world, in front of him and behind him, seemed to be merely hostile, and where all the horizons were blocked, and from which all attempts at action in principle appeared to be doomed to failure. However, if the purifying reflection, which we have asked to unveil for us the structures and implications of the natural attitude, is effectively valid, then there must be a possibility for this man to be liberated from his freedom: there must be "roads to freedom."

Indeed, the first two volumes of Sartre's novel that bears this promising title barely provide us with practical indications, except for those taken from a negative point of view. But they are, for that matter, no less clear. From the beginning of L'âge de raison, Mathieu appears to us as a man who has lost his freedom because he willed to escape all situation. "Your life is full of missed opportunities, Marcelle said to him. . . . Nowadays you are very seldom in the mood. . . . It is always that lucidity you fuss about so much. . . . You are so absurdly scared of being your own dupe that you would back out of the finest adventure in the world rather than risk telling yourself a lie. . . . Do you know what I do believe? That you are beginning to sterilize yourself a little. . . . Everything is so neat and tidy in your mind; it smells of clean linen; it is as though you had just come out of a drying-room. But there is want of shade. There is nothing useless, or hesitant, or underhand about you now. It is all high noon. . . . You have acquired the taste for self-analysis. . . . It helps you to get rid of yourself; to contemplate and criticize yourself: that is the attitude you prefer. When you look at yourself, you imagine you are not what you see, you imagine you are nothing. That is your ideal: you want to be nothing."

And Mathieu tries to rectify: "To be nothing? No, it is not. Listen, I—I recognize no allegiance except to myself. . . . If I did not try to assume responsibility for my own existence, it would seem utterly absurd to go on existing."[7]

One recognizes here the classical "freedom of indifference," the trivial conception of a total availability, the attempt of a personal consciousness to withdraw on the level of transcendental consciousness, to adopt "God's point of view" of the world. Mixed with detachment, Mathieu's freedom, which is similar to that of Orestes in *Les Mouches*, makes him a fluctuating being, a stranger to everyone, alone among the other human beings, non-existent for himself. And this is not equivalent to the feeling of strangeness that Camus describes for us: the freedom that destroys itself, this is the one that Mathieu has willed as such. He willed to *be* free, that is to say, to be nothing. He willed to "recover" his freedom; he has ignored that essential aspect of human reality that ontology has unveiled to us: it is that being which has to be what it is, that is to say, which is not what it is—but which is also what it is not. Mathieu has only tried not to be what he is. He has disengaged himself from himself, forgetting that such a disengagement is meaningless except in favor of an engagement he evaluates, and that to be free means to choose and to act.

Brunet is the antithesis of Mathieu. He adheres to the meaning life proposes to him without questioning it. He engages himself once and for all. This is a perfect illustration of the spirit of seriousness; "he makes himself such that he is waited *for* by all the tasks placed along his way."[8] He thinks of his life as a destiny, as a mission that is inscribed in things. He justifies his existence by means of objective values to which his freedom submits. Contrary to Mathieu, he has willed to be engaged, that is to say, to be something. He has willed to "recover" his project, coincide with it, to be what he is not. He, too, has lost his freedom.

And all the other characters of these two volumes have lost

---

[7] Jean-Paul Sartre, *The Age of Reason*, trans. Eric Sutton (New York: Knopf, 1947), pp. 8–11.

[8] *Being and Nothingness*, p. 626.

their freedom, too. Until the end of *Le Sursis*, we are on the level of ontological failure. But it is also the level of solitude, and without a doubt one must see in this an indication that has a positive value. Let us recall the solitude of Roquentin in *Nausea*. In this novel, the theme of the other is not touched upon for him. Roquentin always envisages that he must save himself alone, act alone, albeit to impress the others, in order to have others talk about him: at any rate, it never occurs to his mind that he could act *with others*. Likewise, the only action that seems to be possible to him is ultimately an act by means of the imaginary, an act of artistic creation.

However, there is one single passage in Roquentin's diary that seems to have an inkling of the falsehood of this solitary search: "I am all alone, but I march like a regiment descending on a city. At this very moment, there are ships on the sea resounding with music; lights are turned on in all the cities of Europe; Communists and Nazis are shooting it out in the streets of Berlin, the unemployed are pounding the pavements of New York, women at their dressing tables in a warm room are putting mascara on their eyelashes. And I am here, in this deserted street, and each shop from a window in Neukölln, each hiccough of the wounded being carried away, each precise gesture of women at their toilette answers to my every step, to my every heartbeat."[9] It turns out also that this passage is the only one in which Roquentin knows real anxiety, not only the fear that his Nausea will return, but the crushing weight of his freedom. "I am full of anguish: the slightest movement irks me. I cannot imagine what they want with me. Yet I must choose. . . ."[10] But he then commits the mistake of believing that something is waiting for him, an "adventure." And his freedom, of which he had barely caught a glimpse, is made a laughingstock.

What does it matter? We have recognized here the central theme of *Le Sursis*. This brilliant counterpoint is going to pose the problem of the relationships between a man and

[9] Jean-Paul Sartre, *Nausea*, trans. Lloyd Alexander (New York: New Directions, 1949), p. 77.
[10] Ibid.

other men in all its fullness. If freedom must preserve the value which little by little we have recognized in it, then from a social point of view this can be done only in the bosom of human groups that are not simply indifferent collectivities in which everyone lives in his own solitude, and that cannot be a kind of tribe, either, where the individual finds himself swallowed up in his participation in the "collective spirit." From the primitive man who *is* his totem, to the civilized man who locks himself in, in an exasperated individualism, no progress whatsoever seems to have taken place in the direction of authenticity; the one is engaged, the other refuses to engage himself.

But the moment of Munich, with its obsession of the war, will force man to transcend at the same time both the notion of one society and the notion of the individual. The war is neither a "social" fact (for it is unthinkable in its totality) nor an "individual" fact (for everyone feels himself suddenly bound together with all others). Let us say that it is neither a determinate object for all, nor a personal project for each individual; neither a common destiny, nor an individual vocation. Such is the ambiguous character of everything that concerns the presence of a human world around us. We undergo this presence first either in voluntary abasement or in mistrust and hostility; later we believe we can disengage ourselves from it in indifference and contempt. These two social attitudes are evidently inauthentic, and we cannot make ourselves free without being willing to overcome the one as well as the other, toward free relationships with the liberties of the others, toward an interhuman communication which would be a recapturing of the ambiguous fact of the existence of the other on the moral level.

There, too, it seems that there is a misunderstanding in reproaching Sartre's ontology, or the first two volumes of *Chemins de la liberté*, envisaging only the fact without manifesting its evaluation: if the two were confused, then no effort would have had to be made, everything would have been given, and nothing would have had any value. But neither the genuine community nor our authentic humanity—and we shall see shortly that these two values are essentially connected

—waits for us at birth to give itself to us ready-made: we must invent them. Man must make himself man, in himself and with his fellow men.

It is in this framework that Sartre's remarks about literature, and more precisely about the responsibility of the author, find their proper place: "Each literary work is an appeal. . . . The author appeals to the freedom of the reader so that it may collaborate in the production of his work. . . . If he is willing to be the creator of injustices, it is in a movement that overcomes them by abolishing them. As far as I, the one who reads, am concerned, if I create and maintain in its existence an unjust world, I can do nothing except make myself responsible for it. . . . We, the two of us, bear the responsibility for the universe. . . . If one gives me this world with its injustices, then this is not in order that I may contemplate these injustices calmly, but so that I may animate them with my indignation and unveil them and show the nature of their injustice, that is to say, as abuses that are to be suppressed. Thus the universe of the author reveals itself in all its profundity only to the investigation, admiration, and indignation of the reader; and generous love is an oath to maintain, generous indignation an oath to change, and admiration an oath to imitate; although literature is one thing and morals a completely different thing, at the root of the aesthetic imperative we discern the moral imperative. For, because he who writes, by the very fact that he takes the trouble to write, recognizes the freedom of his readers, and because he who reads, by the simple fact that he opens the book, recognizes the freedom of the author, the work of art, from whatever point of view one takes it, is an act of confidence in the freedom of man."[11]

In reading the preceding chapters one may already have grasped the distance that separates Sartre's thought from classical philosophies. The criteria that apply to them do not hold for him. For this reason his philosophy requires, more than any other, that one penetrate into its spirit before criticizing it in its formulation. That is without a doubt the rea-

[11] Jean-Paul Sartre, *What Is Literature?* trans. Bernard Frechtman (New York: Philosophical Library, 1963).

son why it is almost impossible, in the course of a conversation, to answer the question that has become a ritual: "What is existentialism?" Even if one takes care to focus attention on the fact that there are several existentialisms, which are very different from one another, that Sartre's existentialism, about which one is talking, is not complete, and that perhaps it asks never to be completed, that Sartre deplores the use of this expression which has gradually lost its entire meaning, one must nevertheless endeavor in one way or another to characterize this thought, whose repercussions are all the more unforeseeable as our minds are not prepared to receive it in its most fundamental rhythm.

But let us nonetheless maintain its "Christian name," and let us closely adhere to the clue that has directed us throughout our entire study, and let us for the last time, by means of successive interlacing steps, try to capture in our net this disturbing monster that sometimes bathes itself in clarity . . . in order to better escape our view.

Existentialism is the philosophy of human ambiguity. As a matter of fact, the recognition of this ambiguity is perhaps not a very new fact in the history of ideas. What is newer, and what at first appears "strange to every Mediterranean mind"—according to a formula that in the opinion of its author[12] constitutes a decisive condemnation—is a philosophy that attempts to make itself sufficiently objective in order to adapt itself to its object: namely, human subjectivity. That a being is capable of interrogating itself about itself is without a doubt a fact that necessarily must be taken into consideration, for this fact must immediately imply the choice of a special method whose point of departure is constituted by some attempt at definition in which it appropriates being only with reservation and in an equally special sense. This "appropriation with reservation" seems necessarily to characterize the primordial step of the philosopher: Descartes has missed this by committing the mistake of doubting about all existing things, but at that very moment taking himself— the one who doubts—for a thinking *thing*. This means, in fact,

[12] Namely, Lucien Fabre.

that doubt in regard to the world is always hyperbolic: one can never doubt except concerning this or that thing; but on the other hand, doubt about oneself could never be of the same type as doubt in regard to a determinate thing. More precisely, I cannot "doubt" my own existence, and in that sense the question cannot even be posed; but if it does not make sense to doubt that I exist, it certainly makes sense to doubt *what I am*. And there I realize that what is characteristic of my "being" is not-to-be-what-it-is—because it calls itself into question in regard to itself. In short, my existence is an evidence that no ulterior reflection can threaten; my essence, on the contrary, is a problem that a reflection in bad faith wishes to ignore, but which a purifying reflection must manifest as such.

Let us go further: my essence is not only a problem. *To exist is tantamount to being a problem for oneself.* And just as I do not cease to exist until my death, each attempt I make at ceasing to be this living problem will manifest my desire for blindness, my resignation *vis-à-vis* myself. One sees here the relations that, according to the viewpoint we have adopted, can be validly established between essence and existence. Either I consider only my essence, that is, the completion, the fixation of myself by death (in that case one must say that existence precedes essence), or I call "essence" that which defines me essentially as human subjectivity—the fact of being my own problem—and then I must say that essence and existence are contemporaries in me, because my essence is merely the fundamental character of my mode of being, namely an existence that is absolutely different from that of things.

Now, that is a way of looking at things that totally escapes classical philosophy. It is, indeed, a fact that the latter, even if it is aware of the philosophical problem raised by the sole existence of the philosophical attitude, quite soon considers this original "problem" like any other problem, of the same type as those which present themselves to the sciences. In short, for classical philosophy the issue is merely one of a problem *to be solved*, and it simply forgets to see in it the inescapably problematic origin of all problems. Forced to exist in order to explain the world, one nevertheless pretends to explain his own existence as well—employing the same methods science invented in regard to the world. Captured by his own attitude of objectifying things, he comes to objectify this very attitude—and in so doing, he renounces all positivity in order to deliver himself to the imaginary: for he wishes then to take God's point of view for himself, a point of view that is contradictory in that it excludes all situation and consequently all attitude. In this way, man suppresses himself in order to know himself, and forms—even if he is an atheist— the fiction of a supra-existence whose task it is to define his own human essence. And so the problem is solved at the cost of having been passed by in silence. If I grant an absolute consciousness the role of founding myself and the world, then I become a part of the world of this consciousness, and I am no more than an object among other objects: essence is passivity in being, it is made in order to be known; thus I will know myself through the intermediary of some fictive existence that is capable of conceiving (that is, at the same time creating and knowing) my essence.

One sees the contradiction, for after everything is said without any reservation, I attribute to myself the essential characteristics of all being, and then nevertheless pretend to preserve the benefit of my knowledge of myself. That is to say, philosophy, taken in its traditional form, is dependent upon an accessory reflection—on whose level we know that human reality makes itself the slave of its desire *to be*. From this, follow various consequences we have already met: the explicitly admitted, or more or less explicitly disguised, theory of psychological determinism; the mystification of morals, metamorphosed either into a sterile idealism or into some science of morals. In this way, the philosopher becomes a mechanic or a "moralist"—that is to say, a rationalist on the theoretical level, and on the practical level a "politician," who is convinced that the main issue is never about anything except pulling strings.

But to reconstruct human beings (that is to say, to reconstruct oneself at the same time), with their "failures" and "qualities," and then to judge them or to maneuver them, is always tantamount to being in contradiction with oneself, tantamount to being willing to conceal from oneself that the principles upon which one rests—by the very fact that one formulates them—are called into question. I can easily say that Paul is a kind of machine whose levers I feel capable of setting in motion: this means that Paul has adopted the attitude of self-suppression, through which he tends to make an object of himself, to repudiate his freedom, to be no more than a mechanism with foreseeable reactions. But if I pretend that every man is a similar machine, then I affirm the same thing in regard to myself, and in so doing I withdraw all meaning from my affirmation.

To declare that human reality is ambiguous, then, means nothing—as long as one refuses to recognize in a practical sense this essential characteristic, by treating it the way one treats things that are what they are. Psychology, then, becomes an inventory, and the moralization of the self becomes the training—of the other. But if one has truly understood that man is that "being" who perpetually remains in question for himself, one must renounce once and for all any attempt to account for what is human, and philosophy will, in turn, appear as a perpetual struggle of thought with itself.

The starting point is the fact that the world appears, but the world is indissolubly bound to my own appearance to myself. And this presence to myself assumes the character of a fact as well as that of an obligation. I *am* this presence to myself—and it is in this way alone that I can progressively accede to personality—but one must say equally that I *have to be this*, and that is why my own personalization is not a natural evolution but a moral activity. The subjectivity is given to me, but I have to conquer it in a process of subjectivation. I exist, but I cannot attain this existence except by assuming it. This question which I am—I have barely asked it, and look, I find myself tied to myself, responsible for myself, at once unified in the act of this "I" who poses it. To know oneself and to make oneself, these are one and the same thing, for one cannot know oneself without, by positing oneself as subject, contesting the objectivation toward which the act of knowledge tends.

I exist. This is a declaration that should not be confused with the establishment that *there is* a scratch-pad in front of me: in fact, this finding even implies that I exist. All philosophies speak of the subject, the ego, the person—but this is done only to make them enter into the category of Existence, which amounts to omitting the "I" in "I exist." And this omission bears heavily on all that follows, for then the ego is no more than an object of knowledge, an essence—and the knowing subject is thrown back into the impersonality of some "transcendental consciousness."

The first finding of the existentialist philosophy bears upon the irreality of such a non-existing consciousness, that is to say, of that "metaphysical error" which consists in pretending to explain my consciousness by means of the products of its own activity. I can aim at a depersonalization, but I cannot situate myself in the impersonal, outside each situation. In short, I cannot desert myself, I always take myself with me; there is no domain in which I could situate myself in order to account for this "I" which I can never cease to be.

Indeed, the classical illusion has its origin in the fact that one sunders the ambiguity in order to disclose it, on the one hand, as a natural behavior rooted in the world, and on the other, as the moral behavior of self-realization. But first, if the natural behavior is merely natural, if the issue were a form of behavior in the sense that one can say that a ball on an inclined plane will behave in such or such a way, then the transition to man's moral behavior would be completely unintelligible. Some philosophers have clearly seen this—but they have simply suppressed it. But the fact continues to be that the moral problem, once it is expressed, does not let itself be dismissed in this way, because (whether you like it or not) it is implied in the one fact that man can *attribute* a natural behavior *to himself*: from this it follows that the latter constitutes an *attitude* that on its part is open to a naturalization that is always pushed further, as well as to the struggle that is implied in its very definition. "I am a brute animal" means above all that I *am* not an animal and that a question poses itself for me concerning whether I should sink deeper into such a way of being, or, on the contrary, disengage myself from it, just as I have already had to do in order to become aware of it.

Thus, to become aware does not signify noticing that one *is* this or that; I exist, that is to say, I carry in me my own understanding, my own relationship to myself. When I picture the face of my girl friend, I need not reflect in order to understand the absence of my girl friend: I do not confuse this image with the objects that surround me. In short, I cannot imagine without being conscious of the fact that I imagine. To exist implies a becoming-aware-of; and that which one generally takes for this conscious grasp is the revival of this spontaneous consciousness, the attempt that one makes in order to recover it on the level of reflection. Classical philosophies assimilate consciousness to knowledge, perception to representation, self-presence to reflection on one's self. They deliberately omit *consciousness as consciousness*. They end by wanting to explain the latter from that which can be understood only through it. This is tantamount to committing the error of accounting for man through the material results of his work, of explaining the pioneer through the gold-bearing sill, and the ingot of gold through the roll of currency.

I exist; that is to say, I am a perpetual signification for myself. Even in the midst of the most exaggerated conformism I cannot forget myself completely: I cannot cease to be present to myself except at the cost of adopting an attitude of blindness. Such is the case, for instance, of an emotion in which I attempt to ignore the choice that the situation demands of me: but this attempt, however spontaneous it may be, is still a choice I make, I understand it implicitly as such, I persist in taking refuge in it even after my reflection has demanded of me some "voluntary" act of self-control. And if, working with the psychology of emotions, I later declare that there is an "essence" of the emotion, one then sees that the issue is about a lived essence, about an "existential essence," about an implicit comprehension of my own attitude; and although it is capable of being isolated, described, and fixed into concepts, it is nonetheless without any relationship to the traditional "essences" that the philosophers posit in the realm of the imaginary as pre-existing with respect to all existence, essences made to be known, objects of knowledge, and conceptions that are fully realized before every act of conceptualization. Its mode of being consists in a call toward its own *essentialization*.

In short, my attitude, whatever it may be, taken on each occasion, *means* something. But this signification itself is ambiguous precisely to the extent to which it must not be confused with a sign. In order to grasp the entire difference, it is useful to refer here to the work of Kafka. In Kafka's universe there are signs that offer themselves objectively everywhere; and if this universe appears to be absurd, it is because at each moment in this world the characters have the experience of the absolute emptiness of these signs, each one of which demands that a signification be resolutely bestowed upon it by a subject who engages himself in it. This door is here, open for everyone who feels a need to pass through it, and the guard in front of the door pronounces very firm words. These are so many signs that objectively are what they are. And man chooses to interpret them as if they represented the impossible: he waits humbly in front of the door—in order to learn at the moment of his death that this door was made for him, and for him alone.

In this sense, one could say that Camus stands exactly opposite Kafka, and that, at any rate, Sartre's existentialism opposes the absurdist statement "One must maintain the absurd" with this theme which is undoubtedly more fertile: "One must maintain the ambiguity."

Between a rigid consciousness which tends to suppress itself in its respect for absolute values, for signs without signification, and a rebelling consciousness which renounces all signification, from these two *attitudes* existentialism draws a lesson and describes consciousness as the presence to oneself, non-coincidence with oneself, the absolute origin of all meaning and all evaluation. No consciousness, as long as it exists, can completely coincide with itself in order to *be*, nor dissolve itself in order to be done with its own responsibility. But it can try to go in either one of these two directions; this very effort, however, manifests a bad faith that precedes the choice of either one of them.

This is the point of departure. The whole of existentialism springs from it—to the extent to which it remains faithful to it. As a system of struggle, it must struggle with itself. And the greatest risk that it will incessantly encounter is that of disavowing the ambiguity by passing from description to moral imperative. Having recognized in the human fact itself the position of the moral problem, it will have to deny itself all solutions to this problem, because otherwise it would precisely suppress the human fact. For it, the moral attitude will not consist in the total passage from a natural world to a universe of values; this attitude cannot consist in the suppression of what is human. It is in this sense that existentialism calls itself an authentic humanism.

This is to say that authenticity cannot be taken as a *state* that is accessible to man, a level at which he will be able to install himself. No one has ever come to grips with himself. To say that freedom is ambiguous because it must liberate itself, is still saying too little: one must add that it must will itself to be ambiguous, and know that it is not total liberation. No authenticating of myself can free me from the incessant problem that is my situation: my relationship to the world and my relationship to the other. I can exist only by engaging myself, and my engagement can never content itself with having been lucid once and for all; the authentic choice I make in regard to myself is not a solution, but a starting point of new problems. As far as the style of life I adopt following a moral conversion is concerned, I could very well say that in each particular situation "it causes the rules to be cancelled": but it is not without me that, from now on, it guides my behavior. Just as does the natural attitude, it carries within it its own struggle. And from this point of view the only difference between the two—the genuine result of the conversion—is to be found in the fact that, from now on, that which was first a spontaneous struggle turns into an obligation to struggle.

In this sense, the unique moral recommendation of existentialism, which is a simple transposition of its description of what is human, could be "to live with the laceration of consciousness." One sees that the issue here is one of an equilibrium, which is always to be invented and which always remains unstable, between action (requiring a coherent engagement) and reflection (necessitating ratification in the form of distance from one's self of this latent laceration that is the self-presence). And this is to say that the effort toward authenticity is not an evasion of action: disengagement, which it indeed implies as a means, must not be taken for its own goal. The human condition can be ignored in bad faith, or understood and lived in such an effort toward authenticity: in no case can it be dismissed. The conversion from natural bad faith is not inscribed in the process of any necessitating dialectics; but neither does it permit the individualist suppression of the problem that everyone keeps constituting for himself, to the extent that his existence is inevitably situated. Each man ties himself to himself from the moment in which he accepts this situation as his, in which he formulates this implicit relation to himself that has already constituted him in his presence to the world.

The first consequence of these remarks is that each solution is simultaneously provisional, individual, and practical: this means that its author cannot rest in the choice he has made in its regard, that he must not ask it of someone else, and finally that he will derive his consistency only from the unfolding of his efforts in the world. I cannot choose freedom without engaging myself in an enterprise of liberation: the approach of a consciousness toward authenticity would itself be inauthentic if this consciousness—in order to reach the end faster—were to forget that it is situated. Freedom is not immediately salvaged by an abstraction from the situation; but it is the situation that must be progressively penetrated by freedom. Thus I cannot choose my freedom without choosing a mode of free relationship with the other. And if my freedom needs the freedom of the other in order not to deny itself, I can, for instance, will the emancipation of women. But it is clear that if, given a country in which women do not have the right to vote, I fight against giving that right to them, I must at least never lose sight of the fact that this right is theirs as women, and that the issue concerns a situation that no passage toward the universal could ever suppress. And what is more, I must take into account the ability of the women in that country to enjoy such emancipation. That is to say, my enterprise should not be a political one, but above all a moral one—for the political attitude attempts to create a new situation in the name of certain principles, whereas the moral attitude tends toward transforming the existing situation in order to make it accessible to these principles.

It is here that the error of all artificiality appears: the conservative wants to artificially maintain a state of affairs, the revolutionary wishes to artificially impose some ideal norm upon concrete individuals who are in different situations. The one believes in the absolute value of the fact, the other in the absolute value of the ideal. But positivism as well as idealism are equally at fault: they refuse to recognize that ambiguity of the human fact that carries in itself its own ideal in the choice that each one makes of himself in his situation. Generally speaking, artificiality consists in pretending to impose, or imposing, on oneself a solution from the outside—before assuring oneself that it can be lived as an effective solution and as a point of departure for authentic problems. Emotion is an artificial solution that consists in rejecting the genuine problem; the same holds true for the act of imagining to the extent to which it pretends to obtain satisfaction. Similarly, the political attitude wants immediate solutions: it eludes what is human, and refuses to recognize that, in man, progress does not mean technical transformation, but subjective conversion and conscious grasp of the natural attitude.

One sees that existentialism finds itself here at a dangerous turning point. The temptation is great to turn either toward a transcendental philosophy ignorant of individual historical situations, or toward an exclusive preoccupation with historicity, where the risk is great that one will forgo all concern for authenticity. In this sense, it is permissible to say that the ambiguity cannot be maintained to the end, except under the condition of establishing some synthesis between radical conversion and historical progress, or, if you wish, between the realism of authenticity in Husserl or even Heidegger, and the realism of history in Marx.

Such is undoubtedly the road that suggests itself here as a

way to overcome the dilemma between individualism and communism. If man could abstract from human beings, he would accede to authenticity from the height of his ivory tower. And if he could abstract from himself, the question could no longer be posed. But the question *remains*: man himself is that question. To will to save oneself all by oneself alone means, properly speaking, to run away from oneself; to will to save the others, without them, means to withdraw all value from the salvation one imposes upon them. Everyone must decide about the means he has at his disposal to engage in the liberation of what is human, without isolating himself in his own case and without transcending the limits beyond which his action is no more than a useless constraint.

This is to say, no solution must be left on its own; no conviction can cease to be indefinitely contested; and yet one has to invent solutions and begin as someone who is convinced. The essential point is to understand that the conviction must not be belief, but faith, for a belief addresses itself *to what is* —either in the order of facts or in the order of ideas; but faith is concerned with the *one who exists* and who makes his existence his own, without ever pretending to justify it by assuming it, for assuming it is carrying it further, hollowing it out further, and making the question that it poses more urgent.

As a philosophy of the "prise de la conscience," existentialism involves a mediatization of the immediate, a reflexive recoil in regard to the natural attitude, in which man has not yet disengaged himself from himself. But since this mediatory thought is a purifying thought, it can neither contest itself nor hold as inauthentic a "conscious grasp" in which the subject would satisfy itself by placing the world between brackets and "rolling itself in itself"—according to an ancient saying of Montaigne, which very aptly characterizes the accompanying reflection.

As Alain writes: "To believe is enjoyable. It is a rapture of which one must deprive oneself. . . . Man is not in a situation in a way that he could ever offer himself the luxury of believing. Belief means slavery, war, and misery. And in my opinion faith stands opposite to belief. Faith in man is hard for a man, for it is faith in a living spirit; it is faith that lashes the mind, that pierces it, that puts it to shame; it is faith that shakes up the sleeper."

If you have faith in man, do not believe any man. If you pretend to exist, do not accept any answers: invent your answers. To write is a useless act if one writes for those who are expecting answers. The greatest respect one could pay to Sartre's work is to contest incessantly its practical efficacy; by doing just that, one has already allowed it to reach its essential goal. "It is to be wished that the whole of literature would become moral and problematic. . . . Moral—not moralizing: that it would show simply that man is *also* value and that the questions he asks are always moral questions. Above all, that it shows the inventor in man. In a sense, each situation is a trap, with walls everywhere: I express myself badly: there are no exits to *choose*. An exit—that is to be invented. And everyone, by inventing his own exit, invents himself. Man must be invented every day."

But finally, if I wish to attach no importance to the humanization of man, and if it pleases me to choose myself as resigned, resigned to being trapped, resigned to degradation, resigned to bad faith . . . this is the last and supreme struggle: "What purpose does all this serve?" Through this contestation the moral problem, the questioning of man by man himself, finds itself, in turn, called into question. It is in this way that even the decision to adopt the moral attitude does not allow man to take himself seriously; it rests on nothing; it does not found itself upon any absolute sign; no guarantee justifies it from the outside. In it resides the radical invention of man by man himself, and if this invention is human, it is because it proceeds from the nothingness of that which *is* not, because nothing, absolutely nothing, indicates its value in advance, and this is because the freedom from which it proceeds is free to repudiate itself as well as to conquer itself.

". . . the collectivity passes the reflection and meditation by means of literature, it acquires an unhappy conscience, a lopsided image of itself that it constantly tries to modify and improve. But, after all, the art of writing is not protected by immutable decrees of Providence; it is what men make it; they choose it in choosing themselves. If it were to turn into pure propaganda or pure entertainment, society would wallow in the immediate, that is, in the life without memory of hymenoptera and gasteropods. Of course, all this is not very important. The world can very well do without literature. But it can do without man still better."[13]

Selective Bibliography

L'être et le néant: Essai d'ontologie phénoménologique (Paris: Gallimard, 1943) English: *Being and Nothingness*, trans. Hazel Barnes (New York: Philosophical Library, 1956)

L'existentialisme est un humanisme (Paris: Nagel, 1946). English: *Existentialism [Is a Humanism]*, trans. B. Frechtman (New York: Philosophical Library, 1947)

Situations, 6 vols. (Paris: Gallimard, 1947–65)

Simone de Beauvoir, *Pour une morale de l'ambiguïté* (Paris: Gallimard, 1947) English: *The Ethics of Ambiguity*, trans. B. Frechtman (New York: Philosophical Library, 1948)

Francis Jeanson, *Le problème moral et la pensée de Sartre* (Paris: Seuil, 1965)

Norman N. Greene, *Jean-Paul Sartre: The Existentialist Ethic* (Ann Arbor: University of Michigan Press, 1960)

Thomas C. Anderson, "Is a Sartrian Ethics Possible?" *Philosophy Today*, 14 (1970), pp. 117–40.

13 *What Is Literature?*, p. 297.

Chapter 10

INTRODUCTION

SIMONE DE BEAUVOIR (1908–   ), novelist, drama-
tist, and philosopher, was educated at the Sorbonne, receiving her degree in philosophy in 1929. From then until 1943
she held teaching positions at various lycées in Marseilles,
Rouen, and Paris, deciding finally to devote her time exclusively to literary and philosophical work. Her first novel,
L'Invitée, was published in 1943 and was followed almost
immediately by an essay entitled *Pyrrhus et Cinéas*. *Le Sang
des autres* was published in 1944 and *Les Bouches inutiles* in
1945. By 1947 she had completed two works that are mainly
philosophical in character: a novel, *Tous les hommes sont
mortels*; and *Pour une morale de l'ambiguïté*. *Le deuxième
sexe* appeared in 1949, and what is considered to be her best
novel, *Les Mandarins*, in 1954.

Simone de Beauvoir has been one of Sartre's most devoted
disciples. She has contributed considerably to the promulga-
tion of his ideas and has made her own personal contributions
to existentialism as well, particularly in the realm of ethics.
Pour une morale de l'ambiguïté, for example, is a work in
which she attempts to justify Sartre's position in ethics and
to further develop his view; she then proceeds to present the
view systematically in outline form.

The selection that follows is Chapter 5 from *The Ethics
of Ambiguity*, in which the author is explaining why, and in
what sense, an existentialist conception of ethics should be
characterized by the label "ambiguity."

AMBIGUITY

Simone de Beauvoir

The notion of ambiguity must not be confused with that of
absurdity. To declare that existence is absurd is to deny that
it can ever be given a meaning; to say that it is ambiguous is
to assert that its meaning is never fixed, that it must be constantly won. Absurdity challenges every ethics; but also the
finished rationalization of the real would leave no room for
ethics; it is because man's condition is ambiguous that he
seeks, through failure and outrageousness, to save his existence. Thus, to say that action has to be lived in its truth,
that is, in the consciousness of the antinomies which it involves, does not mean that one has to renounce it. In *Plutarch
Lied* Pierrefeu rightly says that in war there is no victory
which can not be regarded as unsuccessful, for the objective
which one aims at is the total annihilation of the enemy and
this result is never attained; yet there are wars which are won
and wars which are lost. So is it with any activity; failure and
success are two aspects of reality which at the start are not
perceptible. That is what makes criticism so easy and art so
difficult: the critic is always in a good position to show the
limits that every artist gives himself in choosing himself;
painting is not given completely either in Giotto or Titian or
Cézanne; it is sought through the centuries and is never finished; a painting in which all pictorial problems are resolved
is really inconceivable; painting itself is this movement toward its own reality; it is not the vain displacement of a mill-

This essay is from *The Ethics of Ambiguity*, by Simone de Beauvoir, trans. Bernard Frechtman (New York, 1967), pp. 129–55. Copyright © 1948 by Philosophical Library, Publishers.

stone turning in the void; it concretizes itself on each canvas as an absolute existence. Art and science do not establish themselves despite failure but through it; which does not prevent there being truths and errors, masterpieces and lemons, depending upon whether the discovery or the painting has or has not known how to win the adherence of human consciousnesses; this amounts to saying that failure, always ineluctable, is in certain cases spared and in others not.

It is interesting to pursue this comparison; not that we are likening action to a work of art or a scientific theory, but because in any case human transcendence must cope with the same problem: it has to found itself, though it is prohibited from ever fulfilling itself. Now, we know that neither science nor art ever leaves it up to the future to justify its present existence. In no age does art consider itself as something which is paving the way for Art: so-called archaic art prepares for classicism only in the eyes of archaeologists; the sculptor who fashioned the Korai of Athens rightfully thought that he was producing a finished work of art; in no age has science considered itself as partial and lacunary; without believing itself to be definitive, it has however, always wanted to be a total expression of the world, and it is in its totality that in each age it again raises the question of its own validity. There we have an example of how man must, in any event, assume his finiteness: not by treating his existence as transitory or relative but by reflecting the infinite within it, that is, by treating it as absolute. There is an art only because at every moment art has willed itself absolutely; likewise there is a liberation of man only if, in aiming at itself, freedom is achieved absolutely in the very fact of aiming at itself. This requires that each action be considered as a finished form whose different moments, instead of fleeing toward the future in order to find there their justification, reflect and confirm one another so well that there is no longer a sharp separation between present and future, between means and ends.

But if these moments constitute a unity, there must be no contradiction among them. Since the liberation aimed at is not a *thing* situated in an unfamiliar time, but a movement which realizes itself by tending to conquer, it can not attain itself if it denies itself at the start; action can not seek to fulfill itself by means which would destroy its very meaning. So much so that in certain situations there will be no other issue for man than rejection. In what is called political realism there is no room for rejection because the present is considered as transitory; there is rejection only if man lays claim in the present to his existence as an absolute value; then he must absolutely reject what would deny this value. Today, more or less consciously in the name of such an ethics, we condemn a magistrate who handed over a communist to save ten hostages and along with him all the Vichyites who were trying "to make the best of things": it was not a matter of rationalizing the present such as it was imposed by the German occupation, but of rejecting it unconditionally. The resistance did not aspire to a positive effectiveness; it was a negation, a revolt, a martyrdom; and in this negative movement freedom was positively and absolutely confirmed.

In one sense the negative attitude is easy; the rejected object is given unequivocally and unequivocally defines the revolt that one opposes to it; thus, all French anti-fascists were united during the occupation by their common resistance to a single oppressor. The return to the positive encounters many more obstacles, as we have well seen in France where divisions and hatreds were revived at the same time as were the parties. In the moment of rejection, the antinomy of action is removed, and means and end meet; freedom immediately sets itself up as its own goal and fulfills itself by so doing. But the antinomy reappears as soon as freedom again gives itself ends which are far off in the future; then, through the resistances of the given, divergent means offer themselves and certain ones come to be seen as contrary to their ends. It has often been observed that revolt alone is pure. Every construction implies the outrage of dictatorship, of violence. This is the theme, among others, of Koestler's *Gladiators*. Those who, like this symbolic *Spartacus*, do not want to retreat from the outrage and resign themselves to impotence, usually seek refuge in the values of seriousness. That is why, among individuals as well as collectivities, the negative moment is often the most genuine. Goethe, Barrès, and Aragon, disdainful or rebellious in their romantic youth, shattered old conformisms and thereby proposed a real, though incomplete, liberation. But what happened later on? Goethe became a servant of the state, Barrès of nationalism, and Aragon of Stalinist conformism. We know how the seriousness of the Catholic Church was substituted for the Christian spirit, which was a rejection of dead Law, a subjective rapport of the individual with God through faith and charity; the Reformation was a revolt of subjectivity, but Protestantism in turn changed into an objective moralism in which the seriousness of works replaced the restlessness of faith. As for revolutionary humanism, it accepts only rarely the tension of permanent liberation; it has created a Church where salvation is bought by membership in a party as it is bought elsewhere by baptism and indulgences. We have seen that this recourse to the serious is a lie; it entails the sacrifice of man to the Thing, of freedom to the Cause. In order for the return to the positive to be genuine it must involve negativity, it must not conceal the antinomies between means and end, present and future; they must be lived in a permanent tension; one must neither retreat from the outrage of violence nor deny it, or, which amounts to the same thing, assume it lightly. Kierkegaard has said that what distinguishes the pharisee from the genuinely moral man is that the former considers his anguish as a sure sign of his virtue; from the fact that he asks himself, "Am I Abraham?" he concludes, "I am Abraham"; but morality resides in the painfulness of an indefinite questioning. The problem which we are posing is not the same as that of Kierkegaard; the important thing to us is to know whether, in given conditions, Isaac must be killed or not. But we also think that what distinguishes the tyrant from the man of good will is that the first rests in the certainty of his aims, whereas the second keeps asking himself, "Am I really working for the liberation of men? Isn't this end contested by the sacrifices through which I aim at it?" In setting up its ends, freedom must put them in parentheses, confront them at each moment with that absolute end which it itself constitutes, and contest, in its own name, the means it uses to win itself.

It will be said that these considerations remain quite abstract. What must be done, practically? Which action is good? Which is bad? To ask such a question is also to fall into a naive abstraction. We don't ask the physicist, "Which hypotheses are true?" Nor the artist, "By what procedures does one produce a work whose beauty is guaranteed?" Ethics does not furnish recipes any more than do science and art. One can merely propose methods. Thus, in science the fundamental problem is to make the idea adequate to its content and the law adequate to the facts; the logician finds that in the case where the pressure of the given fact bursts the concept which serves to comprehend it, one is obliged to invent another concept; but he can not define *a priori* the moment of invention, still less foresee it. Analogously, one may say that in the case where the content of the action falsifies its meaning, one must modify not the meaning, which is here willed absolutely, but the content itself; however, it is impossible to determine this relationship between meaning and content abstractly and universally: there must be a trial and decision in each case. But likewise just as the physicist finds it profitable to reflect on the conditions of scientific invention and the artist on those of artistic creation without expecting any ready-made solutions to come from these reflections, it is useful for the man of action to find out under what conditions his undertakings are valid. We are going to see that on this basis new perspectives are disclosed.

In the first place, it seems to us that the individual as such is one of the ends at which our action must aim. Here we are at one with the point of view of Christian charity, the Epicurean cult of friendship, and Kantian moralism which treats each man as an end. He interests us not merely as a member of a class, a nation, or a collectivity, but as an individual man. This distinguishes us from the systematic politician who cares only about collective destinies; and probably a tramp enjoying his bottle of wine, or a child playing with a balloon, or a Neapolitan lazzarone loafing in the sun in no way helps in the liberation of man; that is why the abstract will of the revolutionary scorns the concrete benevolence which occupies itself in satisfying desires which have no morrow. However, it must not be forgotten that there is a concrete bond between freedom and existence; to will man free is to will there to *be* being, it is to will the disclosure of being in the joy of existence; in order for the idea of liberation to have a concrete meaning, the joy of existence must be asserted in each one, at every instant; the movement toward freedom assumes its real, flesh and blood figure in the world by thickening into pleasure, into happiness. If the satisfaction of an old man drinking a glass of wine counts for nothing, then production and wealth are only hollow myths; they have meaning only if they are capable of being retrieved in individual and living joy. The saving of time and the conquest of leisure have no meaning if we are not moved by the laugh of a child at play. If we do not love life on our own account and through others, it is futile to seek to justify it in any way.

However, politics is right in rejecting benevolence to the extent that the latter thoughtlessly sacrifices the future to the present. The ambiguity of freedom, which very often is occupied only in fleeing from itself, introduces a difficult equivocation into relationships with each individual taken one by one. Just what is meant by the expression "to love others"? What is meant by taking them as ends? In any event, it is evident that we are not going to decide to fulfill the will of every man. There are cases where a man positively wants evil, that is, the enslavement of other men, and he must then be fought. It also happens that, without harming anyone, he flees from his own freedom, seeking passionately and alone to attain the being which constantly eludes him. If he asks for our help, are we to give it to him? We blame a man who helps a drug addict intoxicate himself or a desperate man commit suicide, for we think that rash behavior of this sort is an attempt of the individual against his own freedom; he must be made aware of his error and put in the presence of the real demands of his freedom. Well and good. But what if he persists? Must we then use violence? There again the serious man busies himself dodging the problem; the values of life, of health, and of moral conformism being set up, one does not hesitate to impose them on others. But we know that this pharisaism can cause the worst disasters: lacking drugs, the addict may kill himself. It is no more necessary to serve an abstract ethics obstinately than to yield without due consideration to impulses of pity or generosity; violence is justified only if it opens concrete possibilities to the freedom which I am trying to save; by practising it I am willy-nilly assuming an engagement in relation to others and to myself; a man whom I snatch from the death which he had chosen has the right to come and ask me for means and reasons for living; the tyranny practised against an invalid can be justified only by his getting better; whatever the purity of the intention which animates me, any dictatorship is a fault for which I have to get myself pardoned. Besides, I am in no position to make decisions of this sort indiscriminately; the example of the unknown person who throws himself in to the Seine and whom I hesitate whether or not to fish out is quite abstract; in the absence of a concrete bond with this desperate person my choice will never be anything but a contingent facticity. If I find myself in a position to do violence to a child, or to a melancholic, sick, or distraught person the reason is that I also find myself charged with his upbringing, his happiness, and his health: I am a parent, a teacher, a nurse, a doctor, or a friend. . . So, by a tacit agreement, by the very fact that I am solicited, the strictness of my decision is accepted or even desired; the more seriously I accept my responsibilities, the more justified it is. That is why love authorizes severities which are not granted to indifference. What makes the problem so complex is that, on the one hand, one must not make himself an accomplice of that flight from freedom that is found in heedlessness, caprice, mania, and passion, and that, on the other hand, it is the abortive movement of man toward being which is his very existence, it is through the failure which he has assumed that he asserts himself as a freedom. To want to prohibit a man from error is to forbid him to fulfill his own existence, it is to deprive him of life. At the beginning of Claudel's *The Satin Shoe*, the husband of Dona Prouheze, the Judge, the Just, as the author regards him, explains that every plant needs a gardener in order to grow and that he is the one whom heaven has destined for his young wife; beside the fact that we are shocked by the arrogance of such a thought (for how does he know that he is this enlightened gardener? Isn't he merely a jealous husband?) this likening of a soul to a plant is not acceptable; for, as Kant would say, the value of an act lies not in its *conformity* to an external model, but in its internal truth. We object to the inquisitors who want to create faith and virtue from without; we object to all forms of fascism which seek to fashion the happiness of man from without; and also the paternalism which thinks that it has done something for man by prohibiting him from certain possibilities of temptation, whereas what is necessary is to give him reasons for resisting it.

Thus, violence is not immediately justified when it opposes willful acts which one considers perverted; it becomes inadmissible if it uses the pretext of ignorance to deny a freedom which, as we have seen, can be practised within ignorance itself. Let the "enlightened élites" strive to change the situation of the child, the illiterate, the primitive crushed beneath his superstitions; that is one of their most urgent tasks; but in this very effort they must respect a freedom which, like theirs, is absolute. They are always opposed, for example, to the extension of universal suffrage by adducing the incompetence of the masses, of women, of the natives in the colonies; but this forgetting that man always has to decide by himself in the darkness, that he must want beyond what he knows. If infinite knowledge were necessary (even supposing that it were conceivable), then the colonial administrator himself would not have the right to freedom; he is much further from perfect knowledge than the most backward savage is from him. Actually, to vote is not to govern; and to govern is not merely to maneuver; there is an ambiguity today, and particularly in France, because we think that we are not the master of our destiny; we no longer hope to help make history, we are resigned to submitting to it; all that our internal politics does is reflect the play of external forces, no party hopes to determine the fate of the country but merely to foresee the future which is being prepared in the world by foreign powers and to use, as best we can, the bit of indetermination which still escapes their foresight. Drawn along by this tactical realism, the citizens themselves no longer consider the vote as the assertion of their will but as a maneuver, whether one adheres completely to the maneuvering of a party or whether one invents his own strategy; the electors consider themselves not as men who are consulted about a particular point but as forces which are numbered and which are ordered about with a view to distant ends. And that is probably why the French, who formerly were so eager to declare their opinions, take no further interest in an act which has become a disheartening strategy. So, the fact is that if it is necessary not to vote but to measure the weight of one's vote, this calculation requires such extensive information and such a sureness of foresight that only a specialized technician can have the boldness to express an opinion. But that is one of the abuses whereby the whole meaning of democracy is lost; the logical conclusion of this would be to suppress the vote. The vote should really be the expression of a concrete will, the choice of a representative capable of defending, within the general framework of the country and the world, the particular interests of his electors. The ignorant and the outcast also has interests to defend; he alone is "competent" to decide upon his hopes and his trust. By a sophism which leans upon the dishonesty of the serious, one does not merely argue about his formal impotence to choose, but one draws arguments from the content of his choice. I recall, among others, the naiveté of a right-thinking young girl who said, "The vote for women is all well and good in principle, only, if women get the vote, they'll all vote red." With like impudence it is almost unanimously stated today in France that if the natives of the French Union were given the rights of self-determination, they would live quietly in their villages without doing anything, which would be harmful to the higher interests of the Economy. And doubtless the state of stagnation in which they choose to live is not that which a man can wish for another man; it is desirable to open new possibilities to the indolent Negroes so that the interests of the Economy may one day merge with theirs. But for the time being, they are left to vegetate in the sort of situation where their freedom can merely be negative: the best thing they can desire is not to tire themselves, not to suffer, and not to work; and even this freedom is denied them. It is the most consummate and inacceptable form of oppression.

However, the "enlightened élite" objects, one does not let a child dispose of himself, one does not permit him to vote. This is another sophism. To the extent that woman or the happy or resigned slave lives in the infantile world of ready-made values, calling them "an eternal child" or "a grown-up child" has some meaning, but the analogy is only partial. Childhood is a particular sort of situation: it is a natural situation whose limits are not created by other men and which is thereby not comparable to a situation of oppression; it is a situation which is common to all men and which is temporary for all; therefore, it does not represent a limit which cuts off the individual from his possibilities, but, on the contrary, the moment of a development in which new possibilities are won. The child is ignorant because he has not yet had the time to acquire knowledge, not because this time has been refused him. To treat him as a child is not to bar him from the future but to open it to him; he needs to be taken in hand, he invites authority, it is the form which the resistance of facticity, through which all liberation is brought about, takes for him. And on the other hand, even in this situation the child has a right to his freedom and must be respected as a human person. What gives *Emile* its value is the brilliance with which Rousseau asserts this principle. There is a very annoying naturalistic optimism in *Emile*; in the rearing of the child, as in any relationship with others, the ambiguity of freedom implies the outrage of violence; in a sense, all education is a failure. But Rousseau is right in refusing to allow childhood to be oppressed. And in practice raising a child as one cultivates a plant which one does not consult about its needs is very different from considering it as a freedom to whom the future must be opened.

Thus, we can set up point number one: the good of an

individual or a group of individuals requires that it be taken as an absolute end of our action; but we are not authorized to decide upon this end *a priori*. The fact is that no behavior is ever authorized to begin with, and one of the concrete consequences of existentialist ethics is the rejection of all the previous justifications which might be drawn from the civilization, the age, and the culture; it is the rejection of every principle of authority. To put it positively, the precept will be to treat the other (to the extent that he is the only one concerned, which is the moment that we are considering at present) as a freedom so that his end may be freedom; in using this conducting-wire one will have to incur the risk, in each case, of inventing an original solution. Out of disappointment in love a young girl takes an overdose of phenobarbital; in the morning friends find her dying, they call a doctor, she is saved; later on she becomes a happy mother of a family; her friends were right in considering her suicide as a hasty and heedless act and in putting her into a position to reject it or return to it freely. But in asylums one sees melancholic patients who have tried to commit suicide twenty times, who devote their freedom to seeking the means of escaping their jailers and of putting an end to their intolerable anguish; the doctor who gives them a friendly pat on the shoulder is their tyrant and their torturer. A friend who is intoxicated by alcohol or drugs asks me for money so that he can go and buy the poison that is necessary to him; I urge him to get cured, I take him to a doctor, I try to help him live; insofar as there is a chance of my being successful, I am acting correctly in refusing him the sum he asks for. But if circumstances prohibit me from doing anything to change the situation in which he is struggling, all I can do is give in; a deprivation of a few hours will do nothing but exasperate his torments uselessly; and he may have recourse to extreme means to get what I do not give him. That is also the problem touched on by Ibsen in *The Wild Duck*. An individual lives in a situation of falsehood; the falsehood is violence, tyranny: shall I tell the truth in order to free the victim? It would first be necessary to create a situation of such a kind that the truth might be bearable and that, though losing his illusions, the deluded individual might again find about him reasons for hoping. What makes the problem more complex is that the freedom of one man almost always concerns that of other individuals. Here is a married couple who persist in living in a hovel; if one does not succeed in giving them the desire to live in a more healthful dwelling, they must be allowed to follow their preferences; but the situation changes if they have children; the freedom of the parents would be the ruin of their sons, and as freedom and the future are on the side of the latter, these are the ones who must first be taken into account. The Other is multiple, and on the basis of this new questions arise.

One might first wonder for whom we are seeking freedom and happiness. When raised in this way, the problem is abstract; the answer will, therefore, be arbitrary, and the arbitrary always involves outrage. It is not entirely the fault of the district social-worker if she is apt to be odious; because, her money and time being limited, she hesitates before distributing it to this one or that one, she appears to others as a pure externality, a blind facticity. Contrary to the formal strictness of Kantianism for whom the more abstract the act is the more virtuous it is, generosity seems to us to be better grounded and therefore more valid the less distinction there is between the other and ourself and the more we fulfill ourself in taking the other as an end. That is what happens if I am engaged in relation to others. The Stoics impugned the ties of family, friendship, and nationality so that they recognized only the universal form of man. But man is man only through situations whose particularity is precisely a universal fact. There are men who expect help from certain men and not from others, and these expectations define privileged lines of action. It is fitting that the Negro fight for the Negro, the Jew for the Jew, the proletarian for the proletarian, and the Spaniard in Spain. But the assertion of these particular solidarities must not contradict the will for universal solidarity and each finite undertaking must also be open on the totality of men.

But it is then that we find in concrete form the conflicts which we have described abstractly; for the cause of freedom can triumph only through particular sacrifices. And certainly there are hierarchies among the goods desired by men: one will not hesitate to sacrifice the comfort, luxury, and leisure of certain men to assure the liberation of certain others; but when it is a question of choosing among freedoms, how shall we decide?

Let us repeat, one can only indicate a method here. The first point is always to consider what genuine human interest fills the abstract form which one proposes as the action's end. Politics always puts forward Ideas: Nation, Empire, Union, Economy, etc. But none of these forms has value in itself; it has it only insofar as it involves concrete individuals. If a nation can assert itself proudly only to the detriment of its members, if a union can be created only to the detriment of those it is trying to unite, the nation or the union must be rejected. We repudiate all idealisms, mysticisms, etcetera which prefer a Form to man himself. But the matter becomes really agonizing when it is a question of a Cause which genuinely serves man. That is why the question of Stalinist politics, the problem of the relationship of the Party to the masses which it uses in order to serve them, is in the forefront of the preoccupations of all men of good will. However, there are very few who raise it without dishonesty, and we must first try to dispel a few fallacies.

The opponent of the U.S.S.R. is making use of a fallacy when, emphasizing the part of criminal violence assumed by Stalinist politics, he neglects to confront it with the ends pursued. Doubtless, the purges, the deportations, the abuses of the occupation, and the police dictatorship surpass in importance the violences practised by any other country; the very fact that there are a hundred and sixty million inhabitants in Russia multiplies the numerical coefficient of the injustices committed. But these quantitative considerations are insufficient. One can no more judge the means without the end which gives it its meaning than he can detach the end from the means which defines it. Lynching a Negro or suppressing a hundred members of the opposition are two analogous acts. Lynching is an absolute evil; it represents the survival of an obsolete civilization, the perpetuation of a struggle

of races which has to disappear; it is a fault without justification or excuse. Suppressing a hundred opponents is surely
an outrage, but it may have meaning and a reason; it is a
matter of maintaining a regime which brings to an immense
mass of men a bettering of their lot. Perhaps this measure
could have been avoided; perhaps it merely represents that
necessary element of failure which is involved in any positive
construction. It can be judged only by being replaced in the
ensemble of the cause it serves.

But, on the other hand, the defender of the U.S.S.R. is
making use of a fallacy when he unconditionally justifies the
sacrifices and the crimes by the ends pursued; it would first
be necessary to prove that, on the one hand, the end is unconditioned and that, on the other hand, the crimes committed in its name were strictly necessary. Against the death
of Bukharin one counters with Stalingrad; but one would
have to know to what effective extent the Moscow trials in-
creased the chances of the Russian victory. One of the ruses
of Stalinist orthodoxy is, playing on the idea of necessity, to
put the whole of the revolution on one side of the scale; the
other side will always seem very light. But the very idea of
a total dialectic of history does not imply that any factor
is ever determining; on the contrary, if one admits that the
life of a man may change the course of events, it is that one
adheres to the conception which grants a preponderant role
to Cleopatra's nose and Cromwell's wart. One is here playing,
with utter dishonesty, on two opposite conceptions of the
idea of necessity: one synthetic, and the other analytic; one
dialectic, the other deterministic. The first makes History
appear as an intelligible becoming within which the particularity of contingent accidents is reabsorbed; the dialectical
sequence of the moments is possible only if there is within
each moment an indetermination of the particular elements
taken one by one. If, on the contrary, one grants the strict
determinism of each causal series, one ends in a contingent
and disordered vision of the ensemble, the conjunction of the
series being brought about by chance. Therefore, a Marxist
must recognize that none of his particular decisions involves
the revolution in its totality; it is merely a matter of hasten-

ing or retarding its coming, of saving himself the use of other and more costly means. That does not mean that he must retreat from violence but that he must not regard it as justified *a priori* by its ends. If he considers his enterprise in its truth, that is, in its finiteness, he will understand that he has never anything but a finite stake to oppose to the sacrifices which he calls for, and that it is an uncertain stake. Of course, this uncertainty should not keep him from pursuing his goals; but it requires that one concern himself in each case with finding a balance between the goal and its means.

Thus, we challenge every condemnation as well as every *a priori* justification of the violence practised with a view to a valid end. They must be legitimized concretely. A calm, mathematical calculation is here impossible. One must attempt to judge the chances of success that are involved in a certain sacrifice; but at the beginning this judgment will always be doubtful; besides, in the face of the immediate reality of the sacrifice, the notion of chance is difficult to think about. On the one hand, one can multiply a probability infinitely without ever reaching certainty; but yet, practically, it ends by merging with this asymptote: in our private life as in our collective life there is no other truth than a statistical one. On the other hand, the interests at stake do not allow themselves to be put into an equation; the suffering of one man, that of a million men, are incommensurable with the conquests realized by millions of others, present death is incommensurable with the life to come. It would be utopian to want to set up on the one hand the chances of success multiplied by the stake one is after, and on the other hand the weight of the immediate sacrifice. One finds himself back at the anguish of free decision. And that is why political choice is an ethical choice: it is a wager as well as a decision; one bets on the chances and risks of the measure under consideration; but whether chances and risks must be assumed or not in the given circumstances must be decided without help, and in so doing one sets up values. If in 1793 the Girondists rejected the violences of the Terror whereas a Saint-Just and a Robespierre assumed them, the reason is that they did not have the same conception of freedom. Nor was the same republic being aimed at between 1830 and 1840 by the republicans who limited themselves to a purely political opposition and those who adopted the technique of insurrection. In each case it is a matter of defining an end and realizing it, knowing that the choice of the means employed affects both the definition and the fulfillment.

Ordinarily, situations are so complex that a long analysis is necessary before being able to pose the ethical moment of the choice. We shall confine ourselves here to the consideration of a few simple examples which will enable us to make our attitude somewhat more precise. In an underground revolutionary movement when one discovers the presence of a stool-pigeon, one does not hesitate to beat him up; he is a present and future danger who has to be gotten rid of; but if a man is merely suspected of treason, the case is more ambiguous. We blame those northern peasants who in the war of 1914-18 massacred an innocent family which was suspected of signaling to the enemy; the reason is that not only were the presumptions vague, but the danger was uncertain; at any rate, it was enough to put the suspects into prison; while waiting for a serious inquiry it was easy to keep them from doing any harm. However, if a questionable individual holds the fate of other men in his hands, if, in order to avoid the risk of killing one innocent man, one runs the risk of letting ten innocent men die, it is reasonable to sacrifice him. We can merely ask that such decisions be not taken hastily and lightly, and that, all things considered, the evil that one inflicts be lesser than that which is being forestalled.

There are cases still more disturbing because there the violence is not immediately efficacious; the violences of the Resistance did not aim at the material weakening of Germany; it happens that their purpose was to create such a state of violence that collaboration would be impossible; in one sense, the burning of a whole French village was too high a price to pay for the elimination of three enemy officers; but those fires and the massacring of hostages were themselves parts of the plan; they created an abyss between the occupiers and the occupied. Likewise, the insurrections in Paris and

Lyons at the beginning of the nineteenth century, or the revolts in India, did not aim at shattering the yoke of the oppressor at one blow, but rather at creating and keeping alive the meaning of the revolt and at making the mystifications of conciliation impossible. Attempts which are aware that one by one they are doomed to failure can be legitimized by the whole of the situation which they create. This is also the meaning of Steinbeck's novel *In Dubious Battle* where a communist leader does not hesitate to launch a costly strike of uncertain success but through which there will be born, along with the solidarity of the workers, the consciousness of exploitation and the will to reject it.

It seems to me interesting to contrast this example with the debate in John Dos Passos' *The Adventures of a Young Man*. Following a strike, some American miners are condemned to death. Their comrades try to have their trial reconsidered. Two methods are put forward: one can act officially, and one knows that they then have an excellent chance of winning their case; one can also work up a sensational trial with the Communist Party taking the affair in hand, stirring up a press campaign and circulating international petitions; but the court will be unwilling to yield to this intimidation. The party will thereby get a tremendous amount of publicity, but the miners will be condemned. What is a man of good will to decide in this case?

Dos Passos' hero chooses to save the miners and we believe that he did right. Certainly, if it were necessary to choose between the whole revolution and the lives of two or three men, no revolutionary would hesitate; but it was merely a matter of helping along the party propaganda, or better, of increasing somewhat its chances of developing within the United States; the immediate interest of the C.P. in that country is only hypothetically tied up with that of the revolution; in fact, a cataclysm like the war has so upset the situation of the world that a great part of the gains and losses of the past have been absolutely swept away. If it is really *men* which the movement claims to be serving, in this case it must prefer saving the lives of three concrete individuals to a very uncertain and weak chance of serving a little more effectively by their sacrifice the mankind to come. If it considers these lives negligible, it is because it too ranges itself on the side of the formal politicians who prefer the Idea to its content; it is because it prefers itself, in its subjectivity, to the goals to which it claims to be dedicated. Besides, whereas in the example chosen by Steinbeck the strike is immediately an appeal to the freedom of the workers and in its very failure is already a liberation, the sacrifice of the miners is a mystification and an oppression; they are duped by being made to believe that an effort is being made to save their lives, and the whole proletariat is duped with them. Thus, in both examples, we find ourselves before the same abstract case: men are going to die so that the party which claims to be serving them will realize a limited gain; but a concrete analysis leads us to opposite moral solutions.

It is apparent that the method we are proposing, analogous in this respect to scientific or aesthetic methods, consists, in each case, of confronting the values realized with the values aimed at, and the meaning of the act with its content. The fact is that the politician, contrary to the scientist and the artist, and although the element of failure which he assumes is much more outrageous, is rarely concerned with making use of it. May it be that there is an irresistible dialectic of power wherein morality has no place? Is the ethical concern, even in its realistic and concrete form, detrimental to the interests of action? The objection will surely be made that hesitation and misgivings only impede victory. Since, in any case, there is an element of failure in all success, since the ambiguity, at any rate, must be surmounted, why not refuse to take notice of it? In the first number of the *Cahiers d'Action* a reader declared that once and for all we should regard the militant communist as "the permanent hero of our time" and should reject the exhausting tension demanded by existentialism; installed in the permanence of heroism, one will blindly direct himself toward an uncontested goal; but one then resembles Colonel de la Roque who unwaveringly went right straight ahead of him without knowing where he was going. Malaparte relates that the young Nazis, in order to become insensitive to the suffering of others, practised by plucking out the eyes of live cats; there is no more radical way of avoiding the pitfalls of ambiguity. But an action which wants to serve man ought to be careful not to forget him on the way; if it chooses to fulfill itself blindly, it will lose its meaning or will take on an unforeseen meaning; for the goal is not fixed once and for all; it is defined all along the road which leads to it. Vigilance alone can keep alive the validity of the goals and the genuine assertion of freedom. Moreover, ambiguity can not fail to appear on the scene; it is felt by the victim, and his revolt or his complaints also make it exist for his tyrant; the latter will then be tempted to put everything into question, to renounce, thus denying both himself and his ends; or, if he persists, he will continue to blind himself only by multiplying crimes and by perverting his original design more and more. The fact is that the man of action becomes a dictator not in respect to his ends but because these ends are necessarily set up through his will. Hegel, in his *Phenomenology*, has emphasized this inextricable confusion between objectivity and subjectivity. A man gives himself to a Cause only by making it *his* Cause; as he fulfills himself within it, it is also through him that it is expressed, and the will to power is not distinguished in such a case from generosity; when an individual or a party chooses to triumph, whatever the cost may be, it is their own triumph which they take for an end. If the fusion of the Commissar and the Yogi were realized, there would be a self-criticism in the man of action which would expose to him the ambiguity of his will, thus arresting the imperious drive of his subjectivity and, by the same token, contesting the unconditioned value of the goal. But the fact is that the politician follows the line of least resistance; it is easy to fall asleep over the unhappiness of others and to count it for very little; it is easier to throw a hundred men, ninety-seven of whom are innocent, into prison, than to discover the three culprits who are hidden among them; it is easier to kill a man than to keep a close watch on him; all politics makes use of the police, which officially flaunts its radical contempt for the individual and which loves violence for its own sake. The thing that goes by the name of political necessity is in part the laziness and brutality of the police. That is why it is incumbent upon ethics not to follow the line of least resistance; an act which is not destined, but rather quite freely consented to; it must make itself effective so that what was at first facility may become difficult. For want of internal criticism, this is the role that an opposition must take upon itself. There are two types of opposition. The first is a rejection of the very ends set up by a regime: it is the opposition of anti-fascism to fascism, of fascism to socialism. In the second type, the oppositionist accepts the objective goal but criticizes the subjective movement which aims at it; he may not even wish for a change of power, but he deems it necessary to bring into play a contestation which will make the subjective appear as such. Thereby he exacts a perpetual contestation of the means by the end and of the end by the means. He must be careful himself not to ruin, by the means which he employs, the end he is aiming at, and above all not to pass into the service of the oppositionists of the first type. But, delicate as it may be, his role is, nevertheless, necessary. Indeed, on the one hand, it would be absurd to oppose a liberating action with the pretext that it implies crime and tyranny; for without crime and tyranny there could be no liberation of man; one can not escape that dialectic which goes from freedom to freedom through dictatorship and oppression. But, on the other hand, he would be guilty of allowing the liberating movement to harden into a moment which is acceptable only if it passes into its opposite; tyranny and crime must be kept from triumphantly establishing themselves in the world; the conquest of freedom is their only justification, and the assertion of freedom against them must therefore be kept alive.

SELECTIVE BIBLIOGRAPHY

Pour une morale de l'ambiguïté (Paris: Gallimard, 1947). English: *The Ethics of Ambiguity*, trans. Bernard Frechtman (New York: Philosophical Library, 1948)

Le deuxième sexe (Paris: Gallimard, 1949). English: *The Second Sex,*
    trans. H. M. Parshley (New York: Knopf, 1953)

Tous les hommes sont mortels (Paris: Gallimard, 1946). English:
    All Men Are Mortal, trans. Leonard M. Friedman (Cleveland:
    World Publishing Co., 1955)

L'existentialisme et la sagesse des nations (Paris: Nagel, 1948)

Chapter 11

INTRODUCTION

ALBERT CAMUS (1913–60) received his education at the University of Algiers. After completing his formal education he wrote a number of plays for a drama group he founded in Algiers (1934–39). In 1939 he began his career as a journalist, and in that function moved to Paris in 1940. Camus was active in the resistance movement, and in 1944 he became the editor of the previously clandestine newspaper *Combat*. In the years following the war, Camus was still very active in political and social life; at first he was closely associated with Sartre and the existentialist movement, but in 1951 he separated from the movement and gradually withdrew more and more from direct political action. In 1960 he died in an automobile accident.

Although Camus is not a philosopher in the common sense of the term, being known mainly as novelist and essayist, nonetheless he has written several important philosophical works, and almost all of his literary work is deeply influenced by his philosophy.

Camus's name is often connected with the phenomenological or the existentialist movement. It seems to me that there is no real ground for this. Camus was not influenced by either Husserl or Heidegger, nor by Sartre, nor by any other French "existentialist." He is a rather individual thinker whose thought is (mainly negatively) determined by Plotinus, St. Augustine, Spinoza, Pascal, and Nietzsche. Camus is skeptical of any form of metaphysics. As he says, "I wish to limit myself to what I know and what I can justify." His main interest is in moral and political problems, and, in general, one may say that he defends a kind of moralistic humanism. This humanism is explained somewhat systematically in *The Myth of Sisyphus* and *The Rebel*. Although Camus defends basically the same view in both works, there is nonetheless an obvious difference between them. In *The Myth of Sisyphus* Camus explains his "absurdist position," which at first sight comes very close to what other people have called "nihilism." In *The Rebel* he clearly distinguishes between nihilism and his own absurdist position. Combining both books, one might say that Camus's basic intention was to develop a moral view of man and his world without ever bringing any "absolute" into the view. The reason for this is that man does not know of any absolutes, nor does he have any other access to them. This is almost the opposite view of that defended by Plotinus, St. Augustine, Pascal, Spinoza, and Hegel. To defend a moral humanism without any appeal to absolutes, however, is not tantamount to defending nihilism. True, for Camus there is no absolute. The consequence of this is that everything is "absurd" in the sense of lacking any *ultimate* justification. Man must object to this basic absurdity by rebellion; not by appealing to absolutes, but just by changing the absurd into the humanly meaningful. In creating what is humanly meaningful and valuable, man has to use human life as an unquestionable value. Camus explains his basic view concretely in *The Myth of Sisyphus* by asking the question of whether or not the absurdist position implies the acceptability of suicide; in *The Rebel* the same is done by asking the question of whether or not there can be any political justification for the killing of human beings.

Since I was unable to find a selection in Camus's works giving a really clear, succinct idea of what he intends, I decided to substitute an essay *on* Camus. It is my conviction that Professor Hochberg's essay although perhaps too critical, gives an objective and clear idea of Camus's basic concern.

ALBERT CAMUS AND
THE ETHIC OF ABSURDITY

Herbert Hochberg

ALBERT CAMUS sought, in *The Myth of Sisyphus*, to establish the absurdity of the human condition.[1] There and in *The Rebel* he further sought to derive an ethic from that condition—the ethic of the absurd man. Here we shall see that in the second task he failed completely, while, in the first, partial success is purchased at the price of triviality and, even so, rests on paradoxical ambiguities in his notion of "absurdity."

To grasp Camus's notion of the absurd, one must juxtapose it against a background of the philosophical ideas of the Greek Neo-Platonist, Plotinus. Plotinus envisioned the world as a "chain of Being." That is, he conceived of reality as a hierarchical arrangement of different sorts of entities culminating in the *One* or *Absolute*. Embracing the eternal and unchanging Platonic ideas, or essences, as a pattern for "explaining" or "accounting for" the varied and changing world of ordinary experience, Plotinus felt that the Platonic forms themselves required an explanation. He did so primarily

This paper was first read to the Philosophy Club at Indiana University in 1962 and later delivered at the University of Göteborg in 1963. From *Ethics* 75 (1964–65), pp. 87–102. Reprinted by courtesy of the author and the Editor of the University of Chicago Press.

[1] Notes are to the Vintage editions of *The Myth of Sisyphus*, trans. Justin O'Brien (New York: Vintage Books, 1959), hereinafter referred to as *MOS*; and *The Rebel*, trans. Anthony Bower (New York: Vintage Books, 1958), hereinafter *R*.

from one of the most basic and pervasive motives that has entranced philosophers from the days of the Greeks to the present—the idea that diversity has to be explained in terms of some ultimate unity. For, where distinctions remain, the monist feels that the relationships among the diverse things require explanation. The search for an explanation, on this pattern, can only come to rest in some all-embracing unity, which, allowing of no distinctions within itself, somehow accounts for all the diversity that there is and, in turn, requires no explanation. It is, in its way, the old idea of the one and the many. Plato sought to account for the many particulars of a certain kind in terms of the universal form in which they all participated. But, for Plotinus, the Platonic forms, being many, could not then be the ultimate source of explanation and, hence, of reality. The ultimate sources of explanation and reality coalesce, since to explain a thing is to account for its being in terms of some other entity. Thus the explanatory order reflects the "chain of Being." The ultimate level of explanation and source of reality could then only be some absolute unity. Being the source of the Platonic forms, the One was not, in turn, a form or idea itself. Since the ideas or forms also functioned as the objects and means of rational thought, the One was held to be incapable of being rationally comprehended. Another line of reasoning led to the same conclusion. Rational thought, for Plotinus, inescapably involved two dualisms: that of knower and known and that of subject and predicate. First, in thought there was the distinction between the knower and the object of knowledge and, second, judgments involved ascribing a predicate to a subject. Rational thought, involving such dualisms, was thus held to be incapable of comprehending *absolute unity*. The comprehension of the One must then go beyond rational thought and beyond all dualisms. Platonic rationalism, pushed to this extreme, lapses or, perhaps, leaps into mysticism. In the mystic experience the One is finally reached and grasped. But the diversity characteristic of reason and ordinary experience must be avoided, hence the soul, in experiencing and comprehending the Absolute, becomes "one with the One." The mystic finally escapes diversity and gains comprehension by being absorbed into the Absolute.

By providing the ultimate explanation for, and source of, all things, the One constitutes the productive cause of all else. The pattern of Plotinus thus provides a dividend, for not only does the soul fulfill its desire to comprehend in the obliterating mystical experience, but it attains the very source and cause of its existence. In reaching the One, it joins the highest link in the chain of being and, consequently, achieves salvation. Starting out to explain the ordinary world, one thus ends by discovering its insignificance and the need to flee from it to something higher. The Absolute provides a haven as well as an explanation. By so doing, it gives man an end or destiny, union with it, as well as an ethic. One's life is to be lived so as to prepare for salvation. This is a union not only with the ultimate source of reality but with the absolute good, for the One, as man's final end, is the ultimate source of value. The "chain of being" is simultaneously a "chain of value," and something is good insofar as it is real. If one then asks how evil can come from the ultimate source of all, which is the absolute good, one is told that evil is simply the absence of goodness or reality and, as such, is non-being. The further one gets from the Absolute, the lower one sinks on the chain of being and of value. Since the ordinary world is the lowest link, to flee it is to flee from a lesser state of being and of value to the highest of both—to the true, the good, and the beautiful.

One can see, on the basis of the preceding sketch of Plotinus' view, some of the things that would appeal to Christians eager to find a metaphysical defense for their faith. However, there are pitfalls. One is the so-called problem of evil. Unlike Augustine, some may feel that there is still a puzzle in reconciling the absolute goodness of God with the evils of the world. The contrast seems, if we may anticipate, "absurd." A second problem is found in the deterministic element of Plotinus' world view. The Absolute is not modeled on a mind confronted with choices about which it exercises its free will. The things of this world are explained by the

Absolute's being their necessary ground or condition. Hence all flows from it as rigorously as theorems from axioms in deductive systems. Orthodox Christianity obviously cannot make its peace with such a theme. In part the issue erupted in the Middle Ages in the scholastic attempts to reconcile a personal God's "knowledge" of all with man's freedom to create the future. For, some wondered, in what sense does man freely create what God knew he would do? These problems are not confined to Christians. They will bother anyone simultaneously intoxicated with the Plotinian pattern, man's freedom, and evil. Camus is such a one. Around these themes he attempts to construct an ethic.

The Myth of Sisyphus is purportedly an examination of the absurdity of man's condition and an attempt to provide a rationale for not committing suicide in the face of that absurdity. What does Camus mean by "absurdity"? Actually, he means several things, and, as we shall see, his arguments depend on these different senses. But, basically, he simply means that there is no Plotinian absolute—no ultimate unity, divine or secular, which explains all.[2] Camus thinks in terms of absurdity since he accepts Plotinus' pattern but rejects its culmination in the One. That is, he holds to the idea that explanation and understanding of the things of this world are to be had if and only if there is such an absolute, and yet he rejects it. Camus opts for "all or nothing" since, as he sometimes puts it, "to understand is, above all, to unify." The lack of such an ultimate unifying principle or entity forces us to accept the fact that all is absurd. This is Camus's thesis. Unfortunately, he obscures the simplicity of his route to the absurd by rehearsing some bad and irrelevant arguments from various philosophical sources, which supposedly show the impossibility of any knowledge.[3] But he need not have bothered with these feathery buttresses. Once he has rejected the Absolute, after accepting the theme that such an ultimate unity is a necessary ground for comprehending the things of the world, it follows, in his terms, that the world is incomprehensible and, consequently, absurd.

[2] MOS, pp. 13–16, 20, 27, 33–39.
[3] MOS, pp. 13–14.

One may wonder why Camus, after adopting the monist's pattern, rejects the Absolute, and suffers from a "nostalgia for unity." There are several reasons, none original.

First, Camus notes the paradoxical nature of the Plotinian solution—its culmination in a mystical irrationalism, and he is not one to accept the verbal solution that this irrationalism culminates in something "above" reason rather than below it. For Camus, as for many before him, to accept the Absolute is to relinquish the search for an explanation, since one explains things in terms of something that is rationally incomprehensible. In short, while Camus requires that an explanation culminate in absolute unity, he also requires that an explanation be rationally comprehended and meaningful in terms of ordinary experience.[4] Here he is irretrievably caught between two themes. The criterion of unity requires the Absolute; the criterion of rational comprehension rejects it. Camus's incompatible criteria for what may constitute an explanation of the things of the world lead him to conclude that there can be no explanation and no comprehension. Actually the paradox stems from a deeper incompatibility that Camus accepts. I spoke above of "meaningful in terms of ordinary experience." "Empiricism" is an ambiguous term. But one theme that may be associated with this viewpoint is the contention that there is no extraordinary experience, whether it be mystical union with the Absolute or the intuitive grasp of certain eternal truths, that is philosophically significant. To the empiricist those who claim to experience the Absolute require analysis of a non-philosophical variety. In one way or another empiricists have suggested that what is comprehensible must be found so in terms of ordinary experience. In keeping with this they have tended to formulate criteria of meaning and have held as meaningless attempts to explain the realm of ordinary experience in terms of something which transcends that realm. Camus is such an empiricist. For him, in one sense of the trio of terms "meaningful," "comprehensible," and "rational," only things of this world can fall under them. Yet, to give a meaning to, a ra-

4 MOS, pp. 32, 34, 38, 42.

tionale for, or comprehension of the things of this world is, on the Plotinian pattern, to do so in terms of something beyond this world—some absolute unity. Accepting this, Camus is also a monist. Thus the Absolute, or God, is required to give a meaning to this world and yet is, at the same time, meaningless, since it is not of this world. In one sense of the term, the world is "meaningless" because there is no absolute; in another sense, there is no absolute, since any such "thing" would be "meaningless" in not being of this world. Camus's combination of empiricism and the Plotinian pattern leads him to the view that all is meaningless and absurd—the things of this world and whatever transcends this world.[5]

Closely intertwined with this first point is a second. One motive of an advocate of a transcendent absolute is the desire to give a point or purpose and, consequently, a value to the world and life. Yet, in doing so, he automatically depreciates the world of ordinary experiences in virtue of its insignificance when compared to its source. In giving a "value" to the world and life one *minimizes* the "values" of both. Since this world is the only one Camus comprehends and its joys and values the only ones he grasps, he can only be satisfied with giving the world, somehow, an *intrinsic value*. Doing this necessitates the rejection of a transcendent absolute. But in such rejection one foregoes giving the world value in the sense of purpose or meaning. Thus the world will have to be, ultimately, with value and meaning and without value and meaning. This will be the contradiction of the absurd condition that Camus will face in The Rebel.[6] But, again, the paradox depends on different senses of the same term and is thus no paradox. What is involved, as we shall see, is Camus's failure to provide the intrinsic value he seeks.

[5] By a meaning criterion, either explicit or implicit, a consistent *empiricist* would avoid Camus's dilemma by rejecting both "the Absolute" and the sense of "explanation" that an Absolute provides as meaningless notions. Hence any Plotinian scheme would be rejected. It is no accident that the empirically oriented Thomists resort to a doctrine of "analogy" to speak of God or refer to him in terms of his effects.

[6] R, p. 8.

Third, Camus rejects the transcendent One in that it provides a cue for the entrance of the Christian God. He rejects God, in part, due to the problem of evil.[7] He cannot see any reconciliation between the existence of God and the existence of unwarranted suffering. In short, reason cannot comprehend how God can exist in the face of such evil. Since there is such evil, God cannot then exist. The paradox here is in requiring a rational explanation for there being a God with certain qualities and a world containing evil. Since, for Camus, this situation allows of no such explanation, it is absurd; but here the absurdity is a ground for the rejection of God. The point is that God, taken as an explanation, leads one to absurdity and, hence, cannot constitute an explanation. Nor is Camus one to accept the piety, be it that of priest or commissar, that all is for the best in the end. Such sentiments, to him, may be used to justify anything while really only covering up the absence of any justification. For the ultimate appeal is then to a mystique of faith and not to reason or experience. He is not tempted to trade future glories for present miseries. To buttress this sentiment he goes back to one of his uses of "meaning." He comprehends what he experiences. Future heavens, beyond the pale of experience, are incomprehensible. Thus to act in their name is incomprehensible or irrational, while to be rational is to act in terms of what one comprehends, the joys and experiences of this world. As we shall see, the absurd man is, ultimately, the rational man.

A fourth reason for rejecting the Absolute is based on the deterministic element it contains. Camus sees the Absolute as a threat to man's freedom. "Freedom," linked to "spontaneity," is opposed to what is *explainable*. Recall, for a moment, the discussions one hears time and again centering around purported proofs that there cannot be, in principle, scientific explanations of human behavior. In a sense the behavior scientist has replaced God in our current variations of the scholastic perplexity. But whereas God was above attacks on the logical limitations of his knowledge, the behav-

[7] MOS, p. 42. It would also be relevant to recall *The Plague*.

ior scientists are not granted such divine immunity. Camus deals with the issue in its original form; he denies the Absolute to assert his freedom.[8]

For these reasons Camus denies the Absolute, hence God, and "establishes" the "absurdity" of the world. Following this he attempts to work out what some call the logic of the absurd, using, I take it, absurdist logic. The program is simple enough. He asserts, in Cartesian fashion, that he knows two things for certain—his own existence and the world's. Starting with what he knows for certain, his systematic construction begins. But, as we have seen, man cannot grasp rationally an explanation of his and the world's existence. This is, as we saw, one meaning of the absurd condition: the lack of explanation. But, as Camus uses the term, he finds it absurd that there is no explanation while one is craved. In this latter sense he speaks of the absurdity arising from the confrontation of man and the world, while belonging to neither alone.[9] He speaks this way for several reasons.

First, many contemporary writers, particularly on the Continent, are entranced by the notion of "contradiction." Historically, the absurd or irrational has been linked with the

---

[8] There are suggestions of this in MOS, p. 16, where Camus links "universal reason" with "determinism," and again on p. 41, where he touches on the classical problem of free will and holds that the very notion that makes the problem possible (that of God as a transcendent master) also makes it meaningless. Preoccupied with the question of evil, Camus chooses to see the "paradox" of God in terms of the problem of evil. Nevertheless, in proceeding (MOS, p. 42), by his empiricism, to declare that "the only conception of freedom I can have is that of the prisoner or the individual in the midst of the State," he rejects the traditional problem of free will as meaningless; for it involves a "notion which eludes me and loses its meaning as soon as it goes beyond the frame of reference of my individual experience." This also serves to reject any suggestion of a "deeper freedom" granted by God. The theme is taken up again in R where Camus holds that absolute justice destroys freedom (p. 288) and in a footnote writes: "Jean Grenier lays the foundation for an argument that can be summed up thus: absolute freedom is the destruction of all value; absolute value suppresses all freedom. Likewise Palante: 'If there is a single and universal truth, freedom has no reason for existing.'"

[9] MOS, pp. 22–23, 16.

contradictory. In a loose sense of this term we may speak of a contradiction involved in craving for the impossible, in our "nostalgia for the Absolute." Hence, this situation is absurd. Second, speaking in this way permits Camus to juxtapose man to the rest of the world. This emphasizes his place, his difference, and his importance. Man becomes the creator of the absurd condition. When we recall that ever since Descartes, the problem of man's role in a physical universe has bothered commentators on the human condition, we can understand the need Camus feels for giving him a unique place. The destruction of the Absolute gives man his freedom, the absurd condition guarantees him a unique and independent role. Note that this role is due, in part, to the existence of his rational faculty, his seeking to comprehend rationally what is incomprehensible. In traditional fashion man's reason is what ultimately distinguishes him. As Camus sometimes puts it, man is the only creature that seeks a meaning for things. Third, this juxtaposition presents us with the feel of a tense dialectical situation. Camus has an affinity for the confrontation of opposites, be they "contradictions" or conflicts. We shall see how this permeates his view and how he makes use of the theme of "conflict" in his ethic. It is almost as if, having destroyed the Absolute as a sort of final cause to draw men to it, one requires an inherent tension to get things moving. One may here note that Camus, like many continental thinkers, while critical of Hegelian philosophy is impregnated with Hegelian patterns of thought. Fourth, and basically, he has to put the matter in terms of a juxtaposition of man and the universe to get his solution to the problem he raised: to show that life is worth living and that metaphysical suicide is to be rejected. This now follows from the absurd situation which arises out of the polarity between man and the universe—between man's desire to know and the world's silence. Having rejected the Absolute, Camus takes the absurd condition as a fact. It follows from the two previously stated facts of one's existence and the world's existence, plus, as we saw, a healthy dose of Greek metaphysics. If man removes himself, he destroys the situation and hence the absurd condition. Since the absurd condition is taken as a fact, one who destroys himself denies this fact. But he who denies a fact puts himself in opposition to what is, to, in short, the truth. To oppose the truth, recognizing it to be true, is to contradict oneself. Recognizing a truth, one ought to preserve it, rather than deny it. It follows that one ought not to commit metaphysical suicide in the face of the meaningless universe. In sum and in substance this is the argument of *The Myth of Sisyphus*.[10] One hopes that it is not the sole barrier holding some from suicide, for it commits a twofold blunder. First, there is the unfortunate play on the notion of preserving or, alternatively, denying a truth or a fact. Need one do more than point out that it is quite one thing to deny that some one has a wart by stating that it is not so; it is quite another thing to "deny" that fact by removing the wart. Of course, in Camus's case one removes the disease by removing the patient, but the point is still the same. Second, Camus has leaped from the factual premise that the juxtaposition of man and the universe is absurd, to the evaluative conclusion that this state ought to be preserved. As we noted, his play on the term "preserve" provides the verbal bridge. For this transition we have no justification. Without such justification, Camus has not, in the least way, made his point. He has simply begged the question. To produce such a justification would obviously involve the construction of an ethic. But it is precisely on this point that Camus builds his ethical view. Hence all that follows leans on a hollow argument. His lack of coherence may be explained by the fact that, having denied a transcendent source of value, he must, if he is to have an ethic at all, anchor his values somehow in the world of ordinary experience. Values must come about from the factual condition of the world as it is. This being so, one might be led to think that values must "emerge" from facts, and what is more natural than to have one's values emerge from what is for Camus one of the most fundamental facts of all—man's absurd condition?

Whatever explains his logical lapses, they remain with us. Hence, unlike some who find his logic impeccable and his

10 MOS, pp. 23–24, 38–41; and R, p. 6.

premise about the absurd unfortunate, I find his logic quite inadequate while his premise, given the Plotinian framework, quite understandable. If by the world being absurd all one means to assert is that there is no Plotinian absolute or Christian God, many will accept Camus's thesis; but then, it has been said before and doesn't say very much.

Be that as it may, on the basis of the concept of the absurd and some absurd logic, Camus has repudiated metaphysical suicide. He has done so by discovering an absolute value through "reasoning" about the absurd condition. The value is life, since the preservation of life is necessary to maintain the absurd polarity between man and the world. Camus has denied a transcendent source of value and yet seems to have found a basic value, one created by man. This fact even further enhances man's place in the universe as the creator of values. With this value Camus will attempt to construct an ethic and repudiate nihilism, which is an ever present threat to him. We can see why nihilism is such a threat. Recall that adherents of the Absolute tend to minimize the ordinary world of change, becoming, and decay—the stage of ordinary living and experience. Camus repudiates any attempt to minimize the ordinary world and the pleasures of the senses. He has then a further ground for rejecting the Absolute. In rejecting any transcendent absolute, he is left with this world and this life. These, as we saw, become the sole possible sources of value. Since there is no external standard, one may be tempted to hold that differences of value can only arise from quantitative differences in this world—from the amount of it, in the form of experience or living, that one partakes of. In this way one can be led to hold that a life with more experiences is preferable to one with less. Thus an "ethic of quantity" may arise from holding this life to be an absolute value. Indeed, in *The Myth of Sisyphus* Camus is taken with such a view, but it obviously contains the seed of nihilism—a potential justification for a future Marquis de Sade.[11]

Camus is also led to assert the absolute value of life by

11 MOS, pp. 45–46.

his well-known preoccupation with death. In death he finds, paradoxically, a satisfaction for "nostalgia for unity." Death in its way "unifies" all men, and, in so doing, furnishes an "absolute." Unlike the One, it is not an end we seek, but one we seek to avoid. Yet we cannot do so. The conflict of fact and desire thus breaks out once again. We seek to understand the world and cannot; we seek to avoid death and cannot. Just as the first conflict led him to speak of absurdity, so does the second. Death becomes a further sense of the absurd. However, like the absolutes of Plotinus and Christianity it provides us with a source of value. The point here is to oppose the new absolute or absurd, not join it. In seeking to avoid it and to oppose it unconditionally, we create an absolute rule: Do not kill. Again life becomes an absolute value, and the drama of man is viewed as a struggle against death. Note that in struggling against the absurd, in the form of death, we preserve the absurd, in the form of the polarity between man and the world. But in speaking of death as an enemy to be opposed, Camus can introduce a further notion—that of rebellion, for rebellion needs an antagonist. The *absurd*, in the earlier senses, does not provide it explicitly enough; death does. It also provides as we saw, an ultimate unity that Camus always seeks, so deep is the Plotinian pattern imbedded in his thought. That men die becomes an ultimate sad fact beyond which we cannot go. This fact is also taken to be absurd in that it is inexplicable. But there is a further air of paradox about all this. Death is absurd on three counts: the conflict of our desire for immortality with our mortality, the inexplicability of it, and its denying or negating the only meaningful existence we know. Alternatively, death would not be absurd if we were immortal, if there was a point to it, and if this was not the only meaningful existence. In short, death would not be absurd if we introduce God and subservient immortal souls. But, paradoxically, it is also absurd on other grounds with God. For, recall, Camus is struck by the problem of evil, and he views death as an absolute evil. God, responsible for death, is both an abomination and a contradiction. Thus, death is absurd if God exists, and absurdity results with or without God. Death destroys God, and, in a sense, takes his place in Camus's scheme of things as an absolute opponent. It is almost as if Camus rejects God as a source of value but finds such a source in man's opposition to the devil, as absolute evil. With a transcendent God or One, we face a deterministic framework and loss of freedom. Death, too, seems to be a limit on our most basic freedom—to exist. But, Camus also sees it as a liberator.[12] Not only does it free us from a transcendent absolute, but it frees us in smaller ways. For just as we lose our freedom with a transcendent absolute that defines our purpose, we tend to lose it by thinking in terms of the future. We propose roles for ourselves and hence limit our freedom by living within these roles, be they those of bank teller, professor, or what have you. Realizing, through death, that there is no future, we may reject these roles and be free.[13] So the realization of death brings us freedom. In one sense Camus simply speaks nonsense and here makes contact with the "existentialist" of left-bank café society and the "authentic man" of recent literature. But in another sense, he is merely advocating the life of his "lucid" or "absurd" man. This will be elaborated in a moment. Death, in addition to being a "liberator," finally provides us with an absolute unity that is not transcendent. For, in a sense, death is part of the world of ordinary experience. We have found a unity which, in this sense, we can comprehend. But, as we saw, being inexplicable it is still absurd. Hence, even the unity we find does not provide us with comprehension but again demonstrates the lack of such. Yet through it we gain freedom. Thus Camus has another fundamental value. In destroying the Absolute we become free, and this fact too must be "preserved." We have, then, two values, life and freedom, while death is an absolute opponent. However, we face the threat of nihilism through an ethic of quantity. This threat must be removed and the two values integrated. In short, all the grounds Camus uses for asserting the absolute value of life must be

12 MOS, pp. 43–44.
13 MOS, p. 43.

coherently put together. The intellectual glue is provided by his notions of *lucidity* and *limitation*.

Recall the three basic grounds. The first was the necessity for preserving the truth of the absurd condition. It can lead us to look at Camus as a lonely but courageous bearer of the burden of life—as one who does one's duty solely by living— in short, as Sisyphus. The second was the upholding of the joys of sensual life in the face of their deprecation by a transcendent absolute. Here one can look at Camus as a sort of happy pagan, shuttling between beach, bedroom, and bar, decrying moral codes, and rhapsodizing about the quantity and variety of experience. Finally in the third, we find the rebel, the resolute opponent of death. In him some see the ground of a social ethic finally propounded in Camus's later work. We shall deal with that shortly. First, let us see how all these themes are put together.

We have seen how the absurd condition may be said to arise from man's consciousness. Once it is produced one may then recognize it or not. He who does is lucid. Thus, once again, as with the Greeks, we have a distinction between men on the basis of knowledge. Except the knowledge here is of the absurd condition, not of Platonic forms or mystical absolutes. But then this has become the ultimate fact concerning man's relation to the world. The lucid man then knows the ultimate truth. Moreover, his knowledge is rational, having been arrived at by reason and in terms of this world. The lucid man further recognizes that he must preserve the absurd condition. In this way he comes to advocate the absolute value of life. In recognizing the absurd condition, he rejects all transcendent values and notes that this life is all we have. He will enjoy it to the full, but with limits. For in recognizing the absolute value of life and the absolute opposition of death, the lucid man recognizes these *in general*. He has found the absolute value of all life, not just of his; and he opposes death in all its forms, not just his own death. In maintaining life to be an absolute value, the lucid man maintains the equality of all lives, with respect to the right to live. The lucid man will not kill himself or another, since the maintaining of the absurd condition weighs equally against suicide and murder. This imposes a limitation on the enjoyment of life and avoids the nihilism implicit in the ethic of quantity. Likewise, one's freedom is limited by the absolute value of life. Hence, this second value, freedom, is subordinate to the first, life. Even so, it, in turn, provides a further limitation on the way one lives one's life. The lucid man does not interfere with the "legitimate" freedom of others. Thus the lucid man becomes the moral man, and out of absurdity emerges morality. But, within the limits so imposed, the lucid man will reap the sensual fruits of this life. This is the point of the "freedom" the absurd man finds in death and the rejection of "roles." All this is implicit in *The Myth of Sisyphus*, though the preoccupation with freedom and the rebellion against death are explicitly the themes of *The Rebel*. But nowhere does Camus overcome the basic defects we noted earlier. This, in its way, is the whole story. We have seen how it stands on weak ground. What we shall see next is how, aside from its inadequate origins, it collapses of its own weight.

In the early pages of *The Rebel* Camus states two things. First, he holds that there seems to be a contradiction in his "absurdist" view, for he has introduced the value of life after claiming that there are no values. Second, he holds that murder and suicide are linked together in the absurdist position.[14] We have already seen that this second point is implicit in *The Myth of Sisyphus* and that there is really no contradiction in his "absurdist" view, since what he denies is a *transcendent* source of value. *The Rebel* is devoted to showing how a value, and hence an ethic, arises from the absurdist position. But this too adds nothing to *The Myth of Sisyphus*. There is, however, an elaboration of his ethical view in *The Rebel* and an attempt to reconcile the possible conflicts that may arise due to his holding life and freedom to be basic values.

The Rebel is dominated by Camus's opposition to nihilism, of which he sees two kinds. One is the nihilism of "all is permitted," the rejection of all moral standards; the other is

14 R, pp. 6–8.

the nihilism of absolutists who permit all means in the name of some absolute end.[15] Together, these two forms of nihilism pose a dilemma that must be avoided. The absolute value of life serves as a reply to the second form of nihilism as well as the first. For the basic crime of nihilists of the second kind is the subversion of human life to some other-worldly goal—other-worldly either in the sense of not of this world or of it but in some utopian future. In the name of such goals nihilists do not hesitate to murder and in this way deny the absolute value of life. In so doing they align themselves with man's eternal enemy—death. To rebel against death, as the lucid man does, is thus to reject these tyrannies, be they of church or state. And, in so doing, the lucid man becomes the rebel.

Camus considers rebellion to contain essentially the commitment to the struggle against death, by limiting it.[16] The revolt against death is, in fact, the archetype for all rebellion. Thus nihilists of either kind cannot be rebels. Much of the argument of *The Rebel* is devoted to this point. In establishing this betrayal of rebellion in history Camus feels he has established the intellectual impotency of nihilism. His ethic of rebellion furnishes him with a basis of criticism for all forms of nihilism. But it is tailored for the denunciation of injustice rather than the propounding of justice. One may, as Camus does, criticize all who seek to subvert human life and freedom to other ends, for, on Camus's view, this constitutes injustice. Thus the rebellion against death becomes the model for the denunciation of injustice and is the dominant motif of *The Rebel*. One can see why Camus's ethic must be one of opposition and condemnation from the very structure of his position. To specify some long-range program as embodying justice aside from the values of life and freedom would involve either other standards of value or at least a proposal as to what, in the long run, would be the closest realization of these two values. In the first case one clearly has the possibility of subjecting the values of life and freedom

15 R, pp. 57–60, 102–4.
16 R, pp. 100–101.

to these other standards. In the second case, the same thing may happen, since such programs for the realization of values tend to subvert the values themselves. In short any utopian program contains the seeds of nihilism since it leads us to the acceptance of an absolute other than life and hence, ultimately, to tyranny. Yet Camus feels he must say something more specific about the "good society." This leads him to the role of the artist.

In speaking of the artist Camus almost portrays a utopian community where all are artists. His pattern is simple. Recall that the absolute value of life involves the equality of all lives. If one then notes with Marx that political equality depends on one's role in the social and economic hierarchy, one may, with Camus, hold that true equality will involve men working at tasks to which we attach equal dignity. Since we must have plumbers as well as painters, Camus's solution lies in turning the plumber into an artist. Being an artist, he will take pride in his work and achieve equality with all other artists. Thus art or craftsmanship, rather than the dictatorship of the proletariat, becomes the great equalizer and hope for the future.[17] There are other reasons for Camus's intoxication with the role of the artist. The artist is a creator. As such he is the embodiment of the absurd condition on three counts. First, creation is opposed to destruction and hence "death." Second, the artist rebels against and "makes over" reality just as the rebel rejects his condition. Moreover, both the artist and the rebel reject existing reality in the name of some unifying principle. Third, the absurd condition, recall, is maintained by a tense opposition between man and the world. The problem of the artist is also one of maintaining such a tense opposition—between form and matter. A work of art is, in effect, a model of the absurd condition, and the artist the absurd man par excellence.[18] In creation the artist, like

[17] R, pp. 273–74.

[18] R, pp. 257–58, 270–76. Camus apparently makes use of the traditional dichotomy of "art and science" in his thesis of the absurd condition. *Explanation* is impossible, but art can both describe the world in its diversity as well as create new experiences. Thus art, rather than *rationalist* science and philosophy, is more "in

man as the creator of values, replaces God. Perhaps this too enhances the role of the artist for Camus. Be that as it may, from Camus's conception of the artist it is obvious how an aesthetic can emerge that may condemn, however unprecisely, the art of social realism on the one hand and highly abstract art on the other. This, of course, fits with Camus's rejection of the different forms of nihilism pervasive in the political societies that these forms of art represent. Perhaps from the inherent "dialectical" tensions a new art and a new society may be thought to emerge. If so, the Hegelian strain in his thought would offer Camus a hope for the future.

But Camus does not, in the end, offer any utopia, for all utopias tend to become tyrannies. Also he sees in the prevalence of evil and death signs of the imperfection of man. Our task must be the more mundane one of limiting hell rather than trying to attain heaven. Man's condition is perpetually one of injustice and death which all men face. This condition, in its way, insures the rejection of all absolutes. For if injustice were thought to be conquerable, we would face an ideal in whose name all might be permissible—the condition of absolute justice. Thus the perpetual state of injustice guarantees the inadequacy of any utopia. Simultaneously, it guarantees the perpetual timeliness of Camus's ethic of rebellion. For man's opponents are always with him and man's rebellion always relevant.[19] Our common struggle need never cease and this struggle, in turn, reflects a further "unity" in the face of death. This struggle also provides Camus with a rhetorical device. He puts the philosophical questioner of his ethic in the position of playing intellectual games while, so to speak,

---

tune" with "the absurd." In fact science and philosophy must merge with art in describing and creating, since neither can, ultimately, explain anything. Hence the traditional and "arbitrary" opposition between art, on the one hand, and science and philosophy, on the other, is "overcome" (MOS, pp. 70–74).

[19] R, pp. 286–92, 303. Also, Camus believes that a notion of absolute justice or value (aside from that of life) is inconsistent with freedom (see n. 7 above). Thus just as Camus has his version of original sin by holding to the perpetual injustice of man's condition, he also adheres, in his way, to the idea that injustice and evil are necessary conditions for human freedom.

the nihilists are at the door. Times of conflict are not compatible with intellectual searching into one's basic values. One declares them and struggles for them. Camus makes dramatic use of this persuasive device in *The Rebel*. At times he seems to hold that values are things one cannot, ultimately, reason about. Yet he often attempts not only to reason about them but to "prove" them.

In *The Rebel* Camus offers what seems to be a further argument for his "ethic of rebellion." It is perhaps on the basis of this particular argument that some see in his work the basis of a "new" social ethic. He argues that one rebels in the name of universal properties inherent in men. Thus rebellion is based on something common to men and not on egotistical grounds. He concludes that one rebels in the name of all men, or universally. The rebel even includes his master in this "natural unity" in whose name he rebels. Camus sees the fact that rebels give up their lives to struggle for rights as evidence that they hold these rights to be more important than their lives. These rights or values thus "transcend" the individual and are common to all. This shows, to Camus, that man rebels in the name of a universal "human nature" or essence which all men share.[20] Thus the value of the rebel, life, is anchored in the essence of man. Here, Camus's reasoning rests on a twofold confusion and is patently circular. Universals, or properties, are sometimes said to "transcend" the individuals that have them in that they "belong" to more than one particular thing and their existence is independent of any one particular exemplification. Values may be said to "transcend" an individual in that (a) he is willing to die for them; (b) other individuals may subscribe to these values; (c) they provide a standard by which one judges actions, rather than arising out of one's actions. But subscribing to values and holding that they "transcend" individuals in senses (a), (b), and (c) does not imply that there is a universal "human nature," something permanent in man that "transcends" any given man in the sense that a universal property "transcends" any exemplification of it. That both universals, as philosophers have thought of them, and values are spoken of as "transcending" individuals provides *part* of the bridge whereby Camus proceeds from the premise that one rebels for values to the conclusion that there is a universal human nature. The remaining part is supplied by the term "universal." A "universal" in the sense of a *common property* need not be "universal" in that it applies to all things. To be trite, the property of being a man applies to all men but that of being tall only to some. Yet both are "universals" in the sense of common properties. Camus thinks that because one rebels in the name of common properties, or universals, one rebels *universally*, in the name of all men. One might think, however, that a slave could rebel in the name of properties that only some men have in common or in the name of "transcendent" values that do not require him to rebel for "all men." Part of Camus's rejection of this line is explained by the confusions about "transcend" and "universal." But the link between "universal" as a property and "universal" in application involves another, circular thread. Camus holds that to rebel against the condition of slavery is to assert that *no one* ought to suffer the indignities of slavery. Since the slave rebels for all men, he rebels in the name of his master as well. Thus he cannot, consistently, either kill or enslave his master. So Camus's argument runs from (*a*) rebellion in the name of a transcendent value to (*b*) rebellion in the name of a "universal" or "essence" to (*c*) rebellion in the name of all instances of that universal to (*d*) rebellion in the name of all men, since that universal is common or "essential" to all men. But the contention that *no one* ought to suffer the indignities of slavery or be murdered can mean *at least* two things. First, one can take it in some ideal sense to the effect that a world without such indignities would be a better world, other things "being equal." Second, one can mean that, no matter what the consequences or the context, no man must be enslaved or murdered. Taking the first sense, the rebel might justify political murder as a necessary step for "progress." If so, Camus's case would not have been made, and, moreover, this is just what he wishes to avoid as a form of nihilism and absolutism. Taking the second sense, Camus patently begs the question. For the rebel then simply and explicitly adheres to the assertion that lives may not be taken. Thus the discussion of *The Rebel* does not take us beyond the "argument" of *The Myth of Sisyphus*. That is why for Camus to rebel is to rebel against the condition of man, that is, death and absurdity. This being so, Camus believes he has shown that the rebel cannot kill. Aside from the circularity, all this is comprehensible if we recall Camus's preoccupation with nihilism. Consider the three propositions: (*a*) life is the only absolute value; (*b*) all lives are of equal value; (*c*) one may not take a life. Camus takes (*b*) and (*c*) to follow from and "explicate" (*a*). Thus from the absolute value of life, he argues that one cannot kill at all. For, the ambiguity of adhering to life as the only absolute value may still allow one to hold that a life may be taken if such a course of action leads to less loss of life "on the whole." And if one does this, he is on the verge of an ethic of quantity, of absolutism, and of nihilism since, again, in the name of saving life in the "long run," all may be permitted. This is why, in *The Rebel*, Camus thinks in terms of an unrelenting and absolute opposition to death. Consequently, the rebel, the embodiment of Camus's ethic, cannot kill. To avoid any danger of absolutism in the name of some positive "good" or value, the absolute value becomes opposition to death; hence the rebel's ethic is one of ceaseless opposition, rebellion, and conflict.

Put in this way it is clear how the "equality of all lives," with respect to being killed, follows from the absolute opposition to death. It is also clear that, again, no argument has been offered in support of the "ethic" of the rebel. What further becomes clear, in the context and terms of Camus's own work, is the inadequacy inherent in the simplicity of his biblical stricture. This we see when he considers the possible justification of political murder in his concept of the "just assassin." Before discussing that concept it is interesting to note that in appealing to "human nature" to anchor his ethic, Camus seems to desert one of the basic themes of *The Myth of Sisyphus*. For he offers a variant of those views which hold objective values to be grounded in the very nature of man. And, insofar as one speaks of such values as deriving from man's essence and that essence "transcending" man, one is led to hold that such values have a transcendent source. Man's values, then, in some sense, come from his essence rather than arise out of his existential condition. One cannot help but wonder if this traditional pattern appeals to Camus as providing an anchor and an objective ground for the values which are created in rebellion. But one can also see why he might feel that he has not abandoned his earlier view. For the rebel's value, the rejection of death, is "created" by man's "absurd" confrontation of the world and his "metaphysical" rebellion. Thus man, not God, is the source of man's values. Perhaps Camus would even feel that, in holding both that there is a human essence which is presupposed by the rebel's value and that this value emerges from man's existential condition, he has reconciled any conflict between "essence" and "existence." It may be relevant to recall the mixing of the two senses of "universal" we noticed earlier. For one sense has to do with essence; the other with instances, or existences, of such essence. Whatever the relevance of such "metaphysical" intrusions, man's existential condition, involving death, murder, and slavery, is unjust. Man opposes it, or rebels against it, by asserting his essence or value—by opposing death. But sometimes in our unjust condition we will be faced with choosing between murder and slavery—between our two values of life and freedom. What choice are we to make? Camus is not a pacifist. Nor can he avoid the problem. To assassinate for the cause of freedom is to reject the absolute value of life, that is, the absolute opposition to death. The assassin contradicts the ultimate value of the rebel and betrays rebellion, even though he does so in the name of another value—freedom. Yet to avoid doing so in some cases is to perpetuate slavery. This too must not be allowed. Camus thus faces a dilemma. His solution is disarmingly simple, novel, and incoherent. He introduces the notion of the "just assassin."[21] The assassin murders and contradicts the value of life. Contradictions must be removed. The way out is for the assassin to "remove" the contradiction by killing himself. Here we have come full circle. On the basis of the absolute value of life Camus has rejected suicide, capital punishment, and murder. He ends by acquiescing in certain cases to all three, for the suicide of the just assassin is suicide in the form of self-imposed capital punishment.[22] Obviously all this is a way of saying that the just assassin's act is both right and wrong. It is right in that it can be done, in the cause of freedom; it is wrong in that it must be punished for implementing death. Usually when principles conflict, we reconcile them either by altering one or recognizing an order of precedence. This can "remove" the conflict. Camus in recognizing a "just assassin" acknowledges a breach with the absolute value of life. But he must cling to that value or his whole intellectual edifice crumbles. Hence he sees the conflict as existing not in his principles but in the life of the assassin. The suicide of the assassin removes the contradiction and enables Camus to keep his conflicting principles intact until the next embodiment of their conflict.[23] It, in turn, will be removed in the same way. By this act of intellectual juggling Camus both acknowledges and denies that life is an absolute value.

Camus's notion of the "just assassin" is, in some ways, symbolic of his thought. Recognizing that murder and expediency can become institutionalized and yet that freedom may

[22] Strictly speaking Camus has rejected only "philosophical" or "metaphysical" suicide, i.e., suicide based on the realization that the human condition is absurd. Thus no formal contradiction is involved. However, his rejection of philosophical suicide and his advocacy of the assassin's suicide both stem from his "discovery" of the absurdity of life. (In this paper I have not gone into any question of the legitimacy of suicide in other contexts, and, if Camus approved of suicide in some cases, what complications this would involve him in regarding the absolute value of "life." Such points would take us out of the context of MOS and R.)

[23] Perhaps Camus does not see the conflict as imbedded in his principles as they, as such, are "abstractions." Thus a contradiction or conflict only arises in an actual or existential situation. A contradiction then only arises in the person of one who embraces conflicting principles—in the rebel who murders. The rebel's suicide removes the actual or existential, as opposed to abstract, contradiction. One who thinks, like Camus, of essence and existential conditions may have something vaguely like this in mind.

require one to kill, the "just assassin" serves freedom and avoids, in his suicide, the institutionalization of murder. He pays for his principles with his life.[24] This embodies, as so much of Camus's work does, a noble thought. Yet it is symptomatic of a desperately inadequate consideration of, and proposed solution to, the problems of ethics.

This combination of nobility without lucidity is what seems so disturbing about Camus. But then something he wrote might serve as a commentary on his thought.

> Even if the novel describes only nostalgia, despair, frustration, it still creates a form of salvation. To talk of despair is to conquer it. Despairing literature is a contradiction in terms.[25]

Camus consistently wrote of man's absurd condition. Perhaps in this way he sought to conquer it. Indeed, it may be true that just to talk of despair and our absurd condition is to conquer it—psychologically. But to "conquer" it in another sense, as Camus sought to do, a bit more is required.

SELECTIVE BIBLIOGRAPHY

Le Mythe de Sisyphe (Paris: Gallimard, 1942). English: The Myth of Sisyphus and Other Essays, trans. Justin O'Brien (New York: Random House, 1955)

L'Homme révolté (Paris: Gallimard, 1951). English: The Rebel, trans. Anthony Bower (New York: Random House, 1956)

Théatre, Récits, Nouvelles, ed. Roger Quillot (Paris: Gallimard, 1962)

---

[24] Camus is much taken by the nobility of sacrifice. In fact he sometimes seems to value the sacrifice of one's life for one's fellows almost as much as he values life itself. This is understandable in that sacrifice signifies (a) a "unity" with one's fellow men, and (b) submission to a "value" over and above one's own life. For Camus, as we have seen, both (a) and (b), in different senses, inject "meaning" into a meaningless universe. Sacrifice, so to speak, is the test of the absurd man's commitment.

[25] R, p. 263.

Germaine Brée, *Camus* (New Brunswick, N.J.: Rutgers University Press, 1959)

John Cruickshank, *Albert Camus and the Literature of Revolt* (Oxford: University Press, 1959)

Philip Thody, *Albert Camus: A Study of his Work* (London: Hamish Hamilton, 1957)

Chapter 12

INTRODUCTION

MARTIN HEIDEGGER (1889–   ) is certainly one of the leading European philosophers of this century. Since his first major work, *Being and Time* (1927), Heidegger has always maintained that the basic concern of his philosophical endeavor is connected with the question of the meaning of Being. We find this view defended in the opening remarks of *Being and Time*, and we still find it in his latest publications.

In trying to formulate the precise meaning of this question and in attempting to point to various directions in which, perhaps, one might find a preliminary suggestion as to a possible answer to this question, Heidegger has touched upon a great number of issues that at first sight are not connected with one another, but that in his view nonetheless are all related to his basic concern: an existential analysis of man's mode of Being, commentaries on the writings of great philosophers of the past, reflections on Hölderlin's poems and other works of art, reflections on science, technology, language, etc.

A remarkable trait of Heidegger's philosophy as a whole is certainly the fact that he has never written on ethical problems. True, a great number of people have interpreted several parts of *Being and Time* in an ethical sense, but Heidegger has always explicitly objected to this. Others have pointed to rather fragmentary remarks in other publications, such as *Introduction to Metaphysics* (1953) and his *Letter on Humanism* (1947), which could somehow suggest a concern for moral problems. However, if one studies these passages carefully, it becomes clear that, even there, Heidegger's concern is not with ethics but with the question concerning the meaning of Being.

One could perhaps give three different explanations for the fact that Heidegger has never explicitly dealt with ethical problems. First, one could argue that Heidegger preferred to limit himself to the question concerning the meaning of Being. However, one could say then that such a limitation on Heidegger's part does not necessarily exclude the possibility of developing a philosophical ethics on the basis of his thought.

Second, one could argue that in Heidegger's view a *philosophical* ethics is impossible, since philosophy's task is not to constitute meaning but merely to focus its attention on the historically developing totality of meaning, which is Being. Finally, one could argue that although ethical problems are not explicitly dealt with in Heidegger's philosophy, nonetheless the moral aspect of man's life and the world in which he lives are implicitly present in his thought, precisely because it refuses to explicitly articulate the different realms of meaning that can be legitimately distinguished in "Total-Meaningfulness." In this case one might even go so far as to say that Heidegger's view is basically ethical.

Given the texts available to us today, the second explanation seems to be the more reasonable. Adopting this explanation as a *possible* one, it seems reasonable, then, to assume that Heidegger leaves room for the view that the concern for moral problems is one of the tasks that religion sees placed before itself. Without trying to solve the problem, I have chosen some selections from Heidegger's *Letter on Humanism* that should shed some light on the issue.

In 1947 Beaufret wrote a letter to Heidegger asking him the following three questions: 1) How can we restore a meaning to the word "humanism"? 2) Precisely what is the relationship between ontology and an eventual ethics? 3) How can we preserve the element of adventure, which all research comports, without making philosophy mere venturesomeness? The selection that follows is Heidegger's reply to the first and second questions. The attentive reader will see that Heidegger purposely leaves room for the three possible interpretations of his "humanism" that are briefly indicated above.

ON HUMANISM

Martin Heidegger

You ask: *Comment redonner un sens au mot "Humanisme"?*
"How can one restore meaning to the word humanism?" Your
question not only presupposes that you want to retain the
word "humanism," but it also contains the admission that
the word has lost its meaning.

It has lost it through the realization that the essence of humanism is metaphysical and this now means that metaphysics
not only does not ask the question of the truth of Being, but
even abstracts asking it, insofar as metaphysics persists in its
oblivion of Being. The thought, however, that leads to this
realization of the questionable essence of humanism has at
the same time brought us to think of the essence of man more
originally. In view of this more essential *humanitas* of the
homo humanus, the possibility follows of restoring to the
word humanism an historical meaning that is older than what
"history" considers the oldest. This restoration is not to be
understood as though the word humanism were without
meaning at all and a mere *flatus vocis*. The "*humanum*" in
the word points to the *humanitas*, the essence of man. The
"ism" indicates that the essence of man would like to be understood essentially. The word "humanism" has this meaning
as a word. To give back a meaning to this word can mean
only to redetermine its meaning. This requires first that we
experience the essence of man more originally; and then show

This essay is from *Letter on Humanism*, by Martin Heidegger,
trans. Edgar Lohner, and reprinted from *Philosophy in the Twentieth Century*, ed. William Barrett and Henry D. Aiken (New York,
1962), Vol. III, pp. 291–301. Copyright © 1962 by Random House,
Inc.

in what degree this essence becomes in its own way a destiny. The essence of man rests in ex-sistence. This essence derives from Being itself, insofar as Being raises man as the ex-sisting one for the guardianship of the truth of Being. "Humanism" means now, should we decide to retain the word: the essence of man is essential for the truth of Being, and apart from this truth of Being man himself does not matter. So we think of a "humanism" of a strange sort. The word offers a term which is a *lucus a non lucendo*.

Should one still call "humanism" this view which speaks out against all earlier humanism, but which does not at all advocate the in-human? And this only in order to swim perhaps in the dominant currents, which are stifled in a metaphysical subjectivism and find themselves drowned in the oblivion of Being? Or should thought, resisting the word "humanism," make an effort to become more attentive to the *humanitas* of the *homo humanus* and what grounds this *humanitas*? So, if the world-historical moment has not already gone that far itself, a reflection might be awakened that would not only think of man, but of the "nature" of man, and even more than this, of his nature as the original dimension in which the essence of man, determined as coming from Being itself, is at home. But perhaps we should rather suffer for a while the inevitable misinterpretations to which the way of thought that centers on Being and time has so far been exposed and let them gradually be worn out? These misinterpretations are the natural reinterpretations of what people had read or rather, what they later thought they had read, but which, in fact, was preconception. They all show the same structure and the same basis.

Because "humanism" is argued against, one fears a defense of the inhuman and a glorification of barbaric cruelty. For what is more "logical" than that for one who negates humanism only the affirmation of inhumanity can remain?

Because "logic" is argued against, one believes that we renounce the rigor of thinking and in its place enthrone the despotism of instincts and emotions, and so proclaim "irrationalism" as the truth. For what is more "logical" than that one who argues against the logical defends the a-logical?

Because "values" are argued against, one is shocked by a philosophy that allegedly dares to neglect the highest goods of humankind. For what is more "logical" than that thinking which negates values must necessarily declare everything valueless?

Because it is said that the Being of man consists of "Being-in-the-World" (*In-der-Welt-sein*), one considers man to have been degraded to the level of a mere this-worldly being, and that philosophy thereby sinks into positivism. For what is more "logical" than that one who maintains the worldliness of man only admits the this-worldly, thereby negating the other-worldly and renouncing all "transcendency"?

Because reference is made to Nietzsche's expression of "God's death", one declares such a procedure to be atheism. For what is more "logical" than that one who has experienced "God's death" is a godless person?

Because in all that has been said I have argued everywhere against what mankind values as high and holy, this philosophy therefore teaches an irresponsible and destructive "nihilism." For what is more "logical" than that one who negates everywhere what is truly being, places himself on the side of the non-being and with that advocates mere nothingness as the meaning of reality?

What is happening here? One hears talk of "humanism," of "logic," of "values," of "world," of "God." One hears talk of an opposition to these. One knows and takes these things as positive. What is expressed against them, one immediately takes as their negation and thus "negative" in a sense of the destructive. This is a question of what, in a certain part of *Sein und Zeit*, we called "the phenomenological destruction." One believes that with the help of logic and *ratio* [Reason] that all that is not positive is negative and so would reject reason; and therefore, deserves to be branded as an infamy. One is so full of "logic," that everything which is repugnant to the usual somnolence of opinion is immediately charged to a censurable contrariness. One casts all that does not remain in the well-known beloved positive into the prearranged pit of bare negation that negates everything and therefore ends in nothingness and so achieves nihilism. In this logical way one lets everything succumb to a nihilism that one has fabricated with the help of logic.

But is it certain that the apparition that thought brings up against common opinion necessarily points to mere negation and to the negative? This occurs only when (but then so inevitably and so definitively, that is, without a free view of other directions) one fixes beforehand what is meant by "the positive" and from this decides absolutely and negatively against the sphere of possible oppositions to it. Such a procedure hides the refusal to expose to scrutiny the preconceived "positive," together with the black and white opposition, in which it believes that it has preserved itself. Through the constant appeal to logic one produces the illusion that one has yielded to thought, while one has abjured it.

That the opposition to "humanism" by no means implies the defence of the inhuman, but opens other prospectives must have become clearer to some extent now.

"Logic" understands thought as the representation of beings in their Being, and this Being as producing this representation as a universal concept. But how is it with the consideration of Being itself, i.e., with thought that thinks of the truth of Being? Such thought reaches the original essence of the λόγος, which in Plato and Aristotle, the founder of "logic," had already been dead and buried. To think "counter to logic" does not mean to stick up for the illogical, but only means to think the *logos*, and its essence as it appeared in the early days of thought; i.e. to make an effort first of all to prepare such an act of re-flecting (*Nach-denkens*). Of what use are all such prolix systems of logic to us, when even without knowing what they are doing they immediately avoid the task of asking after the essence of the λόγος? If one wanted to retaliate with objections, which is frankly fruitless, then one could more rightly say that irrationalism, as a renunciation of *ratio*, rules as unrecognized and undisputed master of that "logic" which believes it can avoid a consideration of the *logos* and of the essence of *ratio*, which is founded on the *logos*.

The thinking that runs counter to "values" does not state that all that one declares "values"—"culture," "art," "science," "human dignity," "world," and "God"—is worthless. One should rather come to understand that it is exactly through the characterization of something as "value," that it loses its dignity. This is to say that through the estimation of something as a value, one accepts what is evaluated only as a mere object for the appreciation of man. But what a thing is in its Being is not exhausted by its being an object, much less when the objectivity has the character of value. All valuing, even when it values positively, subjectivises the thing. It does not let beings be, but makes them valuable as the object of its action. The extravagant effort to demonstrate the objectivity of values does not know what it is doing. When one proclaims "God" as altogether "the highest value," this is a degradation of the essence of God. Thinking in values here and in general is the greatest blasphemy that can be thought of in the face of Being. To think counter to values, therefore, does not mean to beat the drum for the worthlessness and nullity of the existent, but means to bring—against the subjectivization of the existent as mere object—the clearing of the truth of Being before thought.

To refer to "Being-in-the-World" as the basic trait of the *humanitas* of the *homo humanus* is not to claim that man is simply a secular being, in the Christian sense, and so turned away from God and devoid of "transcendency." What is meant by this last word might be more clearly called: the Transcendent. The Transcendent is the super-sensual being. This is valued as the supreme being in the sense of the first cause of every being. God is thought of as this first cause. "World," however, does not in any way signify, in the term "Being-in-the-World," the earthly being in contrast to the heavenly, nor does it mean the "secular" in contrast to the "spiritual." "World" does not signify in this determination a being at all and no realm of beings, but the openness of Being. Man is and is man insofar as he is the existing. He stands exposed to the openness of Being, an openness which is Being itself, that has projected the essence of man into "care." So thrown, man stands "in" the openness of Being. "World" is the clearing of Being, wherein man stands out from his thrown essence. "Being-in-the-World" names the essence of ex-sistence in relation to the cleared dimension out of which the "ex" of the ex-sistence essentially arises. Thought of from the point of view of ex-sistence, "world" is in a way transcendence within and for existence. Man is never this-worldly and of the world as a "subject," whether this "subject" be understood as "I" or as "We." He is also not essentially a subject who is also always in reference to an object, so that his essence lies in the subject-object relation. Man is rather in his essence ex-sistent in the openness of Being; this Open only clears the "between," within which the "relation" between subject and object can "be."

The statement that the essence of man rests in Being-in-the-World contains no resolution about whether man is in the theological-metaphysical sense a mere this-worldly creature or an other-worldly one.

Therefore, with the existential determination of the essence of man nothing has yet been decided about the "existence" or "non-existence" of God, not about the possibility or impossibility of God. It is thus not only precipitate but erroneous to assert that the interpretation of the essence of man in its relation to the truth of Being is atheism. This arbitrary classification, besides everything else, lacks carefulness in reading. One ignores the fact that since 1929 the following statement could be found in the work *Vom Wesen des Grundes* (p. 28, fn. 1): "Through the ontological interpretation of *Dasein* as Being-in-the-World, there is neither a positive nor a negative resolution made about a possible Being-towards-God. However, through the elucidation of the transcendency there is first obtained *an adequate concept of Dasein*, in consideration of which one may now ask what exactly is, ontologically, the relationship between God and *Dasein*." Now when this observation, too, is, as usual, taken too narrowly, one is likely to say that this philosophy makes no decision either for or against the existence of God. It remains indifferent. Thus, the religious question does not concern it. Such "indifferentism" must surely turn into nihilism.

But does the quoted remark really teach indifferentism? Why, then, are some words, and not others, printed in italics in the footnotes? Only to indicate, surely, that thought that thinks from the question of the truth of Being questions more originally than metaphysics can. Only from the truth of Being can the essence of the holy be thought. Only from the essence of the holy can the essence of divinity be thought. Only in the light of the essence of divinity can it be thought and said what the word "God" is to signify. Or must we not first be able to understand and hear these words carefully if we as men, i.e., as ex-sisting beings, are to have the privilege of experiencing a relation of God to man? How, then, is the man of the present epoch even to be able to ask seriously and firmly whether God approaches or withdraws when man omits the primary step of thinking deeply in the one dimension where this question can be asked: that is, the dimension of the holy, which, even as dimension, remains closed unless the openness of Being is cleared and in its clearing is close to man. Perhaps the distinction of this age consists in the fact that the dimension of grace has been closed. Perhaps this is its unique disgrace.

But with this indication, which points to the truth of Being as what-has-to-be-thought, this thought would in no way wish to have declared itself for theism. It can no more be theistic than it can be atheistic. This, however, is not because of any indifferent attitude but out of respect for the limits which have been set upon thought as thought, and precisely through which it is understood as that which has-to-be-thought, through the truth of Being. In so far as thought does not exceed the limits of its task, at the moment of present world destiny it gives man an indication of the original dimension of his historical abode. In so far as thought expresses in this way the truth of Being, it has entrusted itself to what is more essential than all values and all beings. Thought does not overcome metaphysics by surpassing and cancelling it in some direction or other and ascending even higher: it descends into the nearness of the nearest. The descent, especially where man has ascended too far into subjectivity, is more difficult and more dangerous than the ascent. The descent leads to the poverty of the ex-sistence of the *homo humanus*. In ex-sistence, the sphere of the *homo animalis* of metaphysics is abandoned. The domination of this sphere is the indirect and very old reason for the delusion and arbitrariness of what is denominated as biologism, but also for what is known as pragmatism. To think of the truth of Being means at the same time to think of the *humanitas* of the *homo humanus*. What is at stake is *humanitas*, in the service of the truth of Being but without humanism in the metaphysical sense.

But if the thought of Being is so essentially focussed on humanitas, must ontology then not be completed by "ethics"? Is not that effort essential which you express in the sentence, "*Ce que je cherche à faire, depuis longtemps déjà, c'est préciser le rapport de l'ontologie avec une éthique possible*"?

Shortly after *Sein und Zeit* appeared, a young friend asked me, "When are you going to write an ethics?" Where the essence of man is thought of so essentially, i.e., only from the question of the truth of Being, but without raising man to the center of beings, there the desire must arise for personally relevant directives and rules that tell how man, having gathered from his ex-sistence experience for Being is to live "fatefully." The wish for an ethics needs to be fulfilled, all the more urgently, because the overt no less than the concealed, perplexity of man increases to immeasurable dimensions. Every care must be given to ties to be suggested by ethics, in an age of technology when the individual, subject to the nature of a mass society, can be brought to a dependable steadfastness only by means of ordering and gathering his plans and actions as a whole in a way that corresponds to a technological age.

Who can ignore this crisis? Should we not preserve and secure the ties we now have, even if they only hold human beings together precariously and in mere immediacy? Certainly. But does this crisis ever absolve thought of the responsibility of thinking of that which primarily remains to-be-thought and, as Being, remains the guarantee and truth prior to every being? Can thought continue to retreat from the thought of Being after this has lain so long hidden in oblivion and at the same time announces itself at this very moment of world history through the uprooting of every being?

Before we attempt to determine more precisely the relationship between "ontology" and "ethics," we must ask what "ontology" and "ethics" themselves are. It is necessary to consider whether what can be designated by these terms still remains adequate and close to what has been assigned to thought, which as thought has to think before all else of the truth of Being.

Should, however, "ontology" as well as "ethics" and all thinking in disciplines become untenable and our thinking thereby become more disciplined, what happens then to the question of the relationship between these two disciplines of philosophy?

Ethics appeared for the first time, along with logic and physics in the school of Plato. These disciplines were born at a time that converted thought into "philosophy," but philosophy into *episteme* (science) and science itself into a matter for schools and school administrations. In passing through philosophy, so understood, science was born and thought [*Denken*] vanished. Thinkers up to then had known neither a "logic," nor an "ethics," nor a "physics." Yet their thinking is neither illogical nor immoral. But their conception of *physis* had a profundity and breadth which all the later "physics" was never again able to attain. The tragedies of Sophocles, if such a comparison can be made at all, hold the *ethos* more originally concealed in their telling than Aristotle's lecture on "ethics." A saying of Heraclitus that only consists of three words says something so simple that from it the essence of the *ethos* immediately comes to light.

The saying of Heraclitus goes (fragment 119): ἦθος ἀνθρώπῳ δαίμων. This is usually translated as: "A man's character is his daimon." This translation is modern but not Greek thinking. ἦθος means abode, place of dwelling. The word designates the open sphere in which man dwells. The openness of his abode allows that to appear which approaches toward the essence of man and so arriving abides near him. The abode of man contains and maintains the advent of that to which man in essence belongs. This, according to Heraclitus' saying, is δαίμων, God. The fragment says: Man, insofar as he is man, dwells in the nearness of God. A story that Aristotle relates (de part. anim. A 5, 645 a 17) coincides with this saying of Heraclitus. It runs:

"An anecdote tells of an explanation that Heraclitus is said to have given strangers who wanted to approach him. Upon approaching they found him warming himself at a stove. They stopped surprised and all the more so because as they hesitated he encouraged them and bade them come in with the words: 'For here too there are Gods present.'"

The story speaks for itself, yet some aspects should be stressed.

The group of unknown visitors in its inquisitive curiosity about the thinker is disappointed and puzzled at first by his abode. It believes that it must find the thinker in conditions which, contrary to man's usual way of living, show everywhere traits of the exceptional and the rare, and, therefore, the sensational. The group hopes to find through its visit with the thinker things which, at least for a time, will provide material for entertaining small talk. The strangers who wish to visit the thinker hope to see him perhaps precisely at the moment when, sunk in profound meditation, he is thinking. The visitors wish to experience this, not in order to be affected by his thinking, but merely so that they will be able to say that they have seen and heard one who is reputed to be a thinker.

Instead, the inquisitive ones find Heraclitus at a stove. This is a pretty ordinary and insignificant place. True enough, bread is baked there. But Heraclitus is not even busy with baking at the stove. He is there only to warm himself, and so he betrays the whole poverty of his life at this spot which is in itself prosaic. The glimpse of a freezing thinker offers little of interest. And so the inquisitive ones at this disappointing sight immediately lose their desire to come any closer. What are they to do there? This ordinary dull event of someone cold and standing by the stove one can find any time in his own home. Then, why look up a thinker? The visitors are about to leave again. Heraclitus reads the disappointed curiosity in their faces. He realizes that with the crowd the mere absence of an expected sensation is enough to make those who have just come leave. Therefore, he heartens them. He especially urges them to enter with the words εἶναι γὰρ καὶ ἐνταῦθα θέους. "There are Gods present even here."

This statement puts the abode (ἦθος) of the thinker and his doing in a different light. Whether the visitors have understood the statement immediately or at all and then seen everything in this different light, the story does not tell. But that the story was told and transmitted to us today, is due to the fact that what it reports is of the bearing of this thinker and characterizes it. καὶ ἐνταῦθα. "Even here," at the baking oven, at this common place, where all things and every condition, each act and thought, are familiar and current, i.e., securer, "even there" in the sphere of the secure εἶναι θεούς, it is so "that even there there are gods present."

ἦθος ἀνθρώπῳ δαίμων as Heraclitus says: "The (secure) abode for man is the open quality of the presence (Anwesung) of God (of the, insecure, the strange) (des Un-geheuren).

If now, in accord with the basic meaning of the word ἦθος, ethics dwells in the abode of man, then that thought which thinks the truth of Being as the original element of man as ex-sisting is already in itself at the source of ethics. But then this kind of thinking is not ethics, either, because it is ontology. For ontology always thinks only the being (ὄν) in its Being. As long as the truth of Being, however, is not thought, all ontology remains without its base. Hence the thought, which with Sein und Zeit tried to think forward into the truth of Being, called itself fundamental ontology. It attempts to go back to the basic essence, from which the thought of the truth of Being derives. The formulation of different questions removes this thinking from the "ontology" of metaphysics (including that of Kant). The reason, however, why "ontology," be it transcendental or precritical, is subject to criticism is not that it thinks the Being of beings and thereby forces Being into a concept, but that it does not think the truth of Being and so fails to realize the fact that there is a mode of thinking more rigorous than the conceptual. Thinking which tries to think forward into the truth of Being, in the struggle of the first breakthrough expresses only a small part of this entirely different dimension. And the latter is further distorted in that it no longer retains the essential help of phenomenological vision and has not yet abandoned its inadequate pretensions toward "science" and "research." In order to make this attempt of thinking recognizable and understandable within philosophy, it was possible at first to speak only within the horizon of the existing philosophy and within the usage of the terms familiar to it.

In the meantime I have come to be convinced that even these terms must immediately and inevitably lead astray. For the terms and their corresponding conceptual language were not rethought by the readers from the thing which had-to-be-thought first; instead, this thing was imagined through terms maintained in their usual signification. Thinking that seeks for the truth of Being and thereby determines the essential abode of man from Being is neither ethics nor ontology. Therefore, the question of the relationship of the two to each other has no longer any basis in this sphere. Nevertheless your question, if it be thought more originally, continues to make sense and be of essential importance.

One must, of course, ask: If thought, considering the truth of Being, determines the essence of the *humanitas* as existence from its pertinence to Being, does this thought only remain a theoretical imagining of Being and of man, or is it possible to extract from knowledge directives for action and put them to use for life?

The answer is that such thinking is neither theoretical nor practical. It occurs before such a differentiation. This thinking is, insofar as it is, the recollection of Being and nothing else. Belonging to Being, because it is thrown by Being into the trueness of its truth and claimed by it, it thinks Being. Such thinking results in nothing. It has no effect. It suffices its own essence, in that it is. But it is, in that it expresses its matter. At each epoch of history one thing only is important to it: that it be in accord with its matter. Its material relevance is essentially superior to the validity of science, because it is freer. For it lets Being—be.

Thinking works at building the house of Being; in which house Being joins and as such the joining of Being enjoins that man, according to destiny, dwell in the truth of Being. This dwelling is the essence of "Being-in-the-world" (cf. *Sein und Zeit*). The reference there to the "in-Being" (*In-Sein*) as "dwelling" is no etymological game. The reference in the essay of 1936 to Hölderlin's phrase, "Laboring, yet poetically man dwells on this earth" is no mere gilding of a thought that abandoning science, takes refuge in poetry. To talk of the house of Being is not to transfer the image of "house" to Being, but from the materially understood essence of Being we shall some day be more easily able to think what "house" and "dwelling" are.

Nonetheless, thought never creates the house of Being, Thought accompanies historical existence, i.e., the *humanitas* of the *homo humanus,* to the domain where grace arises.

With grace, evil appears in the clearing of Being. The essence of evil does not consist in pure wickedness of human action, but in the malice of anger. Both grace and anger can, however, essentially only be in Being, insofar as Being itself is the Contentious. In it is hidden the essential source of nihilation (*das Nichten*). What nihilates, is manifest as the nothing-like (*das Nichthafte*). This can be approached in the "No." The "Not" does not arise from the Nay-saying of negation. Each "No" which is not misinterpreted as a self-willed insistence on the positing power of subjectivity, but remains letting-be of ex-sistence, answers the claim of the manifest nihilation. Every "No" is only the affirmation of the "Not." Every affirmation rests in recognition. This lets that towards which it goes approach it. It is believed that nihilation cannot be found anywhere in beings themselves. This is true as long as one seeks for nihilation as something that is being, as an existing quality of the existent. But that is not the place to seek for nihilation. Being, too, is no existing quality which characterizes the being. Nevertheless, Being is being more than any actual being. Because nihilation is essentially in Being itself, we can never become aware of it as something that is being in the existent. But this impossibility does not prove that the source of the Not is from Nay-saying. This proof only seems conclusive if one posits the existent as the object of subjectivity. From this alternative it then follows that each Not, since it never appears as something objective, must inevitably be the product of a subjective act. Whether, however, the Nay-saying constitutes the Not as something merely thought, or whether the nihilation only demands the "No" as what-is-to-be-said in the letting-be of beings, certainly can never be distinguished from the subjective reflection of thinking, which has already been posited as subjectivity. In such a reflection, the dimension for the formulation of the questions adequate to the matter has not yet been reached. It remains to be asked, granted that thought belongs to ex-sistence, whether all "Yes" and "No" is not already existent in the truth of Being. If so, then "Yes" and "No" are already in themselves bound to Being. As bondsmen, they can never first posit that to which they themselves belong.

Nihilation is essentially in Being itself and by no means in the *Dasein* of man, insofar as this is thought as subjectivity of the *ego cogito*. The Dasein by no means nihilates, insofar as man as subject performs the nihilation in the sense of rejection, but the Da-sein nihilates, insofar as, as essence, wherein man ex-sists, it itself belongs to the essence of Being. Being nihilates—as Being, Therefore, in the absolute idealism of Hegel and Schelling, the Not appears as the negativity of the negative in the essence of Being. This, however, is thought there in the essence of absolute actuality as the unconditioned will, which wills itself and, indeed, as the will of knowledge and love. In this will, Being is still concealed as the will to power. Why, however, the negativity of the absolute subjectivity is the "dialectical" and why, through the dialectic, the nihilation is discovered, but at the same time is concealed in its essence cannot here be discussed.

The nihilating (*das Nichtende*) in Being is the essence of what I call the Nothing. Because it thinks Being, thought thinks the Nothing.

Only Being lends to grace the ascent to graciousness and to anger the push toward disgrace.

Only so far as man, ex-sisting in the truth of Being, belongs to it, can the assigning of all the directions which must become for man law and rule, come from Being itself. The verb "assign" in Greek is νέμειν. The νόμος is not only law, but more originally the assigning concealed in the destiny of Being. Only this is capable of ordering man in Being. Only such ordering is capable of bearing up and binding. Other-

wise, all law remains but the handiwork of human reason.
More essential than any establishment of rule is the abode
in the truth of Being. Only this abode yields the experience
of the tenable (*das Haltbare*). The hold (*Halt*) for all behavior (*Verhalten*) is given by the truth of Being. "Hold" in
our language means "shelter." Being is the shelter that
in view of its own truth shelters man in his ex-sisting essence
in such a way that it lodges ex-sistence in language. Thus
language is at once the house of Being and the dwelling of
human beings. Only because language is the dwelling of the
essence of man, can the historical ways of mankind and men
not be at home in their language, so that for them it becomes
the shell of their machinations.

In what relationship now does the thought of Being stand
to theoretical and practical behavior? It is superior to all
contemplation, because it cares for the light in which only a
seeing as theory can abide and move. Thought attends to the
clearing of Being by putting its speaking of Being into language as the dwelling of ex-sistence. Thus thought is an action. But an action that is superior at the same time to all
practice. Thinking surpasses doing and producing, not
through the magnitude of its performance, nor through the
consequences of its activity, but through the humbleness of
the achievement that it accomplishes without result.

Thinking, as you know, brings into language in its saying
only the unspoken word of Being.

The expression used here, "to bring into language," is now
to be taken quite literally. Being, clearing itself, comes into
language. It is always on its way towards it. As it arrives, it in
its turn brings ex-sisting thought to language in its telling,
which is thus elevated into the clearing of Being. Only thus,
language *is* in its mysterious and yet humanly pervasive way.
Insofar as language, thus brought fully into its essence, is
historical, Being is preserved in remembering. Ex-sistence in-
habits as it thinks the house of Being. In all this, it is as if
nothing had happened at all through the utterance of thought.

But we have just seen an example of this insignificant act
of thinking. For while we specifically think the expression "to
bring to language," which was given to language, only this

and nothing else, and while we retain in the observance of speaking what we have thought as something that always has-to-be-thought in the future, we have ourselves brought something essential of Being into language.

The strange thing in this thought of Being is its simplicity. This is precisely what keeps us from it. For we seek for the thought that in the name of "philosophy" has its world-historical prestige in the form of the unusual, which is only accessible to the initiate. At the same time we represent thought to ourselves in the manner of scientific knowledge and research. We measure the act against the impressive and successful achievements of practice. But the act of thinking is neither theoretical nor practical, nor is it the coupling together of both ways or behavior.

Through its simple essence the thought of Being is disguised for us. But when we become friends with the unusualness of the simple, another affliction befalls us at once. The suspicion arises that this thought of Being may lapse into the arbitrary; for it cannot cling to beings. From whence does thought derive its rule? What is the law of its action?

SELECTIVE BIBLIOGRAPHY

Sein und Zeit (Halle: Niemeyer, 1927). English: Being and Time, trans. John Macquarrie and Edward Robinson (London: SCM Press, 1962)

Platons Lehre von der Wahrheit. Mit einem Brief über den Humanismus (Bern: Francke Verlag, 1947). English: Letter on Humanism, trans. Edgar Lohner, in Philosophy in the Twentieth Century, 2 vols., ed. William Barrett and Henry D. Aiken (New York: Random House, 1962), vol. II, pp. 270–302

Einführung in die Metaphysik (Tübingen: Niemeyer, 1953). English: Introduction to Metaphysics, trans. Ralph Manheim (New Haven, Conn.: Yale University Press, 1958)

Chapter 13

INTRODUCTION

OTTO BOLLNOW (1903–   ) first studied mathematics
and physics, obtaining his doctorate at Göttingen in 1925. He
then studied philosophy and pedagogy at Göttingen and Freiburg. He taught at Göttingen as an instructor from 1931 to
1939 and at Giessen as Professor from 1939 to 1946. From
Giessen he went to Mainz (1946–53), and since 1953 he has
been teaching at Tübingen.

Bollnow's publications focus on two separate themes:
philosophical anthropology and ethics. He conceives of the
former as the hermeneutic of human life, which must interpret every individual phenomenon within the context of the
whole of a man's life as it develops in a still larger totality of
meaning—man's world as it is historically and culturally determined. Bollnow adopts a rather critical attitude in regard
to existentialism, not only as Sartre conceives of it, but even
taken in the form in which we find it in Heidegger's *Being
and Time* and in the numerous authors influenced by
Heidegger. Bollnow argues that most "existentialists" put too
much stress on the "negative" phenomena in man's life, such
as anxiety, or require too much of man, such as is implied in
Heidegger's conception of authenticity. This is why Bollnow
focuses most of his attention on positive and "happy" moods;
in his view, life becomes intolerable without hope. Existentialism overlooks the fact that freedom of decision and authenticity are possible only when based on a sustaining sub-
soil of security (*Geborgenheit*). Security does not mean
naïve safety or certainty, but signifies that condition under

which man's life-tensions can be endured. It is obvious that such an anthropology is closely related to an "optimistic" view in ethics.

The selection that follows is the first section of *Neue Geborgenheit*, in which Bollnow himself explains his major concern vis-à-vis the "existentialists."

EXISTENTIALISM'S BASIC ETHICAL POSITION

Otto Bollnow

1   THE REPROACH OF IMMORALISM

The problem of overcoming existentialism can best be approached from an ethical point of view, because it is here that the immediately practical consequences of its basic decisions come most clearly to the fore; it is here that, above all, the errors of its decisions manifest themselves most irrefutably in its consequences. It is true that a widespread conception holds that existentialism contains no ethics at all, but rather that according to its innermost essence it undermines all ethical behavior since it abrogates all stable norms and surrenders man's behavior to subjective arbitrariness. However, this conception is no less superficial than the confusing of existentialism with any form of nihilism, which rests for the most part on confusing it with certain fashionable concomitant phenomena in the realm of literature.

On the other hand, it could barely be held accidental that until now existentialism has not brought forth a systematically developed ethical system, and one can correctly point to the fact that its main interest goes in another direction. Heidegger, at least, has always declined an ethical evaluation of his thought. True, in the concluding sections of his main work, *Being and Nothingness*, Sartre has sketched ethical per-

This essay is from *Neue Geborgenheit*, by Otto Friedrich Bollnow (Stuttgart, 1960), pp. 33–50. Copyright © 1960 (second edition) by W. Kohlhammer Verlag, Stuttgart. The present essay was translated into English expressly for this edition by Joseph J. Kockelmans.

spectives with a few strokes and promised a more penetrating ethical investigation,[1] but the fact that, so many years after the work mentioned, this investigation has not yet appeared, might point to the fact that for him, too, the ethical interest is not so decisive. To date there is only a project of an ethics available; written by Simone de Beauvoir, it is essentially in harmony with Sartre's thought.[2]

All of this notwithstanding, the absence of a systematically developed philosophical ethics does not exclude the fact that existentialism is carried by a basic ethical conception that is completely determinate, and even defended very passionately. This conception is contained in its basic philosophical treatises, that is, in the general anthropological determinations given in them, and is in principle simply to be made explicit in an investigating reflection. The ethical attitude, however, perhaps comes even more clearly to the fore in the poetic witnesses of this movement, in that they constitute an immediate expression of its conception of life.

2 Basic Ethical Concepts

An in-depth explanation of existentialist ethics cannot be given here;[3] it should suffice to accentuate briefly those decisive characteristics that are indispensable for our present discussion. The starting point for an understanding of the ethical conception of existentialism is found where we said that man does not simply let himself be driven by the anxiety that crowds in on him, but courageously opposes it with a decisive turn and thus materializes the existential summit of his *Dasein* in an active endurance of anxiety.

[1] Jean-Paul Sartre, *Being and Nothingness. An Essay on Phenomenological Ontology*, trans. Hazel E. Barnes (New York: Philosophical Library, 1956), pp. 625–28.

[2] Simone de Beauvoir, *The Ethics of Ambiguity*, trans. Bernard Frechtman (New York: The Citadel Press, 1967).

[3] Otto Friedrich Bollnow, *Existenzphilosophie* (Stuttgart: Kohlhammer, 1960); "Existentialismus," *Die Sammlung*, 2(1947), pp. 654 ff.; "Existentialismus und Ethik," *Die Sammlung*, 4(1949), pp. 321 ff.

This holds true in an even more general way: while man finds himself confronted with a threatening and basically hopeless situation, he feels pressed to come to a clear *decision*, and with this decision the situation itself receives at once a determinate form. However, if man attempts to withdraw from the decision, or if he tries to mediate between the oppositions in a non-decisive way, then his life escapes from him and falls into indeterminate meaninglessness. Kierkegaard had already argued passionately for this attitude of "either-or," in opposition to Hegel's spirit of mediation and reconciliation, and up until now the difficulty of this decision has been stressed repeatedly in the realm of theology. But beyond all this, one may say generally that that tendency toward compromise and synthesis is basically repugnant to the existentialist spirit.

On the basis of such a clearly executed decision it becomes necessary at once, then, that man collect his *Dasein* in the firm determinateness of his will, which until then was in danger of losing itself in the indeterminateness of vague possibilities.

In this way we are led to the necessity of resoluteness, as Heidegger more than any other has clearly worked out. Only in the resoluteness of his will does man wrench himself from the "fallenness" of his everyday *Dasein*, and thus gain the "authenticity" of his ek-sistence.

And finally a third element: this resoluteness cannot be just understood as a mere inner state of man, but according to a necessary trait of its own essence, it changes immediately into action. Thus resoluteness materializes in an unconditioned engagement, *dans l'engagement*, as French existentialism originally framed it. It is only because, and in so far as, man becomes engaged, actively takes part in something, and devotes all his energy to this realization, that he gains a foothold in a reality of some sort and secures his own innermost reality by tearing himself away from a state of mere noncommittal possibility.

Decision, resoluteness, and engagement therefore are the three basic concepts of existentialist ethics. They are so closely related to one another, that one is better advised to conceive of them as three different aspects of the basic ethical conception of existentialism, which, taken in its essence, constitutes a homogeneous phenomenon. It is a conception of an ultimate (*letzter*), *heroic* greatness, which is expressed here, and thus by no means can be criticized. Rather, it must be seen and recognized in its entire greatness.

3 THE POINT OF DEPARTURE FOR A CRITICISM

Nevertheless, when the necessity of a critical discussion arises, then the issue is not one of making these virtues as such questionable, but involves merely the fact that through the absolutizing of these virtues a completely *distorted image* of man's *Dasein* emerges, and that in so doing one then also brings moral behavior into a completely inadequate and false perspective. Thus these virtues are by no means false; but the anthropological presuppositions that have led to their one-sided representation are false, and it is thus necessary to gain a broader anthropological foundation on which these relationships can be properly corrected.

While toward this end we begin first on the ethical level, it is once and for all vital (for our purpose) to examine the disastrous consequences of existentialist one-sidedness in the realm of ethics, and to show that if they and they alone determine the picture, they will lead us to the situation with which we have just preliminarily dealt and in which a human life becomes altogether impossible. On the other hand, it is, secondly, vital to develop certain "countervirtues," that is to say, develop the essential structures of certain basic attitudes of a different nature that cannot be understood from the standpoint of existentialism, to acknowledge these in their particular and partly even superior right, and in this way to provide certain building stones for the development of a more comprehensive anthropological foundation. Such "countervirtues," which are contrary to the existentialist world, are composure (*Gelassenheit*), ever-available willingness, hopeful courage under all threats, never-relaxing patience, the capacity for thankfulness, and unshakable hope, just to mention a few of the most important virtues for a first consideration.

One of the dangers of the existentialist conception suggests itself immediately. We characterize it in a short formula as "the danger of existential adventurousness." For if one asks the question concerning the motives on the basis of which the decision becomes determined, and about the goals toward which the resoluteness must turn, and for which the engagement sets itself in motion, then existentialism as such is unable to give an answer to these questions. When Sartre formulates this as follows: "What counts is the total commitment,"[4] it can be taken to stand for a characterization of the existentialist position as such. It leads necessarily to an ethics that is purely "formal," for which existence as such—and correspondingly resoluteness and resolution, also —gains an absolute value that is independent from the uncertainty found in the question concerning the determination of man's goal. The grounds that have led to such a formal ethics cannot be discussed here in detail. In any case they spring from all the deep shocks that in general have led to existentialism and in which, in this connection, the relativizing of historic consciousness and the fatal blow to all material goals play important parts.

From this background alone the greatness of existentialist ethics begins to stand out. On the basis of modern historical relativism it materializes once again a wholly decisive moral conception. But with this we encounter at once the danger that emerges in the possibility of an existential adventurousness. The adventurer, who has become free from any commitment in regard to substantial content and lacks the stability that rests upon faith, enjoys the venture of his commitment as a last and most sublime fascination. It is precisely in the indeterminateness of the engagement, which, at each time, is momentary, that the existentialist is delivered in a particularly great degree to the temptation toward instability and infidelity. The danger of such existential adventurousness is not just a theoretically constructed possibility, but is realized in existentialist poetry, or the poetry of our time that is closely related to existentialism.

[4] Jean-Paul Sartre, *L'existentialisme est un humanisme* (Paris: Nagel, 1946), p. 62. Cf. also the two articles quoted in note 3.

SITUATION AND DECISION

1 THE EXAGGERATION IN THE DEMAND TO DECIDE FOR ONESELF

In order to realize the consequences of the one-sided exaggeration of an existentialist virtue, and to detect the necessity of a "countervirtue," we choose as a first example the relationship between situation and decision. The problem found here is not only of importance for existential philosophy in the narrow sense, but in addition to this, for contemporary consciousness determined by existential experiences as well. This is even the case, too, where this consciousness has perhaps not yet come in contact with the explicit, philosophical sharpening of this problem. But that is not an objection to asking this question here in the beginning, for what is at stake in the problem concerning the discussion with existentialism is certainly not so much its deeper philosophical coining of expression, but rather, even much more, its effects, which have passed over to a broader publicity; for it is precisely here that the fateful consequences of such a beginning have come to light most clearly.

When one looks around in contemporary spiritual life, it becomes conspicuous how much people ask about "situation" and how much they search for a clear "decision." These questions keep returning repeatedly as themes for conferences and lectures.[5] This can easily be understood and is perfectly in order; for our times are so intricate, confused, and opaque that they precisely ask of themselves for a clarification; and then so many heterogeneous and conflicting powers crowd in on man, that it becomes necessary to decide

[5] On the philosophical level we must mention the symposium on "Situation and Decision," led by Theodor Litt during the Congress of Philosophy held in Bremen in 1950. In this symposium these relationships were fruitfully clarified from various perspectives. Cf. *Symphilosophein. Bericht über den Dritten Deutschen Kongress für Philosophie: Bremen, 1950* (München: Kösel Verlag, 1952), pp. 273 ff. The conception defended here was developed by the author for the first time at the Bremen colloquium.

between them. Man can hope to get out of this unsettled condition of the present time and finally get a firm footing again only by means of a determinate and clarifying decision. The search for a clear decision, therefore, is not just to be understood, it is even necessary, and in this necessity, to be affirmed. To that extent, it would be completely wrong to try to deny this will to decision its high moral value.

And yet, there is *something* that is *cramped* in this continuous pressing for a decision, and often there is even something dangerous in it, and it is to this reverse of the problem that we must draw attention in the present context. Frequently one can even speak of a *hunger after decision,* of a sickly exaggerated desire for decision. But here one hides from oneself the fact that this desire by no means emerges from the power of an unbroken life, but on the contrary, merely from its weakness: because one is simply unable to endure the indecision any longer, he therefore forces the decision at any price and withdraws to the fatal statement: that a false decision is better than no decision at all. One acts as if the genuine greatness of mankind materializes only and exclusively in the unconditional decision. But this is a conception in regard to which, as far as its very origin is concerned, existential philosophy is not completely without guilt. On the other hand, however, we shall have to show that decision is by no means always and necessarily the highest form of man's life.

2   Position and Situation

In order to understand the one-sidedness of a conception of man's life that is wholly oriented toward decision, it is first necessary to clarify briefly the two concepts employed in this context. On the one hand, we must determine the relationship between the concepts "situation" and "decision." When these two are mentioned together repeatedly and understood within the unity of an all-encompassing problematic, then this is done with good reason; for they necessarily belong together and mutually refer to one another. For if we take the concept "situation" in a strict sense, then not every arbitrary position in which a man finds himself deserves to be characterized as situation. It is appropriate, rather, to make a distinction between these two concepts.

Position is the more general of the two. Taken in a very broad sense, we define "position" as the living environment of man, the totality of all the circumstances that influence him in a stimulating as well as restraining way. All life—not only human, but also animal life as well—finds itself at each moment in a determinate position. This position itself can then be of a very heterogeneous nature: it can mean pressure, and stimulate man's efforts to change his living conditions, but it may be as well a position of rest, in which he feels well and which he by no means plans to change.

In contrast with this, we define "situation" as a determinate critical position, namely a position that places man before the necessity of making a decision. Situation, therefore, designates a position in which man has to make a determinate choice between different possibilities that offer themselves to him, and to organize his life in harmony with this choice. Thus it is only with respect to the decision to be taken that there is a situation; one can even further sharpen the issue in the sense of Heidegger, who was the first to develop this aspect of the problematic in a very precise way, and say: even in those exceptional moments the situation is not simply present-at-hand as a given fact, but it constitutes itself as a determinate one only in so far as man sees himself placed before the choice to make a decision either in this way or in the opposite way. It is such a clearly comprehended decision-question, which alone forces the position, which until then was still ambiguous and undetermined before the unequivocality of a determinate situation.

3   MAN IN CRISIS

In the sense of such a distinction, one may say that human life, indeed, at all times finds itself in a determinate position, but not at all times in a determinate situation. It is only in a certain crisis that position becomes sharpened into situation in the proper sense. In this sense the concept of situation includes the one of crisis, that is, each situation is according to its essence a crisis-situation. This is indeed the conception of existential philosophy, also, when it puts so much stress upon decision: it believes that the essence of man's *Dasein* as such is to be found in crisis, that is, that only in it does *Dasein* reveal itself in its depth, and only by going through it, in decision, come to its own innermost essence.

True, the significance of crisis for gaining an essentially genuine *Dasein* can by no means be contested. What is wrong with it again is the exaggeration, as if crisis were the *only* genuine form of man's *Dasein*, and for that reason human life must necessarily be oriented in regard to the decision. That, however, is a fatal error, for in this way two connected things are misunderstood, the essence of crisis as well as that of human life in so far as it is not marked by crises. That is why we must first try to realize that there are broad and no less important realms of man's life that cannot be properly understood in their innermost essence if one considers them from that point of view.

According to their own essence, crises are not states that last long, but exceptional situations. Although it is true that they are very important, they are nonetheless interruptions of the normal course of life, and they fulfill their genuine function only when they lead beyond themselves toward a liberating solution. In between these crises, however, life often passes through very long periods of time in quiet continuity, without there being any need for a decision in the pregnant sense of the term, and without it being the case, on the other hand, that for that reason life should have to be "inauthentic" in the existential-philosophical sense of the term, that is, less real and less essential. The demand for a continuous resoluteness is rather a false and very fatal heroization, and it is precisely here that we find one of the most essential sources of the existential "cramp," to which we have pointed already. That is why Landmann, with very good reason, said at the congress in Bremen: "The idea of decision is the gateway of activism and irrationalism in ethics (Viking-philosophy)."[6]

6 Ibid., p. 302.

4 LIFE OUTSIDE THE CRISIS

The different forms of a state in which life develops through long periods of time without there being any necessity for a decision, cannot be discussed here in detail; we must limit ourselves to outlining them in three directions in a brief summary:

1. Life passes without decision where a decision made is changed into reality through systematic work, as in the *execution of a plan*, and it would mean to withdraw all continuity from this work, and make the execution of such a plan completely impossible, were one to demand that this decision be taken anew at each moment. In that case it could also be executed again at each moment in a different way, and that would finally lead in the direction of an existential adventurousness that, precisely because of the decision to be executed anew at each moment, could become faithless. In contrast to this, man must have the force to continuously build up his life on the basis of a decision once made. Such continuity, however, cannot develop from the existential attitude.

2. Secondly, life passes without decision as long as it develops within the perspective of determinate, *supporting habits and convictions*; these may be those which each individual forms in the course of his own life, or those which he has tacitly adopted from his environment. For they always predelineate how he must behave in any new case he may encounter. The necessity of making a new decision is here, thus, always already taken away from man through the convictions and habits on hand. Something like this is, however, not only possible where life takes place without history and in courses that eternally remain the same, but also within historical development as long as the latter happens without ruptures, somehow organically, and from within.

3. And finally, all development of life takes place without decision when it is executed in the manner of a genuine *expression* with inner necessity. These circumstances can best be explained with the help of a *work of art*, although this is just one example, albeit perhaps the most impressive example

of such an expressive creation.[7] For when this emerges from the depths of the unconscious life of the soul, then it occurs almost with uncanny sureness from an inner necessity, and thus does not require a decision that always presupposes leeway between two different possibilities. The artist does not decide, where he is really at work in his creative work. At the most, he makes decisions in those particular situations in which he must choose between two different plans, where he, for instance, gives up a work he has already started and instead falls back upon another plan, which had previously been discontinued. It is obvious that this does not mean that artistic creation takes place completely in the realm of the unconscious, rather it is certainly compatible with full consciousness in the choice of means, at least so long as it is guided in the setting of its last goal from an unconscious inner necessity.

And thus, generally, life takes place, at least in so far as it unfolds itself according to a hidden inner necessity, without being in need of any particular decision. Rather, such a decision becomes necessary only where the natural certainty is lost or where obstacles that intrude from the outside get in the way of the inner development. The necessity of a decision occurs only where the harmonious relationship of man to his environment is disturbed; such a decision aims at removing the disturbance.

Thus it becomes clear that human life in its sound development happens without the necessity of a decision, and that it is wrong, for that reason, to derive from this necessity the standard for that life as a whole.

5   ESCAPE INTO THE DECISION

A slightly different direction in the problematic is more essential for the present context: the issue is not only that life is not in all circumstances in need of a decision, but that it is also true that man is not *permitted* everywhere to push

[7] For the problematic concerning this expression, see my description in *Dilthey: Eine Einführung in seine Philosophie* (1936) (Stuttgart: Kohlhammer, 1955), pp. 167 ff.

for decisions, and that a continuous orientation toward the decision blocks the view for other, more pressing necessities of life. The impatient pushing toward decision of which our present time is full, is itself merely the result of a highly disquieting demoralizing phenomenon, which, in turn, is closely connected with existential consciousness in so far as it rests on a lack of faith in the supporting powers of life. The impatient drive for decision itself is the result of the feeling of being helplessly lost.

But we do not speak here only of the so-called sound, that is unthreatened, life. In contrast to this, one could rightly point to the whole, presently really critical menace to our *Dasein*. Over and above this, it can be shown that even in a crisis, and precisely there, all hurried striving for decisions is disquieting. For it appears that, even in the cases of a disturbed and an endangered life, it is not always possible to force a freeing solution by means of a clear decision, and that it often requires greater strength to leave patiently unsettled what cannot be decided.

This becomes clear in the theoretical questions concerning our world view. Today an impatient drive goes through most people toward a definitive settlement of all questions concerning our last convictions, and in those cases the will to resoluteness must often cover the lacking objective foundation. Here, too, one wants a decision at all cost. On the other hand, however, it is the spirit of the genuine scientific approach to recognize the problems in their entire complexity and to withhold all judgment so long as it does not secure the foundation necessary for a founded decision; however, this approach also demands that we be able to leave unsettled what cannot be decided upon with its own means. This cautious approach of science has often been attacked in past years as a sign of weakness. And yet in this endurance and in this great patience, there is found that superiority of the scientific attitude that today we must slowly try to regain.

But in man's immediate life, too, there are agonizing circumstances that one cannot force to decision even with all his power. I am thinking here, first of all, of the distressing experiences, during the Second World War, in which this difficulty came to the fore in an impressive way. In the desperate need, one longed for a clear decision, but the atrocious fact was precisely that this will to decision had to lapse in emptiness because one was delivered to an extrinsic fate that took its course in such an excruciatingly slow way and upon which one could not have any influence, all willingness to make a decision notwithstanding. One could not do anything except wait. True, one was even compelled to realize that he uselessly consumed his strength in the fulfillment of tasks that the present moment offered him, when he was always already involved far beyond the present in decisions that were still to come in the future. One is unable to overpower in advance those decisions that were menacing in the future, and what one has to learn is something completely different: that is the art of being able to wait patiently.

There is no doubt that the capability of making a clear decision is a great moral virtue. But it is not the only virtue, and it is held in balance by a "countervirtue" that is no less important and that for us today is much more difficult to materialize than the resoluteness of a decision that has been made. This is tranquillity, or composure, with whose help man can let things approach him, that is, the art of being able to wait patiently without wishing on one's own initiative to force overhasty decisions, that is, speaking generally, the capability of settling down in the present moment in faith and full of hope. In this way we have circumscribed a realm of spiritual and moral attitudes that are of great importance for the conquering of the existential "cramp," and to whose analysis we must now turn.

6   THE VIRTUE OF AVAILABILITY; GABRIEL MARCEL

Gabriel Marcel, the representative of so-called Christian existentialism in France, with his fortunate ability of coining new words, has introduced a concept here that receives special importance in this connection. This is the concept of *disponibilité*, the availability, the keeping-oneself-open for the new possibilities of the future, which can never be foreseen. This availability is for that reason the precise counterconcept of resoluteness, which springs from the definitively made decision. Resoluteness gathers, so to speak, all the forces of man together into a sharp point, with which it runs counter to the future. It concentrates completely on this task. But precisely for that reason it also closes itself to all other possibilities in order to be able to fulfill this one and only task. *Resoluteness* is necessarily and at the same time *closedness*, also. It isolates man and determines him on an entirely determinate and predelineated course. That is why, if it were the only determining factor, it would make our entire life into an issue that could be predicted in advance, that is planned by man, and that as such is completely in his power.

But this is a presumption that, for its part, again, does not spring from a natural force, but inversely from uncertainty. It is a flight from the unpredictable demands of life, from which a certain hardening originates, such as is characteristic for the existentialist attitude in general, when one attempts to make the decision made in a determinate moment, into a lasting standard. And immediately, this leads again to the question concerning the possibility of avoiding such a hardening and overcoming it—thus the question concerning the possibility of a *relaxation* after the exaggerated existentialist strain. And for this, that availability then becomes necessary, that openness and this readiness for the demands of life that, new and unpredictable, approach man at each moment.

In this way, then, it becomes manifest how one-sided is the picture that man, who is always guided only by the will to decision, projects of his own future. Any attempt at coming to grips in advance with the possibility of the future can beforehand only take its threats into account; for only what is evil is predelineated beforehand. All that is enchanting and liberating, however, comes unexpectedly to man, as a gift. That is why one covers up ungratefully one's view of the enjoyable sides of life when one constantly strives exclusively for resoluteness in order to meet pressing situations. That is precisely why one must learn to be open in a relaxed mood and in tranquillity for the gift of the moment. This is the great virtue of availability, for which we must learn slowly to gain the right view. In contrast to the pride of existentialism, which is often downright fanatic, availability means a deeply humble and modest attitude.

But the virtue of availability contains yet a second side, which is equally important to our present discussion. Compared with the subjective self-preoccupation of existentialism, man opens himself here to what confronts him from the outer world, opens himself particularly to the justified demands of other people. When man is available, this, then, means that he has freed himself from his own being-captured-by-himself and thus has again become free for his tasks in the world.

This meaning of availability is stressed by Marcel in a very clear way when he says: "Being unavailable means being preoccupied with one's self."[8] And in contrast to this on availability: "This word by no means signifies emptiness, just as when one speaks of an 'available space,' but it signifies rather the capability of surrendering to that which encounters us and binding oneself through this surrender; or the capability of changing mere circumstances into occasions, or even into favorable situations; that is, to co-operate in regard to one's own destiny by stamping one's own identification mark on it."[9] It is clear that availability taken in this sense is not just a spiritual disposition that is (or is not) present at hand, but a virtue that must be acquired with difficulty, in which man overcomes his own natural self-preoccupation.

SELECTIVE BIBLIOGRAPHY

Die Ehrfurcht (Frankfurt a.M.: Klostermann, 1947)
Einfache Sittlichkeit (Göttingen: Vandenhoeck & Ruprecht, 1947)
Neue Geborgenheit. Das Problem der Überwindung des Existentialismus (Stuttgart: Kohlhammer, 1955)
Wesen und Wandel der Tugenden (Frankfurt a.M.: Taschenbücher Verlag, 1958)

[8] Gabriel Marcel, *Être et Avoir* (Paris: Aubier, 1935), p. 103.
[9] Gabriel Marcel, *Homo Viator* (Paris: Aubier, 1945), p. 20. Cf. my essay "Gabriel Marcel (Christlicher Existentialismus)," in *Die Sammlung*, 2 (1954), no. 3.

Part IV: SITUATION ETHICS

Situation ethics, to which English-speaking people often refer as "the new morality," is almost exclusively found in the works of philosophers who developed their philosophical views within the realm of a religious perspective; most authors who have written on situation ethics are of a Lutheran background.

The origin of this movement in contemporary ethics, as well as of its name, goes back to Eberhard Grisebach's book *Gegenwart: eine kritische Ethik*, which appeared in 1928 (Halle, Niemeyer). In this book, Grisebach (1880–1945) claimed that an ethics that allows for a religious perspective is unable to talk about principles, laws, norms, and rules that are universally valid for everyone. Each moral problem is unique and can be solved only by the one who is concretely confronted with this problem. Each human being finds himself at each moment in a concrete situation that is his and that he cannot share with anyone else. Although it is true that one can formulate purely formal norms such as "Love your neighbor" and "Thou shall not kill," these purely formal norms do not yet have a real *moral* meaning, because it is only in the unique situation in which each one of us continually finds himself that he is able to creatively determine what the moral meaning of such a formal norm might be.

As I understand it, it was *not* Grisebach's idea to suggest that philosophy and religion can no longer be distinguished from one another. He only pointed out that wherever a philosophical view and the Lutheran conception of Christianity are found together in one human individual, the philosophical conception has to take into account there the fact that as far as moral decisions are concerned, the concrete relationship between this individual and God is all-decisive, and that in such a decision God's grace and man's free creativity must go hand in hand in a mysterious way.

It is important, also, to note that situation ethics does *not* defend the thesis that there are no norms and values. It merely hopes to overcome all formalist and legalist interpretations of moral laws. As far as values are concerned, it does *not* state that ethics is not axiological; ethics certainly is a doctrine of meaning and value. Here situation ethics merely argues that meaning and value are not pre-given, passively and objectively; values are to be created, and this can be done only within and on the basis of the concrete situation in which the one who creates values finds himself.

Many people who defend a form of situation ethics have taken their inspiration from Kierkegaard and Nietzsche. This is certainly true for Grisebach, who originated the movement. In a later phase, Heidegger's *Being and Time* (1927) has had a considerable influence on the development of the movement, in which Émile Brunner, Bonhoeffer, Buber, Berdyayev, and Joseph Fuchs have played important parts. From the English-speaking world, the names of John A. Robinson and Joseph Fletcher must be mentioned.

The selection by Steinbüchel was included here because it contains a relatively clear explanation of Grisebach's original view and points to a number of difficulties to which this view necessarily leads. For a more detailed exposition of Grisebach's view, I must refer the reader to G. A. Rauch, *The Philosophy of Actuality* (Fort Hare, S. Africa: Fort Hare University Press, 1964). The selections by Bonhoeffer and Thielicke are written from a Lutheran point of view, whereas Buber, obviously, wrote from a Jewish background.

Chapter 14

INTRODUCTION

THEODOR STEINBÜCHEL (1888–1949), former professor at Tübingen, was one of the leading neo-Thomist philosophers in Germany during the first half of this century. His publications include several important books on the history of philosophy, but his original contributions to philosophy have been mainly in philosophical anthropology and ethics.

The following selection was taken from *Die philosophische Grundlegung der katholischen Sittenlehre* (1938). The main goal of the book was to clarify the *philosophical* foundation of a Catholic conception of ethics. The first part of the book is devoted to a careful description and comparison of the philosophical and theological conceptions of the humanity of man, and to the establishment of relationships between moral theology and ethics. The last chapter in this section deals with critical reflections on philosophical views that are somehow antithetical to the *ethos* of Christianity. The second part contains reflections on the ontological and anthropological presuppositions of any ethical theory. After a short chapter on the relationship between anthropology and ethics, Steinbüchel tries to answer the question of how deeply one can meaningfully speak about the "essence" of man. In the last chapter of his book, he develops an outline of a philosophical anthropology that, in his view, is in complete harmony with the theological conception of man. The selection here was taken from Chapter V: *Wesen und Existenz* (*Essence and Existence*). I have chosen this selection because I believe it gives a rather accurate account of the origin and development of situation ethics as found in Grisebach, Bonhoeffer, and others, and also points to serious difficulties with which situation ethics is necessarily confronted.

SYSTEMATIC ESSENTIALIST ETHICS AND
EXISTENTIAL SITUATION ETHICS

Theodor Steinbüchel

The nature of situation ethics (2) must be understood in terms of the historical situation in which the mind finds itself in this era (1). After such a critical evaluation (3) it will then be possible to understand (a) as well as to test (b) its main concern.

1. Situation ethics originates in the existential-philosophical ethos, which no longer subscribes to the notion that man is sheltered in a closed world order; it seeks to show him, without any illusions, his own naked being. Man himself is de-substantialized, his essence is found in the fact that he does not have an essence, thus he lacks any essential constancy. An ethics that does not wish to bolster him with a Self, as idealism tries to do, which in the situations in which it continuously finds itself placed can never say out of itself what it will do in such situations, can only consist in a "critical task." "The positive goal of such a criticism is the liberation from false beliefs in oneself."[1] Whereas in Emil Brunner, Friedrich Gogarten, and others, an ethos that is concerned with the existential self-being of man wishes to place him within the "order" where, alone, he can live his existence in

This article is from *Die philosophische Grundlegung der katholischen Sittenlehre*, by Theodor Steinbüchel (Düsseldorf, 1947), Vol. I, pp. 237-57. Copyright © 1947 by Patmos Verlag. The present essay was translated into English expressly for this edition by Joseph J. Kockelmans.

[1] Eberhard Grisebach, *Gegenwart. Eine Kritische Ethik* (Halle: Niemeyer, 1928) p. 199.

a genuine way, Eberhard Grisebach's ethics leads man away from all firmly established order, and lets him find himself immediately in a "present" that is always different and incalculable, that cannot be determined from his self-knowledge, and in which, thus, he can never experience in himself what he must do. Grisebach is the most radical opponent of all ethics based on essences, norms, or values. His own ethics is the "destructive criticism" of these kinds of ethics. Therefore what follows about Grisebach may be taken as typical for all existentialist situation ethics. However, the only thing he does is to express for the realm of ethics what Nietzsche and Kierkegaard passionately stressed for our knowledge of the world and the interpretation of man in the world from completely different world views and religious attitudes, namely the impossibility of a systematic world view and thus, also, of any ethics that might try to found itself upon such a view as a system of values and norms. It is precisely through this criticism that the deep, metaphysical rootedness of ethics has become clearer than it was in times when, without questioning, ethics was related to such a world view. For even Kant's denial of a "scientific" metaphysics had not prevented a metaphysics of morals; on the contrary, his denial reserved the metaphysics of morals for the practical belief of reason and secured the moral through the denial of a scientific metaphysics. For according to the famous words found in the Preface to the second edition of the *Critique of Pure Reason*, words revealing Kant's entire intention with his "critical business," Kant precisely intended to supersede theoretical knowledge in order to make room for that belief which is more important for man, a belief that is able to interpret man's being, that determines his action and fulfills his hope.

The intention of Kierkegaard's position in regard to Hegel's system[2] was to save the "individual" from degrading into a moment of the universal found in the suprapersonal and divine world process. The existential and temporal determination that Kierkegaard appropriated to man is not "moment"

[2] Cf. Walter Ruttenbeck's interpretation in *Sören Kierkegaard* (Berlin: Older, Trowitzseh, 1929) pp. 150 ff., 172 ff., 184 ff., and 245 ff.

but "instant" (*kairos*); that is, the special situation that transcends all temporal development (*chronos*), the human situation in which the "individual" as a person encounters the eternal God in the order of time, a situation in which he is claimed by Him here and now and as an individual, a situation in which he must respond to Him personally and with responsibility, and in such a special decision, which is completely given over to him as an individual, becomes a self "before" God. This form of personalism, which opposes itself to Hegel's process of the universal "Idea," thus seeks to establish a genuine revelation, not an unfolding of God in man. Hegel's impersonalism could not know of both these insights; for Hegel, there was no personal encounter between God and man in this special instant, which occurs only once and in which God calls man and addresses Himself to him, as once to Adam, by using his name, that is, *as this* man. In Hegel, man is no longer placed before God in this decisive situation of his personal being. Man's temporality, namely the instant, had to be lacking in Hegel's dialectical scheme of development, the process of the Spirit. And yet even in ethics, where for Kierkegaard everything depends on authenticity (*Selbstsein*), on personal freedom, there is still the danger that the Self will be submerged in the Universal. For here the being-a-self (*Selbstsein*) still has the meaning of an expression of our universal being-human (*Menschsein*), and the task is given to man to fulfill this being of a universal "Idea" of man which is precisely characteristic for man in general. Thus we find here the "paradigmatic man" placed higher than the particular individual in his own peculiar situation before his God, and no longer faced with a decision that only he himself can make and that alone will bring him to his innermost and inalienable self. Here in this belief in the personal God of the revelation, and not in a pantheistic All-God with whom an encounter from person to person is impossible, here alone man is the individual and, as such, himself. Here he no longer flees into a Universal, as is the case in a universally valid ethics as well as in a pantheistic religiosity; here he no longer saves himself in a system of world order that he is able to understand. Man "ek-sists" in the "paradox" of his belief in a God Who unconditionally transcends him, and thus can no longer be understood from himself and his own "world" view, that is, can no longer be mastered in his thinking about man.

In Kierkegaard, however, "existence" refers to man's way of being. And it consists in the fact that man relates himself to himself on the basis of his relationship to that God Whom he himself is not. This God is the Lord, the sovereign God without qualification, thus Lord in regard to all the ethical systems man has built up. His demand upon man can never be calculated, nor can it be inserted into an ethical system, nor even derived from it. Abraham's sacrifice is the most striking revelation of the sovereign God, the attitude of obedience to a God Who cannot be understood by man, the only attitude toward God that is possible for man and demanded of him. And yet the Christian Kierkegaard lives the belief[3] that the care for what is human retains its relative value, under the condition that man as believer in God is prepared to renounce everything for the sake of God, the Lord, to possess things as if he did not possess them (cf. I *Cor.* 7, 29 ff.), and to believe that renunciation for the sake of the one and only Absolute, God, will give him back everything he has sacrificed to God. The respect of his faith, however, leaves the mode of this return to God alone. Thus man lives in this world, works at it within this ethos of faith, but he does not consider this work and all that is human as something final—an attitude of which we, too, have found that it is the only possible one for someone who believes, and which is what St. Augustine meant in his distinction between *uti* and *frui* in regard to the world and human goods, namely the relative use of things that does not dwell on them as something ultimate, but rather sees and uses them in relation to the highest Good. But in this way it continues to remain possible to understand the work in regard to what is human as a meaningful situation that is willed by God.

Nietzsche, on the other hand, knew that with the tidings of "God's death" this ethical relationship to the world is im-

[3] Ibid., pp. 249 ff.

possible. At that moment, the world lost all of its order and
man the entire invariability of his essence (*Wesenskonstanz*),
which would have to stand the test in it. In a contradiction
that cannot be reconciled, Nietzsche rebels against the idea
that the world is still somehow to be understood (albeit even
in a pantheistic interpretation) as an ordered universe and
a movement that aims at an ordered unity. It is only in an
aimless and meaningless world that man really renounces a
helping God, a Saviour, and at the same time a "logic," which
in the final analysis is invented only to give him certainty
in a world of order and to hide his being-endangered in the
real, chaotic world. "Logic" thus is the will to power, and not
the ordered structure that can only hamper and would like
to master the power as the will to one's own "dangerous" and
daring life beyond an abyss of ultimate meaninglessness.
Man finds himself only by "despairing" of world order and
an ordering God. Under this condition, indeed, there will be
left only incalculable situations that imply inalienable ven-
tures, which, at the same time, however, can no longer be
subjected to norms. The "venture" of man's existence shows
its result, which was foreseen, namely the renunciation of a
system of values, goals, or norms as the only possible ethos
in man and the world as they are.[4]

Although it is true that today both these world views which
are functioning here as background have been swept away,
namely Kierkegaard's belief in God and Nietzsche's Dionysian
belief in life, nonetheless one thing has remained: the inability to believe in ultimate classifications and systems, or
at least in man's capacity to recognize them as such. It is on
this fact that *situation ethics* rests. It is a more clearly declared enemy of metaphysics than Nietzsche ever was or
wanted to be. Grisebach objects to a systematic ethics as the
imperative foundation of all "ought" based upon a metaphysics, because "the unreasonable demands of metaphysics

[4] Cf. Nietzsche, *Menschliches Allzumenschliches* (Taschenausgabe,
Leipzig: Kröner 1922 ff.) Vol. III, p. 51; *Die fröhliche Wissenschaft*
(Taschenausgabe VI), pp. 241, 243, 351; *Der Wille zur Macht*
(Taschenausgabe X), pp. 224–30.

cannot be made in regard to "modern man."[5] Nietzsche's pathos for "honesty," which denied itself belief in God[6] on epistemological grounds, is continued here in the attitude regarding rational metaphysics, however little of Nietzsche's fundamental atheism and his ethos of power, which is still a systematical ethics, has been taken up here. But Grisebach also denies himself the "dogmatic offer of theology,"[7] because it, too, is, as a doctrine, a form of knowledge. However, knowledge is never reality itself, it is "interiorization" (*Erinnerung*), that is, representation (*Vorstellung*) formed by the Self and taken into it, interiorized in it, but not that "which is outside," which is never adequate in regard to what is inside, and which certainly cannot be derived from representations, concepts, and ideas of the "humanist" consciousness. The entire "humanist" world of science and philosophy, of our culture as a whole, is built upon the Self and is its work. This is the only thing the Self has at its disposal, but to take this as what is real is to credit an illusion. The attempt to found, on the basis of such a representation and "interiorization," a systematic ethics containing demands for our practical actions, in reality is an enterprise that can never lead out of the circle of the Self, and thus is basically a falsification of genuine existential behavior in the world of underivable situations in the real life within which man finds himself. It may be that essentialist ethics is possible as a systematic-logical structure of judgments, but it cannot be "employed as an ethical doctrine in a positive way for the development of a moral life."[8] It is not a concrete ethics of encounter be-

---

[5] Eberhard Grisebach, op. cit., p. 184.

[6] Cf. Nietzsche, *Die fröhliche Wissenschaft*, pp. 327–28; *Menschliches Allzumenschliches*, pp. 116–17.

[7] Eberhard Grisebach, op. cit., pp. 198 ff. Cf. Herrigel's interesting comparison between Grisebach and Leo Schestov, who challenges a philosophical systematization of right precisely from the viewpoint of revealed faith: *Zwischen Frage und Antwort* (Berlin: Schneider, 1930) pp. 168 ff. Leo Schestov, *Potestas clavium oder die Schlüsselgewalt* (Berlin: Schneider, 1926), pp. 307 ff.; *Aufs Hiobs Wage. Über die Quellen der ewigen Wahrheit* (Berlin: Schneider, 1929) pp. 524 ff.

[8] Eberhard Grisebach, op. cit., p. 182; cf. pp. 179 ff.

tween me and the world; it is a product of the ego and nothing more.

2. The essentialist ethics of idealism thus stands opposite to situation ethics. It is oriented toward reality, and reality is "Present,"[9] that is, the limitation of man's existence (the real, living, particular man) through that which is independent of the Self and thus cannot be derived from it nor explained by it. In existential philosophy, which was so decisively codetermined by Kierkegaard, the concepts of limit and finitude taken in connection with man received the privileged position. They now become fruitful for existentialist situation ethics, also, and are elevated so as to become its founding concept. The reality which limits is not a universal reality in itself, but the particular, changing reality of the situation that at each time limits each particular man. The boundary drawn for him is not one that is connected with his universal human essence and the universal finitude that founds his essence, but that which here and now limits each particular man in a changing and always different way, and before which he finds himself in a special mode of his finitude. The "situation" now becomes completely understandable in its existential signification: it consists in the fact that man is determined concretely and unrepeatably, in an always different way in this moment of time in which he finds himself here and now, whereas his essence is abstract, always remains the same, time and again can bring back what it is, and always moves in a circle. However, if man, who is determined, is limited by situations that are always determined then the latter are not phases of his own development, but rather that which is "outside," which limits him from the outside, and lets him encounter something that does not originate from the circle of his essence, and thus is certainly not something universal. This, however, is the "Present," which as the German word (Gegen-wart) suggests is that which is waiting (warten) in the face of (gegen) existence By this, one does not mean a point in the continuous stream

[9] Ibid., pp. 173–219.

of time, but the instant (*Augenblick*), which cannot be derived from the past, within which an encounter between I and Thou takes place. The situations can never be determined in advance, either, as far as the persons or the mode of their encounter is concerned, but they determine and limit one another mutually; and here the moral demand manifests itself which, since it cannot be derived from principles, is at each time a different demand.

This "reality" taken as "Present" is not a speculative, but an existential, concept; it does not refer to the reality of an outer world, for instance, but to that which limits the ego personally, and encounters it: the Thou. "The life space of the Present is . . . not the space of nature, but rather the narrow distance between two human beings who limit one another mutually in address and response (*Spruch und Widerspruch*)." And precisely this mutual boundary in the instant of the encounter, the one and only "reality" that is important from the ethical point of view, is "certainly in all cases a breathtaking narrowness which the free mind may shun."[10] For here the ego as the limitless, creative "being," which as the idealist "Self" releases the whole world from itself and yet carries it in itself as its world, this ego finds itself here in a position in which a limit is imposed on it, which replaces this world-wide essence of the "Mind" by an existence that at each moment is always limited. It can become itself only by waiting for that which places itself opposite to it, thus for the Thou who encounters it.[11]

A radical revolution of all essentialist ethics can be derived from this "Present":[12] all value tables are smashed here, and the same is true for all remaining virtues of a humanist ethics that attempt to bring man's being to completion. There are

---

[10] Ibid., p. 149.

[11] Thus Grisebach remains essentially within the manner of thinking that originates from Ebner and that, as do many others today, conceives of "Reality" in terms of the I-Thou relation, considering this relation as the one that alone is ethically relevant. And yet it is certainly Kierkegaard who stimulated Grisebach and who was also highly estimated by Ebner.

[12] Ibid., pp. 550 ff.

no longer any moral "principles" from which one could derive commandments and value goals that would perfect the Self of man.[13] For the "critical" ethics of the "crisis" of the Self, and all moral doctrines founded upon it, can therefore never tell man what he has to do here and now. It is impossible as material value ethics, as well as non-formal ethics built upon laws. In this ethos there are only two attitudes that never become concretized into a non-formal, concrete command, and that certainly are not rooted in values taken as ideal contents that stand above man. For this precisely means the negation of the isolated ego and thus of the possibility of opening oneself up to the Thou.

As that ethos which precisely urges us in the direction of the Self, Grisebach's ethics does away with the Self as essence in a much more radical way than is the case in Heidegger's existential philosophy. He was even one of the first to reject Heidegger.[14] He could not help but see through this pressing for an "authentic" being and understand it as an idealist attitude, and recognize that man (true, no longer as consciousness, but as *Dasein*) remained the starting point for all understanding of Being. And yet Grisebach, too, wishes to come to a "genuine" relationship, even to that which in the I-Thou situation is and remains dependent upon itself and its decision. But no systematic ethics can give man a "grasp" when he stands before this incalculable situation. There is no more-critical opponent of a personalist ethics than Grisebach. The "human Self" is "the origin of all evil," the "true Satan"— we find here the Lutheran who fights philosophy, and makes no secret of it in the strict demarcation of his view in regard to Catholic ethics, which is founded upon an ontology of essences.[15] The ego *must* isolate itself, because it produces the norms for its behavior out of its own Self, and with those can pursue only the "egoistic purpose" of the completion of

[13] Ibid., pp. 187 ff.
[14] Ibid., pp. 511 ff. Cf. also Grisebach's criticism of Heidegger in *Deutsche Vierteljahrschrift für Literaturwissenschaft und Geistesgeschichte* 8(1930), pp. 199 ff.
[15] Ibid., pp. 185 ff.

its essence. Thus he must shut himself off against the other (*das Andere*). But this means that he must avoid the encounter with the Thou, which nonetheless also is his own reality situation, and remain locked up in the circle of his own "egoity" (*Egoität*). "At that moment humanness becomes Satany, in which man arrogantly claims it for himself to conceive of this development of his own essence as a creation of the world"—but that he must do if his own Self is the absolute Self that contains in itself all norms in their universal validity, and thus does not will, and cannot let itself be determined by someone else.[16]

This individualism which makes itself into God is *the* evil, which thus has its origin in man himself.[17] His *genuine* attitude (and we must use this expression in Grisebach's perspective, also), his one and only morally good attitude, can consist only in that he puts himself in the I-Thou situation, or perhaps in taking up this attitude which is precisely *essential* to him. Community, not taken here as an organism that factually comprises the ego, but rather as the I-Thou relation that is to be established, now becomes still an *imperative*. The ego *must* even resist the continuous temptation to "destroy" the other in the affirmation of its own Self, exactly in the same way as the other, too, is exposed to this temptation and is put under this commandment. Evil is therefore the wickedness of the ego in its relation to the Thou, in which it attempts to materialize its "tendency toward self-development," which is "threatened" by the Thou. Thus Grisebach's ethics, too, is a form of ethics that originates from a determinate belief, namely from the Christian belief in the *demand* of our neighbor. True, this belief is not reinterpreted in a humanitarian way as universal equality; this would contradict all denial of an eternally identical Self. Our neighbor remains here completely in the sense of the biblical concept, the particular man, the "other," to be taken always in a determinate situation of encounter and limitation of the ego. And this encounter occurs in the "Word" that meets with

16 Cf. ibid., pp. 183, 196 ff., 203, 467 ff., 472 ff.
17 See for what follows here: ibid., pp. 478 ff.

(*wider-fahrt*) the ego and breaks into its closed circle in a way that is at the same time disturbing and contradicting. This is certainly first of all a "fact" of our "experience." But, for Grisebach, it is more: man *must* yield to this fact, he *must* give an answer to this Word, that is to say, not the negative answer of sealing oneself off, but the positive one of knowing that one is responsible, and of a responsible, obeying, and loving behavior. After philosophy has laid bare the experience of the Present, which simultaneously has the character of an encounter and a limitation, and has made manifest the crisis of the Self that is self-sufficient and declines all that is other and different, Grisebach leaves all further ethics to *theology*, an ethics that must be one of love between I and Thou. And yet we must admit that his philosophy has done preparatory work for this Christian theology. In his "critical ethics" Grisebach has for the first time laid the foundation on the basis of which any moral theology can perceive the particular *ontological* possibility of man which enables it to make understandable the demands of the neighbor and the charity that originates from God. But although it is true that Grisebach is indeed unable to interpret this demand as a principle from which the theologian might derive laws for the behavior of man in his situation, and although it is also true that he explicitly states that he speaks of "experience" and by no means of ontology, this experience nonetheless *is and remains* an existential possibility of man. This "nominalist" *situation ethics*, which denies all knowledge of essences and all that follows from essences, *cannot circumvent an ontology of man.*

3. With these explanations, our criticism has set in clearly enough. However, this criticism should be positive and for that reason should first appreciate what situation ethics contains of genuine, moral knowledge and real, moral concern.

a) In continuous repetitions and new illustrations, Grisebach points to the dissimilarity of each situation in which man is called to make a moral decision. This is the basic objection to an essentialist ethics, which we saw emerge from existential thought. Situation ethics has taken up a genuine, moral concern: the personal decision of conscience in the doubts and conflicts of life, in the changing situations and unavoidable circumstances of life, in which man is left to his own decisions and must fight for the verification of his moral convictions. It is in these exceptional cases, which break into the quiet everydayness of our moral habit that has become self-evident, that man grows to moral greatness and independence. No moral casuistry can, from pure general principles, try to construct life in its always surprising manifoldness. All its "cases" are time and again differently circumstanced in individual life, as they were once present and certainly different from those which the theory is capable of constructing. That is why no casuistry, even if it follows experience as closely, prudently, and circumspectly as possible, can each time anticipate situations in their historically unique and unparalleled concreteness. To deny all rights to casuistry in regard to pedagogical and pastoral praxis would be equally unreal, and would mean that again one makes a principle of the assumed impossibility of casuistry. Casuistry seeks to explain "typical" cases, situations that *more or less* frequently return and in this way guide one to a moral decision. It has its relative value in so far as it is heuristic, that is an effort to show the realization of the moral decision, as an educational help toward knowledge of one's self and toward a decision, and also as a guide toward a more prudent grasp of the situation.[18] In addition, someone who is aware of the particularity and uniqueness of the conflict-and-doubt situation, as Linsenmann is,[19] cannot deny its value in this regard. A moral theology that seeks to set down norms for our moral life based on the example of Jesus, and yet at the same time is aware of the fact that imitation means individual imitation in historical relationships that are completely different from those Jesus Himself found before Him in His life, wills "far-reaching renunciation" of casuistry and must will this renunciation in that it, itself, wants to relate genuine life to the

[18] Max Pribilla, "Klugheit und Kasuistik," *Stimmen der Zeit:* 133(1937–38), pp. 205–16; Joseph Pieper, *Traktat über die Klugheit* (Leipzig: Hegner, 1937).

[19] Linsenmann, *Lehrbuch der Moraltheologie* (Kempten: Kösel, 1922) pp. 25 ff.

genuine life of Christ and supports the free, joyful, and personal development of Christian life after Him. But precisely it, too, in its fundamental resort to the sources of revelation, knows that St. Paul issued decisions for a concrete case, but without "schematizing" it. And it is not so far away from the pastoral praxis it precisely seeks to serve, by referring to Christ as the One to Whom all Christian spiritual care would lead; that it does not know that scientific-theological morals can and must find their completion through practical instruction oriented toward directing man's spiritual life in the moral doubts of life, as well.[20] However, the meaning of education is and remains found in *maturity*—not in a decrease, but in the cultivation and facilitation of the personal decision, according to the conscience of the free children of God, that commits itself to Christ (*Rom.* 8: 21). The Christian must *prove* his own being-a-Christian in a personal engagement in the situations that occur in his own life.

Situation ethics is correct when it conceives of the situation as something which is not merely the general "position" in which man as man essentially finds himself as a historical and social being; nor is the situation identical with the sociological relation in which he stands within the social relationships of family, profession, status, nation, state, and state federation; and finally the situation is not to be identified either with his entrenchment in the spiritual life of his time which also puts its stamp upon each historical individual, just as the latter carries the former together with the others. *Situation* is much more related to each person's own existence. It is not merely the *external* position in which each particular man finds himself, even if it were a completely individual one. It is more: it is at the same time his own innermost *interior* feeling of finding himself in the historically determined time at the special and incomparable moment that belongs to his own personal reality. And it "belongs" to him. For it is *that* reality in which *his* special

---

[20] Tillmann, *Die Idee der Nachfolge Christi* (Düsseldorf: Schwann, 1934) 2d ed., pp. 25, 41–42.

mode of Being constitutes itself, just as, correlatively, he constitutes that reality. He is determined by that reality, by its peculiarity and uniqueness, which cannot be derived from any "idea," and he lives this mode of Being of his, which is thus determined and is in that sense peculiar, by inserting it into that reality. As individuality, he can never be completely derived from any past whatsoever, and yet he bears responsibility for it and its *heritage*, since this, too, is co-given in his own Being, a moral responsibility that proves itself to be his "faithfulness."[21] He takes up his past as his own existence in a free "yes" in regard to it; he makes what merely has been handed down his *own* past, and carries it with him into *his own* present and future. Present and future are equally *his* modes of existence. Man, who chooses himself as Self, has in regard to the future his own, determinate "possibility." In the present, his task, however, consists in making a personal and unavoidable decision that he alone can make, and from whose "how" his future, in so far as it is in his power, depends. But *what* awaits him and is coming toward him, is what he can merely anticipate. But a moral man does not wait for it in passivity and resignation, but in the willingness to take it as a test of his own morality. Thus ethics ascribes to the situation of the present a very special, moral signification, and the present must mean more to it than a neutral point in physically lapsing time whose instants are all alike. The situation of the present in which man finds himself, acts, undergoes, fights, denies, conquers, and becomes changed, is never the same.

Ethics taken in all forms in which it strives for a decision on the part of the individual person is deeply convinced of the moral significance of the present situation for each unique man. That is why not only existential, but also contemporary value, ethics can stress the moral importance of the situation, as for instance does Nicholai Hartmann[22] when he

[21] Karl Jaspers, *Philosophie*, 3 vols. (Berlin: Springer, 1932), I, p. 16; cf. *Die geistige Situation der Zeit* (Berlin: Springer, 1934) pp. 19 ff.
[22] Nicholai Hartmann, *Ethik*, pp. 330 f.

claims to find the "value" of the "life positions," *independent* of their "typicalness and uniqueness," first and foremost in the fact "that they confront man with his tasks, provoke his attitude, and wait for his decisions." "No conceptual combination, however, and no phantasy, however daring it may be, reaches the depth and richness of the living situation." An idealist ethics, which substitutes the suprapersonal process of a world-spirit for the personal decision, cannot give any meaning to the situation in which a decision is to be made; thus it is not ethics, but a metaphysics of culture or history, in which the personal man is devalued to an occasion of a suprapersonal event. In the situation, the issue is about the questions concerning what and for whom decisions must be made. And it is here that different forms of morals first part: does man settle on values, on biological or cultural societies, on his own Self, on the Thou of the personal fellow man who is always connected with each particular ego, or on the Thou of a personal God? And does a decision in favor of God not also include a decision for His entire creation? Here, too, the unavoidable question thus announces itself again: *who is* the man who in a situation settles on something, who *is* that personal Self that must make the decision? Without an explanation of this ontological question, no situation ethics will be capable of taking even one single step toward a foundation, or even an explanation, of morality. Nowhere can one proceed in ethics without *knowledge* of the *humanitas* and without an *attitude* in its regard.

One cannot deny the deep seriousness with which Grisebach's ethics is particularly concerned about the reality of man and our knowledge of a form of morality that seeks to grasp in a realistic way precisely this reality of the man who is placed in his situations of the "Present" and is called upon in these situations to make a decision. Man should not be idealized here, but considered in his guilty condition, in which he closes himself off from the other, thus in his failure and "*hybris*," which makes his own ego into something absolute. But he should not be led astray into a dream-reality either, where an ethical system hides the continuous threat from him and takes away his having to make a decision. But is this not precisely what is to be avoided here: knowledge of man's essence and the foundation even of situation ethics, itself, upon it?

b) It is precisely at this point that the first starting point for a criticism of a pure situation ethics manifests itself. The second point consists in the impossibility of a decision, which is stressed here above anything else and does not include a Self that has an essence. The third point will be to demonstrate the risk of endangering man's Being as moral Being when the changing situation is considered in isolation and attention is no longer paid, at the same time, to a constant Self which is found in it.

1) The anti-individualistic *type of being* that Grisebach requires as moral conduct on the part of man is the ontological basis upon which his ethics rests. The anti-individualistic *ethos* that is demanded here as corresponding to the being of man and sets for man the task to realize himself in his experience of the presence of the other, originates from man's being as it should be, from his I-Thou relationship. Grisebach, consequently, denies the Self which is locked up in itself, and to which he ontologically reduces the egoistic attitude as immoral. He does not deny, however, but rather founds the being-essence of man in, the ego of this man as opened up toward a Thou. But here, too, to live morally means to live in harmony with Being, that is, to be what one is: the man who opens himself up to the Thou in a personally responsible way and decides to serve this Thou. Thus, here too, man becomes the moral man only by means of a free "yes" in regard to his own *Being*. Here, also, there is a highest commandment: to be what one is in each situation whatever it may be, the commandment that always remains the same in the changing situation. The *essentialist* conception thus forces its way into the *situation* ethics, and the essence of man is necessarily fulfilled in the morally good action in the situation. "Whether Grisebach wants to or not: he, too, has to establish a moral *law*, which perhaps can be formulated as follows: Man should not develop his essence without contradiction from an individualistic point of view and build up a

culture that comes to pass in the unfolding of an identic essence, but he should let himself, as someone who stands in the present, be limited by the other (*das Andere*), which is not essentially identical, which just comes to him (*Zufallendes*) and comes toward him (*Zu-Künftiges*), and endures his contradictions."[23] Neither can Grisebach by any means avoid the idealist distinction that separates man's authentic being from his inauthentic being. He also shares the ethos of existential philosophy, which he opposes in its Heideggerian form because it takes its point of departure in the Being-a-Self of the subject, but with which he has in common the resolute will to Being-a-Self, however differently he may conceive of the Self in its real essence.

This essential I-Thou relationship of man cannot be overlooked in its material-ontological significance for the conception of man's essence. It manifests itself as the ontological fundament of an existential ethos, which in Jaspers' interpretation of existence proves to be also of the same kind, Jaspers' fundamental opposition to all ontology notwithstanding. Ethics precisely remains a disclosure of the essence of the moral Being of man; and the free decision concerning what is characteristic of this essence remains ethical in the sense of what is morally good, whereas missing it freely remains evil. Neither the attempt to desubstantialize the essence of man and make it a pure existence of relating itself, nor the attempt to eliminate the essence from ethics in favor of the situations, which are always changing and always different, can build up an ethics and determine and found an ethos. How will Grisebach found his view that the limitation of the ego to itself is immoral, whereas the responsible orientation of the ego toward a Thou addressing him to it is morally good, except by interpreting the former as a failure in regard to man's essence and the latter as its affirmation? Why is it that both are not forms of man's being-able-to-be with equal rights? Why is it that the ego that closes itself off is "satanic," and why is man good when he places himself in

23 Cf. E. Brunner, "Grisebachs Angriff auf die Theologie," *Zwischen den Zeiten* 6(1928) pp. 219–32, 234–35.

the service of the Thou? Generally speaking, why can the Thou lay claim to me in *my* Being in a moral sense? Why is the responsibility for the Thou a morally good attitude? In all these cases the Christian faith announces itself as the basis of this "critical" ethics, which tries to found the crisis of the ego, the Christian *humanitas* as the *a priori* that is accepted here without question, all demarcation of philosophy in opposition to theology notwithstanding. Each situation ethics *has* an ontological *a priori*. Why does Grisebach not decide in favor of man as will to power, which in Nietzsche's situation ethics constitutes the *a priori*: why does he decide in favor of the Being of the I in regard to the Thou as it was uncovered by Ebner, and in whose affirmation alone the Self becomes as it should be? This is merely because he presupposes an ontology of the Self and assesses his own conception as the one that corresponds to Being, whereas he assesses those proposed by Idealism and by Nietzsche as false because of their silence in regard to the Thou.

Grisebach generalizes the idealistic Self that denies itself a Thou into the only possible and real Self. He does not know any other ontology except the idealist, and yet he himself defends another kind. He is too much caught up in the asceticism of a "criticist" philosophy, which is hostile toward metaphysics, to be able to do justice to man's being open toward God in his own "critical" ethics. Following Kant, he has led knowledge through criticism into crisis, but he leaves explicitly[24] empty the place that Kant conquered for faith through his critique. Using the genuinely existential philosophical method of indirect communication,[25] which was employed above all by Kierkegaard and Jaspers, Grisebach speaks of faith only indirectly by pointing to the experience that disturbs the self-sufficient Self of idealism, and in which something else, thus something that is somehow transcendent in regard to the ego, places itself ahead of the ego and enters its circle. There faith may speak of God, but the philosopher can say only that the believing man now maintains *his* right

[24] Eberhard Grisebach, op. cit., p. 485.
[25] Cf. Karl Jaspers, *Psychologie der Weltanschauungen* (Berlin: Springer, 1922) pp. 332 ff.

where the philosopher must keep silent. That is why the theologians soon began to follow Grisebach, when Forsthoff, among others, took up the former's findings and sealed the "end of the humanist illusion" by means of a theology that reminds one of Kierkegaard: "Man with his claim to authority must completely give way to the absolute authority of God; he sees that his entire existence is made questionable before God and becomes degraded to an object of His governing of the world, to an object of God's mercy. It is not he who decrees, but he is at God's disposal. It is not he who decides, but decisions are made about him."[26]

2) Just as little as situation ethics itself can manage without an essential Self in man, which as human is the same in spite of and precisely in all individual forms and within all different situations, so it is impossible that there could ever be the execution of a concrete decision without the reality of this living Self. For it is precisely the concrete man as being-a-Self that must open himself to the Thou, and it is his constant possibility of Being that must prove itself in each situation as extending itself to the Thou, and even as one that wins its Self merely in so doing, and that is time and again seizing it in the temptation to break away from its own innermost reality. If man were so fluid, so unequal in himself as the situation in which he finds himself, then there would be neither a decision that decides on one and only one, permanent ought, on the I-Thou relation that is to be established, nor a test that endeavors to fulfill just this one imperative continuously, and through it saves and deepens one's own Self. What else will education, with which Grisebach precisely is concerned, establish except to educate man for this essential being in the I-Thou relationship? Does the entire endeavor of situation ethics in regard to the education of the genuine Being of man in all its situations not equally presuppose something universal that transcends all particularization? Is it not true that each one of its moments, each statement, and each piece of knowledge is a tiding about the

[26] Heinrich Forsthoff, *Das Ende der humanistischen Illusion* (Berlin: Furche-Verlag, 1933) p. 138; cf. especially pp. 48–67.

permanent Self of the moralist and the teacher himself, who knows that he is permanently responsible for the one for whom he works and whom he wishes to educate? He, as well as the other, is a Self; between himself and the other, the dialogue of communicating and understanding, exercising an influence and responding to it, must develop; but without a permanent and common element, this is impossible. And finally, the moralist is by no means the perfect one who already has all knowledge; he, too, learns from the one to whom he speaks; the dialogue is also creative in that what it establishes rouses knowledge and will; creative, that is, in the I as well as in the Thou, in the correlation of address and response. It is in this way that the dialogue brings to the fore from hidden depth what is possible in the I and in the Thou themselves, and what still remains there to be awakened as far as the reality of Being, knowing, and acting are concerned—this is precisely the experience that repeatedly breaks through in Plato's dialogues and that the dialogues let be re-experienced continually.[27] And in that case it is certainly not so that everything is extracted from a Self; on the contrary, the possibility of transcendence of the I in the direction of the Thou, the possibility of communicating and the will to learn, the readiness to receive and give back, are all presupposed. This dialogical knowledge depends as much upon what is "outside" and the "other," as it depends on one's own Self which wants to learn and is able to understand. And the decision of the I for the Thou, to which a correlative decision of the Thou for the I exists, is, in turn, each time a decision of the Self of a reality, of a permanent spiritual will of this very Self in a "moment" that is awakened and to be tested; and this moment does not consist in romantic *self-enjoyment*, but requires the seriousness of the moral *engagement* of the Self. Thus what Grisebach correctly objects to is the decisionlessness of a Self that already possesses everything or fancies itself in possession of everything. But if he wishes to make his I-Thou ontology acceptable, to posit it as a moral task,

[27] For the history of the discovery of the dialogical character of the Self, see Steinbüchel, *Der Umbruch des Denkens*, pp. 26 ff.

then obviously he cannot object to the life of the Self in the
decision that is awakened by it and allows it to come to itself
in itself. To be a Self is to be a living, non-self-contained
being, and this being, which becomes by opening itself, is a
dead substance no more than it is the insubstantiality of a
denied personal self-sufficiency (*Substanzlosigkeit—verleug-
neter Selbstand*). The personal Self is that which always
comes to itself in its relationship to what is different from it.
But the dynamics of the decision for the Thou awakens in the
ego that which it, itself, is, as far as possibility is concerned.
Without this, there would be as the fruit of the denial of the
ego neither the decision of a self-sufficient person, nor the
desire to be a Self.

In our critical position regarding situation ethics, we found
that it, too, knows of a law that is of supra-individual validity:
the surrender to the Thou. We found it as an essential law
of man's Being, without whose fulfillment this Being of man
itself remains unfulfilled. And thus, all of this notwithstanding, *essentialist and situation ethics still meet one another*.
Anticipating some insights that will be established later, we
may therefore say now: a systematic ethics takes its norms
from the law of action—does not exclude the wholly personal
position in regard to the general law, but precisely includes
it. "In truth," says such a strict Thomist as A. D.
Sertillanges,[28] who, however, has penetrated the objective
spirit of the system in such an individual manner, "*the* man
is never found, except in my thought or beyond me in an
ideal world, but one still has to determine such a world for
me." I am as man *a* man, *this* man, I myself. All that is materialized in my moral conduct is my essence in its individual
character, in the situations of my life, and it is never without
a decision that is characteristic of my Self, that is possible for
me and demanded of me. I can obey man and God only as
the one *who I am* and who I am as a Self, and as this unique
Self in which man's essence materializes itself and in which

---

28 A. D. Sertillanges, *Der heilige Thomas von Aquin*, (Leipzig:
Hegner, 1928) p. 785.

man's moral Being crystallizes in a form in which *I* fulfill it. It is in this sense that, as Heinrich Barth[29] has correctly stressed in regard to the indeterminable individual situation, the reality of our moral Being lies "always beyond everything universal." And further, there cannot be any practical decision "whose content of meaning could not be transcended in principal." But all the deficiency of the moral act in each concrete situation, and all limitation resulting from the fact that one can do only what is possible, all of this notwithstanding, the moral is just as everything else that is human, that which concretely grows together out of the universal act in the particular, out of man's essential Being and the individual act in the particular situation. The moral attitude that corresponds to our finite human Being does not consist in a fanaticism for the law, but in the humility that is characteristic for a moral claim that can be fulfilled by us only in a finite and limited way, and factually is so fulfilled. Each fanaticism is, in the final analysis, nothing but the elevation of one's own Self to a morally perfect and morally absolute being, which no *man* is, nor any *man* ever can be. Rigorism, which recognizes as good merely what is good *without qualification* and condemns the morality of our concrete actions, which shows itself in our real life as more or less great, and thus as gradually different, is the easiest position possible, but it is also the most inhuman, the most pharisaic, and the most unrealistic position. "In itself" the good is obviously good without qualification, but no man is good in that way. God alone is good in that sense. Man can in his own Being only approach Him without in any way comparing himself with others, and the situation of his finitude as such, as well as the situation that limits his activity in each case, determines his morality then, too.

3) Situation ethics is an anti-idealistic interpretation of man's Being, at all cost. Its motive is truthfulness in the conception of man, who in his existential situation as limited by

[29] Heinrich Barth, *Philosophie der praktischen Vernunft* (Tübingen: Mohr, 1931) pp. 229, 231. Cf. H. Diem, *Kritischer Idealismus in theologischer Sicht* (Berlin: Kaiser, 1934) pp. 33–38.

the Thou is not the infinite Self, but finitude pure and simple. But just as the autonomy of an ego that is self-sufficient in its own eyes can lead to an overestimation of its own Self and even to the titanism of a Self-divinization, and thus falsifies the being called man and makes it something supra-human, so the one-sided stress upon the situation that no longer seeks to consider the constant Self, can also lead to a misconception of man's Being. But *both* constitute an endangering of our *moral* Being, because the latter cannot be separated from man's essence. The idealistic interpretation of man's Being overlooks the I-Thou relationship of man's essence, the growth toward the Self in this, his own way of existing. In so doing, it necessarily denies the finitude of the Self, which is founded by the Thou. It misunderstands man's morality and interprets it as the self-affirmation of a Self that is self-sufficient. It makes the Self limitless and infinite at the moment when, in a pantheistic interpretation of Being, it conceives of the Self as a moment of the one and only, really being, World-Spirit. At the same moment, personal freedom, the necessary presupposition for morality, becomes impossible; and equally impossible, then, is a moral conduct that always involves limitation of egoism and is always enacted in the surrender to the other who stands opposite to the Self, to the person who lays claim on it and calls it to account for its activity and, thus, demands commitment and limitation of the ego. Only a person can bind another person, but in Hegel's idealism there is only *one* person, and this is not even the Self, but the Divinity that develops into a person in this Self.

However, situation ethics is not so far from the danger of another misconception and exaggeration of man's Being, as in view of its *pathos* for finitude it could seem to be. And this danger threatens in two different directions: first, as a misjudgment in regard to what is human in man, and then as a misinterpretation of his finitude.

The first danger is given together with the denial of an essential constancy. This disavowal must deny the meaningful content of everything that is humanly valuable and that, like human culture in all realms of the mind, is real and can be real only on the basis of the spirituality that characterizes man as that typical being he is. For here man is taken merely as that being which changes from moment to moment. Here, Being-a-spirit is no longer the ontological principle that creates cultural solidarity and spiritual community between human beings, a principle that links man to man in religion, language, common historical destiny, common responsibility for the heritage that has been handed down as well as for the future that is to be created, and thus establishes the moral connections of our *lives*. They harbor their own moral goods (i.e., goods that concern *man*); and the care for them constitutes a moral task that originates from the essence of the historical, spiritual man. The "situation" about which situation ethics speaks, is conceived of in such an individual manner that it overlooks the *common* historical situation, which belongs to the essence of man and lays moral claims on him as much as does the personal situation. The morality of situation ethics indeed sees the I and the Thou, but not the We in which they encounter one another. It pays attention to the relationships between person and person, but it does not understand that society, as a moral-human relation, is more than a relationship between I and Thou. Its deeper ethical meaning is the reference to the fact that the human community is more than an impersonal collectivity and that it itself can exist only where the personal-moral relationship of the common service of the ego in regard to the Thou, and of the Thou in regard to the ego, holds sway between those who carry the society. But its imperfection remains the isolation of these relationships as that which is only moral. That is why pure situation ethics, although it is true that it is not individualistic, nonetheless is inhuman in so far as it does not take into consideration a vast domain of man's Being and his moral Being. If one may designate the exaggeration of the Self in the idealist ethos as *supra*-human, then one may call the one-sided stress on the Self as found in the ethos of situation ethics *in*-human in the sense that it is unable to do justice to the richness of the *humanitas* and poses opposite to the supra-human fullness of the idealist Self an inhuman poverty, which is a misjudgment, in the other direction, of man's morality.

However, there is also a kind of coquetry with respect to this poverty which now more than ever must misrepresent finitude as the essential human condition. Situation ethics need not elicit this danger, but it can easily do so. And it can involve another revolt, which can change the poverty of the finitude into an insisting upon it. This titanism of the finite Being of man is a denial of the genuine essence of man just as much as is the titanism of an infinite Self. The poverty of finitude changes into the pride of the poor for whom poverty suffices, just as the idealist autarchy found its self-sufficiency in the divine wealth of the Self that has become full of God. There is also the hardening pride of finitude, which closes itself from Transcendence and perseveres in a delimitation that no longer sees the double character of the limit, that is, its dialectic essence: one's own being-limited *and* the relationship of what is so limited to that which delimits it. Jaspers has described this form of pride. But Goethe has confronted his Faustus at the end with the grace from above which breaks that titanism and is the only thing that can crown the eternally struggling endeavor from beyond the boundaries of what is human. And in his deepest psychological interpretation of sin, Kierkegaard[30] has described the gradual loss of the existential Self in the despair of one's own Self. It raises itself beyond pride and becomes self-induration which no longer believes in remission by God, in order then to lead to the creature's denial of God in the sin against the Holy Spirit. Time and again one finds *this* accentuation of man's finitude, which sees only the limit and no longer the one who delimits, and for whom the human-personal finitude precisely begins to exist—a denial of the very essence of gen-

[30] Sören Kierkegaard, *Die Krankheit zum Tode* (Jena: E. Diederichs, 1911). For the question concerning the relationship between sin and existence in Kierkegaard, cf. Ruttenbeck, *Kierkegaard*, pp. 172 ff.; Romano Guardini, *Unterscheidung des Christlichen* (Maintz: Mathias-Grünewald-Verlag, 1935), pp. 480–81.

uine finitude, which is delimited by the other. The finitude of the real man consists merely in this ontological *dialectic* of being limited and yet relating oneself to something beyond the limitation in which one's own limit is precisely understood as such. However, if the finitude is absolutized in such a way that it, in turn, is now sufficient for itself, then it constitutes an exaggeration of man's Being from the other direction, a parallel toward the negative of the positive exaggeration of the human Self in its idealistic self-understanding. Just as little as the latter, it no longer knows the other, its dependence on it, and its Being toward it. And it is even more denial and loss of itself than *as* finitude it precisely *is* relational Self which can be finite only before the Infinite. It cancels itself as Being when it hardens itself toward and in itself. But in so doing, it at the same time cancels the ethos of its Being toward the other. It then becomes as lonely as the idealist who perseveres in a loneliness without a Thou. And by misjudging its own Being, it misjudges its innermost morality.

Finitude, too, is a constant essential trait of man, and without its fulfillment there is no answer to the demand of the situation. Situation ethics and essentialist ethics require one another, and the opposition between the two is merely a seeming one. Situation ethics is unable to push aside the ethics of *humanitas*. There is not only room in it for the situation, but it also recognizes that essential fulfillment takes place only in the situation.

However, if moral values are founded upon the essence of man as material moral contents, then there is a determinate content that in all moral conduct materializes itself in each situation. Then values no longer float freely above man, but their content is the realization of his essential Being: each instance of moral conduct, each act of goodness, each true and pure attitude, each good intention, all these contain a moral value that is inherent only in a personal being, that only he can realize in his characteristic conduct, working and acting in a situation. But *essentialist ethics, situation ethics, and value ethics are related to one another* in this way, since all of them are oriented toward man's Being, and *a priori* attribute to him a meaning, and appropriate a value to him, and it is solely on this basis that it is worth while to occupy oneself with man. . . .

SELECTIVE BIBLIOGRAPHY

Der Zweckgedanke in der Philosophie des Thomas von Aquino (Münster: Aschendorff, 1912)

Das Grundproblem der hegelschen Philosophie (Bonn: Haustein, 1933)

Nietzsche: Ein christliche Besinnung (Stuttgart: Deutsche Verlags Anstalt, 1946)

Grosse Gestalten des Abendlandes (Trier: Paulinus Verlag, 1951)

Der Umbruch des Denkens (1936) (Darmstadt: Wissenschaftliche Buchgemeinschaft, 1966)

Ehrfurcht (Stuttgart: Mittelbach, 1947)

Die philosophische Grundlegung der katholischen Sittenlehre (Düsseldorf: Patmos, 1947, 3d ed.)

Chapter 15

INTRODUCTION

MARTIN BUBER (1878–1965) studied philosophy at the Universities of Vienna, Leipzig, Berlin, and Zürich between 1896 and 1900. From 1900 to 1924 he spent most of his time in the Zionist movement. He was professor of the philosophy of Jewish religion and ethics in Frankfurt from 1924 until 1933. From 1938 on, he taught at the Hebrew University in Jerusalem.

One of the basic themes found in almost all of Buber's work is the realization that there is a basic difference between a man's relation to a thing or an object and to a person, a "Thou." A thing and an object are watched or observed; a person is spoken to. Quite often we observe other persons as objects; then the other is no longer a "Thou" but an "It." The "I-It" relationship is typical for the "objective" attitude, which attempts to understand everything as part of an objective world and is caught in its causal chain. The "I-It" relationship is not a genuine relationship, in that it does not take place between the I and the It, but is found merely in the I, who watches, observes, analyzes, and thus objectifies. The "I-Thou" relationship is genuine, since it is between me and the other, who addresses himself to me. The "Thou" is not encountered as a thing among things in the world, nor is the "Thou" seen in the light of an objective world, but rather the whole universe is seen precisely in the light of the "Thou."

The "I-Thou" relation may also take place between me and an animal, a tree, a work of art, etc., but this is possible only under the condition that I genuinely "meet" it in its uniqueness and let it have its impact upon me. It is through all the "I-Thou" relations that I meet God, the "eternal Thou."

For Buber, all genuine living is "meeting"; this takes place in the realm of the "in-between": and this sphere of the "between" constitutes for him the "really real," to which we must attribute ontological reality. While meeting the other in the sphere of the "between," I must respect the other as a person, but at the same time, I must also hold my own ground when I meet him. It is in the "I-Thou" relation that the person, the "single One," emerges. The primary relation in which man achieves his authentic personality is the "Between-man-and-man," *das Zwischenmenschliche*. In this, Buber shows certain affinities and differences with Kierkegaard. As does Kierkegaard, he defends the idea that only the man who has become a *single One*, a Self, a real person, is able to have a complete relation to another Self. But Buber refuses to limit the encounter, or dialogue, to the Self and God. In Buber's view, this relation is essentially triadic, including God, the Self, and the Other. "Real relationship with God cannot be achieved on earth if real relationship to the world and mankind are lacking," just as a real relationship with other human beings is possible only in terms of a real relationship to God.[1] I shall return to this point in a moment, but first a few words on Buber's conception of God are in order.

According to Buber, "the eternal Thou" addresses Himself to me in and through His creation; each created thing and each situation or event is a sign of the address of the "eternal Thou." In other words, in all the signs of life, we are addressed by the "eternal Thou," but under the "guise" of the God of a moment, a momentary God. Out of the momentary Gods there arises for us with a single identity the Lord-of-the-Voice, the One. The world of God and the world of men are inseparable, as are the Creator and His creation. One cannot speak

[1] See Buber, Martin, "The Silent Question," in *At the Turning: Three addresses on Judaism* (New York: Farrar, Straus, and Young, 1952, p. 39; and Herberg Will, *The Writings of Martin Buber*, New York: World, pp. 15–16).

to God without speaking with men; one cannot speak with men without speaking with God. *Above* and *below* are bound to one another. Man comes to authenticity when he responds genuinely to the address of the "eternal Thou," which comes to him in what happens to him, in what is to be seen, heard, and felt in each concrete situation. "God is not met by turning away from the world or by making God into an object of contemplation. . . . God is met only as Thou. As I know the person of the Other only in the dialogue with him, I know God only in dialogue. But this is the dialogue that goes on moment by moment in each new situation, the dialogue that makes my ethical 'ought' a matter of real response with no preparation other than my readiness to respond with my whole being to the unforeseen and the unique. I can know neither God nor moral values as transcendent realities knowable in themselves apart from the dialogue in which I meet God and discover values . . ." (Maurice Friedman, Introduction to *Between Man and Man*, p. xviii).

The following selection was taken from the essay "The Question to the Single One." In this essay, Buber explains how, according to Kierkegaard, each man has to "reduce himself" to a "Single One" by complete renunciation in order to be able to encounter God. Buber explains Kierkegaard's view by comparing it with Stirner's conception of the "Unique One," according to which the authentic man has no essential relation except to himself. As far as Kierkegaard is concerned, Buber argues that the former was convinced that in order to love God, one has to remove all "objects." To this, Buber answers as follows: "That is sublimely to misunderstand God. Creation is not a hurdle on the road to God, it is the road itself. We are created along with one another and directed to a life with one another. Creatures are placed in my way so that I, their fellow creature, by means of them and with them find the way to God. A God reached by their exclusion would not be the God of all lives in Whom all life is fulfilled. . . . God wants us to come to Him by means of the Reginas he has created, not by renunciating them. . . ." (Ibid., p. 52).

This view led Kierkegaard to an absolute separation of ethics and religion. Toward the end of his life, Kierkegaard realized that this is impossible and that an autarkic ethic as well as an autarkic religion are inadmissible, and that just as the ethical cannot be freed from the religious, neither can the religious be separated from the ethical without doing injustice to both. Concerning this change of view, Buber writes: "The ethical no longer appears here, as in Kierkegaard's earlier thought, as a 'stage' from which a 'leap' leads to the religious, a leap by which a level is reached that is quite different and has a different meaning; but it dwells in the religious, in faith and service. This ethical can no longer mean a morality belonging to a realm of relativity and time and again overtaken and invalidated by the religious; but it means *essential* action and suffering in relation to men, which are co-ordinated with the essential relation to God. But only he who has to do with men essentially can essentially act and suffer in relation to them. If the ethical is the only means by which God communicates with man, then I am forbidden to speak essentially only with God and myself. And so indeed it is. . . ." (Ibid., pp. 55–56).

From what has just been said, it will be clear that Buber's thought is profoundly religious in that he conceives of man as essentially oriented to God. But his thought is equally existential, in that he sees man equally primordially as oriented toward the world and his fellow men. The combination of these two characteristics leads almost necessarily to a situational conception of ethics. In Buber's view, responsibility is the basic notion of every genuine ethics, but then the term is to be taken in its literal meaning: genuine responsibility exists only where there is real responding. This responding and answering presupposes someone who addresses me primarily from a realm independent of myself and to whom I am answerable. "Our answering for ourselves is essentially our answering to a divine address." This address, however, does not come to me in the form of a universally valid law or norm; it rather comes over me in the "lived moment" of existence and takes place in the concreteness of each situation in which I may find myself. Responsibility thus means listening to the unreduced claim of the hour and answering it out of the fullness of one's being. "Many are the ways in which the Self tries to evade the responsibility in the existential dialogue of life, but they all add up in the end to the erection of some protective structure of fixed and final general rules . . . to stand between the individual and the concrete here-and-now that makes its demand upon him, so that it is not he who is deciding, but the general rule that decides for him. No responsible person remains a stranger to norms. But the command inherent in a genuine norm never becomes a maxim, and the fulfillment of it never a habit. . . . What it has to tell him is revealed whenever a situation arises that demands of him a solution of which till then he had perhaps no idea. . . . [The situation] demands nothing of what is past; it demands presence, responsibility: it demands you." (Ibid., pp. 16, 45, 114; Will Herberg, op. cit., p. 20.)

THE QUESTION OF THE SINGLE ONE

Martin Buber

THE SINGLE ONE AND THE BODY POLITIC

. . . Kierkegaard's thought circles round the fact that he essentially renounced an essential relation to a definite person. He did not resign this casually, or in the relativity of the many experiences and decisions of life, or with the soul alone, but essentially. The essential nature of his renunciation, its downright positive essentiality, is what he wants to express by saying, "In defiance of the whole nineteenth century I cannot marry." The renunciation becomes essential through its representing in concrete biography the renunciation of an essential relation to the world as that which hinders being alone before God. Moreover, as I have already said, this does not happen just once, as when a man enters a monastery and has thereby cut himself off from the world and lives outside it as one who has done this; but it is peculiarly enduring: the renunciation becomes the zero of a spiritual graph whose every point is determined in relation to this zero. It is in this way that the graph receives its true existential character, by means of which it has provided the impulse to a new philosophy and a new theology. And certainly there goes along with this secularly significant concreteness of biography the curiously manifold motivation—which is undoubtedly legitimate, and is to be found piecemeal in the soundings of inwardness—of the renunciation which Kierkegaard expresses

This essay is from *Between Man and Man*, by Martin Buber, trans. Ronald Gregor Smith (London, 1948; New York, 1965). Copyright © 1948 by Routledge and Kegan Paul Ltd. and The Macmillan Company 1965. Reprinted with permission of The Macmillan Company.

directly and indirectly, by suggestion and concealment. But beyond that, on a closer consideration it is to be noted that there arises, between the renunciation and an increasingly strong point of view and attitude which is finally expressed with penetrating clarity in the *Two Notes* to the *Report to History*, a secret and unexpressed connexion important for Kierkegaard and for us.

"The crowd is untruth." "This consideration of life, the Single One, is the truth." "No-one is excluded from becoming a Single One except him who excludes himself by wanting to be crowd." And again, " 'The Single One' is the category of the spirit, of spiritual awakening and revival, and is as sharply opposed to politics as possible." The Single One and the crowd, the "spirit" and "politics"—this opposition is not to be separated from that into which Kierkegaard enters with the world, expressing it symbolically by means of his renunciation.

Kierkegaard does not marry "in defiance of the whole nineteenth century". What he describes as the nineteenth century is the "age of dissolution", the age of which he says that a single man "cannot help it or save it", he can "only express that it is going under"—going under, if it cannot reach God through the "narrow pass". And Kierkegaard does not marry, in a symbolic action of negation, in defiance of this age, because it is the age of the "crowd" and the age of "politics". Luther married in symbolic action, because he wanted to lead the believing man of his age out of a rigid religious separation, which finally separated him from grace itself, to a life with God in the world. Kierkegaard does not marry (this of course is not part of the manifold subjective motivation but is the objective meaning of the symbol) because he wants to lead the unbelieving man of his age, who is entangled in the crowd, to becoming single, to the solitary life of faith, to being alone before God. Certainly, "to marry or not to marry" is the representative question when the monastery is in view. If the Single One really must be, as Kierkegaard thinks, a man who does not have to do essentially with others, then marriage hinders him if he takes it seriously—and if he does not take it seriously then, in spite of Kierkegaard's remark about Luther, it cannot be understood how he as an existing

person can be "the truth". For man, with whom alone Kierkegaard is fundamentally concerned, there is the additional
factor that in his view woman stands "quite differently from
man in a dangerous rapport to finitude". But there is still a
special additional matter which I shall now make clear.

If one makes a fairly comprehensive survey of the whole
labyrinthine structure of Kierkegaard's thought about renunciation it will be recognized that he is speaking not solely
of a hard, hard-won renunciation, bought with the heart's
blood, of life with a person; but in addition of the downright
positively valued renunciation of the life (conditioned by life
with a person) with an impersonal being, which in the foreground of the happening is called "people", in its background
"the crowd". This being, however, in its essence—of which
Kierkegaard knows or wants to know nothing—refutes these
descriptions as caricatures and acknowledges as its true name
only that of a *res publica*, in English "the body politic". When
Kierkegaard says the category of the "Single One" is "as
sharply opposed as possible to politics" he obviously means an
activity that has essentially lost touch with its origin the *polis*.
But this activity, however degenerate, is one of the decisive
manifestations of the body politic. Every degeneration indicates its genus, and in such a way that the degeneration is
never related to the genus simply as present to past, but as in
a distorted face the distortion is related to the form persisting
beneath it. The body politic, which is sometimes also called
the "world", that is, the human world, seeks, knowingly or
unknowingly, to realize in its genuine formations men's turning to one another in the context of creation. The false formations distort but they cannot eliminate the eternal origin.
Kierkegaard in his horror of malformation turns away. But
the man who has not ceased to love the human world in all
its abasement sees even to-day genuine form. Supposing that
the crowd is untruth, it is only a state of affairs in the body
politic; how truth is here related to untruth must be part and
parcel of the true question to the Single One, and that warning against the crowd can be only its preface.

From this point that special matter can be made clear of
which I said that it is an additional reason for Kierkegaard's

considering marriage to be an impediment. Marriage, essentially understood, brings one into an essential relation to the "world"; more precisely, to the body politic, to its malformation and its genuine form, to its sickness and its health. Marriage, as the decisive union of one with another, confronts one with the body politic and its destiny—man can no longer shirk that confrontation in marriage, he can only prove himself in it or fail. The isolated person, who is unmarried or whose marriage is only a fiction, can maintain himself in isolation; the "community" of marriage is part of the great community, joining with its own problems the general problems, bound up with its hope of salvation to the hope of the great life that in its most miserable state is called the crowd. He who "has entered on marriage", who has entered into marriage, has been in earnest, in the intention of the sacrament, with the fact that the other *is*; with the fact that I cannot legitimately share in the Present Being without sharing in the being of the other; with the fact that I cannot answer the lifelong address of God to me without answering at the same time for the other; with the fact that I cannot be answerable without being at the same time answerable for the other as one who is entrusted to me. But thereby a man has decisively entered into relation with otherness; and the basic structure of otherness, in many ways uncanny but never quite unholy or incapable of being hallowed, in which I and the others who meet me in my life are inwoven, is the body politic. It is to this, into this, that marriage intends to lead us. Kierkegaard himself makes one of his pseudonyms, the "married man" of the *Stages,* express this, though in the style of a lower point of view which is meant to be overcome by a higher. But it is a lower point of view only when trivialized, there is no higher, because to be raised above the situation in which we are set never yields in truth a higher point of view. Marriage is the exemplary bond, it carries us as does none other into the greater bondage, and only as those who are bound can we reach the freedom of the children of God. Expressed with a view to the man, the woman certainly stands "in a dangerous rapport to finitude", and finitude is certainly the danger, for nothing threatens us so sharply as that we remain clinging to it. But our hope of salvation is forged on this very danger, for our human way to the infinite leads only through fulfilled finitude.

This person is other, essentially other than myself, and this otherness of his is what I mean, because I mean him; I confirm it; I wish his otherness to exist, because I wish his particular being to exist. That is the basic principle of marriage and from this basis it leads, if it is real marriage, to insight into the right and the legitimacy of otherness and to that vital acknowledgment of many-faced otherness—even in the contradiction and conflict with it—from which dealings with the body politic receive their religious ethos. That the men with whom I am bound up in the body politic and with whom I have directly or indirectly to do, are essentially other than myself, that this one or that one does not have merely a different mind, or way of thinking or feeling, or a different conviction or attitude, but has also a different perception of the world, a different recognition and order of meaning, a different touch from the regions of existence, a different faith, a different soil: to affirm all this, to affirm it in the way of a creature, in the midst of the hard situations of conflict, without relaxing their real seriousness, is the way by which we may officiate as helpers in this wide realm entrusted to us as well, and from which alone we are from time to time permitted to touch in our doubts, in humility and upright investigation, on the other's "truth" or "untruth", "justice" or "injustice". But to this we are led by marriage, if it is real, with a power for which there is scarcely a substitute, by its steady experiencing of the life-substance of the other as other, and still more by its crises and the overcoming of them which rises out of the organic depths, whenever the monster of otherness, which but now blew on us with its icy demons' breath and now is redeemed by our risen affirmation of the other, which knows and destroys all negation, is transformed into the mighty angel of union of which we dreamed in our mother's womb.

Of course, there is a difference between the private sphere of existence, to which marriage belongs, and the public sphere of existence. *Identification* takes place in a qualitatively different way in each. The private sphere is that with which a man, at any rate in the healthy epochs of its existence, can in all concreteness identify himself without regard to individual differentiation, such as the bodily and spiritual one between members of a family. This identification can take place by his saying in all concreteness *We, I*, of this family or band of his. (A genuine band stands in this respect on the side of the private sphere, in another respect it is on the side of the public sphere.) And when he says this he means not merely the whole, but also the single persons recognized and affirmed by him in their particular being. Identification with the public sphere of existence, on the other hand, is not really able to embrace the concrete persons in a concrete way. Thus I say of my nation "we", and this can be raised to the power of an elementary "That is I". But as soon as concretion, direction to the persons of whom the nation consists, enters in, there is a cleavage, and knowledge of the unbridgable multiple otherness permeates the identification in a broad stream. If the like happened to a province of private existence then it would either itself become of questionable value or it would pass over into public existence. For the relation to public existence every such test can be a proof and strengthening.

There are, however, two basic attitudes in which identification with public existence wards off the concretion, the direction to actual persons, and either transitorily or enduringly asserts itself. Very different from one another though they are, they often exercise almost the same effect. The one derives from the act of enthusiasm of "historic" hours: the crowd is actualized, enters into the action and is transfigured in it, and the person, overpowered by delirious ecstasy, is submerged in the movement of public existence. Here there is no contesting and impeding knowledge about the otherness of other persons: the transfiguration of the crowd eclipses all otherness, and the fiery impulse to identification can beget a real "family" feeling for the unknown man who walks in a demonstration or in the enthusiastic confusion of the streets runs into one's arms.

The other basic attitude is passive and constant. It is the accustomed joining in public opinion and in public "taking of a position". Here the crowd remains latent, it does not appear as a crowd, but only becomes effective. And, as is known, this happens in such a way that I am either completely excused from forming an opinion and a decision, or as it were convicted, in a murky recess of inwardness, of the invalidity of my opinions and decisions, and in their stead fitted out with ones that are approved as valid. By this means I am not in the least made aware of others since the same thing happens to them and their otherness has been varnished over.

Of these two basic attitudes the first is of such a kind that it snatches us out and away from confrontation with the great form of otherness in public existence, from the most difficult of the inner-worldly tasks, and raises us enthusiastically into the historical paradise of crowds. The second undermines the ground on which confrontation is to be carried out; it rubs out the pathetic signs of otherness and then convinces us by the evidence of our own eyes that uniformity is the real thing.

It is from this point that Kierkegaard's confusion of public existence, or the body politic, with the crowd, is to be understood. He knows the body politic, indeed, also in the form of the State, which is for him, however, only a fact in the world of relativity which is foreign to transcendence; it is respectable, but without significance for the individual's religious relation. And then he knows a crowd which is not respectable, but which has the deepest negative significance, indeed concerning transcendence, but as compact devilry.

This confusion which is in increasing measure heavy with consequences for the thought of our time must be opposed with the force of distinction.

A man in the crowd is a stick stuck in a bundle moving through the water, abandoned to the current or being pushed by a pole from the bank in this or that direction. Even if it seems to the stick at times that it is moving by its own motion it has in fact none of its own; and the bundle, too, in which it drifts has only an illusion of self-propulsion. I do not know if Kierkegaard is right when he says that the crowd is untruth—I should rather describe it as non-truth since (in distinction from some of its masters) it is not on the same plane as the truth, it is not in the least opposed to it. But it is certainly "un-freedom". In what un-freedom consists cannot be adequately learned under the pressure of fate, whether it is the compulsion of need or of men; for there still remains the rebellion of the inmost heart, the tacit appeal to the secrecy of eternity. It can be adequately learned only when you are tied up in the bundle of the crowd, sharing its opinions and desires, and only dully perceiving that you are in this condition.

The man who is living with the body politic is quite different. He is not bundled, but bound. He is bound up in relation to it, betrothed to it, married to it, therefore suffering his destiny along with it; rather, simply suffering it, always willing and ready to suffer it, but not abandoning himself blindly to any of its movements, rather confronting each movement watchfully and carefully. that it does not miss truth and loyalty. He sees powers press on and sees God's hands in their supreme power held up on high, that the mortal immortals there below may be able to decide for themselves. He knows that in all his weakness he is put into the service of decision. If it is the crowd, remote from, opposed to, decision which swarms round him, he does not put up with it. At the place where he stands, whether lifted up or unnoticed, he does what he can, with the powers he possesses, whether compressed predominance or the word which fades, to make the crowd no longer a crowd. Otherness enshrouds him, the otherness to which he is betrothed. But he takes it up into his life only in the form of *the* other, time and again the other, the other who meets him, who is sought, lifted out of the crowd, the "companion". Even if he has to speak to the crowd he seeks the person, for a people can find and find again its truth only through persons, through persons standing their test. *That* is the Single One who "changes the crowd into Single Ones"—how could it be one who remains far from the crowd? It cannot be one who is reserved, only one who is given; given, not given over. It is a paradoxical work to which he sets his soul, to make the crowd no longer a crowd. It is to bring out from the crowd and set on the way of creation which leads to the Kingdom. And if he does not achieve much he has time, he has God's own time. For the man who loves God and his companion in one—though he remains in all the frailty of humanity—receives God for his companion.

"The Single One" is not the man who has to do with God essentially, and only unessentially with others, who is unconditionally concerned with God and conditionally with the body politic. The Single One is the man for whom the reality of relation with God as an exclusive relation includes and encompasses the possibility of relation with all otherness, and for whom the whole body politic, the reservoir of otherness, offers just enough otherness for him to pass his life with it.

THE SINGLE ONE IN RESPONSIBILITY

The category of the Single One has changed. It cannot be that the relation of the human person to God is established by the subtraction of the world. The Single One must therefore take his world, what of the world is extended and entrusted to him in his life, without any reduction into his life's devotion; he must let his world partake unabated of its essentiality. It cannot be that the Single One finds God's hands when he stretches his hands out and away beyond creation. He must put his arms round the vexatious world, whose true name is creation; only then do his fingers reach the realm of lightning and of grace. It cannot be that the spirit of reduction reigns in the relation of faith as well. The Single One who lives in his relation of faith must wish to have it fulfilled in the uncurtailed measure of the life he lives. He must face the hour which approaches him, the biographical and historical hour, just as it is, in its whole world content and apparently senseless contradiction, without weakening the impact of otherness in it. He must hear the message, stark and untransfigured, which is delivered to him out of this hour, presented by this situation as it arrives. Nor must he translate for himself its wild and crude profaneness into the chastely religious: he must recognize that the question put to him, with which the speech of the situation is fraught—whether it sounds with angels' or with devils' tongues—remains God's question to him, of course without the devils thereby being turned into angels. It is a question wondrously tuned in the wild crude sound. And he, the Single One, must answer, by what he does and does not do, he must accept and answer for the hour, the hour of the world, of all the world, as that which is given to him, entrusted to him. Reduction is forbidden; you are not at liberty to select what suits you, the whole cruel hour is at stake, the whole claims you, and you must answer—Him.

You must hear the claim, however unharmoniously it strikes your ear—and let no-one interfere; give the answer from the depths, where a breath of what has been breathed in still hovers—and let no-one prompt you.

This arch-command, for whose sake the Bible makes its God *speak* from the very time of creation, defines anew, when it is heard, the relation of the Single One to his community.

The human person belongs, whether he wants to acknowledge it and take it seriously or not, to the community in which he is born or which he has happened to get into. But he who has realized what destiny means, even if it looks like doom, and what being placed there means, even if it looks like being misplaced, knows too that he must acknowledge it and take it seriously. But then, precisely then, he notes that true membership of a community includes the experience, which changes in many ways, and which can never be definitively formulated, of the *boundary* of this membership. If the Single One, true to the historico-biographical hour, perceives the word, if he grasps the situation of his people, his own situation, as a sign and demand upon him, if he does not spare himself and his community before God, then he experiences the boundary. He experiences it in such agony as if the boundary-post had pierced his soul. The Single One, the man living in responsibility, can carry out his political actions as well—and of course omissions are also actions—only from that ground of his being to which the claim of the fearful and kind God, the Lord of history and our Lord, wishes to penetrate.

It is obvious that for the man living in community the ground of personal and essential decision is continually threatened by the fact of so-called collective decisions. I remind you of Kierkegaard's warning: "That men are in a crowd either excuses a man of repentance and responsibility or at all events weakens the Single One's responsibility, because the crowd lets the man have only a fragment of responsibility." But I must put it differently. In practice, in the moment of action, it is only the semblance of a fragment, but afterwards, when in your waking dream after midnight you are dragged before the throne and attacked by the spurned calling to be a Single One, it is complete responsibility.

It must, of course, be added that the community to which a man belongs does not usually express in a unified and unambiguous way what it considers to be right and what not right in a given situation. It consists of more or less visible groups, which yield to a man interpretations of destiny and of his task which are utterly different yet all alike claim absolute authenticity. Each knows what benefits the community, each claims your unreserved complicity for the good of the community.

Political decision is generally understood to-day to mean joining such a group. If this is done then everything is finally in order, the time of deciding is over. From then on one has only to share in the group's movements. One no longer stands at the cross-roads, one no longer has to choose the right action out of the possible ones; everything is decided. What you once thought—that you had to answer ever anew, situation by situation, for the choice you made—is now got rid of. The group has relieved you of your political responsibility. You feel yourself answered for in the group; you are permitted to feel it.

The attitude which has just been described means for the man of faith (I wish to speak only of him here), when he encounters it, his fall from faith—without his being inclined to confess it to himself or to admit it. It means his fall in very fact from faith, however loudly and emphatically he continues to confess it not merely with his lips but even with his very soul as it shouts down inmost reality. The relation of faith to the one Present Being is perverted into semblance and self-deceit if it is not an all-embracing relation. "Religion" may agree to be one department of life beside others which like it are independent and autonomous—it has thereby already perverted the relation of faith. To remove any realm basically from this relation, from its defining power, is to try to remove it from God's defining power which rules over the relation of faith. To prescribe to the relation of faith that "so far and no further you may define what I have to do; here your power ends and that of the group to which I belong begins" is to address God in precisely the same way. He who does not let his relation of faith be fulfilled in the uncurtailed measure of the life he lives, however much he is capable of at different times, is trying to curtail the fulfilment of God's rule of the world.

Certainly the relation of faith is no book of rules which can be looked up to discover what is to be done now, in this very hour. I experience what God desires of me for this hour —so far as I do experience it—not earlier than *in* the hour. But even then it is not given me to experience it except by answering before God for this hour as *my* hour, by carrying out the responsibility for it towards him as much as I can. What has now approached me, the unforeseen, the unforeseeable, is word from him, a word found in no dictionary, a word that has now become word—and it demands my answer to him. I give the word of my answer by accomplishing among the actions possible that which seems to my devoted insight to be the right one. With my choice and decision and action—committing or omitting, acting or persevering—I answer the word, however inadequately, yet properly; I answer for my hour. My group cannot relieve me of this responsibility, I must not let it relieve me of it; if I do I pervert my relation of faith, I cut out of God's realm of power the sphere of my group. But it is not as though the latter did not concern me in my decision—it concerns me tremendously. In my decision I do not look away from the world, I look at it and into it, and before all I may see in the world, to which I have to do justice with my decision, my group to whose welfare I cling; I may before all have to do justice to it, yet not as a thing in itself, but before the Face of God; and no programme, no tactical resolution, no command can tell me how I, as I decide, have to do justice to my group before the Face of God. It may be that I may serve it as the programme and resolution and command have laid down. It may be that I have to serve it otherwise. It could even be—if such an unheard-of thing were to rise within me in my act of decision —that I might be set in cruel opposition to its success, because I became aware that God's love ordains otherwise. Only one thing matters, that as the situation is presented to me I expose myself to it as to the word's manifestation to me, to the very ground where hearing passes into being, and that I perceive what is to be perceived and answer it. He who prompts me with an answer in such a way as to hinder my perceiving is the hinderer, let him be for the rest who he will.

I do not in the least mean that a man must fetch the answer alone and unadvised out of his breast. Nothing of the sort is meant; how should the direction of those at the head of my group not enter essentially into the substance out of which the decision is smelted? But the direction must not be substituted for the decision; no substitute is accepted. He who has a master may yield "himself", his bodily person, to him, but not his responsibility. He must find his way to that responsibility armed with all the "ought" that has been forged in the group, but exposed to destiny so that in the demanding moment all armour falls away from him. He may even hold firm with all his force to the "interest" of the group— till in the last confrontation with reality a finger, hardly to be perceived, yet never to be neglected, touches it. It is not the "finger of God", to be sure; we are not permitted to expect that, and therefore there is not the slightest assurance that our decision is right in any but a personal way. God tenders me the situation to which I have to answer; but I have not to expect that he should tender me anything of my answer. Certainly in my answering I am given into the power of his grace, but I cannot measure heaven's share in it, and even the most blissful sense of grace can deceive. The finger I speak of is just that of the "conscience", but not of the routine conscience, which is to be used, is being used and worn out, the play-on-the-surface conscience, with whose discrediting they thought to have abolished the actuality of man's positive answer. I point to the unknown conscience in the ground of being, which needs to be discovered ever anew, the conscience of the "spark", for the genuine spark is effective also in the single composure of each genuine decision. The certainty produced by this conscience is of course only a personal certainty; it is uncertain certainty; but what is here called person is the very person who is addressed and who answers.

I say, therefore, that the Single One, that is, the man living in responsibility, can make even his political decisions properly only from that ground of his being at which he is aware of the event as divine speech to him; and if he lets the awareness of this ground be strangled by his group he is refusing to give God an actual reply.

What I am speaking of has nothing to do with "individualism". I do not consider the individual to be either the starting-point or the goal of the human world. But I consider the human person to be the irremovable central place of the struggle between the world's movement away from God and its movement towards God. This struggle takes place to-day to an uncannily large extent in the realm of public life, of course not between group and group but within each group. Yet the decisive battles of this realm as well are fought in the depth, in the ground or the groundlessness, of the person.

Our age is intent on escaping from the demanding "ever anew" of such an obligation of responsibility by a flight into a protective "once-for-all". The last generation's intoxication with freedom has been followed by the present generation's craze for bondage; the untruth of intoxication has been followed by the untruth of hysteria. He alone is true to the one Present Being who knows he is bound to his place—and just there free for his proper responsibility. Only those who are bound and free in this way can still produce what can truly be called community. Yet even today the believing man, if he clings to a thing that is presented in a group, can do right to join it. But belonging to it, he must remain submissive with his whole life, therefore with his group life as well, to the One who is his Lord. His responsible decision will thus at times be opposed to, say, a tactical decision of his group. At times he will be moved to carry the fight for the truth, the human, uncertain and certain truth which is brought forward by his deep conscience, into the group itself, and thereby establish or strengthen an inner front in it. This can be more important for the future of our world than all fronts that are drawn today between groups and between associations of groups; for this front, if it is everywhere upright and strong, may run as a secret unity across all groups.

What the right is can be experienced by none of the groups of today except through men who belong to them staking their own souls to experience it and then revealing it, however bitter it may be, to their companions—charitably if it may be, cruelly if it must be. Into this fiery furnace the group plunges time and again, or it dies an inward death.

And if one still asks if one may be certain of finding what is right on this steep path, once again the answer is No; there is no certainty. There is only a chance; but there is no other. The risk does not ensure the truth for us; but it, and it alone, leads us to where the breath of truth is to be felt.

ATTEMPTS AT SEVERANCE

Against the position outlined here of the Single One in responsibility there is bound to rise up that powerful modern point of view, according to which in the last resort only so-called objectives, more precisely collectives, are real, while significance is attached to persons only as the workers or the tools of the collectives. Kierkegaard's merely religious category, to be sure, may be indifferent to this point of view: according to his category only the person is essential and the objective either has only a secondary existence or, as crowd, is the negative which is to be avoided. If, however, the Single One as such has essentially to do with the world, and even with the world in particular, with the body politic, but not in order, consciously and with the emphasis of faith, henceforth to let himself be used, but in responsibility for that in which before God he participates, then he is bound to be opposed and if possible refuted once for all by that point of view. It can set about this by means of arguments taken from

a certain contemporary trend of thought which conforms to
the time and is apparently its expedient. It is a trend of
which the representatives, first of all, with all their various
differences, have in common one object of attack—it may be
described as liberalism or individualism or by any other
slogan you please. (In this they usually neglect—as, under-
standably, often happens in cases of this kind—to analyze the
attacked "ism" conceptually, nor do they make a distinction
between what they mean and what they do not mean, that is,
between what is worth contesting and what should be spared.
If such an analysis should be applied to, say, "liberalism", individual concepts of varying tendency would arise, towards
which it would be possible to adopt a standpoint in quite
different clarity and unambiguousness. Thus, for example,
there would be libertinism, the poor mode of thought of the
released slave who only knows what is or what ought to be
permitted to him, to "man"; on the other hand there would
be liberism, the mode of thought of the free-born man for
whom freedom is the presupposition of binding, of the true
personal entry into a binding relation, no more and no less—
a mode of thought worthy of being preserved in the treasure-
house of the spirit and defended along with it by everyone
who knows about the spirit.) But it is more significant that
the representatives of this trend have also a common purpose
or at least a common effect: they give the political province
an exaggerated autonomy, they contrast public life with the
rest of life, they remove it from the responsibility of the
Single One who takes part in it.

In order to indicate what might be replied to such arguments from the standpoint of the transformed category of
the Single One, [an] example of the trend of thought under
consideration may be discussed [here]. . . .

Gogarten explains in his *Political Ethics* that all ethical
problems receive their ethical relevance only from the political problem. That is, the ethical is valid as the ethical only
by its connexion with man's political being. In saying this he
abandons Kierkegaard's category of the Single One. Gogarten
believes that he is only fighting against individualism but at
the same time he is fighting against the position of personal

life in the rigour of its total responsibility. If ethical problems receive their relevance from the political realm, they cannot also receive them from the religious, not even if the political has a religious basis. But if they do not receive them from the religious realm, then we have reached again, within the life of the "religious" man—even if in a politicized form—the disconnected ethic which Kierkegaard helped us to overcome. Gogarten may speak in theological terms as emphatically as he pleases, he narrows down the Single One's fundamental relation with God when he lets his action receive its validity from some other source, even if it is from the destiny, considered in itself, of the community to which the Single One belongs. (And what else are "ethical problems" but man's questions about his actions and their meaning?) True as it is that he, the Single One, cannot win to a legitimate relation with God without a legitimate relation to the body politic, it is nevertheless also true that the defining force has to be ascribed not to the latter but to the former alone. That is, I must always let the boundary between co-operation and non-co-operation within my relation to my community be drawn by God. You say that often you hear nothing? Well, we have to be attentive with the unreserved effort of our being. If even then we hear nothing, then, but only then, may we turn in the direction Gogarten indicates. But if we are not attentive or if we hear but do not obey, then our omission, and not our invoking of some kind of relation of ethical problems to the political, will persist in eternity.

In Gogarten's view man is "radically and therefore irrevocably evil, that is, in the grip of evil". The relevance of the political arises from the fact that "only in the political" does man have, "in face of this recognition, the possibility of existence". The ethical quality of the State consists "in its warding off the evil to which men have fallen prey by its sovereign power and by its right over the life and property of its subjects". (Incidentally, this is a theological version of the old police-state idea.) For "whence shall the State derive sovereign power if not from the recognition of man's fallen state"?

The concept to which Gogarten refers, of the radical evil of man, his absolute sinfulness, is taken from the realm where man confronts God and is significant there alone. What to my knowledge and understanding is taught by Christian theology, in whose name Gogarten speaks, is that man, more precisely, fallen man, considered as being unredeemed, is "before God" (*coram Deo*) sinful and depraved. I do not see how his being unredeemed can be broken off from its dialectic connexion with redemption (*ab his malis liberemur et servemur*) and used separately. Nor do I see how the concept of being evil can be translated from the realm of being "before God" into that of being before earthly authorities, and yet retain its radical nature. In the sight of God a state of radical evil can be ascribed to man because God is God and man is man, and the distance between them is absolute, and because precisely in this distance and in virtue of it God's redeeming deed is done. In the sight of his fellow-men, of human groups and orders, man, it seems to me, cannot be properly described as simply sinful, because the distance is lacking which alone is able to establish the unconditional. Nothing is changed if a human order is considered as established or empowered by God. For that absolute distance to man, which establishes the unconditional (but at the same time discloses the place of redemption)—the distance from which alone man's radical evil could appear also in face of the body politic—can by no means be bestowed in this way upon the human order. Hence no legitimate use can be made in politics or political theory of the concept of human sinfulness.

In my view, however, man generally is not "radically" this or that.

It is not radicality that characterizes man as separated by a primal abyss from all that is merely animal, but it is his potentiality. If we put him alone before the whole of nature then there appears embodied in him the character of possibility inherent in natural existence and which everywhere else hovers round dense reality only like a haze. Man is the crystallized potentiality of existence. But he is this potentiality in its factual limitation. The wealth of possibility in existence from which the animals are kept away by their exiguous reality is exhibited in man in a sign that is incomprehensible from the standpoint of nature. Yet this wealth of possibility does not hold free sway, so that life might be able time and again to follow on wings the anticipation of spirit, but it is confined within narrow limits. This limitation is not essential, but only factual. That means that man's action is unforeseeable in its nature and extent, and that even if he were peripheral to the cosmos in everything else, he remains the centre of all surprise in the world. But he is fettered surprise, only inwardly is it without bonds; and his fetters are strong.

Man is not good, man is not evil; he is, in a pre-eminent sense, good and evil together. He who eats of him, as he who ate of that fruit, has the knowledge of good and evil together. That is his limitation, that is the cunning of the serpent: he was to become as God, knowing good and evil; but what he "recognizes", what in being mixed up with it he has recognized as something mixed up, is good and evil together: he has become good and evil together; that is the nakedness in which he recognizes himself. The limitation is only factual, it does not transform his essence or destroy God's work. To ascribe to the serpent the power of destruction is to elevate it to rivalry with God and make it for the time superior to him (as Ahriman was for a time to Ormuzd), since it perverts God's creation. But the serpent in the Bible is not that. It is not an opposing god, it is only the creature which desires to undo man by man's own doing. It is the "cunning" creature, the cunning of the secretly poisonous creature which foments disorder; and out of the disorder comes history which, groping and striving and failing, is concerned with God's order. The primal event pointed out by the images of the Bible does not lie under the principle of contradiction: A and not-A are here strangely concerned with one another.

Good and evil, then, cannot be a pair of opposites like right and left or above and beneath. "Good" is the movement in the direction of home, "evil" is the aimless whirl of human potentialities without which nothing can be achieved and by which, if they take no direction but remain trapped in themselves, everything goes awry. If the two were indeed poles the man who did not see them as such would be blind; but the man would be blinder who did not perceive the lightning flash from pole to pole, the "and".

As a condition of the individual soul evil is the convulsive shirking of direction, of the total orientation of the soul by which it stands up to personal responsibility before God. The shirking can take place from passion or from indolence. The passionate man refuses by his passion, the indolent man by his indolence. In both cases the man goes astray within himself. The real historical dæmonias are the exploiting by historical powers of this shirking.

But the State *as such* cannot indicate the one direction of the hour towards God, which changes time and again by concretion. Only the Single One, who stands in the depth of responsibility, can do that. And indeed a statesman can also be this Single One.

Gogarten puts *the* State in place of the historical State, that is, of the government of the particular time (ἄρχοντες). This government cannot ward off the "evil" as an impersonal State but can do it only on the basis of its own personal responsibility, and is for the rest itself exposed to the dynamic between good and evil. The State is the visible form of authority, and for Gogarten authority is simply what is established, the diaconal; power is full power. But if the establishment of power is taken seriously, theologically and biblically seriously, the establishing turns out to be a precise commission and the power a great duty of responsibility. The Old Testament records, in the history of the kings of Israel and the history of foreign rulers, the degeneration of legitimacy into illegitimacy and of full power into antagonistic power. As no philosophical concept of the State, so likewise no theological concept of the State leads beyond the reality of the human person in the situation of faith. None leads beyond his responsibility—be he servant or emperor—for the body politic as man in the sight of God.

THE QUESTION

In the human crisis which we are experiencing to-day these two have become questionable—the person and the truth.

We know from the act of responsibility how they are linked together. For the responsible response to exist the reality of the person is necessary, whom the word meets in the happening claiming him; and the reality of the truth is necessary to which the person goes out with united being and which he is therefore able to receive only in the word, as the truth which concerns himself, in his particular situation, and not in any general way.

The question by which the person and the truth have become questionable to-day is the question to the Single One.

The person has become questionable through being collectivized.

This collectivizing of the person is joined in history to a basically different undertaking in which I too participated and to which I must therefore confess now. It is that struggle of recent decades against the idealistic concepts of the sovereign, world-embracing, world-sustaining, world-creating *I*. The struggle was conducted (among other ways) by reference to the neglected creaturely bonds of the concrete human person. It was shown how fundamentally important it is to know in every moment of thought this as well—that the one who thinks is bound, in different degrees of substantiality but never purely functionally, to a spatial realm, to a historical hour, to the genus man, to a people, to a family, to a society, to a vocational group, to a companionship in convictions. This entanglement in a manifold We, when known in an actual way, wards off the temptation of the thought of sovereignty: man is placed in a narrow creaturely position. But he is enabled to recognize that this is his genuine width; for being bound means being bound up in relation.

But it came about that a tendency of a quite different origin and nature assumed power over the new insights, which exaggerated and perverted the perception of bonds into a doctrine of serfdom. Primacy is ascribed here to a collectivity. The collectivity receives the right to hold the person who is bound to it bound in such a way that he ceases to have complete responsibility. The collectivity becomes what really exists, the person becomes derivatory. In every realm which joins him to the whole he is to be excused a personal response.

Thereby the immeasurable value which constitutes man is imperilled. The collectivity cannot enter instead of the person into the dialogue of the ages which the Godhead conducts with mankind. Human perception ceases, the human response is dumb, if the person is no longer there to hear and to speak. It is not possible to reduce the matter to private life; only in the uncurtailed measure of lived life, that is, only with the inclusion of participation in the body politic, can the claim be heard and the reply spoken.

The truth, on the other hand, has become questionable through being politicized.

The sociological doctrine of the age has exercised a relativizing effect, heavy with consequences, on the concept of truth, in that it has, in the dependence of the thought processes on social processes, proved the connexion of thought with existence. This relativization was justified in that it bound the "truth" of a man to his conditioning reality. But its justification was perverted into the opposite when its authors omitted to draw the basic boundary line between what can and what cannot be understood as conditioned in this way. That is, they did not comprehend the person in his *total* reality, wooing the truth and wrestling for it. If we begin with the Single One as a whole being, who wishes to recognize with his total being, we find that the force of his desire for the truth can at decisive points burst the "ideological" bonds of his social being. The man who thinks "existentially", that is, who stakes his life in his thinking, brings into his real relation to the truth not merely his conditioned qualities but also the unconditioned nature, transcending them, of his quest, of his grasp, of his indomitable will for the truth, which also carries along with it the whole personal power of standing his test. We shall certainly be able to make no distinction, in what he has, time and again, discovered as the truth, between what can and what cannot be derived from the social factor. But it is an ineluctable duty to accept what cannot be so derived as a border concept and thus to point out, as the unattainable horizon of the distinction made by the sociology of knowledge, what takes place between the underivable in the recognizing person and the underivable in the object of his recognition. This duty has been neglected. Consequently, the political theory of modern collectivisms was easily able to assume power over the principle which lay

ready, and to proclaim what corresponded to the (real or supposed) life interests of a group as its legitimate and unappeal-
able truth. Over against this the Single One could no longer
appeal to a truth which could be recognized and tested by
him.

This marks the beginning of a disintegration of human
faith in the truth, which can never be possessed and yet may
be comprehended in an existentially real relation; it marks
the beginning of the paralysis of the human search for the
truth.

"What I speak of," says Kierkegaard, "is something simple
and straightforward—that the truth for the Single One only
exists in his producing it himself in action." More precisely,
man finds the truth to be true only when he stands its test.
Human truth is here bound up with the responsibility of the
person.

"True is what is Mine," says Stirner. Human truth is here
bound up with the human person's lack of responsibility.
Collectivisms translate this into the language of the group:
"True is what is Ours."

But in order that man may not be lost there is need of
persons who are not collectivized, and of truth which is not
politicized.

There is need of persons, not merely "representatives" in
some sense or other, chosen or appointed, who exonerate the
represented of responsibility, but also "represented" who on
no account let themselves be represented with regard to responsibility. There is need of the person as the ground which
cannot be relinquished, from which alone the entry of the
finite into conversation with the infinite became possible and
is possible.

There is need of man's faith in the truth as that which is
independent of him, which he cannot acquire for himself,
but with which he can enter into a real relation of his very
life; the faith of human persons in the truth as that which
sustains them all together, in itself inaccessible but disclosing
itself, in the fact of responsibility which awaits test, to him
who really woos the truth.

That man may not be lost there is need of the person's

responsibility to truth in his historical situation. There is need of the Single One who stands over against all being which is present to him—and thus also over against the body politic—and guarantees all being which is present to him—and thus also the body politic.

True community and true commonwealth will be realized only to the extent to which the Single Ones become real out of whose responsible life the body politic is renewed.

SELECTIVE BIBLIOGRAPHY

Ich und Du (Leipzig: Insel Verlag, 1923). English: *I and Thou*, trans. Ronald Gregor Smith (New York: Charles Scribner's Sons, 1937)

Die Frage an den Einzelnen (Berlin: Schocken Verlag, 1936). English: *Between Man and Man*, trans. Ronald Gregor Smith (New York: Macmillan, 1948)

Pfade in Utopia (Heidelberg: Schneider, 1950). English: *Paths in Utopia* trans. R. F. C. Hull (New York: Macmillan, 1950)

Bilder von Gut und Böse (Cologne: Hegner, 1952). English: *Good and Evil: Two Interpretations*, trans. R. G. Smith and M. Bullock (New York: Charles Scribner's Sons, 1953)

Eclipse of God: Studies in the Relation Between Religion and Philosophy, trans. Maurice Friedman et al. (New York: Harper and Brothers, 1952)

Der Glaube der Propheten (Zürich: Menesse Verlag, 1950). English: *The Prophetic Faith*, trans. Carlyle Wittson-Davies (New York: Macmillan, 1949)

The Writings of Martin Buber, ed. Will Herberg (New York: Meridian Books, 1956)

Maurice Friedman, *Martin Buber: The Life of Dialogue* (Chicago: University of Chicago Press, 1955)

The Philosophy of Martin Buber, ed. Paul Arthur Schilpp and Maurice Friedman (La Salle, Ill.: The Open Court Publishing Company, 1965)

Manfred Vogel, "Buber's Ethics and Contemporary Ethics," *Philosophy Today*, 13(1969) 2–18

Paul E. Pfuetze, *The Social Self* (New York: Bookman Associates, 1954)

Chapter 16

INTRODUCTION

DIETRICH BONHOEFFER (1906–45) was the son of a well-known professor of psychiatry at the University of Berlin. He studied theology at the same university (1924–28) under Harnack, Seeberg, and Lietzman. At first his interest was in theology; he attempted to reconcile sociological views of the church, taken as a human organization, with a theological conception of the "divine society." His doctoral thesis, *Communio Sanctorum* (1927), was devoted to this complex theme. His inaugural thesis, *Akt und Sein* (1928), was mainly concerned with the philosophical presuppositions of his theological view; in this book, Bonhoeffer tried to find his way by carefully comparing Kant and Heidegger; in applying the result of this comparison to theology, he was guided mainly by Grisebach and Karl Barth.

After a short period as a pastor in Barcelona (1928–29) and a year's study at the Union Theological Seminary in New York (1929–30), Bonhoeffer taught at the University of Berlin, from 1930 to 1933. He then became a pastor in London (1933–35), after which he returned to Berlin University (1935–36). In 1936 he became the rector of a new "emergency" seminary for Lutheran ministers in Pomerania. Bonhoeffer was in the United States on a lecture tour in 1939. During the war he became gradually more and more involved in the resistance movement in Germany and in an attempt to overthrow the Hitler regime. On April 5, 1943, he was imprisoned in Berlin, from where he was taken later to Buchenwald, Schönberg, and Flüssenburg. He died on April 9, 1945, in the concentration camp of Flüssenburg.

Bonhoeffer basically disagreed with the commonly defended view that ethics aims at the knowledge of good and
evil. He wanted to write a Christian ethics whose first task
it would be to invalidate this thesis. Such an attempt sets a
Christian ethics apart from all other forms of ethics, and it
even becomes questionable whether it makes sense to speak
of a Christian ethics at all. "But if one does so notwithstanding, that can only mean that Christian ethics claims to discuss the origin of the whole problem of ethics, and this pro-
fesses to be a critique of all ethics simply as ethics."
(*Ethics*, p. 17.)

When a man claims that he knows good and evil, then he
has already fallen away from his origin. According to the
Christian view, Bonhoeffer claims, man's origin is God. And
at his origin he knows only one thing: God. All other things
he knows in God, and he only knows God in all things. When
this man thus claims to have knowledge of good and evil,
then this shows that he is no longer at one with his origin. "In
the knowledge of good and evil, man does not understand
himself in the reality of the destiny appointed in his origin,
but rather in his own possibilities, his possibility of being
good or evil. He knows himself now as something apart from
God, outside God, and this means that he now knows only
himself and no longer knows God at all. . . . The knowledge of good and evil is therefore separation from God. Only
against God can man know good and evil." (Ibid., pp. 17–
18.) The moment man turns away from his genuine origin,
he knows himself as an origin. He interprets himself according to his own possibilities of being good or evil, and thus
conceives of himself as the origin of good and evil. In so
doing, man becomes like God and makes himself his own
creator and judge. (Ibid., p. 18.)

When a man reflects upon what has taken place here and
perceives himself in his disunion with God and thus with
men and things, he finds himself laid bare. Then shame
arises. Shame is man's indelible recollection of his estrange-
ment from his genuine origin; it is grief for this alienation,
and the powerless desire to return to unity with his origin.
Man is ashamed because he has lost something that is some-

how essential to him. Shame is not the same as remorse. Man feels remorse when he has done something wrong; he feels shame because he lacks something. Thus shame is more original than remorse. (Ibid., p. 20.)

In shame, man is reminded of his disunion with God. After he has become separated from his origin, God, conscience is the sign of his disunion with himself. Conscience, thus, is concerned not with man's relation to God, but with man's relation to himself. But such a relation is possible only after man becomes detached from his relation to God and via God to other men. Conscience "is the voice of apostate life which desires at least to remain one with itself. It is the call to the unity of man with himself." That this is true is clear from the fact that the call of conscience is always a prohibition: "Thou shalt not. . . ." Conscience is satisfied as long as the prohibition is not disobeyed. For conscience, whatever is not forbidden is permitted. For conscience, there is no positive commandment. What is permitted is good. (Ibid., pp. 24–25.)

This world of disunion with God, conflict, and moral problems must be overcome in a reconciliation with man's origin; and this can be brought about only by Christ. But as soon as man is reunited with God through Christ, the law as that which teaches us the difference between what is permissible and what is forbidden, what is good and what is evil, immediately becomes meaningless. A man cannot live simultaneously in reconciliation and in disunion, in freedom and under the law. There are no intermediate stages here; it is one thing or the other. (Ibid., p. 25.) After the reconciliation through Christ has taken place, a man has to do only one thing: to do the will of God. This will is not known to him by "intuition"; he must search for it. However, one thing is certain, the will of God is not a system of rules that is established once and for all. The will of God "is something new and different in each different situation in life, and for this reason a man must ever anew examine what the will of God may be." (Ibid., p. 36.)

This view brings Bonhoeffer very close to a basic thesis of Kierkegaard and to what Grisebach called "situation ethics."

As we have seen, according to this view there are no universal rules or judgments that can "automatically" guide our moral behavior; each moral problem is unique and must be decided individually on its own condition. Almost in the same sense, Bonhoeffer writes that the question of good and evil always finds us in a situation that cannot be reversed. This means that we can no longer raise and answer the question of good and evil as though we had first of all to create what is beautiful and good. It is as creatures, and not as creators, that we inquire about good and evil. "The question of good is posed and is decided in the midst of each definite, yet unconcluded, unique, and transient situation of our lives, in the midst of our living relationships with men, things, institutions, and powers, in other words, in the midst of our historical existence. The question of good cannot now be separated from the question of life, the question of history. Ethical thought is still largely dominated by the abstract notion of an isolated individual man who applies the absolute criterion of a good that is good in itself. . . . These isolated individuals do not exist, and we do not dispose over any such absolute criterion of a good that is good in itself; nor do good and evil display themselves in history in their pure form. . . ." (Ibid., pp. 214–15.)

Many people believe that situation ethics teaches that ethics is concerned with man's personality and with this personality only, and that all other things of the world remain untouched by this ethos. Bonhoeffer strongly objects to this view and defends the thesis that a Christian ethics can and must make assertions with regard to worldly institutions and conditions such as the State, economics, science, etc. (Ibid., pp. 320–21.)

The following selection was taken from *No Rusty Swords*. The selection is an essay that Bonhoeffer wrote while he was in Barcelona, in 1929. At that time, he became interested in finding a theological foundation for ethics, a problem that was to occupy him until his death. His main concern was to find a way to dispense with the outworn codes of a previous generation ("rusty swords") and to fashion ethical attitudes to match contemporary moral problems.

WHAT IS A CHRISTIAN ETHIC?

Dietrich Bonhoeffer

We will speak today of the basic questions raised by the demand for a Christian ethic, not by making the attempt to lay down generally valid, Christian norms and precepts in contemporary ethical questions—which is in any case completely hopeless—but rather by examining and entering into the characteristic trend of contemporary ethical problems in the light of fundamental Christian ideas. The reason for a limitation of this nature lies in the fact, still to be elaborated in detail, that there are not and cannot be Christian norms and principles of a moral nature; the concepts of 'good' and 'evil' exist only on the completion of an action, i.e. at any specific present, and hence any attempt to lay down principles is like trying to draw a bird in flight. But more of this later.

Ethics is a matter of history; it is not simply something which has descended from heaven to earth, but is rather a child of the earth. For this reason it changes its appearance with the trends of history and the shift of generations. There is a German ethic and a French ethic, just as there is an American ethic, and none is more ethical or less ethical than the others, but all are firmly fixed in the nexus of history, and all have in our time been decisively influenced by the

From pp. 39–48 of *No Rusty Swords*, by Dietrich Bonhoeffer, edited by Edwin H. Robertson, translated by Edwin H. Robertson and John Bowden. Copyright © 1965 in the English translation by William Collins Sons & Co. Ltd., London, and Harper & Row, Publishers, Inc., New York. By permission of Harper & Row, Publishers.

tremendous experience of the world war, as it has been seen through different eyes. . . .

We said that there was a German, a French, an American ethic, for ethics is a matter of blood and of history. But in that case how does the idea of a so-called *Christian ethic* stand? Are these two words, Christian and ethic, not perhaps completely disparate? Does not the idea 'Christian' in this way become secularised, and the so-called Christian ethic become one alongside many, one of many, perhaps rather better or perhaps rather worse, but still in any event completely implicated in the relativity of history? In that case there is a Christian ethic as well as a German ethic, and neither of them is allowed to lay claim to superiority. It is therefore extremely hazardous to speak of a Christian ethic and at the same time to maintain the absolute claim for such an ethic.

In the last address a remark was made which was perhaps not completely comprehensible: that Christianity was basically amoral, i.e. that Christianity and ethics were in fact divergent entities. And why? Because Christianity speaks of the single way of God to man, from the merciful love of God for unrighteous men and sinners, and because ethics speaks of the way of man to God, of the encounter of the holy God with unholy man; because the Christian message speaks of grace and ethics speaks of righteousness. There are countless ways from man to God, and therefore there are also countless ethics, but there is only one way from God to man, and that is the way of love in Christ, the way of the cross. The question of Christianity is not the question of good and evil in man, but the question whether it is God's will to be gracious or not. The Christian message stands beyond good and evil; and that must be the case, for should the grace of God be made dependent upon the extent of man's good or evil, the basis would be laid for a claim of man upon God, and in this way God's sole power and glory would be assailed. It is an extremely profound thing that in the old story of the Fall, the reason for the Fall is eating from the tree of the knowledge of good and evil. The original—shall we say childlike—communion between God and man stands beyond this knowledge of good and evil; it knows only of one thing, of the boundless love of God towards man. Thus the discovery of what is beyond good and evil was not made by Friedrich Nietzsche, who from this standpoint utters polemics against the hyprocrisy of Christianity; it belongs to the original material of the Christian message, concealed, of course, as it is.

If the argument up to this point is correct, then the conclusion appears to be quite clear: Christianity and ethics do indeed have nothing to do with one another; there is no Christian ethic and there can be no transition from the idea of Christianity to that of ethics. Yet it is immediately obvious that at this point we are on the wrong track. For we must ask, Why then are the Gospels full of evidently ethical directions? What business does the Sermon on the Mount have in the New Testament? The question, obvious as it is important, which confronts us is: What is the significance of the so-called New Testament ethic?

Since the third and fourth centuries there have always been movements which gave out that the preaching of a new ethic was the centre of Christianity, and the new commandment was the commandment of love. Such a view, while of course superficial, was possible and tenable right up to the last century. Since, however, investigations into the history of religion and literature have concerned themselves exhaustively with the Rabbinic literature of the time of Jesus and earlier, and with the philosophical and ethical tractates of the philosophical schools of that time, it may be held that to make such claims for the New Testament is demonstrably false. The commandment of love is not exclusively Christian, but was already generally recognised and widespread at the time of Jesus. . . .

Had the proclamation of this commandment really stood in the middle of Jesus' preaching, he would always have made a fresh beginning from this point. But that is not the case. This also emerges from a comparison of sayings of Jesus with the sayings of Jewish Rabbis and pagan philosophers, which are often similar, right down to their formulation. The Rabbi Hillel is asked what is the greatest commandment and he replies, 'Love your neighbour as yourself. That is the greatest commandment.' Another says, 'Do not do to another what you would not have done to yourself.' The Roman philosopher Seneca says, 'Let us not become weary of exerting ourselves for the general good, of helping individuals, of bringing aid even to our enemies.' To the objection, 'But anger affords pleasure. It is even more comfortable to requite pain,' he replies, 'No, it is honourable in charity to recompense good with good, but not so injustice with injustice. In the one it is disgraceful to let oneself be surpassed, in the other it is disgraceful to prove the victor.'

In that case, however, what now remains of a Christian ethic? Has the Sermon on the Mount really nothing new to say to us? Nothing 'new' in the sense of a new commandment, but at the same time something quite different. The significance of all Jesus' ethical commandments is rather to say to men: 'You stand before the face of God, God's grace rules over you; you are at the disposal of someone else in the world and for him you must act and work. So be mindful in your actions that you are acting under God's eyes, and that his will must needs be done. The nature of this will of God can only be clear in the moment of action; it is only important to be clear that every man's own will must be brought to be God's will, that his own will must be surrendered if God's will is to be realised, and therefore insofar as complete renunciation of personal claims is necessary in acting before the face of God, the Christian's ethical action can be described as love. But this is not a new principle; it derives from the place of man before God. For the Christian there are no ethical principles by means of which he could perhaps civilise himself. Nor can yesterday ever be decisive for my moral action today. Rather must a direct relationship to God's will be ever sought afresh. I do not do something again today because it seemed to me to be good yesterday, but because the will of God points out this way to me today. That is the great moral renewal through Jesus, the renunciation of principles, of rulings, in the words of the Bible, of the Law, and this follows as a consequence of the Christian idea of God; for if there was a generally valid moral law, then there would be a way from man to God—I would have my principles, so I would believe myself assured *sub specie aeternitatis*. So, to some extent, I would have control over my relationship to God, so there would be a moral action without immediate relationship to God. And, most important of all, in that case I would once again become a slave to my principles. I would sacrifice man's most precious gift, *freedom*.

When Jesus places men immediately under God, new and afresh at each moment, he restores to mankind the immense gift which it had lost, freedom. Christian ethical action is action from freedom, action from the freedom of a man who has nothing of himself and everything of his God, who ever and again lets his action be confirmed and endorsed by eternity. The New Testament speaks of this freedom in great words . . .

For the Christian there is no other law than the law of freedom, as the New Testament paradoxically puts it. No generally valid law which could be expounded to him by others, or even by himself. The man who surrenders freedom surrenders his very nature as a Christian. The Christian stands free, without any protection, before God and before the world, and he alone is wholly responsible for what he does with the gift of freedom. Now through this freedom the Christian becomes creative in ethical action. Acting in accordance with principles is unproductive, imitating the law, copying. Acting from freedom is creative. The Christian chooses the forms of his ethical action as it were from eternity, he puts them sovereign in the world, as his act, his creation from the freedom of a child of God. The Christian himself creates his standards of good and evil for himself. Only he can justify his own actions, just as only he can bear the responsibility. The Christian creates new tables, a new Decalogue, as Nietzsche said of the Superman. Nietzsche's Superman is not really, as he supposed, the opposite of the Christian; without knowing it, Nietzsche has here introduced many traits of the Christian made free, as Paul and Luther describe him. Time-honoured morals—even if they are given out to be the consensus of Christian opinion—can never for the Christian become the standard of his actions. He acts, because the will of God seems to bid him to, without a glance at the others, at what is usually called morals, and no one but himself and God can know whether he has acted well or badly. In ethical decision we are brought into the deepest solitude, the solitude in which a man stands before the living God. No one can stand beside us there, no one can take anything from us, because God lays on us a burden which we alone must bear. Our 'I' awakes only in the consciousness of being called, of being claimed by God. Only through the call of God does this 'I' become isolated from all others, drawn into responsibility by God, knowing myself to confront eternity alone. And because in the solitude I come face to face with God, I can only know for myself, completely personally, what is good and what is evil. There are no actions which are bad in themselves—even murder can be justified—there is only faithfulness to God's will or deviation from it; there is similarly no law in the sense of a law containing precepts, but only the law of freedom, i.e. of a man's bearing his responsibility alone before God and himself. But because the law remains superseded once for all and because it follows from the Christian idea of God that there can be no more law, the ethical commandments, the apparent laws of the New Testament must also be understood from this standpoint.

It is the greatest of misunderstandings to make the commandments of the Sermon on the Mount into laws once again by referring them literally to the present. This is not only senseless, because it is impracticable, but still more, it is against the spirit of Christ, who brought freedom from the law. The whole life of, say, Count Tolstoy and so many others has been lived under this misunderstanding. There are no ethical directions in the New Testament which we should have, or even could have, taken over literally. The letter kills, the spirit gives life, says Paul; that means, there is only spirit on the completion of the action, in the present; once fixed, the spirit is no longer spirit. Thus, too, there is ethics only on the completion of the act, not in the letter of the law. Now the spirit which is active in us in ethical action is said to be the Holy Spirit. The Holy Spirit is only in the present, in ethical decision, and not in fixed moral precepts, in ethical principles. For this reason, the new commandments of Jesus

can never be regarded merely as ethical principles; they are to
be understood in their spirit, not literally. And that is no
subterfuge, because things would otherwise be too uncom-
fortable; it is demanded by the idea of freedom and Jesus'
concept of God. That the demands of Jesus have got this
radical acuteness lies in the fact that the position of man in
ethical decision before God demands a radical repudiation
of his own person, his own will; but not every single one of
Jesus' rules of conduct is valid for us, otherwise the imitation
of them would be slavish and unfree. Now it follows from
all this that ethical problems of content can never be discussed in a Christian light; there is simply no possibility of
erecting generally valid principles, because each moment,
lived in God's sight, can bring an unexpected decision. Thus
even in our time only one thing can be repeated, over and
over again: in ethical decisions a man must put himself under
the will of God, he must consider his action *sub specie
aeternitatis* and then, however it turns out, it will turn out
rightly. Now, day by day, hour by hour, we are confronted
with unparalleled situations in which we must make a decision, and in which we make again and again the surprising
and terrifying discovery that the will of God does not reveal
itself before our eyes as clearly as we had hoped. This comes
about because the will of God seems to be self-contradictory,
because two ordinances of God seem to conflict with one
another, so that we are not in a position to choose between
good and evil, but only between one evil and another. And
here it is that the real, most difficult problems of ethics lie.
And if we set to work to deal with them, it is clear, after
what has been said, that we can give no generally valid decisions which we might then hold out to be the only Christian
ones, because in so doing we are only setting out new principles and coming into conflict with the law of freedom.
Rather can we only seek to be brought into the concrete situation of the decision and to show one of the possibilities of
decision which present themselves at that point. The decision which is really required must be made freely by each
person in the concrete situation . . .

We must break off and summarise. Ethics is a matter of

earth and of blood, but also of him who made both; the trouble arises from this duality. There can be ethics only in the framework of history, in the concrete situation, at the moment of the divine call, the moment of being addressed, of the claim made by the concrete need and the situation for decision, of the claim which I have to answer and for which I have to make myself responsible. Thus there cannot be ethics in a vacuum, as a principle; there cannot be good and evil as general ideas, but only as qualities of will making a decision. There can be only good and evil as done in freedom; principles are binding under the law. Bound up in the concrete situation, through God and in God the Christian acts in the power of a man who has become free. He is under no judgment but his own and that of God.

But through this freedom from the law, from principle, the Christian must enter into the complexity of the world; he cannot make up his mind *a priori*, but only when he himself has become involved in the emergency and knows himself called by God. He remains earthbound, even when his desire is towards God; he must go through all the anxiety before the laws of the world; he must learn the paradox that the world offers us a choice, not between good and evil, but between one evil and another, and that nevertheless God leads him to himself even through evil. He must feel the gross contradiction between what he would like to do and what he must do; he must grow mature through this distress, grow mature through not letting hold of God's hand, in the words 'Thy will be done'. A glimpse of eternity is revealed only through the depths of our earth, only through the storms of a human conscience. The profound old saga tells of the giant Antaeus, who was stronger than any man on earth; no one could overcome him until once in a fight someone lifted him from the ground; then the giant lost all the strength which had flowed into him through his contact with the earth. The man who would leave the earth, who would depart from the present distress, loses the power which still holds him by eternal, mysterious forces. The earth remains our mother, just as God remains our Father, and our mother will only lay in the Father's arms him who remains true to her. That is the Christian's song of earth and her distress.

All the examples which we have hitherto chosen have shown us that it is necessary for a man to be involved in the concrete situation and from there to direct his gaze towards eternity, contending afresh in the ambiguity of the situation always to decide in accordance with the will of God; the decision may then turn out as it will. And then ethics does not become once again a way from man to God, but remains like everything that men who know themselves to be freed from the world by Christ can do, a sacrifice, a demonstration of the weak will which springs from thankfulness for what God has done for us; a sacrifice, an offering, a demonstration which God can either accept or refuse; man's action springs from the recognition of the grace of God, towards mankind and towards himself, and man's action hopes for the grace of God which delivers him from the distress of the time. Thus the realm of grace builds itself over the ethical realm. This distress and anxiety of the conscience must find an end, the incomprehensible contradictions of the divine order in the world must become clear, if the kingdom of grace is to take the place of the kingdom of the world, the kingdom of God the place of the kingdom of man. Only the man who has once tasted the utter depth and distress of the kingdom of the world, the ethical realm, longs to be away, and he has one wish, 'Let this world pass away, thy kingdom come.'

SELECTIVE BIBLIOGRAPHY

Gesammelte Schriften, 4 vols. (München: Kaiser Verlag, 1960)
Act and Being (New York: Harper and Row, 1961)
Christ the Center (New York: Harper and Row, 1960)
The Communion of Saints (New York: Harper and Row, 1966)
The Cost of Discipleship (New York: Macmillan, 1966)
Ethics (New York: Macmillan, 1967)
Letters and Papers from Prison (New York: Macmillan, 1967)
No Rusty Swords: Letters, Lectures, and Notes, 1928–36, ed. E. H. Robertson (New York: Harper and Row, 1965)

E. Bethge, "The Challenge of Dietrich Bonhoeffer's Life and Theology," *The Chicago Theological Seminary Register* 60(1961), 1–38

W. Kuhns, *In Pursuit of Dietrich Bonhoeffer* (New York: Image Books, 1967)

Martin E. Marty, ed., *The Place of Bonhoeffer* (New York: Associates Press, 1964)

E. L. Massall, *The Secularization of Christianity* (New York: Holt, Rinehart, and Winston, 1965)

E. H. Robertson, *Dietrich Bonhoeffer* (Richmond, Va.: John Knox Press, 1967)

Benjamin A. Reist, *The Promise of Bonhoeffer* (Philadelphia: Lippincott Press, 1967)

Chapter 17

INTRODUCTION

HELMUT THIELICKE (1908–   ) received his education at Marburg, Erlangen, and Bonn, earning degrees in theology and philosophy. He taught theology at the University of Heidelberg from 1936 to 1940, when he was banned from his professorate by the Nazis. During the war he was active in the resistance movement and for a time was in internment in Ravensburg. In 1945 he became professor of theology and philosophy of religion at Tübingen; in 1954 he went to Hamburg, where he is still teaching. Thielicke has published a very important book on Lessing's philosophy of religion. In addition, he has written several books on theology: among others, *Der Glaube der Christenheit, Geschichte und Existenz,* and *Fragen des Cristentums an die moderne Welt.* His most important work is *Theologische Ethik.*

Thielicke defends a kind of situation ethics. What is to be done from a moral point of view cannot be decided on in advance. To decide ethical questions in advance is possible only within the framework of a natural law which pictures the world as an orderly construct, permeated by eternal norms laid down within the very structure of man and world once and for all. According to this view, the world taken as a whole becomes a hierarchical cosmos, and in principle every case that may arise and every decision that may be required can be prejudged morally by reason of a hierarchy of values. Such a conception of the world and the hierarchy of values, and thus such a conception of natural law, is unacceptable to Thielicke on strictly religious, or perhaps more accurately, theological grounds. We must keep in mind here the fact that Thielicke wrote a *theological* ethics, which makes it understandable why he rejects this view on typically theological grounds. His argument is directed mainly against the Catholic conception of natural law. The latter view presupposes that there is a specific interrelationship between man's original state and the fallen world in which he finds himself, thus between creation and sin. This relationship is determined by the fact that man's sin violates God's creation only in a peripheral way. According to the Reformation, however, the world is totally permeated by both creation and sin, so that it is impossible to suppose the fallen aeon to be still determined by the "orders of creation," and thus to subscribe to the illusion of a hierarchical cosmos of natural law. Furthermore, Thielicke argues, the view that we can ethically prejudge future cases leads necessarily to legalism and certainly not to an "evangelical view" of things. In that view, man is not the acting subject in the making of his own decisions; he becomes merely the object or the executor of a decision that has already been made by others, those in places of authority, or "the" church.

Obviously, Thielicke has other reasons for his view, but from a philosophical point of view these arguments do not seem to be immediately relevant. The conclusion to which Thielicke's criticism ultimately leads is the following: If there can be no legalistic ethics with preformed decisions, decisions must be made within the framework of each existing situation. The ethics of law is replaced by a kind of "situation ethics." According to Thielicke, what this term means can best be illustrated by a careful analysis of the "borderline situation of extreme conflict," "which demonstrates particularly well the absurdity, not merely of arriving by way of theory at advance decisions, but also of attempting in practice to subsume the 'circumstances' under hierarchically ordered norms. . . ." (*Theological Ethics*, pp. 648–50.)

The main reason for my choosing this selection is that Thielicke, unlike most people who write on situation ethics, clearly shows, as do Buber and Bonhoeffer, that the situation in which each man finds himself at each moment, is for the greater part determined by *historical* and *social* factors.

MEANING AND ANALYSIS
OF THE BORDERLINE SITUATION

Helmut Thielicke

. . . Theological ethics usually makes the mistake of taking the "normal case" as its standard for measuring reality. The result is the illusion that by providing certain Christian directives we have actually solved the problems. In ethics, however, the situation is similar to that in medicine. The problems do not arise with the ordinary cases, but with the borderline cases, those involving transitions or complications. It is the abnormal rather than the normal case which brings us up against the real problems. Hence the real test, even in respect of foundational principles, is whether an ethics has been proved in the crucible of the borderline situation and emerged with even deeper insights.

Thus a doctrine of the orders will receive its inner movement and depth from the very fact that it deals with concrete disorders. Similarly, the doctrine of justification and sanctification will have to prove itself by submitting to the acid test of whether and how far it can be practiced in an underground movement of resistance against a perverted government, a movement which cannot get on without lying, deception, and falsehood. If our doctrine of the divine commandments applies only in a Christian culture or a democratic society, but is helpless when the times are "out of joint," what we have is not a doctrine of *God's* commandments at all but simply a religious and ideological superstructure extrapolated out of the "normal" situation.

This essay is from *Theological Ethics*, by Helmut Thielicke, trans. William H. Lazareth (Philadelphia, 1966), pp. 578–604. Copyright © 1966 by Fortress Press.

The Theological Relevance of the Borderline Situation

On the drawing board all ethical problems may be represented with relative ease. This may be seen from the available handbooks. The ease of representation is due to the fact that reality is first of all illegitimately reduced to that which is normal. To put it even less charitably, reality is robbed of the element of caricature; it is divested of its perversion, of its disorderliness. This means that ethics is deprived of its usefulness, inasmuch as the general tendency is for men to turn to ethics for guidance in critical and unusual situations, when available schemes provide no answer to the question "What shall we do?" (Acts 2:37). But the impairing of its usefulness is not the most serious consequence. Beyond that, ethics is also divested of those questions and problems which are theologically decisive.

When the "world" is seen with the normal spectacles of the nature aesthete it is all too easy to contrive a natural theology. But how does this business of natural theology, and its underlying principle of the analogy of being, stand up in the face of earthquakes, air raids, and a few other riddles of history?

It is easy, almost dangerously easy, to speak of the "orders of creation"—and of obedience to "authority" as one such order—when what we have in view is the "ideal" case involving a Christian society and a ruler who is at the same time the foremost member of the church. But what happens in an age such as that of Hitler and Stalin? Do we not have to recognize that the firm stance taken in actual practice at the time of these critical situations could have basic implications for theory as well, and that theology and ethics could have been thrown at this point into a crucible of massive dimensions?

This is the more to be expected because it is in the borderline situation of injustice, where sin is institutionalized as it were, that we learn in no uncertain terms that "this aeon" is not shot through with stable "orders of creation" which have a kind of indelible character and can serve as our standard of measurement. The possibility of total corruption is an indication that there is no such thing as those ontic relics of creation, and that the orders are simply a macrocosmic reflection or objectification of the human heart. And just as a firm line cannot be drawn between creation and sin in the individual heart, so it is impossible to draw any such line in the macrocosmic dimension.

This means that institutionalized evil, the borderline case in which injustice has taken on structural form, is not just a marginal possibility. It is not just an exception, a deviation from the true nature of this aeon. On the contrary—and this is a far cry from all ideology of the orders—it is simply an extreme example of a constitutional perversion of the aeon. So it is not a proclivity for dramatizing the exceptional which leads us to begin with an analysis of the borderline situation. In adopting such an approach we are simply being objective, true to the facts, the fact of the "world" as it is.

It is perhaps because our ethical and theological theories are here forced to undergo an unprecedented death and renewal that treatments of ethics have constantly avoided this issue like a hot potato. There seems to be an unwritten law that one does not speak about certain problems, e.g., the theological problems of an underground movement. Such problems are too painful and shocking. They must be relegated to the private sphere of the quiet chamber, where the most personal decisions of conscience are made. But this chamber is supposed to be a place of prayer, not just a closet for junk or for depositing whatever the theological professor wants to discard from his classroom, whatever he does not wish to be seen—or cannot find a place for—in the sacred precincts of academic theology.

Accepting, then, the thesis of Tillich that the border or boundary [Grenze] is the most fruitful place for gaining knowledge, we first turn to the question of what is meant by the "borderline situation" [Grenzsituation].

THE MEANING OF THE TERM "BORDERLINE"

The concept itself derives from Karl Jaspers, and, although we do not mean to take over all that he has said, we would like to adapt for our theological purposes certain significant elements in his thought.[1]

For Jaspers borderline situations are those in which I cannot live without conflict and suffering, in which I take upon myself unavoidable guilt, in which I must die. What happens when I accept and endure such situations is that I enter into confrontation with myself. I cause being to "surge up" in me. Apart from such situations I do not exist; I simply vegetate. "We become ourselves as we enter into the borderline situations with open eyes . . . to experience borderline situations and to exist are one and the same thing."[2] Only as I stand up to such situations do I cease to live merely in the moment, staggering blindly from one moment to the next along my line of time. Only thus do I grasp myself as a totality, since it is only from the perspective of my boundary or border— only from guilt, suffering, and death, the "outermost" limit of my existence—that I can see myself as a whole. Whether I consciously lay hold of my existence or fail to do so is determined wholly in view of this boundary and solely from the perspective it affords. Only as I stand at this outer limit does my existence become a question for me, and therewith the object of inquiry. It ceases to be the non-objective wrapper which envelops me so tightly that I simply vegetate inside without any awareness of it.[3] Now it seems to me important that we should apply to the mode of being of the whole aeon these thoughts about the boundary or border which Jaspers has expressed in respect only of individual existence. This we could do, of course, without even mentioning the concepts of Jaspers. For the thesis that the boundary is the place of knowledge, and hence—in modern terms—the only place at which I can consciously lay hold of my existence and experience it as the object of decision, is no new discovery. As regards knowledge of the world, for example, it is quite plainly found in the Bible. For what the world is, and what man is within the world, is apparent—in the strict sense—only in the

---

[1] See Karl Jaspers, *Philosophie* (Berlin, 1932), II, 201 ff., esp. 220 ff.

[2] Ibid., p. 204.

[3] Ibid., p. 209.

light of the boundary or limit, i.e., of the fact that the world comes from the hand of the creator and ends on the last day. In other words, it is revealed eschatologically. No statement can be made concerning the world, its guilt, freedom, orders, or history, except with reference to this beginning and this end.

In the light of this it would seem obvious that the "boundary" is not to be understood simply in terms of a temporal horizon embracing the beginning of the world and also its end. It involves also a qualitative horizon, as it were, first in the sense of what God has invested in the world by way of creation, by making man in his own image and by making the phenomena of creation to serve as transparencies for "his eternal power and deity," and second in the sense of what the world has become after the fall, in the extreme perversion of the orders and in times of crisis when sin is not merely present in individual acts but has become crystallized, as it were, into the very form of the world itself.

Here too, then, we are confronted by two limits or boundaries of the world, in the light of which it may clearly be seen in its totality, i.e., in its ultimate possibilities and hence also in its very nature. On the one hand, there is that which was posited in the world as the possibility of creation, that wherein it should attain to its authentic being, truly actualizing God's original plan. On the other hand, there is that which it bears within itself as the extreme possibility of decline and fall, of chaos, and of misappropriation of that wherewith it was endowed at creation.

Somewhere between these two limits stands the world as it is. This is why we think it makes sense to apply to the world, to the aeon in its totality, that which Jaspers describes as the "borderline situation" of individual existence. In other words, there is value in seeing the world in the light of this extreme limit of its possibility, whereby it is confronted with the theme of the destiny which it has missed but which is still set before it, and consequently with the task of understanding itself and of adopting an attitude towards itself.

The borderline situation is thus an instructive example in terms of which to study the fact of the fallen world and to put the problem of ethics in its sharpest form. Here it will become clear whether we did right in rejecting the normativeness of the original order and its natural law on the grounds that we could not find any "formula of transformation" whereby to apply the laws of man's primal state before the fall to the completely different world after the fall. Here it will also become evident whether we were right to follow the New Testament and the Reformation in understanding the fall in such radical terms, as wholly characterizing the order of this world, an order which thus stands in need of forgiveness, and hence to interpret the normative directives given to the world as merely negative imperatives.

This ethical situation is expressed particularly well in the underground movements of the Second World War, especially those in Holland and France, in which Christians took a leading part. The constant problem of underground ethics is that of "behavior in illegality," the question of how to act obediently where injustice reigns supreme. It is the question of how one can expect and claim for himself the forgiveness of God in a world of lies in which it is apparently no longer clear at all what truth means and how it is to be told, a world of the "black market" in which illegal methods of doing business are routinely followed, etc.

The possibility, indeed the necessity of breaking the law of human order—and not just the law of the land but in some cases even the moral law—in order to obey the Law of God, such "legitimate illegality" presupposes a state of injustice in which the fallen nature of the world assumes a particularly extreme and paradigmatic form. "Here law and justice may be so far apart that the former still insists upon being dutifully observed even when it is in fact nothing but codified injustice."[4]

The most distinguishing feature of this state of injustice and illegality is to be found in the inescapable conflict of values for which there is no clear solution, so that whichever way I go I am guilty. . . .

4 Dietrich Oehler, "Die Achtung vor dem Leben und die Notstandshandlung," in *Juristische Rundschau* (1951), XVI, 1.

THE ANALYSIS OF BORDERLINE SITUATIONS

The analysis of borderline situations is best accomplished with the help of the most pertinent possible examples. As a criterion in the selection of these examples we may use the question of how committed Christians—men who were not only aware of the theological responsibility of their decision but also reflected on it—faced up to classical instances of the borderline situation, even though they may have perished in so doing.

We choose this method because of the danger that a purely theoretical and detached approach may involve an oversimplification which can be wholly misleading. To discuss the borderline situation purely in terms of principle, to sketch it, as it were, on the drawing board, is to reduce the actual frictions to which it is subject. Here, if anywhere, we must draw on both sources of knowledge: the perspective afforded by the "existential" threat involved in the borderline situation (which is more than merely a threat to physical existence) and the more aloof and disinterested "theoretical" point of view. The two modes of consideration supplement one another, since each alone has its own particular failings.

The perspective of existential threat is insufficient of itself, for there is a danger that elements of personal weakness will impair the objectivity of decision. The decision may be prejudiced, for example, by anxiety, by a misunderstanding of the situation, or by tactical considerations. When it comes to the question of how Christians ought to decide in a given instance, however, these defects in the concrete situation should not be allowed to deceive us into thinking that the solutions attempted by so-called "prominent" Christians can simply be taken over and made normative, for this would be to misuse them in the manner of legal casuistry. The so-called "prominent" Christians were far too clearly aware of their own fallibility—and of the need that they be forgiven for the decisions they did make—to allow us to treat them casuistically as models to be imitated.

On the other hand, aloof theoretical consideration is also

insufficient of itself, because it cannot take into account specific factors which have also to be decided on the spur of the moment. Thus it is very easy (and can lead us almost to the verge of triviality) to subscribe in the abstract to the saying of Theodor Storm: "One man asks what will be the result, another asks simply is it right; and the difference distinguishes the free man from the slave." This saying has a radically different ring when "the result" involves the lives of many innocent people, when time or new possibilities of negotiation may sometimes be won by compromise, or when out of regard for the prestige of others all doors are not slammed shut but the possibility of retreat is left open in order that the other person may not lose face.

This is why, after 1945, many Germans felt it was far too facile and hence quite illegitimate for neutrals, and for others who had not had to live under a dictatorship and face the dangers involved, to pass sweeping judgments on the "collective guilt" of Germany. Even the factual correctness of this kind of judgment was necessarily felt to be pharisaical by those whose objectivity had been exposed to unheard-of frictions, not merely in terms of such non-objective emotional elements as anxiety and the instinct of self-preservation, but also in terms of conflicts within the region of actual facts, the confusing complications in the way that problems were posed, and the inability to find any obvious criteria for the decisions which had to be made. Even where they themselves were conscious of guilt, they were not disposed to allow this guilt to be foisted upon them by voices from "off stage."

True appreciation of the situation in which decision must be made is thus possible only when we approach it from both standpoints. The existential perspective and the theoretical point of view are both essential for a truly adequate analysis.

CONCRETE FORMS OF CONFLICT

The borderline situation is characterized above all by the fact that in it one is confronted by an opponent who is known to be bent wholly on the exercise of power, and who is obviously on the side of evil. The best examples of such a situation are thus to be found in countries which have been occupied by the representatives of an ideological tyranny. For while the countries in which the tyranny originates undergo a gradual development under the despotism so that they tend to become accustomed to dictatorship, to lose the clarity of judgment afforded by distance, and to be deceived as to its final goal by innumerable tactical tricks, the countries occupied at a later date at least have the chance of arriving at what is essentially a more dispassionate diagnosis.

To fight such an opponent is an obvious duty. But if this is so, the duty is one which can be fulfilled only as we adopt the methods of the opponent. One must necessarily—and this means willingly going against one's own will—share in the depravity of these methods, i.e., get one's hands dirty. The church as such may be obliged to suffer wrong rather than do wrong; it can hardly be said to have the right of putting up political resistance. But by the same token the individual Christian who is called to political responsibility is ineluctably forced into a situation in which he must act within a framework of injustice. As Gebhard Müller, minister-president of Baden-Württemberg, has put it, "He cannot sit back with folded hands and watch the forces of the abyss devastate and destroy his land, the people committed to his care, and the values which he holds sacred." . . .

. . . The essential marks of the borderline situation are as follows. First, the struggle against the blatant representative of injustice is not a personal struggle against a personal enemy but a struggle to preserve orders, values, and the lives of men from external destruction and internal perversion; to make this struggle is thus an inescapable duty. Second, the struggle against the blatant representative of injustice can be carried on only if to a certain degree, which cannot be calculated in advance, one is prepared to use his methods (and thus to incur a measure of guilt), methods which have a logic of their own and a tendency progressively to limit one's freedom of action. Third, the whole sphere of methods or means is thus shown to stand in need of forgiveness. Fourth, the ability to act in this sphere without hatred implies that while one's external actions are indeed bound by the logic of methods, he himself as a Christian never looks upon the opponent as a mere agent of these methods but—in the manner of Francis Drake—as a child of God who has been bound by the chains of evil and thus gone astray; there thus persists a human sphere which is not swallowed up in the autonomous machinery of the conflict.

Having thus surveyed the fundamental structure of the borderline situation, we may now try to gain some impression of its most important variations. There is in fact a certain typology of the borderline situation which arises out of the different values at issue in the conflict.

THE CONFLICT BETWEEN LIFE AND TRUTH

The experiences encountered in rendering illegal assistance to the Jews during the National Socialist persecutions afford classic and terrifying examples of the conflict between life and truth. Such assistance sometimes took the form of striking names from the proscribed list, or of adding them to groups which were not earmarked for liquidation. A high price was exacted by the Gestapo for these steps. Men adopted such dubious means with a sense of anguish about having thus to plunge into direct association with evil without any knowledge of how it might all turn out. But it seemed more important to extend a brotherly hand to the persecuted than to avoid at all costs any personal contamination by association with criminals.[5]

Important from the standpoint of the character of the borderline case in ethics are the means used and the law of logical progression in respect of these means. For example, it was first arranged with an eye clinic to receive a proscribed girl on the staff without her having to report to the police or the rations office. But to get there she had to have a pass which would enable her to secure a railroad ticket. Arrangements were then made for another woman to lend her own pass for this purpose. But this was not enough. The pass could be used only if it were counterfeited. Its owner insisted, too, that the name and number be altered slightly. So a counterfeiter had to be sought. In addition, arrangements had to be

[5] See Helene Jacobs, "Illegalität aus Verantwortung. Dr. Franz Kaufmann zum Gedächtnis," *Unterwegs*, III (1947), 10 ff.

made with the underworld to purchase ration cards, which in some cases had themselves been stolen. In addition, it was often found necessary in dealings with others to connect the assumed name with a detailed life history, which in many cases had to be very far from the truth in order to appear natural and credible. Often those who helped also had to act out a part. In their association with illegality, however, they found their true existence, while the externally inviolate part of their life became increasingly unreal. So it was that they came to be involved in a complete inversion of truth and falsehood, as these were normally understood. The borderline situation can thus bring about a complete reversal of all values, a reversal which is itself nonetheless genuine.[6]

THE CONFLICT BETWEEN LIFE AND LIFE

There are many forms of the conflict between life and life. The best-known is perhaps in relation to the medical problem of a dangerous pregnancy, namely, whether to save the life of the mother or the life of the child.

In view of the techniques of interrogation used by the modern totalitarian state, which involve both torture and the administration of drugs, the same problem arises in the form of the question whether one who has "fallen among thieves" and is in danger of being reduced by chemical means to a depersonalized talking machine is justified in taking his own life. Is it right to sacrifice one's own life in order to protect the lives of others whom he might involuntarily betray by talking? The fact that Carl Goerdeler, for example, when he was in a deranged state and personally no longer responsible, supplied hundreds of names of fellow conspirators and thus condemned them to certain death, shows that what is involved here is a real conflict. We cannot lightly pass judgment on the readiness to make such sacrifice in terms of its being "suicide." "If a prisoner takes his life for fear that under torture he might betray his country, his family or his friend, or if the enemy threaten reprisals unless a certain statesman is surrendered to them and it is only by his own free death that this statesman can spare his country grievous harm, then

[6] Cf. also Gertrud Staewen, "Bilder aus der illegalen Judenhilfe," *Unterwegs*, III (1947), 20 ff.

the self-killing is so strongly subject to the nature of sacrifice that it will be impossible to condemn the deed."[7]

This form of the borderline case, involving the conflict between life and life, is most clearly displayed in an example which is used by Eugen Kogon: "When the SS demanded that the political prisoners in the concentration camps should quickly determine which of their fellow prisoners were 'unfit' —that they might be summarily executed—and threatened that any delay in making the selection would result in an even harsher system of sanctions, there had to be *a readiness to shoulder guilt* [italics by Kogon]. The only choice was between active participation and an abdication of responsibility which, as experience showed, could only bring down even greater evil. The more tender the conscience, the harder was the decision."[8] According to Kogon, Christians were usually unable to make it: "Since it had to be made, and made quickly, it was better that the less sensitive spirits should make it, lest all should become martyrs and none be left to bear witness. Who would dare to condemn such comrades?"

We can correctly assess the dilemma involved in such a conflict situation only if we compare it with the externally similar case of a doctor condemned at Nuremberg.[9] A doctor in a mental institution listed a portion of his patients for extermination in order to make sure that the SS doctor who would otherwise replace him might not condemn all the patients to death. Here too what is involved is the readiness to do wrong in order to prevent an incomparably greater wrong.[10] Yet the case is quite different in principle from that described by Kogon.

[7] Dietrich Bonhoeffer, *Ethics*, ed. Eberhard Bethge, trans. Neville Horton Smith (New York: Macmillan, 1955), p. 126.

[8] Eugen Kogon, *Der SS-Staat* (Berlin, 1947), pp. 343 ff.

[9] See Oehler, op. cit., pp. 3 f.

[10] Many of the church's social missions institutions were confronted by a similar problem (e.g., Bethel, Bielefeld). In order to protect imbeciles, mental patients, and epileptics, they falsified lists, forged death certificates, used every kind of delaying tactic . . . but in the end had to send a hundred, two hundred, a thousand, two thousand to die in order—as it turned out—to rescue ten thousand others from a similar fate. See Kurt Pergande, *Der Einsame von Bethel* (Stuttgart, 1953), p. 157.

In the first place, the command to exterminate the mentally ill was an administrative one, which the doctor concerned could have avoided by resigning his position. Strict obedience to medical ethics, which demands the saving of life rather than its destruction, would certainly have had the force of a demonstration which might have encouraged other doctors to make similar resolves, even though in this particular case the result may have been the ruthless bloodletting of the SS doctor. Readiness to do wrong in order to "prevent something worse" is a very dubious principle, because it implies that the end justifies the means, and because it reposes no confidence in one's own confession and its creative power really to prevent that "something worse" or to bring it under condemnation. Oehler is quite right when he says, "If one believes that the killing of people affords the only way out of a tragic situation, then one must be ready to accept the legal responsibility for it. After all, expiation implies supreme recognition of man as a person; for only man may make expiation, beasts cannot. To take from man the legal responsibility for such action would be to replace guilt by fate."[11] For this would be, not to avert guilt—as "something worse"—but to falsify the whole affair, turn it into a metaethical natural process. The matter of punishing the guilt incurred under such pressures is, of course, a wholly different question.

This case of the doctor can thus be subsumed under fairly clear legal norms. But, as regards the legal and moral criteria, the situation involving killings in the concentration camp is far different. Here it is quite impossible for those compelled to assist in the killing to "resign." Nor is it possible to save the condemned by refusing to co-operate. In view of the total and unrestricted powers of the camp commandant there is in fact the certain prospect that the others will be killed too, and that the command to "survive," which goes far beyond the mere instinct of self-preservation, will thus be violated.

Here too, of course, personal confession and the readiness to sacrifice oneself and all the rest rather than to share in doing wrong is a genuine ethical possibility, in some cases even a binding command. We cannot overlook this aspect of the

[11] Oehler, loc. cit.

gruesome situation. For we owe even to the worst of criminals the preaching of judgment, trusting that the Spirit of God still holds open the possibility of repentance. Yet what preaching of judgment could be more massive and forceful than that done through the sacrifice of one's own life and the lives of others, through the witness of refusing to participate in the killing of people?

This particular line of action, however, cannot be required of everybody. For the contrary decision also has its ethical justification. Furthermore, to take just an example, it is up to each individual to decide whether beyond a certain point the criminal who has rejected every appeal to repent should yet be given one more opportunity, or whether instead he should now be made solely responsible for what must take place. However this individual may decide that question, there can be no doubt that every such decision stands under an ineluctable burden of guilt which apart from forgiveness would be quite unbearable.

THE CONFLICT BETWEEN OUR OBLIGATION TO PEOPLE IN GENERAL AND A PARTICULAR OATH OF LOYALTY

It may be that I can preserve a life, the life of my nation or neighbor, only by trying to overthrow the total order which threatens this life and which is intrinsically corrupt. It may be that I have to become a revolutionary, with all that this entails. It may be that, among other things, I have to break my oath of allegiance.

Military and civil oaths of allegiance pose a particularly complicated ethical problem. I can of course argue that such an oath always involves a mutual obligation. If the state to which I have given it becomes a criminal state it thereby dissolves the oath *de facto*, thereby releasing me from obligation, so that in the strict sense it is quite impossible to speak of my "breaking" an oath at all. This would be a case analogous to that in which all claim to truth was forfeited.

Yet it is not often that the problem arises in a form so simple and comparatively clear. As a rule the oath is given to a state which is already manifestly unjust, so that the state's injustice cannot exempt me from keeping my oath but actu-

ally makes my guilt very real if I do break it. The real ethical decision thus takes place at the point where with open eyes
I take an oath which I cannot keep with a good conscience.[12]
Here there is a clear ethical situation—if this business of keeping my "eyes open" is really that clear and simple. In practice,
even this is always a very complicated matter. For a state
which is manifestly evil is never totally evil. It discharges a
certain function of order which I cannot wholly ignore and
which carries with it a claim to my support. This support is
also to some degree unavoidable inasmuch as the totalitarian
state is usually hermetically sealed against escape. Indeed
within it there is not even a desert to which I can resort and
where I can hide. Unless I am prepared to condemn myself
and my family to destruction, and to leave only the evil men
and supine collaborators alive, I must work out some kind
of *modus vivendi*. Concretely, this means that I cannot rule
out altogether the venture of taking an oath.

We are not to overlook, of course, the two conditions on
which such a compromise—for that is what it is—seems to be
possible. First, there is the explicit proviso, "to the extent
that my Christianity will allow." (This condition could be
fulfilled vicariously through the church's making a corresponding declaration, as was done in connection with the oath taken
by Karl Barth in 1934.) Second, there is the readiness to apply
this restriction in concrete and flagrant cases of injustice.

The conflict in respect to oaths may thus be described as
a conflict between the life entrusted to me (that of my nation
or my neighbor) and my oath of loyalty. Am I not set here
between the Scylla and Charybdis of two responsibilities? On
the one hand, I am guilty if I break the oath for, although
I may be personally justified or even under obligation to do
so, I thereby help to destroy the public validity of the oath,
its power to establish social order. On the other hand, I am
plunged into guilt in a different way if, bound by my oath,
I look on passively while a group of criminals which has

---

[12] An example is the swearing in of the German V*olkssturm* near
the end of the Second World War, when the corruption of the system
which exacted the oath was no longer a potential future development but an accomplished fact.

seized power leads the life entrusted to me to physical and moral destruction.

Christians in the German underground movement were faced by this most difficult conflict. On neither side does there seem to be any easy solution, at least *in re*. Deliverance which is purchased by weakening the validity of oaths, and which will have a disruptive and unsettling effect, especially among those who do not responsibly undergo the rigors of the conflict, is in any case a very doubtful deliverance. But loyalty to a dubious oath, which allows me to be a passive spectator while life goes down to destruction, is also a very doubtful loyalty.

At the Nuremberg trials power politics and propaganda may have caused the thesis to be propounded that morally the only possible course would have been to resist by breaking the oath. Such a judgment, however, should not blind us to the fact that what is involved here is a genuine conflict, one for which no stock solution is possible, and that for this reason the solutions actually proposed and implemented through the personal decision of various individuals could be and were quite different.

The pastoral situation involved in such cases of conflict will always confront the counselor with the fact—and I speak from experience—that he does not have authority to prescribe a specific solution, even though he himself may personally decide in favor of a particular course. He would be a hireling rather than a shepherd if he were to use such authority as he has with the inquirer to make binding upon him this purely personal decision, a decision which cannot be transmitted to anybody else because it is not based on objective criteria. What for one is a response in obedience, a decision ventured in the assurance of forgiveness, might well be for the other a reckless adventure, an act of irresponsibility, or even the line of least resistance.

The typology of the borderline situation, which we have been describing with the help of typical examples, is still incomplete. Many other forms of the conflict might be added, e.g., the question which became only too common as foreign troops began to occupy Germany during World War II, whether a father should kill his wife and daughters rather than allow them to be ravished. But what has been said will suffice to give us some impression of what is actually involved in the situation of thoroughgoing injustice. To the detailed observations already made, and the comments supplied in part by persons who were themselves actually involved, we shall now attempt to add a theological exposition of these phenomena.

A Theological Interpretation of the Borderline Situation

The first point concerning the borderline situation, as has been repeatedly suggested, is that it does not leave open any way of escape. For example, when I am under hostile interrogation, and the fate of a great cause and the destiny of living men lie in my hands, I have to make a choice. Either I "mislead" the opponent or I surrender my cause and my friends. The concept of "misleading" can here include, as we have seen, a wide variety of ethical qualities.

The demonic power, with its usual perspicacity, has also recognized the impossibility of any direct escape. One clear indication of this is the fact that ideological states nowadays artificially create a conflict situation as a tactical means of crippling their opponents. Their diabolical analysis thus leads them to the same conclusions as those of the theological observer. . . .

The second point is that the guilt which we take upon us in the borderline situation constantly increases, that it necessarily gives rise to fresh evil. It is a truism that one untruth sets off a chain reaction of further untruths; a web of lies is never complete but always requires continued spinning. . . .

If the voter in the Soviet Zone should desire the unity of Germany, then a vote in favor of such union is also necessarily a vote for the next step in that direction, i.e., to approve the particular power which has seized the initiative towards this unity as it conceives it, namely, Communism. The conflict situation always issues in a suprapersonal nexus of guilt which not only fixes the course of my own continued sinning but also forces others—perhaps children and relatives—to pursue the same course. Inevitably therefore the time must come when an ideological dictatorship can establish itself, when the personal rot and social decay are such as only a universal guilt could have produced, and these in turn with the passing of time themselves call forth a new sharing of guilt which is greater at every stage than what preceded, intensified by a process of demonic dialectic, a devilish circle.

The process involved here points essentially to a theological circumstance which will repeatedly occupy our attention, namely, that wherever there is a borderline situation we must speak not only of a fate which comes upon us but also of a guilt in which we are implicated. This guilt consists in the fact that our origin and point of departure is always to be found in a complex of wrong decisions, those made by ourselves and by others.

The fact that conflict situations and conflicts of values exist at all in this world is not due to the "structure" of the world itself. More accurately, it is not due to the character imparted to the world by creation, as though "from the beginning" (Matt. 19:8) this included tragic features. It is due rather to the complex of wrong decisions which lie behind us, which have their ultimate root in that primal decision recorded in the story of the fall.

It is not that "the world" is so perverse that it constantly thrusts us into borderline situations. It is rather that man has perverted his world, and no man is exempt from sharing responsibility for this human character of his world, this demonic humanizing of the world. No man is merely the object of a conflict situation. We are all part of the human subject that has helped to bring it about.

Every sin passes over somehow into the suprapersonal sphere and assumes an "aeonic" form. It becomes part of the structure of the world. It becomes, for example, the institutional lie, which atmospherically envelops and pollutes the individual attitude toward truth. As "the best of us cannot live in peace unless it pleases his wicked neighbor," so I am implicated in falsehood and disloyalty if the form of the world—which I have helped to create—secures power over me.

Thus freedom and necessity, volition and ineluctability, are all wrapped up in a single package labeled, not "tragedy," but "original sin." . . .

The third point is that, so far as our guilt *in re* is concerned, in the borderline situation we are in danger of succumbing to the law of the inclined plane. By "inclined plane" we mean that our descending to the level of illegality, our readiness to incur guilt, or the hard and unwelcome realization that we must incur guilt, entails unforseeable consequences, not merely in the sense that guilt has disruptive sociological and institutional effects but also in the sense that it is itself subject to the law of progression. To illustrate the downward movement which it initiates, we may refer to an example of torture adduced . . . by Alexander Miller.[13] In this connection Miller distinguishes two logical steps.

The first is the resolve to use torture. This resolve has its origin in the conflict between two considerations. On the one hand, we may treat our opponent with humanity, and in so doing perhaps miss getting the vital information which might have been secured under the pressure of torture. On the other hand, we may decide to use torture in order to fulfill our human duty to our neighbors and the obligations of service to our cause.

The second step consists in the readiness to torture the family of the prisoner before his eyes, if he is able to resist the dreadful torture himself. Once one descends to this level in the first place, there is a logical progression which finally makes us willing to use the most extreme and dreadful forms of psychical pressure. The first decision in this direction makes it unnecessary that all subsequent steps should be the subject of new and reiterated decision. Instead they are simply logical consequences of the first decision, having the character of automatic advances. Here too the freedom of personal decision is to be found at only one point, namely, in the initial act of decision.

We can also go beyond Miller to distinguish a third step in this downward movement, namely, torture for torture's

[13] Alexander Miller, "Is everything permitted?" *The Student World*, XXXVIII (1945), 288–89.

sake, torture as an end in itself. When humanity collapses, so do other protective walls of division, and there open up desolate background areas in which sinister powers roam unchecked, e.g., the sadistic potentialities of the human psyche. These spirits are not invoked. They are contrary to the original purpose. Yet once they have been unleashed, they cannot be exorcised. They seize the initiative.

The logical progression thus leads us to a fourth and final stage which is particularly acute in respect of the question of the generations. When torture is first used, it is still conceivably possible that those who resort to it may yet be conscious of the dreadful conflict and of the guilt involved in it; at least in their own thinking torture can still have the character of a last resort. There can still conceivably be a sense of good and evil, and hence of an ultimate norm. But in the younger generation which grows up within this unjust order the situation is radically different. For this generation no longer knows the initial conflict. It simply receives what for it is already established norm, namely, the state of lawlessness, the moral flexibility, the inconstancy of all ethical values, the ambivalence and haziness of the world structure. The world order is not an "order" at all. It is a pulp of values through which each must work his own way. It is a scrap heap of rusted norms, a dump of discarded values, a resting place for that which obviously is no longer valid and perhaps never was valid. The only valid law is the law of self-preservation. Thus everything is indeed permitted—and without any safeguarding sense at all of guilt and of forgiveness. . . .

It is thus of fundamental importance that the ethical decision never be regarded as an "isolated" decision affecting only the one who makes it. There is no self-contained ethical subject. My decision is surrounded by a kind of zone of radiation which affects—perhaps adversely—the decisions of others, and which thus entails for me a co-responsibility for their decisions. We have here a fresh indication of the fact that there is no such thing as individual ethics. For there is no individuality which can occupy the realm of decision alone without conveying its movements to other partners in the total system, like a fluid in communicating vessels. . . .

In all this we again see, though this time from rather a different angle, that Christian ethics cannot have the task of prescribing or even recommending casuistical solutions to borderline situations, not even in the sense of offering insights by means of which we may discern in any given instance "the lesser evil." It is of the very nature of the borderline situation that it resists being pigeonholed in any larger or prior framework, and that it refuses to be subsumed under natural law. Here the venture of deciding, under the judgment and the grace of God, is demanded of us. Here we are also given the power to make such a decision.

The task of theological ethics at this point is to teach us how to understand and to endure—not "solve"—the borderline situation, and that from the twofold angle of Law and Gospel, of judgment and grace. We may now sum up our theological analysis of this matter by presenting the decisive insights in the form of theses.

When we undergo and endure the borderline situation this means in the first place, from the angle of Law, that this situation can never be merely a matter of fate, in the sense of being rooted in a suprapersonal cosmic structure which is tragic from the beginning. On the contrary, the borderline situation is provoked through "Adam." It has its origin in a communal guilt which already stands behind our situation and which we for our part ever increase and intensify. We are thus both the object and the subject of this communal guilt: it lays us under the constraint of necessity,[14] yet at the same time we are summoned to act in freedom, responsibly. We are both channels and perpetrators of cosmic guilt. Our own action needs forgiveness, but so too does the situation within which it occurs.

When we thus relate the borderline situation to our own guilt, and thereby rob it of its character as fateful tragedy, we actually understand it as judgment. For it is an essential aspect of divine judgment that what is initially a relatively small evil is condemned by the very fact that it gathers momentum

[14] In this respect we should, of course, pay careful heed to Luther's distinction between "compulsion" [*coactio*] and "necessity" [*necessitas*].

like an avalanche, proceeding under its own power and in its own way. For the voter even to consider the restricted alternatives put before him by the totalitarian regime, as we discussed them a moment ago, seems at first to be a relatively small evil. But the next moment he is the prisoner of the alternatives in which he has acquiesced.

What this means, fundamentally, is not only that injustice calls for judgment, but also that judgment intensifies injustice. Paul expresses this when he speaks of God "giving them up" [παρέδωκεν] in Romans 1:24, 26, 28. The sin of the builders of the tower of Babel (Gen. 11:1 ff.) is so judged that it has effects not merely on the vertical level, between man and God, but also on the horizontal level, between man and man. For when men no longer take God as their norm they come under the dictatorship of their own instincts. They thus become alienated from one another, unpredictable, objects of fear. There thus breaks into human society that centrifugal tendency which leads to disruption and scattering (Gen. 11:7 f.). In this context this is both a judgment and an intensification of the guilt itself.

The same point emerges, for example, in the problem of taxation. Those who for reasons of self-protection—not in the primitive sense of personal survival but in the sense of protecting their business—seek illegal tax advantages gain a step on their competitors momentarily, but as a result they force the others to act in the same way. What was initially a relatively small injustice is thereby condemned by the fact that it necessarily brings about an unforseeable intensification and magnification. The economic order as a whole, which was what seemed to make the first injustice necessary, is as a result itself made even more unjust. Concretely, it necessarily brings about a further tightening of the taxation screw in order to make up the sums illegally lost. Repeatedly we are the "victims" of our initial fault, but at the same time initiators of new faults.

In the second place our dealing with the borderline situation is something that cannot be restricted to the sphere of personal decision. It always puts us also on that downward path which will help to determine not only our own future action but also the action of those around us, not least of all that of the next generation. In some cases it may even lead to basic ethical "mutations." Thus we do not merely act on the *basis* of the suprapersonal nexus of cosmic guilt from which we come. We also for our own part influence and effect it, and thus help to determine the milieu in which others must live and act. "Real" decisions are made only by those who are aware of these factors of action and interaction, and who thus see beyond merely the pressing issue of the moment.

To undergo and endure the borderline situation also raises questions from the standpoint of the Gospel. The ambivalence which attaches to the Word of God in its form as Law and Gospel attaches also to the conflict situation when seen from both these angles. It gives to the conflict situation an ambiguity which cannot be resolved theoretically. This is the same ambiguity as is inherent also in judgment, which as *krisis* implies a crossroads from which the one way leads to life and the other to death. In this sense the borderline situation bears the sign, not only of the fallen world, but also of the grace which bespeaks promise within this world. . . .

SELECTIVE BIBLIOGRAPHY

Geschichte und Existenz (1935) (Gütersloh: Bertelsman, 1964)

Fragen des Christentums und die moderne Welt (Tübingen: Mohr, 1947)

Der Glaube der Christenheit: unsere Welt vor Jesus Christus (1947) (Göttingen: Vandenhoeck und Ruprecht, 1965). English translation of chapters 18 to 32: *Man in God's World*, trans. John W. Doberstein (New York: Harper and Row, 1963)

Theologische Ethik, 3 vols. (Tübingen: Mohr, 1951–58). *Theological Ethics*, trans. William H. Lazareth (Philadelphia: Fortress Press, 1966), is an abridgment of *Theologische Ethik*. *The Ethics of Sex*, trans. John W. Doberstein (London: James Clarke, 1964) is a translation of one chapter of *Theologische Ethik*

The Freedom of the Christian Man: a Christian Confrontation with the Secular Gods, trans. John W. Doberstein (New York: Harper and Row, 1963)

Einführung in die christliche Ethik (München: Piper, 1963)

Der Einzelne und der Apparat: von der Freiheit des Menschen im technischen Zeitalter (Hamburg: Furche Verlag, 1964)

Brauchen wir Leitbilder? Ein Wort an die Jugend über Grosse und Elend der Ideale (Hamburg: Furche Verlag, 1961)

Between Heaven and Earth: Conversations with American Christians, trans. John W. Doberstein (New York: Harper and Row, 1965)

INDEX OF PROPER NAMES

SUBJECT INDEX